Lecture Notes in Computer Science 14420

Services Science

Subline of Lecture Notes in Computer Science

More information about this series at https://link.springer.com/bookseries/558

Flavia Monti · Stefanie Rinderle-Ma ·
Antonio Ruiz Cortés · Zibin Zheng ·
Massimo Mecella
Editors

Service-Oriented Computing

21st International Conference, ICSOC 2023
Rome, Italy, November 28 – December 1, 2023
Proceedings, Part II

 Springer

Editors
Flavia Monti
Sapienza University of Rome
Rome, Italy

Stefanie Rinderle-Ma
Technical University of Munich
Garching, Germany

Antonio Ruiz Cortés
University of Seville
Seville, Spain

Zibin Zheng
Sun Yat-sen University
Guangzhou, China

Massimo Mecella
Sapienza University of Rome
Rome, Italy

ISSN 0302-9743   ISSN 1611-3349   (electronic)
Lecture Notes in Computer Science
ISBN 978-3-031-48423-0   ISBN 978-3-031-48424-7   (eBook)
https://doi.org/10.1007/978-3-031-48424-7

This Springer imprint is published by the registered company Springer Nature Switzerland AG
The registered company address is: Gewerbestrasse 11, 6330 Cham, Switzerland

Paper in this product is recyclable.

Preface

The 21st International Conference on Service-Oriented Computing (ICSOC 2023) took place in Rome (Italy) from November 28 to December 1, 2023. ICSOC is the premier international forum aiming at bringing together academics, industry researchers, developers, and practitioners to report and share ground-breaking work in the area of Service-Oriented Computing. It offers a top-tier platform for unveiling results advancing our understanding of various aspects of the field. This includes everything from application and system considerations to cutting-edge topics like artificial intelligence, machine learning, big data analytics, the Internet of Things (IoT), and emerging technologies such as quantum computing, blockchain, chatbots, and sustainable green IT solutions. Reflecting upon the remarkable history of previous ICSOC editions, including Trento (Italy, 2003), New York (USA, 2004), Amsterdam (the Netherlands, 2005), Chicago (USA, 2006), Vienna (Austria, 2007), Sydney (Australia, 2008), Stockholm (Sweden, 2009), San Francisco (USA, 2010), Paphos (Cyprus, 2011), Shanghai (China, 2012), Berlin (Germany, 2013), Paris (France, 2014), Goa (India, 2015), Banff (Canada, 2016), Malaga (Spain, 2017), Hangzhou (China, 2018), Toulouse (France, 2019), Dubai (United Arab Emirates - virtual, 2020), Dubai (United Arab Emirates - virtual, 2021) and Sevilla (Spain, 2022), ICSOC 2023 continued to build for the next decade upon this rich tradition of excellence.

ICSOC 2023 followed the two-round submission and reviewing process introduced in the previous two editions. Other than a traditional research track, it included four tracks as they relate to service computing research: (1) Artificial Intelligence for Services and as-a-Service, (2) Big Data Analytics for Services and as-a-Service, (3) Novel Service Frameworks for IoT-based and Smart Environments, and (4) Emerging Technologies. Each track was managed by a track chair, hence enhancing the quality and rigor of the paper review process. The conference attracted 208 paper submissions (29 received in the first round) co-authored by researchers, practitioners, and academics from 30 countries across all continents. Three PC members carefully double-blindly reviewed each paper submission, except for a small minority of papers (5%) with two reviews. The reviews were followed by discussions moderated by a senior PC member who made a recommendation in the form of a meta-review to the track chairs and PC co-chairs. The PC consisted of 148 world-class experts in service-oriented computing and related areas (131 PC members and 17 senior PC members) from different countries across all continents. Based on the recommendations and the discussions, 35 papers (16.83%) were accepted as full papers. We also selected 10 short papers (4.81%). In total, 12 of the 29 papers submitted in the first round were recommended for resubmission with minor or major revisions, and 6 were accepted as full or short papers. In addition, 4 papers were submitted to the industry track and 3 of them were accepted as full papers.

The conference program also included three keynotes from distinguished researchers:

– IoTility: Unleashing the Utility of Internet of Things through Microservices Architectural Extensions, given by Abdelsalam (Sumi) Helal (University of Florida, USA)
– Service Governance in a Transforming World - Challenges Ahead, given by Pablo Fernandez (University of Seville, Spain)
– Logic, Automata, and Games in Service Composition, given by Giuseppe De Giacomo (University of Oxford, UK)

Finally, tutorials, a Ph.D. symposium, a demo session and six workshops were organized to broaden the scope of ICSOC 2023. The workshops were:

– The 7th Workshop on Adaptive Service-oriented and Cloud Applications (ASOCA 2023)
– The 3rd International Workshop on AI-enabled Process Automation (AIPA 2023)
– The 19th International Workshop on Engineering Service-Oriented Applications and Cloud Services (WESOACS 2023)
– The 1st International Workshop on Secure, Accountable and Privacy-Preserving Data-Driven Service-Oriented Computing (SAPD 2023)
– The 1st Services and Quantum Software Workshop (SQS 2023)
– The 1st International Workshop on Sustainable Service-Oriented Computing: Addressing Environmental, Social, and Economic Dimensions (SSCOPE 2023)

We would like to express our gratitude to all individuals, institutions, and sponsors that supported ICSOC 2023. We would like to thank all the authors and participants for their insightful work and discussions. We are grateful to the members of the Senior Program Committee, the international Program Committee, and the external reviewers for their rigorous and robust reviewing process. We would like to express our gratitude to the area chairs Fabio Patrizi, Dan Li, Francesco Leotta, and Juan Manuel Murillo Rodriguez, for their tremendous support throughout the review process. ICSOC 2023 paper management was performed through the Conftool Conference Management System.

We would like to thank the ICSOC Steering Committee for entrusting us with organizing the 21st edition of this prestigious conference. We are grateful to all the members of the Organizing Committee and to all who contributed to make ICSOC 2023 a successful event. We are indebted to the local arrangements team from Sapienza Università di Roma for the successful organization of all conference, social, and co-located events, and to Consulta Umbria who acted as organizing agency. We also acknowledge the prompt and professional support from Springer, who published these proceedings as part of the Lecture Notes in Computer Science series.

November 2023

Massimo Mecella
Stefanie Rinderle-Ma
Antonio Ruiz Cortés
Zibin Zheng

Organization

General Chair

Massimo Mecella   Sapienza Università di Roma, Italy

Program Committee Chairs

Stefanie Rinderle-Ma   Technical University of Munich, Germany
Antonio Ruiz Cortés   Universidad de Sevilla, Spain
Zibin Zheng   Sun Yat-sen University, China

Focus Area 1: Artificial Intelligence for Services and as-a-Service Chair

Fabio Patrizi   Sapienza Università di Roma, Italy

Focus Area 2: Big Data Analytics for Services and as-a-Service Chair

Dan Li   Sun Yat-sen University, China

Focus Area 3: Novel Service Frameworks for IoT-Based and Smart Environments Chair

Francesco Leotta   Sapienza Università di Roma, Italy

Focus Area 4: Emerging Technologies Chair

Juan Manuel Murillo   University of Extremadura, Spain
    Rodríguez

Demo Co-chairs

Devis Bianchini   Università di Brescia, Italy
Damian A. Tamburri   TU/e - JADS, The Netherlands and Politecnico di
                                Milano, Italy

Workshop Co-chairs

Pierluigi Plebani   Politecnico di Milano, Italy
Naouel Moha   École de Technologie Supérieure de Montréal, Canada

Ph.D. Symposium Co-chairs

Gowri Ramachandran	Queensland University of Technology, Australia
Helen Paik	University of New South Wales, Australia
Johanna Barzen	University of Stuttgart, Germany

Proceedings and Conference Management System Chair

Flavia Monti	Sapienza Università di Roma, Italy

Local Organization, Finance and Sponsorship Chair

Massimo Mecella	Sapienza Università di Roma, Italy

Publicity, Web and Social Presence Co-chairs

Marco Calamo	Sapienza Università di Roma, Italy
Flavia Monti	Sapienza Università di Roma, Italy

Local Committee

Consulta Umbria	(Organizing Agency)
Filippo Bianchini	Sapienza Università di Roma, Italy
Marco Calamo	Sapienza Università di Roma, Italy
Francesca De Luzi	Sapienza Università di Roma, Italy
Mattia Macrí	Sapienza Università di Roma, Italy
Jerin George Mathew	Sapienza Università di Roma, Italy
Flavia Monti	Sapienza Università di Roma, Italy

Steering Committee

Boualem Benatallah	Dublin City University, Ireland
Athman Bouguettaya	University of Sydney, Australia
Fabio Casati	University of Trento, Italy
Bernd J. Krämer	FernUniversität in Hagen, Germany
Winfried Lamersdorf	University of Hamburg, Germany
Heiko Ludwig	IBM, USA
Mike Papazoglou	Tilburg University, The Netherlands
Jian Yang	Macquarie University, Australia
Liang Zhang	Fudan University, China

Senior Program Committee

Marco Aiello	University of Stuttgart, Germany
Boualem Benatallah	Dublin City University, Ireland

Athman Bouguettaya   University of Sydney, Australia
Carlos Canal   University of Malaga, Spain
Flavio De Paoli   Università di Milano-Bicocca, Italy
Schahram Dustdar   TU Wien, Austria
Hakim Hacid   Zayed University, United Arab Emirates
Brahim Medjahed   University of Michigan-Dearborn, USA
Cesare Pautasso   University of Lugano, Switzerland
Barbara Pernici   Politecnico di Milano, Italy
Manfred Reichert   University of Ulm, Germany
Manuel Resinas   University of Seville, Spain
Michael Q. Sheng   Macquarie University, Australia
Stefan Tai   TU Berlin, Germany
Mathias Weske   HPI / University of Potsdam, Germany
Jian Yang   Macquarie University, Australia
Liang Zhang   Fudan University, China

Program Committee

Alessandro Aldini   University of Urbino, Italy
Moayad M. Alshangiti   University of Jeddah, Saudi Arabia
Andreas Andreou   Cyprus University of Technology, Cyprus
Yacine Atif   University of Skövde, Sweden
Marcos Baez   Bielefeld University of Applied Sciences, Germany
Luciano Baresi   Politecnico di Milano, Italy
Khalid Belhajjame   Université Paris Dauphine, France
Salima Benbernou   Université de Paris, France
Javier Berrocal   University of Extremadura, Spain
Juan Boubeta-Puig   University of Cádiz, Spain
Omar Boucelma   Aix-Marseille University, France
Lars Braubach   Hochschule Bremen, Germany
Uwe Breitenbücher   University of Stuttgart, Germany
Antonio Brogi   University of Pisa, Italy
Antonio Bucchiarone   Fondazione Bruno Kessler, Italy
Christoph Bussler   Robert Bosch LLC, USA
Cristina Cabanillas   University of Seville, Spain
Wing-Kwong Chan   City University of Hong Kong, China
Francois Charoy   University of Lorraine, France
Sanjay Chaudhary   Ahmedabad University, India
Feifei Chen   Deakin University, Australia
Lawrence Chung   University of Texas at Dallas, USA
Marco Comuzzi   UNIST, South Korea
Hoa Khanh Dam   University of Wollongong, Australia
Valeria de Castro   University Rey Juan Carlos, Spain
Martina De Sanctis   Gran Sasso Science Institute, Italy
Bruno Defude   Télécom SudParis, France
Andrea Delgado   Universidad de la República, Uruguay

Shuiguang Deng	Zhejiang University, China
Francesco Di Cerbo	SAP, France
Claudio Di Ciccio	Sapienza Università di Roma, Italy
Gregorio Diaz Descalzo	Universidad de Castilla - La Mancha, Spain
Chen Ding	Toronto Metropolitan University, Canada
Hai Dong	RMIT University, Australia
Khalil Drira	LAAS-CNRS, France
Yucong Duan	Hainan University, China
Joyce El Haddad	Université Paris-Dauphine, France
Rik Eshuis	Eindhoven University of Technology, The Netherlands
Onyeka Ezenwoye	Augusta University, USA
Noura Faci	Université Lyon 1, CNRS, France
Marcelo Fantinato	University of São Paulo, Brazil
Sheik Mohammad Mostakim Fattah	University of Adelaide, Australia
Zhiyong Feng	Tianjin University, China
Pablo Fernandez	University of Seville, Spain
Afonso Ferreira	CNRS, France
Joao E. Ferreira	University of São Paulo, Brazil
George Feuerlicht	University of Technology, Australia
Marios-Eleftherios Fokaefs	École Polytechnique Montréal, Canada
Xiang Fu	Hofstra, USA
G. R. Gangadharan	NIT Tiruchirappalli, India
Felix Garcia	University of Castilla-La Mancha, Spain
José María García	Universidad de Sevilla, Spain
José Garcia-Alonso	University of Extremadura, Spain
Ilche Georgievski	University of Stuttgart, Germany
Mohamed Graiet	ISIMM, Tunisia
Daniela Grigori	Université Paris Dauphine, France
Georg Grossmann	University of South Australia, Australia
Nawal Guermouche	Université de Toulouse, France
Mohand-Saïd Hacid	Université Claude Bernard Lyon 1, France
Jun Han	Swinburne University of Technology, Australia
Chihab Hanachi	IRIT - Toulouse University, France
Qiang He	Swinburne University of Technology, Australia
Richard Hull	IBM Research, USA
Fuyuki Ishikawa	National Institute of Informatics, Japan
Hai Jin	HUST, China
Sokratis Katsikas	Norwegian University of Science and Technology, Norway
Gerald Kotonya	Lancaster University, UK
Hemza Labbaci	University of Tours, France
Philippe Lalanda	UGA, France
Alexander Lazovik	University of Groningen, Netherlands
Weiping Li	Peking University, China
Ying Li	Zhejiang University, China

Jiuyun Xu	China University of Petroleum, China
Sami Yangui	CNRS-LAAS, France
Sira Yongchareon	Auckland University of Technology, New Zealand
Tetsuya Yoshida	Nara Women's University, Japan
Jian Yu	Auckland University of Technology, New Zealand
Qi Yu	Rochester Institute of Technology, USA
Dong Yuan	University of Sydney, China
Gianluigi Zavattaro	University of Bologna, Italy
Uwe Zdun	University of Vienna, Austria
Wei Zhang	University of Adelaide, Australia
Xuyun Zhang	Macquarie University Australia
Weiliang Zhao	Macquarie University, Australia
Zhangbing Zhou	China University of Geosciences, China
Christian Zirpins	Karlsruhe University of Applied Sciences, Germany

Additional Reviewers

Roberto Cipollone
Leandro de Souza Rosa
Matthias Ehrendorfer
Ruibing Jin
Nataliia Klievtsova

Alessandro Trapasso
Silvestro Veneruso
Neng Zheng
Peilin Zheng
Zhijie Zhong

Contents – Part II

Service Frameworks for IoT, Mobile and Smart Environments

Industrial Papers

Contents – Part I

Architecture and System Aspects

Containers and Microservices

Emerging Technologies and Approaches

Processes and Workflows

Artifact-Driven Process Monitoring at Scale

Giovanni Meroni[(✉)] and Szabolcs Garda

Technical University of Denmark, Kgs. Lyngby, Denmark
`giom@dtu.dk`

Abstract. Artifact-driven process monitoring is an effective technique to autonomously monitor business processes. Instead of requiring human operators to notify when an activity is executed, artifact-driven process monitoring infers this information from the conditions of physical or virtual objects taking part in a process. However, SMARTifact, the existing monitoring platform implementing this technique, has been designed to run entirely on edge devices, each of which can monitor only one execution of the process. Thus, monitoring multiple executions at the same time, or reducing the computational requirements of edge devices is not possible. In this paper, we introduce a new artifact-driven monitoring platform that overcomes these limitations and makes artifact-driven monitoring fully scalable.

Keywords: Process monitoring · Scalability · Fog computing

1 Introduction

Business Process Management is the discipline devoted to oversee how organizations perform their work [4]. In particular, process monitoring focuses on gaining insights on how business processes - a set of activities to be performed to achieve a certain goal and the dependencies among them - are performed. This is particularly relevant for so-called multi-party business processes, which require multiple organizations to take part in the same process and to coordinate their activities. In this setting, being able to promptly identify any issue with respect to the planned behavior makes possible for the involved parties to quickly react and take countermeasures.

Among the existing process monitoring techniques, artifact-driven process monitoring [12] is one of the few that specifically targets multi-party business processes. By collecting and processing information coming from physical and virtual objects participating in a process, artifact-driven process monitoring can autonomously identify when activities are executed. Also, by relying on a declarative language named Extended-GSM (E-GSM) to represent the process to monitor, artifact-driven monitoring can immediately detect discrepancies between the planned process and the actual execution.

F. Monti et al. (Eds.): ICSOC 2023, LNCS 14420, pp. 3–12, 2023.
https://doi.org/10.1007/978-3-031-48424-7_1

Despite the advantages brought by artifact-driven process monitoring, SMARTifact, the existing monitoring platform implementing this approach limits its applicability to specific cases. In particular, SMARTifact has been designed to be executed entirely on edge devices (that is, the physical objects in the process). Also, each device can only monitor one execution of the process. If two executions are running, they must be monitored by two distinct devices. Secondly, SMARTifact maintains the monitoring information on the device and in memory. Therefore, if the device experiences a malfunctioning or simply it runs out of battery, all monitoring information is lost.

In this paper we introduce a new monitoring platform, based on the fog computing paradigm, that aims at overcoming the limitations of SMARTifact. In particular, this platform is specifically designed with scalability in mind, making possible to monitor a virtually unlimited number of parallel process executions.

This paper is structured as follows. Section 2 introduces artifact-driven process monitoring and the architecture of SMARTifact. Section 3 discusses the limitations of SMARTifact and identifies a set of requirements that need to be addressed. Section 4 presents the architecture of our monitoring platform. Section 5 discusses how our platform has been validated. Section 6 surveys the state of the art for related work. Finally, Sect. 7 draws the conclusions and outline possible future work.

2   Baseline

To make this paper self-contained, a brief discussion on how artifact-driven monitoring works, and on the architecture of the SMARTifact platform is provided in this section. The reader should refer to [12] for further details.

2.1   Artifact-Driven Process Monitoring

Traditional process monitoring techniques assume that, whenever an activity in a process is executed, an event is always produced. This can be relatively easily achieved when activities are at least partially automated. However, when manual tasks - activities performed by humans without interacting with a computer - are present in the process, events must be manually sent by the operators responsible for the manual tasks and, as such, they are prone to be forgotten or delayed. In addition, most monitoring techniques can detect discrepancies between the expected execution and the actual one only after the execution is complete.

To address these limitations, artifact-driven process monitoring has been proposed. this approach assumes that, whenever an activity is executed, it alters the conditions of one or more physical or virtual objects, named artifacts, that take part in the process. Therefore, by monitoring the conditions of these artifacts during a process execution, it is possible to infer when activities are executed without relying on explicit events.

In order to detect and react to violations, artifact-driven process monitoring represents the process to monitor with a declarative language named E-GSM.

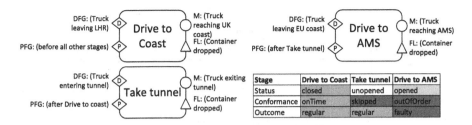

Fig. 1. E-GSM model of LHR-AMS, and monitoring results of an incorrect execution.

In a nutshell, E-GSM represent activities and process portions as stages, which are assessed according to three perspectives: *status, compliance,* and *outcome.* The status of a stage can be *unopened, opened* or *closed,* indicating that the corresponding activity or process portion was never executed, is running, or is complete. The compliance can be *onTime, outOfOrder* or *skipped,* indicating that the activity or process portion follows the process model, has been executed when it should not, or has not been executed when it should. Finally, the outcome can be *regular* or *faulty,* indicating that the activity or process portion was correctly performed, or that something went wrong while it was running. When the process starts, all stages are unopened, onTime, and regular. Stages can be decorated with data flow guards, process flow guards, milestones and fault loggers. Data flow guards and milestones specify the conditions on the artifacts that cause the decorated stage to become, respectively, opened or closed, determining the status. Process flow guards specify control flow dependencies (i.e., which other stages should be executed before the decorated stage), determining the compliance. Fault loggers specify the conditions on the artifacts that cause the stage to become faulty, determining the outcome.

To better understand E-GSM, Fig. 1 shows how it can be used for representing and monitoring the following process. A truck driver is expected to start the process in the LHR airport, and to drive to the coast. Once it reaches it, the driver has to take the Channel tunnel, and finally to drive to the AMS airport. If we consider a process execution where, instead of taking the Channel tunnel, the truck driver takes a ferry, stops before reaching the AMS airport and opens the container, an E-GSM engine will be able to detect activity drive to coast as *closed,* since it completed its execution, *onTime,* since it was the first activity to be executed, and *regular,* since the container was never dropped while the activity was running. The engine also will detect take tunnel as *unopened,* since it was never executed, *skipped,* since it was not executed after drive to the coast ended, and *regular.* Finally, the engine will detect drive to AMS as *opened,* since it is still running, *outOfOrder,* since it was executed before take tunnel, and *faulty,* since the container was dropped while the activity was running.

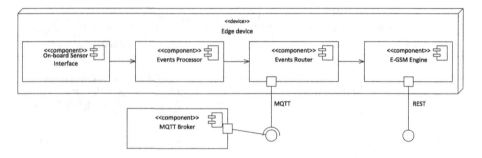

Fig. 2. Architecture of the SMARTifact platform.

2.2   SMARTifact

Originally known as mArtifact [1], SMARTifact is one of the first artifact-driven process monitoring platforms in the literature. Specifically targeting processes involving physical artifacts, SMARTifact has been designed to run on edge devices (e.g., single-board computers) attached to these artifacts. Its architecture, as shown in Fig. 2, consists in the following components deployed on each edge device:

On-Board Sensor Interface. This component is responsible for collecting data from the sensors installed on the edge device attached to a physical artifact.

Event Processor. This component is responsible for aggregating and processing sensor data, in order to determine when the conditions of the attached artifact change.

Events Router. This component is responsible for sending changes in the conditions of the attached artifact to the other edge devices taking part in the same process execution. The events router is also responsible for receiving from the other edge devices changes on the conditions of the other artifacts in the same process execution.

E-GSM Engine. This component contains the E-GSM model of the process to monitor. It is responsible for evaluating the data flow guards, process flow guards, milestones and fault loggers of all stages whenever a change in the conditions of one of the artifacts in the process is detected. It also exposes a Representational State Transfer (REST) Application Programming Interface (API) outside the edge device, which is used to configure the edge device (e.g., by providing the E-GSM model of the process to monitor) and to retrieve information on the process being monitored (e.g., the value of the status, compliance and outcome perspectives for each stage).

To communicate with each other, edge devices rely on an **Message Queue Telemetry Transport (MQTT) broker**. MQTT is a publish-subscribe protocol specifically designed for Internet of Things (IoT) applications. Being a message queue-based protocol, MQTT completely decouples the state of the sender with the recipient.

3 Application Requirements

Despite having proven to be effective in some scenarios, such as smart logistics, SMARTifact suffers from some limitations. Firstly, with the exception of the MQTT Broker, all components are meant to run on an edge device. Although single board computers capable of running SMARTifact are relatively inexpensive, their size and power consumption can be a limiting factor for some processes. For example, although SMARTifact can monitor the conditions of a shipping container and its content, it cannot individually monitor the conditions of each package in the container. To address this issue in our platform, we define the following application requirement. *AR1: Edge devices should only run components needed to process data they directly collect.*

Another limitation of SMARTifact is the inability, for an edge device, to monitor multiple executions of the same process at the same time. This limitation comes from the E-GSM Engine, which is capable of running only one instance of the process to monitor, and makes SMARTifact unsuited to monitor process executions that share the same artifacts. For example, suppose that a truck is shipping two containers that have to be delivered in two different places. Then, the E-GSM Engine running on the truck will consider the two containers as participants of the same execution, rather than to two distinct executions. To address this issue in our platform, we define the following application requirement. *AR2: the platform should allow monitoring multiple instances of the same process at the same time.*

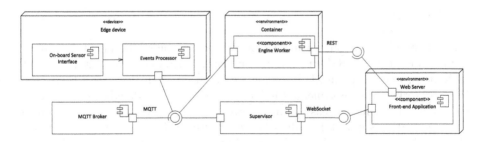

Fig. 3. Architecture of our platform.

4 Proposed Solution

To address the requirements identified in Sect. 3, the architecture shown in Fig. 3 has been designed. This architecture reuses and, when needed, adapts the components present in SMARTifact. In addition, new components and interfaces are introduced.

To address AR1, this architecture embraces the fog computing paradigm [15]. Only the On-board Sensor Interface and the Events Processor are deployed on the edge devices, since they are responsible for processing data created on that device. To accommodate this change, the Events Processor no longer communicates changes in the condition of the artifact to Events Router directly. Instead, it publishes them to an MQTT topic. Therefore, it requires an MQTT interface to the MQTT Broker.

To address AR2, the E-GSM Engine and the Events Router are moved inside the **Engine Worker** component, which is deployed in a cloud environment. To achieve vertical scalability, a software wrapper has been built around the E-GSM Engine, making it multi-instance. Also, to achieve horizontal scalability, the Engine Worker is deployed inside a container, making it easy to deploy multiple instances of this component.

The **Supervisor** and **Front-end Application** components have also been introduced. These components are deployed in a cloud environment as well. The Supervisor keeps track of which Engine Worker instances are in charge of monitoring a specific process execution. It also instantiates, monitors, and destroys Engine Worker instances when needed. The Front-end Application is a web application that allows the user to interact with the monitoring platform. By communicating with the Supervisor through WebSocket, the Front-end Application can know which process executions are monitored and by which Engine Worker. By communicating with the Engine Worker through a REST API, the Front-end Application can pull monitoring information on-demand, and show them to the user. With the exception of the Front-end Application, all components communicate through the MQTT broker. This makes possible for the components to communicate with each other even if some of them change address, new instances are instantiated, or unneeded instances are destroyed.

5   Evaluation

To evaluate our solution, we implemented a prototype of the monitoring platform[1]. Since the E-GSM Engine and the Events Router were originally built in Node.js, and we planned to extend them rather than to rewrite them, the Engine Worker was implemented in Node.js. Also, since Node.js was proven to be resource efficient and easy to port across different environments, and it also provided native support for MQTT, we adopted this programming language also for the Supervisor. The Front-end Application was built in Angular, due to the availability of many data visualization libraries and the tight synergy with Node.js. Like in SMARTifact, we implemented the Events Aggregator with Node-red. Also, to simulate the On-board Sensor Interface, we adopted the simulator that was used by the authors of SMARTifact to test it, which generates

---

[1] Source code available at https://github.com/eGSM-platform.

sensor data from low-level logs. Finally, to deploy the components composing the architecture, we adopted Docker.

To assess how our solution performs in terms of scalability, we compared the memory usage of the Engine Worker components with the one of SMARTifact. To this aim, we initiated an instance of the Engine Worker with a maximum engine limit set to 10. We then proceeded to instantiate and monitor 20 instances of an extended version the LHR-AMS process - which was also used to validate the original version of SMARTifact [12] - 10 of which were compliant and 10 non compliant. As we reached a total of 10 running process instances, we initiated another Engine Worker and continued creating engines until we reached a total of 20 running engines. In order to draw a meaningful comparison with SMARTifact, we enclosed the Event Router and the E-GSM of that platform inside a container. We then deployed 20 instances of that container, and we measured the total memory usage and the time to start monitoring a new execution. The results of this comparison are presented in Fig. 4.

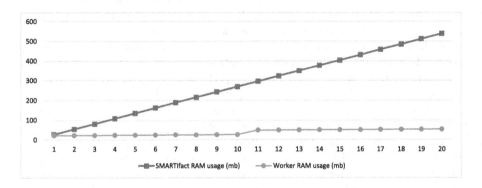

Fig. 4. Memory usage of our solution compared to SMARTifact.

As shown in this figure, the usage of Engine Worker components led to a substantial reduction in memory usage when compared to the individual deployment of SMARTifact instances. The disparity in memory utilization becomes more pronounced as the number of process executions increases. With SMARTifact, monitoring a new execution requires creating two instances of the Event Router and the E-GSM Engine. In contrast, the Engine Worker implementation only adds a negligible amount of data to its internal data structures. This is also the reason why our solution is faster at starting to monitor a new instance. Compared to SMARTifact, which requires on average 76 ms, our solution requires only 28 ms. When the maximum engine limit is reached and an additional Engine Worker is instantiated, memory utilization doubles. Nevertheless, even considering this spike, the memory usage of the Engine Worker remains significantly lower than SMARTifact. This trend is expected to persist as the number of engines continues to increase.

Finally, to verify that no side-effects in process monitoring were introduced in our platform, we compared the monitoring results with the ones obtained by SMARTifact and ensured they were identical.

6   Related Work

Several solutions for runtime business process monitoring exist in the literature. In [2,16], a Complex Event Processing (CEP) engine is adopted to determine if an execution deviates from the expected behavior. Similarly, [13] proposes an alternative platform to detect deviations as soon as they occur. However, all these approaches rely on high-level events explicitly indicating that an activity has started or completed its execution. Therefore, they cannot autonomously infer when activities are running.

To address this limitation, [6,7,14] rely on IoT data to infer when activities are running. [3] focuses on monitoring multi-party business processes. The authors assume that monitoring services are available for each participant, and propose an algorithm to optimize them. It is worth noting that all these solutions are unable to handle deviations from the expected execution.

To handle flexibility in process execution, several architectures relying on artifact-driven process models have been introduced. In [5,8] the authors present a platform for process execution. Similarly, [11] introduces a service-oriented software architecture to integrate business artifacts with social media. [9] presents a platform aiming at optimizing scalability. However, all these solutions are mainly focused on process execution, rather than monitoring.

An artifact-driven monitoring platform is introduced in [10]. Despite allowing for greater flexibility than monitoring platforms relying on imperative process models, this platform still requires the process to behave as specified in the process model. Therefore, it is unable to handle deviations. To our knowledge, SMARTifact [1] is the only artifact-driven monitoring platform capable of detecting and reporting deviations from the expected execution.

7   Conclusion and Future Work

In this paper we presented an artifact-driven monitoring platform capable of handling a virtually unlimited number of process executions. By leaving on edge devices only the components responsible for creating and processing data generated by these devices, it is possible to significantly reduce their computational requirements. Thus, our platform can monitor processes involving small and inexpensive physical objects.

A limitation of the current platform is the lack of security mechanisms in the communication between edge devices and components running in the cloud. Future work will focus on introducing authentication and encryption mechanisms in the communication protocol. We also plan to more extensively validate the platform with real-world use cases.

References

1. Baresi, L., Di Ciccio, C., Mendling, J., Meroni, G., Plebani, P.: martifact: an artifact-driven process monitoring platform. In: BPM Demo Track 2017. vol. 1920. CEUR-WS.org (2017)
2. Burattin, A.: Online conformance checking for petri nets and event streams. In: BPM Demo Track 2017. vol. 1920. CEUR-WS.org (2017)
3. Comuzzi, M., Vanderfeesten, I., Wang, T.: Optimized cross-organizational business process monitoring: design and enactment. Information Sciences **244**, 107–118 (2013). https://doi.org/10.1016/j.ins.2013.04.036
4. Dumas, M., La Rosa, M., Mendling, J., Reijers, H.A.: Fundamentals Of Business Process Management. Springer Berlin Heidelberg, Berlin, Heidelberg (2013). https://doi.org/10.1007/978-3-642-33143-5
5. Eckermann, O., Weidlich, M.: Flexible artifact-driven automation of product design processes. In: Halpin, T., Nurcan, S., Krogstie, J., Soffer, P., Proper, E., Schmidt, R., Bider, I. (eds.) Enterprise, Business-Process and Information Systems Modeling, pp. 103–117. Springer Berlin Heidelberg, Berlin, Heidelberg (2011). https://doi.org/10.1007/978-3-642-21759-3_8
6. Friedow, C., Völker, M., Hewelt, M.: Integrating IoT devices into business processes. In: Matulevičius, R., Dijkman, R. (eds.) Advanced Information Systems Engineering Workshops: CAiSE 2018 International Workshops, Tallinn, Estonia, June 11-15, 2018, Proceedings, pp. 265–277. Springer International Publishing, Cham (2018). https://doi.org/10.1007/978-3-319-92898-2_22
7. Gallik, F., Kirikkayis, Y., Reichert, M.: Modeling, executing and monitoring IoT-aware processes with BPM technology. In: ICSS 2022, pp. 96–103. IEEE (2022)
8. Heath <suffix>III</suffix>, F.T., et al.: Barcelona: a design and runtime environment for declarative artifact-centric BPM. In: Basu, S., Pautasso, C., Zhang, L., Fu, X. (eds.) Service-Oriented Computing: 11th International Conference, ICSOC 2013, Berlin, Germany, December 2-5, 2013, Proceedings, pp. 705–709. Springer Berlin Heidelberg, Berlin, Heidelberg (2013). https://doi.org/10.1007/978-3-642-45005-1_65
9. Lei, J., Bai, R., Guo, L., Zhang, L.: Towards a scalable framework for artifact-centric business process management systems. In: WISE 2016. vol. 10042, pp. 309–323 (2016)
10. Liu, R., Vaculín, R., Shan, Z., Nigam, A., Wu, F.: Business artifact-centric modeling for real-time performance monitoring. In: Rinderle-Ma, S., Toumani, F., Wolf, K. (eds.) Business Process Management, pp. 265–280. Springer, Berlin, Heidelberg (2011). https://doi.org/10.1007/978-3-642-23059-2_21
11. Maamar, Z., et al.: Bridging the gap between the business and social worlds: a data artifact-driven approach. Trans. Large Scale Data Knowl. Centered Syst. **35**, 27–49 (2017)
12. Meroni, G.: Artifact-Driven Business Process Monitoring: A Novel Approach to Transparently Monitor Business Processes, Supported by Methods, Tools, and Real-World Applications. Springer International Publishing, Cham (2019)
13. Schuster, D., Kolhof, G.J.: Scalable online conformance checking using incremental prefix-alignment computation. In: Hacid, H., et al. (eds.) Service-Oriented Computing – ICSOC 2020 Workshops: AIOps, CFTIC, STRAPS, AI-PA, AI-IOTS, and Satellite Events, Dubai, United Arab Emirates, December 14–17, 2020, Proceedings, pp. 379–394. Springer International Publishing, Cham (2021). https://doi.org/10.1007/978-3-030-76352-7_36

14. Seiger, R., Zerbato, F., Burattin, A., García-Bañuelos, L., Weber, B.: Towards IoT-driven process event log generation for conformance checking in smart factories. In: EDOC Workshops 2020, pp. 20–26. IEEE (2020)
15. Yi, S., Hao, Z., Qin, Z., Li, Q.: Fog computing: platform and applications. In: HotWeb 2015, pp. 73–78. IEEE (2015)
16. van Zelst, S.J., Bolt, A., Hassani, M., van Dongen, B.F., van der Aalst, W.M.P.: Online conformance checking: relating event streams to process models using prefix-alignments. Int. J. Data Sci. Anal. 8(3), 269–284 (2019)

LoVizQL: A Query Language for Visualizing and Analyzing Business Processes from Event Logs

María Salas-Urbano[1](✉) ⓘ, Carlos Capitán-Agudo[1] ⓘ, Cristina Cabanillas[1,2] ⓘ, and Manuel Resinas[1,2] ⓘ

[1] SCORE Lab, Universidad de Sevilla, Seville, Spain
{msurbano,ccagudo,cristinacabanillas,resinas}@us.es
[2] I3US Institute, Universidad de Sevilla, Seville, Spain

Abstract. Process event logs record information about the execution of the activities of a business process. Process mining techniques use these event logs to discover, analyze, and optimize business processes. Process mining tools offer many functionalities such as data filtering, process discovery, process visualization, or conformance checking. Process visualization is generally based on Directly-Follows Graphs (DFGs), where each node represents an activity of the process, and each transition represents a directly-follows relation between nodes (activities). A workflow frequently followed by process mining analysts involves manually comparing the DFGs of different event log subsets (e.g., subsets belonging to different product categories in a purchase-to-pay process) to identify patterns or behaviors in the process data (e.g., delays in process execution). However, performing this type of analysis with current process mining tools is usually a time-consuming task, especially if the number of event log subsets analyzed is large. This research aims to address this limitation by presenting LoVizQL, a query language to obtain collections of DFGs that meet specific user-defined conditions in the queries. The language is evaluated using reports belonging to various Business Process Intelligence Challenges. The evaluation demonstrates that LoVizQL covers analyses found in real scenarios and reduces the effort to find specific subsets of event log data and their corresponding DFGs.

Keywords: directly-follows graph · process analysis · query language · LoVizQL · process mining

1 Introduction

Process mining techniques use event logs to discover, analyze, and optimize business processes [1]. Event logs record information about the execution of the activities of a business process. They typically follow a standardized structure based on the eXtensible Event Stream (XES) format [7]. In an XES log, every process instance (or case) corresponds to a sequence (*trace*) of recorded entries, namely,

F. Monti et al. (Eds.): ICSOC 2023, LNCS 14420, pp. 13–28, 2023.
https://doi.org/10.1007/978-3-031-48424-7_2

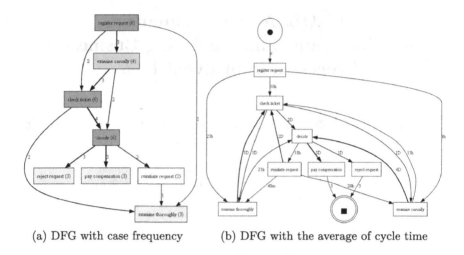

(a) DFG with case frequency   (b) DFG with the average of cycle time

Fig. 1. Examples of DFGs

events. Events are usually characterized by three attributes: case id, activity name and timestamp. The *case id* uniquely identifies the process instance to which the event belongs. The *activity name* is the identifier of the respective activity. The *timestamp* indicates the exact time at which that activity instance was executed [7]. Events can have other attributes, such as the person that performed the activity (i.e., *resource*), the department related to that resource (i.e., *organizational unit*), or more generic attributes (e.g., *cost*).

There are many commercial tools for the practice of process mining (e.g., Disco and Celonis). These tools usually incorporate functionalities for data filtering, process discovery, conformance checking, trace clustering, performance reporting, and process visualization, among others. Regarding process discovery and visualization, most process mining tools use Directly Follows Graphs (DFGs) to explore event data. A DFG of an event log (also called *process map*) is a graph where each node represents an activity of the process, and each transition represents a directly-follows relation between nodes (activities) [7]. Both nodes and transitions can be associated with different metrics, such as the number of traces in which they occur (case frequency) or the average time spent in a node or a transition (average cycle time). Examples are shown in Fig. 1.

DFGs can be used for many types of analyses. Among them, as observed in previous work [3,10], a frequent workflow followed by analysts involves comparing different subsets of cases (e.g., cases grouped by product category of a purchase-to-pay process) to identify patterns or behaviors in the process data (e.g., cases that contain transitions with an unusually high cycle time). Performing this type of analysis with current process mining tools is usually a time-consuming task that involves many steps. First, the analyst filters the event log to keep the cases related to one product. Then, the analyst configures and explores the DFG to find insights related to those cases. Finally, the analyst repeats the same process for all of the products, which may be dozens or hundreds, usually comparing the DFGs with each other or with a pattern the analyst is interested in (e.g., transitions with a high cycle time). This comparison is usually performed applying filters back and forth because most process mining tools can visualize only one process at a time. For example, Disco does not provide the capability to display two DFGs simultaneously, and Celonis only allows comparing cases with similar sequences of activities (i.e., process variants).

In this paper, we aim to support the analyst when performing this type of tedious analysis by developing Log data Visualization Query Language (LoVizQL), a query language to obtain collections of DFGs that satisfy certain conditions desired by the user. It is inspired by the Zenvisage Query Language (ZQL) described in [17]. The goal of ZQL is to automatically find desired visual patterns in collections of visualizations obtained from generic datasets. Each query produces a collection of visualizations (e.g., line charts that represent sales per year for all products sold by an organization), and selects those that fulfill specific conditions (e.g., line charts of products with increasing trends of sales per year). Instead of obtaining general visualizations from generic datasets, LoVizQL is better suited for manipulating event logs, generating DFGs, and performing operations to calculate properties related to them. Using our approach the user can discover process insights without manually manipulating the event log, exploring the data, and comparing the various visualizations that are generated during the analysis. For example, in one single LoVizQL query, the user can filter the log traces by each organizational unit involved in the process, obtain the corresponding DFG for each data subset, and search for those DFGs in which the rework of the activities is higher than the average. Existing query languages in the process mining domain lack of a DFG-based functionality and do not support iterative filtering of event log data based on user-defined conditions.

We have evaluated LoVizQL by studying the analyses found in reports submitted to the Business Process Intelligence Challenges (BPICs). BPIC is an annual contest where a real event log is provided by an organization along with business questions, and the BPIC participants must send a report analyzing that event log to answer them. Our evaluation shows that the type of analysis addressed in this paper is used in a wide variety of real scenarios and that LoVizQL reduces the effort to perform these analyses compared to using existing tools.

The paper is structured as follows. Section 2 describes LoVizQL's syntax and semantics. Section 3 provides details about the evaluation of the language. Section 4 outlines the literature related to this work. Section 5 summarizes the conclusions drawn, limitations and future work.

2   Log Data Visualization Query Language (LoVizQL)

LoVizQL aims to obtain collections of DFGs that contain insights of a process without manually applying several manipulation actions and comparisons between visualizations. The queries of LoVizQL are represented as tables as

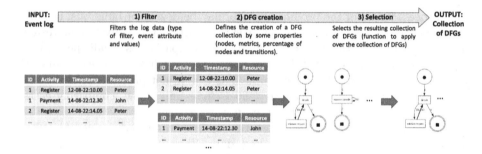

Fig. 2. Query language steps

depicted in Table 1. Each query row specifies and selects a collection of DFGs. The fields are used to specify the characteristics of each collection of DFGs across four main groups of fields: the query identifier (*Name*), the data manipulation properties (*Filter*), the DFG creation (*Nodes, Metrics, %P* and *%A*), and the operation applied to the collection of DFGs to select those of interest (*Selection*).

Figure 2 depicts the main steps of the execution of each query row. All query rows are executed iteratively. The query row receives as input an event log. In the first step (*Filter*), event log subsets are created by filtering operations defined by the user. For instance, in the first row of Table 1, the event log is filtered by each value of the event attribute "case:parts", resulting in a collection of event log subsets, one for each value of the attribute. In the second step (*DFG creation*), a DFG is created for each event log subset according to the properties defined in the query row. Following up the example of Table 1, the corresponding DFG for each filtered subset is created using *absolute frequency* as a metric in the DFGs. In the third step (*Selection*), users can define selection conditions related to DFG properties or metrics to find specific DFGs. For instance, in the example of Table 1, the two DFGs with the maximum number of nodes are selected. Note that the result of the selection is not applied to the collection defined in the first row. Instead, the selected collection of DFGs is stored in a variable *v*2 that is used in the second row to obtain the collection of DFGs that meet the selection condition (cf. Sect. 2.2 for more details). Once all the query rows have been executed, the collection of DFGs of the rows selected as output (marked with an asterisk) are displayed, and the user can inspect them. Next, we describe the syntax of each of the fields and the semantics of the language.

2.1   Syntax

Name. This field uniquely identifies the collection of DFGs specified in each row of the query so that it can be referred to in the *Selection* field. For instance, in the first row of Table 1 a collection of DFGs named f1 is obtained. This collection is then used as input to the function *numberOfNodes()* in the *Selection* field. The *Name* field also specifies which collections of DFGs are part of the output of the query by adding an asterisk before the name like in *f2 in Table 1.

Table 1. Example of query

Name	Filter	Nodes	Metrics	%P	%A	Selection
f1	[Mandatory] v1<- "case:parts".*		Absolute Frequency			v2<- $argmax_{v1}(k=2)$ numberOfN- odes(f1)
*f2	[Mandatory] v2		Absolute Frequency	0.1	0.1	

$\langle Filter \rangle$ ::= '['$\langle Filter\ type \rangle$']' $\langle Attribute\ and\ values \rangle$

$\langle Filter\ type \rangle$ ::= 'Mandatory' | 'Forbidden' | 'Keep Selected' | 'Directly Followed' | 'Eventually Followed' | 'Keep Selected Fragments'

$\langle Attribute\ and\ values \rangle$ ::= (($\langle Var \rangle$ '<-')? $\langle Attribute \rangle$'.'$\langle Values \rangle$) | $\langle Var \rangle$

$\langle Attribute \rangle$ ::= $\langle Value \rangle$ | $\langle ValuesList \rangle$

$\langle Values \rangle$ ::= $\langle Value \rangle$ | $\langle ValuesList \rangle$ | $\langle ValuesOR \rangle$ | '*'

$\langle ValuesList \rangle$ ::= '['$\langle Value \rangle$(','$\langle Value \rangle$)+']'

$\langle ValuesOR \rangle$ ::= $\langle Value \rangle$('OR'$\langle Value \rangle$)+

$\langle Value \rangle$ ::= $\langle String \rangle$

$\langle Var \rangle$ ::= 'v'$\langle Digit \rangle$

$\langle Digit \rangle$ ::= ('0'..'9')+

Grammar 1. Filter's specification in EBNF. $<String>$ is a sequence of alphanumerical characters enclosed between quotes that can contain white spaces (e.g., 'Send submission'), ? denotes that a symbol can appear zero times or once, + denotes that a symbol can appear one or more times, and | is the OR operator.

Filter. This field allows the user to specify the filters to be applied to the event log, such as a filter by attribute value. The language also allows users to carry out multiple consecutive filters by adding additional filter fields (e.g., *Filter 1, Filter 2, ..., Filter N*). The result of each filter field can be a subset of the event log or a collection of subsets (i.e., groupings of events). The syntax of this field is described in Grammar 1 using the Extended Backus-Naur Form (EBNF) [20]. As defined in <Filter type>, LoVizQL offers three filter types related to event attributes and three based on the process control flow, which are those most frequently available in commercial process mining tools. However, new filter types can be added. Attribute-based filters include *Mandatory*, which allows users to keep sets of traces containing specific attribute values; *Forbidden*, which does exactly the opposite, i.e., it is used when users want to filter out traces that contain one or more values of a concrete attribute; and *Keep Selected*, which is used to maintain the events with the selected values of attributes. To specify a filter for each value of an attribute, the character * is used in the <Values> part, as shown in Table 1, where the events in the event log are grouped by each value of the attribute *"case:parts"*. Regarding process control flow filters, the three types (*Directly Followed*, *Eventually Followed*, and *Keep Selected Fragments*) filter the traces by the existence of a process fragment, i.e., a part of the process that occurs between two activities given by the user. The syntax used is *[Filter type] 'activity name attribute'.['ActivityA', 'ActivityB']*. For instance, *[Directly Followed] 'concept:name'.['Registration', 'Payment']* filters the cases where these two activities occur directly after each other[1]. *Eventually Followed* filters cases with a sequence of events without requiring consecutive occurrences. Finally, *Keep Selected Fragments* is used to filter the events that occur between two specified activities. Furthermore, LoVizQL supports the use of variables (<Var>) to store attributes and their values for future reuse, following the structure "variable <- results". For instance, in Table 1, v1 stores all the values of the event attribute *"case:parts"* in the event log.

DFG Creation. This group of fields specifies the characteristics of the DFGs to be generated. In the *Nodes* field, the user specifies the event attribute used as nodes in the DFGs. If empty, activity names are used as nodes by default. Next, in the *Metrics* field, the user specifies the metrics that are associated to nodes, transitions, and the whole DFG. Typically, metrics can be divided into two categories: frequency and performance. Frequency metrics include *Absolute Frequency*, or *Max Repetitions*, among others. For instance, *Absolute Frequency* indicates how many times a node and a transition occur, ignoring repetitions within the same case. Performance metrics include some statistics of cycle time, such as *Mean CT*, which annotates each transition with the average time between the occurrence of the two activities of the transition, and the complete DFG with the average cycle time of the entire process. In any case, the set of available metrics is open and can be extended by the user. Finally, in the *%P* and *%A* fields the user can set thresholds to abstract the number of activities and transitions displayed in the DFGs. The values range from 0 (to show only the activities and paths from the most frequent process variant) to 1 (to display all activities and paths). If no values are specified, 1 is taken by default in both fields.

Selection. This field specifies a user-defined condition to select a subset of the collection of DFGs. Consider Table 1. As aforementioned, the goal of *Selection* in the first row is to identify, from the collection of DFGs generated by each value of the event attribute *"case:parts"*, the two values with the highest number of activities (nodes) in their DFGs. To achieve this, it is necessary to iterate over the collection of DFGs stored in f1 and find the two DFGs that meet the specified conditions, specifically, those with the maximum number of nodes. Thus, this field allows the definition of an optimization function according to the EBNF syntax described in Grammar 2. The <Optimization> parameter

---

[1] According to the XES standard, "concept:name" refers to the activity names.

$\langle Selection\rangle$ ::= $\langle Optimization\rangle$ $\langle Var\rangle_+$ $\langle Condition\rangle$ $\langle Expr\rangle$

$\langle Optimization\rangle$ ::=   '**argany**' | '**argmax**' | '**argmin**'

$\langle Condition\rangle$ ::=   '**(**'$\langle Limiter\rangle$'**)**'

$\langle Limiter\rangle$ ::=   '**k = **'$\langle Digit\rangle$ | '**t > **'$\langle Digit\rangle$ | '**t < **'$\langle Digit\rangle$

$\langle Expr\rangle$ ::= $\langle Function\rangle$'**(**'$\langle Param\rangle$'**)**' ($\langle Operator\rangle$ $\langle Function\rangle$'**(**'$\langle Param\rangle$'**)**')*

$\langle Param\rangle$ = $\langle Id\rangle$ | $\langle Digit\rangle$'**,**'$\langle Id\rangle$

$\langle Function\rangle$ ::= $\langle String\rangle$

$\langle Operator\rangle$ ::=   '**+**' | '**-**' | '*****' | '**/**'

$\langle Var\rangle$ ::=   '**v**'$\langle Digit\rangle$

$\langle Id\rangle$ ::=   '**f**'$\langle Digit\rangle$

$\langle Digit\rangle$ ::=   ('**0**'..'**9**')+

Grammar 2. Selection's specification in EBNF

can be *argmin*, *argmax*, or *argany* to find the minimum, maximum, or any value that satisfies a condition, respectively. The $<Condition>$ parameter limits the number of results: k = N returns the top k values, and t>R or t<R returns values greater than or lesser than a threshold value. The $<Var>$ parameter serves as an iterator over a collection of DFGs. Finally, in $<Expr>$, the user indicates a collection of DFGs ($<Id>$) and the function ($<Function>$) they want to apply to this collection of DFGs to obtain specific properties on the DFGs based on the metrics associated with them. Functions can be combined, such as finding the difference between applying a function to one collection of DFGs and another ($functionA(\mathtt{f2})$ - $functionA(\mathtt{f1})$), or the sum of the results from two functions on the same collection ($functionA(\mathtt{f1})$ + $functionB(\mathtt{f1})$). Some examples of these functions are **meanNodes()** or **maxEdges()**, which return the average value of the metric of the nodes or the maximum value of the transitions, respectively.

2.2 Semantics

To formally describe the semantics of LoVizQL, we introduce some formal definitions and an algorithm that reflects how the processing of a query takes place. We assume the existence of these sets: $\mathcal{C}$ is the set of case identifiers, $\mathcal{A}$ is the set of activity names, $\mathcal{A}tt$ is the set of attribute names, $\mathcal{T}$ is the set of timestamps, and $\mathcal{V}$ is the set of attribute values.

Definition 1 (Event and event log). *An event is a tuple (c, a, t, p) where $c \in \mathcal{C}$ indicates to which case the event belongs, $a \in \mathcal{A}$ is an activity name, $t \in \mathcal{T}$ is a timestamp that indicates when exactly the event occurred, and $p \in \mathcal{A}tt \nrightarrow \mathcal{V}$*

is a partial function that assigns a value to each attribute name. An event log L is a nonempty finite set of events. $\mathbb{U}_L$ *is the universe of all possible event logs.*

Definition 2 (Directly-Follows Graph). *A* Directly-Follows Graph (DFG) *is a tuple (A, T, M) where:*

- $A \subseteq \mathcal{A} \cup \mathcal{V} \cup \{start, end\}$ *are nodes, where start and end are special nodes that are typically used to represent the beginning and the end of the process.*
- $T \subseteq A \times A$ *are transitions.*
- M *is a set of metric functions $m : A \cup T \cup \{\circ\} \nrightarrow \mathbb{R}$ that assign a metric value to nodes, transitions, or the whole DFG, represented by $\circ$.*

$\mathbb{U}_{DFG}$ *is the universe of all possible DFGs.*

Next, we define several key concepts of the semantics of a LoVizQL query. We start with the iteration function, which provides semantics to the variables v_x used in the query:

Definition 3 (Iterator Function). *An iterator function is a partial injective function defined as follows: $it : (\mathcal{A}tt \nrightarrow \mathcal{V}) \nrightarrow \mathbb{U}_L \cup \mathbb{U}_{DFGs}$. This function maps a given assignment of values to attributes $(\mathcal{A}tt \nrightarrow \mathcal{V})$ to a log or DFG. Its inverse function is defined as it^{-1}.* $\mathbb{U}_{it}$ *is the universe of all possible iterator functions.*

For example, consider the query represented in Table 1, specifically, consider the first row (f1) and suppose that the attribute *case:parts* has two values a and b. In this case, an iterator function (it_{v1}) for variable $v1$ would map $\{(case : parts, a)\}$ to the DFG obtained from the events where *case:parts* is a, and $\{(case : parts, b)\}$ to the DFG obtained from the events where *case:parts* is b. Using the iterator function, we can define the semantics of each of the variables used in the queries by mapping each variable id to an iterator function:

Definition 4 (Variable Mapping). *Let $\mathbb{U}_{vid}$ be the universe of all possible variable ids. A variable mapping vmap is a set of tuples $(v, it) \in \mathbb{U}_{vid} \times \mathbb{U}_{it}$ that assigns a variable id to an iterator function. Let $x = (v, it)$ be a set of tuples with a variable v and an interator function it, we use x_v and x_{it} to refer to v and it.* $\mathbb{U}_{vmap}$ *depicts the universe of all possible variable mappings.*

Following up on the previous example, the pair $(v1, it_{v1})$ would map variable $v1$ to its iterator function defined in the *Filter* field.

In addition to defining variables, each query row names a collection of DFGs. This can be captured as follows:

Definition 5 (Collection Mapping). *Let $\mathbb{U}_{fid}$ be an universe of all possible row names. A collection mapping cmap is set of tuples $(n, c, v) \in \mathbb{U}_{fid} \times \mathcal{P}(\mathbb{U}_{DFGs}) \times \mathcal{P}(\mathbb{U}_{vid})$ that assigns a name to a collection of DFGs and specifies the iterators of that collection.* $\mathbb{U}_{cmap}$ *represents the universe of all possible collection mappings.*

For instance, the first row of Table 1 specifies the mapping $(f1, c, \{v1\})$, where $f1$ is the name of the row, c is the collection of DFGs specified in the row, and $v1$ is the variable identifier that iterates over that collection. Using these definitions, we can define a query in LoVizQL.

Definition 6 (Query row). *A query row is a tuple (n, f, g, s), where $n \in \mathbb{U}_{fid}$ is the name of the row specified in the row field and f, g, s are three functions defined as follows:*

- *Filter function (field Filter): $f : \mathbb{U}_L \times \mathbb{U}_{vmap} \to \mathcal{P}(\mathbb{U}_L) \times ((\mathbb{U}_{vid} \times \mathbb{U}_{it}) \cup \bot)$ receives an event log L and a vmap that represents the variables v_x defined in the previous rows of the query and returns a set of event logs that are subsets of L and $(\mathbb{U}_{vid} \times \mathbb{U}_{it}) \cup \bot$ represents the variable v_x and its iterator function assigned to the output of the filter or $\bot$ if no variable is assigned.*
- *DFG creation function (fields $Nodes, Metric, \%A, \%P$): $g: \mathbb{U}_L \to \mathbb{U}_{DFG}$ receives an event log and returns a DFG of the event log.*
- *Selection function (field Selection): $s : \mathbb{U}_{cmap} \times \mathbb{U}_{vmap} \to \mathbb{U}_{vid} \times \mathbb{U}_{it}$ receives a collection mapping and a variable mapping and returns a variable ids assigned to its corresponding iterator.*

Definition 7 (Query). *A query Q is a tuple (O, R), where O represents the outputs as a set of row names $(O \subseteq \mathbb{U}_{fid})$, and R is a sequence of rows such that $O \subseteq \{n \in \mathbb{U}_{fid} | (n, z, g, s) \in R\}$.*

For instance, in Table 1, O is f2, and R is the two rows of the table.

The execution of a query is represented in Algorithm 1, whose input is an event log L and a query Q (line 1) and the output is a collection of DFGs (line 2). The process starts by creating the variable and collection mappings (lines 3 and 4). Then, each row of the query is processed as follows (line 5). First, the filter function of the query receives the log and the variable mapping (line 6) and returns a collection of event log subsets called *logCol* and, optionally, a variable id together with its iterator function. Then, a collection of DFGs (*dfgCol*) and a DFG iterator function (*dfgIt*) are created (line 7). For each event log subset *logCol* (line 8), a DFG is generated with the g function of the query (line 9) and it is added to the collection of DFGs of the query (line 10). In addition, if the filter returned a variable id (line 11), the DFG iterator function is updated to refer to the created DFG (line 12). After processing all event log subsets, if the filter returned a variable id (line 15), both *vmap* and *cmap* are updated (lines 16–17). Otherwise, a tuple with n, *dfgCol* is added to *cmap* (line 19). Finally if the selection function is defined, (line 21), it is executed and the result is added to *vmap* (line 22). Finally, the collection of DFGs is returned (line 25).

3   Evaluation

The evaluation performed aims to show that (i) LoVizQL successfully addresses typical analyses in real-world situations, and that (ii) it simplifies the finding of specific subsets of event log data and their DFGs.

Algorithm 1. Algorithm to process a LoVizQL query.

1: Input: a log L and a query (O, R)
2: Output: a collection of DFGs: $\mathcal{P}(\mathbb{U}_{DFG})$
3: $vmap \leftarrow \emptyset$
4: $cmap \leftarrow \emptyset$
5: **for all** $(n, f, g, s) \in R$ **do**
6:    $(logCol, vm) \leftarrow f(L, vmap)$
7:    $dfgCol \leftarrow \emptyset;\ dfgIt \leftarrow \emptyset$
8:    **for all** $l \in logCol$ **do**
9:       $dfg \leftarrow g(l)$
10:       $dfgCol \leftarrow dfgCol \cup dfg$
11:       **if** $(vm \neq \bot)$ **then**
12:          $dfgIt(vm_{it}^{-1}(l)) \leftarrow dfg$
13:       **end if**
14:    **end for**
15:    **if** $(vm \neq \bot)$ **then**
16:       $vmap \leftarrow vmap \cup \{(vm_v, dfgIt)\}$
17:       $cmap \leftarrow cmap \cup (n, dfgCol, \{vm_v\})$
18:    **else**
19:       $cmap \leftarrow cmap \cup (n, dfgCol, \emptyset)$
20:    **end if**
21:    **if** $(s \neq \bot)$ **then**
22:       $vmap \leftarrow vmap \cup s(cmap, vmap)$
23:    **end if**
24: **end for**
25: **return** $\{dfg \in \mathbb{U}_{DFG} | (n, dfg, x) \in cmap \wedge n \in O\}$

To address the first objective, we have analyzed the reports submitted to the BPIC in 2015 [4], 2019 [5] and 2020 [6]. First, we reviewed the business questions posed in the three challenges by three different organizations in three different domains, and found at least one question in each of them whose objective is to look for process differences, which makes them well-suited to apply LoVizQL. This means that the questions that can benefit the most from LoVizQL can be found in a wide variety of contexts. Next, we reviewed the reports where the answer to these questions is clearly described for each BPIC (9, 13 and 14 reports, respectively), and looked for analyses in which LoVizQL can be directly applied. We identified 5, 3, and 7 reports in which LoVizQL can be directly applied in the analysis. Therefore, we conclude that in at least 40% of the reports, LoVizQL would have been useful to perform part of the analysis.

To address the second objective, we have implemented a functional version of LoVizQL, and applied it to all the cases mentioned above. All details and the implementation of the queries are publicly available.[2] Due to space restrictions, in this paper we focus on two BPIC reports [8,9] as representative examples. In the following, we provide information on each use case. Specifically, for each of them we briefly describe the dataset used, the analysis performed in the report,

---

[2] https://doi.org/10.5281/zenodo.8182758.

how that analysis could be carried out using current process mining tools, and the queries that could be defined to conduct the analysis with LoVizQL. Note that in the analyses using current process mining tools, we have included the steps that are most likely to be performed with tools like Disco and Celonis, but there could be other alternatives.

3.1 Use Case 1: Where Are Differences in Throughput Times Between the Municipalities and How Can These Be Explained?

Dataset. This business question was posed in the BPIC 2015 [4]. The data offered in this challenge consists of five event logs provided by five Dutch municipalities. These logs encompass all building permit applications spanning a period of roughly four years. The dataset has about 263,000 log entries.

Report. Report [8] answers this question as follows. First of all, the authors merge the five event logs to facilitate the manipulation and analysis of the data. Next, they analyze several aspects that could affect the throughput time of each municipality, such as the presence of rework in the processes. To do this, they calculate and compare the percentage of rework of activities of the complete event log with the percentage of each municipality.

Process Mining Tools. Starting from the unified event log, the analysis using a tool like Disco or Celonis involves the following steps. First, the analyst calculates the percentage of rework of activities from the complete log by counting the number of occurrences of each activity in each case but only considering those that are repeated more than once in each case. Second, they compare the percentage that this value represents with respect to the total number of occurrences of all activities. They need to manually check them and calculate these percentages. Third, the analyst filters the event log for one municipality. Fourth, the analyst calculates the percentage of rework for the municipality (similarly to what was done for the complete event log). Fifth, the analyst compares the value with the previous value. Sixth, the analyst repeats the last three steps for each of the municipalities and draws conclusions from the results.

LoVizQL Query. Table 2 translates these actions to LoVizQL. In the first row, the DFG corresponding to the complete event log is stored in f1. Then, in the second row, the event log data is grouped by municipality so that a collection of five DFGs, one for each municipality, is created and stored in f2. In the Selection field of the second row, the difference between the percentage of rework of activities of each DFG and the percentage of rework of the complete log is calculated. Those cases in which this difference is positive (i.e., the municipalities where the percentage of rework is above the average of the five municipalities), are stored in v2. In the last row, v2 is used to filter the data and to generate the respective DFGs. This collection of DFGs (f3) is the output of the query. Only the most frequent activities and transitions are visualized according to the %P and %A fields, and the total number of occurrences of each node and transition is shown as specified by the "Total repetitions" metric.

3.2   Use Case 2: What Is the Throughput of the Invoicing Process, I.e., the Time Between Goods Receipt, Invoice Receipt and Payment (clear Invoice)?

Dataset. This business question pertains to the BPIC 2019 [5]. In this challenge, data from a multinational company in The Netherlands specializing in coatings and paints was gathered. The dataset has about 1.5 million log entries.

Table 2. LoVizQL query for use case 1

Name	Filter	Nodes	Metrics	%P	%A	Selection
f1			[Total Repetitions, Absolute Frequency]			
f2	[Mandatory] v1<-"municipality".*		[Total Repetitions, Absolute Frequency]			$v2<-argany_{v1}(t>0)$ PercReworkAct(f2) - PercReworkAct(f1)
*f3	[Mandatory] v2		Total Repetitions	0.1	0.1	

Report. In report [9], the authors investigate the distributions of case duration for each combination of two event attributes, namely, *"case:Document Type"* and *"case:Item Type"*, which, according to domain knowledge, may have an influence on case duration. There are a total of 13 different combinations. For each of them, they represent a pie chart with the cycle time of the transitions between activities and they identify those that contain some transitions whose cycle time is longer than 30% of the total duration.

Process Mining Tools. To perform this analysis with a process mining tool, the analyst has to manually apply one filter for each of the 13 combinations of values of the *"case:Document Type"* and *"case:Item Type"* attributes. Next, for each of these 13 filtered event logs, they have to identify the transitions whose cycle time is greater than 30% of the total duration. This involves manually converting the duration into a percentage that represents with respect the total duration of the process and *visually* identifying the transitions in each of the 13 DFGs obtained.

LoVizQL Query. The analysis performed in the report can be translated into the query of Table 3. In the first row, we filter the traces by each possible combination of the values of the attribute "case:Document Type" and "case:Item Type". These event attributes and their possible combinations are stored in v1.

Then, we create the collection of DFGs with the average of cycle time ("Mean CT" metric) corresponding to these subsets of data and it is stored in f1. Next, we get the number of transitions whose cycle time is longer than 30% of the total duration using the *CTPorcTransitions()* function for each subset of data in f1. Finally, the combinations of attribute values for which at least one transition is returned are stored in the variable v2. The output of the query is the collection of DFGs with "Mean CT" related to those values that are stored in f2 and represented in the second row of the query.

Table 3. LoVizQL query for use case 2

Name	Filter	Nodes	Metrics	%P	%A	Selection
f1	[Mandatory] v1<- ["case:Document Type","case:Item Type"]."*"		Mean CT			v2<- $argany_{v1}$ (t>0) CTPorc- Transi- tions(30,f1)
*f2	[Mandatory] v2		Mean CT	0.1	0.1	

In conclusion, the previous use cases show that significant manual effort must be put to obtain several groups of traces from the event log. Also, the identification of particular subsets that meet certain conditions, which involves repeating several actions and making comparisons between DFGs, relies heavily on the user. This heavy user workload is caused because process mining tools are not prepared to manage several DFGs at the same time in an homogeneous manner. Instead, the user has to apply all the operations to each DFG one by one. Furthermore, these tools do not usually make it easier to compare DFGs [3]. In contrast, DFG collections are first-class citizens in LoVizQL. This allows performing many of these steps in a single query, which reduces effort and errors.

4 Related Work

In the last decade, specific query languages have been developed in the business process domain to obtain useful information about processes and provide assistance to their executions. These languages have been classified in different categories in the process querying framework [14]. Specifically, some of them were classified as event log query languages [13], which covered different topics.

Some approaches have focused on treating event log data as graphs. For instance, Beheshti et al. [2] developed a framework to model event log data as graphs along with a language called BP-SPARQL to summarize the data and discover hierarchies. Other approaches have focused on facilitating the writing of queries. González López de Murillas et al. [12] designed a language called

DAPOQ-LANG that combines process and data perspectives to make selections and obtain insights more easily. Álvarez et al. [21] designed PIQL, a language with a user-friendly notation to perform queries of Key Performance Indicators (KPIs) and Process Performance Indicators (PPIs) of activities or cases. In addition, some approaches have focused on formulating queries with complex relations between elements of the process (e.g., control flow relations among activities), which are called constrains. Momotko and Subieta [11] designed a query language called BPQL to express constraints for dynamic processes following existing standards and in an understandable way. Schuster et al. [15] designed an event log query language to select case instances using partially ordered activity constraints. Tan et al. [18] designed a query language called IQL, which retrieves information using workflow constraints (e.g., two activities that occur consecutively and with concrete attribute values). Finally, the software company Celonis developed its own language [19] to formalize business questions as queries.

None of the previous query languages is based on the use of DFGs nor allows the user to iteratively filter event log data and select those that meet certain conditions through comparisons between them. To compare them, process mining tools usually provide DFGs, which are manually modified by the user to specify the conditions. Thus, each time the user makes a change, a new DFG is generated. This process is tedious and time-consuming since it is based on a trial-and-error basis. In this regard, Seeliger et al. [16] developed a system to group event log traces into subsets with similar behaviors and recommend those related to the most deviating PPIs (e.g., the average case duration of a subset is higher than that of all cases). However, the conditions in which the user is interested are not considered since the groups are generated by trace clustering.

In data science, some proposals have also addressed the challenge of making comparisons in exploratory data analysis and generating visualizations that meet certain conditions. Our main inspiration is Siddiqui et al. [17], which designed a query language for visual exploration called ZQL, with which the user can indicate a set of desired visual patterns to explore the data. ZQL uses the patterns to obtain the visualizations that fit them best. Thus, the user does not need to generate thousands of graphs to explore the data and find specific graphs.

The work presented in this paper extends the previous research. Specifically, it adapts concepts from ZQL [17] to process mining. We rely on DFGs instead of bar charts or heatmaps, extend filters to consider the concept of case, and provide functions to select DFGs based on their properties. Finally, we show that LoVizQL is useful to ease analyses performed in real process mining reports.

5   Conclusions and Future Work

In this paper, we have introduced LoVizQL, a query language to ease the generation and the identification of DFGs that meet certain conditions from event log data. In our qualitative comparison it can be deducted that LoVizQL reduces the effort of the users compared to some manual tasks performed with current tools which are frequently carried out [3,10] (e.g., manipulations, DFGs comparisons).

Our proposal also has some limitations. First, it is based on DFGs, which suffer from the issues described in [1]. For instance, the application of frequency thresholds in DFGs can lead to interpretation problems. However, we chose DFGs for process visualization because they are the predominant visualization mode in process mining tools (e.g., Disco, Celonis) and also for efficiency reasons. Second, we have shown that LoVizQL is useful for specific types of analysis. It could be suitable in other contexts, but we have not explored that yet.

It should not be assumed that the user will always know what query to define to obtain interesting results, but rather, in practice, they shall interact with a tool that will help them to find the information of interest depending on their objective or business question, and build the LoVizQL query accordingly. Our future research efforts will focus on the development of such tool support as well as a user interface to visually define the queries and interact with the obtained DFG collections. Also, with the evaluation conducted so far we have observed that LoVizQL reduces the effort of performing analyses in terms of steps, but we still need to assess its performance with real users.

References

1. van der Aalst, W.M.P.: A practitioner's guide to process mining: limitations of the directly-follows graph. Procedia Comput. Sci. **164**, 321–328 (2019)
2. Beheshti, A., Benatallah, B., Motahari-Nezhad, H.R., Ghodratnama, S., Amouzgar, F.: BP-SPARQL: a query language for summarizing and analyzing big process data. In: Polyvyanyy, A. (ed.) Process Querying Methods, pp. 21–48. Springer, Cham (2022). https://doi.org/10.1007/978-3-030-92875-9_2
3. Capitán-Agudo, C., Salas-Urbano, M., Cabanillas, C., Resinas, M.: Analyzing how process mining reports answer time performance questions. In: Di Ciccio, C., Dijkman, R., del Río Ortega, A., Rinderle-Ma, S. (eds.) BPM 2022. LNCS, vol. 13420, pp. 234–250. Springer, Cham (2022). https://doi.org/10.1007/978-3-031-16103-2_17
4. van Dongen, B.: BPI Challenge 2015. 4TU.ResearchData (2015). https://doi.org/10.4121/uuid:31a308ef-c844-48da-948c-305d167a0ec1
5. van Dongen, B.: BPI Challenge 2019. 4TU.ResearchData (2019). https://doi.org/10.4121/uuid:d06aff4b-79f0-45e6-8ec8-e19730c248f1
6. van Dongen, B.: BPI Challenge 2020. 4TU.ResearchData (2020). https://doi.org/10.4121/uuid:52fb97d4-4588-43c9-9d04-3604d4613b51
7. Dumas, M., La Rosa, M., Mendling, J., Reijers, H.A.: Fundamentals of Business Process Management, 2nd edn. Springer, Heidelberg (2018). https://doi.org/10.1007/978-3-662-56509-4
8. van der Ham, U.: Benchmarking of five dutch municipalities with process mining techniques reveals opportunities for improvement. Technical report, BPI Challenge (2015)
9. Kim, J., Ko, J., Lee, S.: Business Process Intelligence Challenge 2019: Process discovery and deviation analysis of purchase order handling process. Technical report, BPI Challenge (2019)
10. Klinkmüller, C., Müller, R., Weber, I.: Mining process mining practices: an exploratory characterization of information needs in process analytics. In: Business Process Management (BPM), pp. 322–337 (2019)

11. Momotko, M., Subieta, K.: Business process query language. In: Polyvyanyy, A. (ed.) Process Querying Methods, pp. 345–376. Springer, Cham (2022). https://doi.org/10.1007/978-3-030-92875-9_12
12. González López de Murillas, E., Reijers, H.A., van der Aalst, W.M.P.: Everything you always wanted to know about your process, but did not know how to ask. In: BPM Workshops, vol. 281, pp. 296–309 (2017)
13. Polyvyanyy, A.: Process Querying Methods. Springer, Cham (2022). https://doi.org/10.1007/978-3-030-92875-9
14. Polyvyanyy, A., Ouyang, C., Barros, A., van der Aalst, W.M.P.: Process querying: enabling business intelligence through query-based process analytics. Decis. Support Syst. **100**, 41–56 (2017)
15. Schuster, D., Martini, M., van Zelst, S.J., van der Aalst, W.M.P.: Control-flow-based querying of process executions from partially ordered event data. In: Service-Oriented Computing (ICSOC), pp. 19–35 (2022)
16. Seeliger, A., Sánchez Guinea, A., Nolle, T., Mühlhäuser, M.: ProcessExplorer: intelligent process mining guidance. In: Business Process Management (BPM), pp. 216–231 (2019)
17. Siddiqui, T., Kim, A., Lee, J., Karahalios, K., Parameswaran, A.: Effortless data exploration with zenvisage: an expressive and interactive visual analytics system. Proc. VLDB Endow. **10**(4), 457–468 (2016)
18. Tang, Y., Cui, W., Su, J.: A query language for workflow logs. ACM Trans. Manage. Inf. Syst. **13**(2), 1–28 (2021)
19. Vogelgesang, T., Ambrosy, J., Becher, D., Seilbeck, R., Geyer-Klingeberg, J., Klenk, M.: Celonis PQL: a query language for process mining. In: Polyvyanyy, A. (ed.) Process Querying Methods, pp. 377–408. Springer, Cham (2022). https://doi.org/10.1007/978-3-030-92875-9_13
20. Wirth, N.: What can we do about the unnecessary diversity of notation for syntactic definitions? Commun. ACM **20**(11), 822–823 (1977)
21. Álvarez, J.M.P., Díaz, A.C., Parody, L., Quintero, A.M.R., Gómez-López, M.T.: Process instance query language and the process querying framework. In: Polyvyanyy, A. (ed.) Process Querying Methods, pp. 85–111. Springer, Cham (2022). https://doi.org/10.1007/978-3-030-92875-9_4

On the Nature of Data in RPA Bots

Maximilian Völker[(✉)] and Mathias Weske

Hasso Plattner Institute, University of Potsdam, Potsdam, Germany
`{maximilian.voelker,mathias.weske}@hpi.de`

Abstract. Robotic process automation (RPA) automates tasks traditionally performed by employees, reducing repetitive and error-prone work. While RPA bot models are based on graphical notations, data, a key component of RPA, is often not explicitly represented, making it difficult to understand how data contributes to the automation. This paper explores the role of data in RPA, extends the ontology of RPA operations by data aspects, and proposes a visualization of data in RPA bot models, promoting the design of more comprehensible RPA bot services and enabling different bot analysis techniques.

Keywords: Robotic Process Automation · Ontology · Modeling · Data

1 Introduction

Modeling processes to enable their automation, including the orchestration of services, has been a strong motivation for business process management (BPM) for decades. With robotic process automation (RPA), a new technology emerged that does not require changes to the existing IT systems, as it operates primarily on the user interface level [1] to automate legacy systems, for example. Furthermore, RPA features various capabilities beyond simulating mouse clicks and key presses, like accessing databases or connecting to modern cloud services by using APIs [4], thus bridging the gap between legacy systems and modern services. Tasks automated with RPA are usually of a structured nature and centered around digital data [9], and common use cases include extracting or transferring data between applications [5].

Targeting business users, RPA workflows can typically be defined in a graphical manner by composing predefined building blocks [4,11], such as for clicking a button. However, the configuration of inputs, outputs, and parameters of building blocks is mainly done in a form-like manner. Consequently, data is typically not represented graphically, which is especially problematic as the role of data in the RPA bot and its data-flow cannot be conceived easily. To determine which parts of the bot are dependent from a data-perspective, the configuration of each building block needs to be reviewed individually.

In this paper, we conceptualize the role of data in RPA by refining the ontology of RPA operations [11] (Sect. 3), and suggest an approach for visualizing data and its flow in RPA bot models (Sect. 4). Furthermore, we highlight practical implications in Sect. 5, such as data-flow analysis to prevent run-time errors.

F. Monti et al. (Eds.): ICSOC 2023, LNCS 14420, pp. 29–37, 2023.
https://doi.org/10.1007/978-3-031-48424-7_3

2 Preliminaries and Motivating Example

The lack of RPA standards leads to varied terminology and modeling interfaces across vendors [2,11]. To address this, the ontology of RPA operations (ORPAO) was introduced in [11], featuring the various types of RPA operations (the building blocks), software applications and services that can be automated, and relevant data file types. Figure 1 shows some of the main concepts of the ORPAO, including the taxonomy of RPA operations with its three main classes, where AutomationOperations, for example, represent operations that actually interfere with the system and applications outside the bot.

As shown in Fig. 1, the ontology already includes a rudimentary conceptualization of data based on CSO:Data, originating from the upper *Core Software Ontology (CSO)* by Oberle et al. [6]. For the ORPAO, CSO:Data was extended by File, comprising a taxonomy of different file types [11]. Furthermore, the CSO:accesses relation was refined to hold between RPAOperation and CSO:Data and specialized by the subtypes reads, writes, and transforms [11].

The CSO further includes a notion of inputs and outputs, which was reused in [11] to define that the reads relation defines the input and writes the output of an operation: According to the CSO, CSO:Input and CSO:Output are roles played by certain CSO:Data [6]. The relations CSO:inputFor and CSO:outputFor connect CSO:Inputs and CSO:Outputs to operations, and reads, writes, and transforms were introduced as "shortcut" for this construct [11].

In [12], the ontology was extended by information regarding the control flow by mapping operations to the meta-meta-model for process model languages by Heidari et al. [3]. This mapping enables the vendor-independent modeling of RPA bots based on the concepts in the ORPAO in any common process modeling language, such as BPMN. At the same time, these conceptual models can be translated into RPA bot models of specific vendors and vice versa [12].

The ORPAO recognizes the importance of data in RPA by a separate class of operations, the DataOperations with its subclasses [11]. DataExtractionOperations access external data resources to retrieve data and cache it internally, for example, ReadCell operations that extract a value of spreadsheets for future use. DataInputOperations can write content to external data resources based

Fig. 1. Excerpt of important elements in the ontology of RPA operations, based on [11]

Fig. 2. Exemplary RPA bot model

on internally available data, like `WriteCell` operations write a value to a spreadsheet. `DataTransformationOperations` read the contents of an external data resource, apply a specific transformation to the data, and immediately write the result back to the data resource, like `SortTable`. `DataFileOperations` modify the properties of the data "container", such as creating, moving, or deleting a file.

Consequently, we need to differentiate two types of data in RPA: *External data resources*, such as files, exist independently of the RPA bot itself and are not bound to RPA in any way. *Internal data* is only available within the scope of the RPA bot and thus lost when it terminates. It can be a dynamic value determined at run-time of the bot, i.e., a variable, or a hard-coded value specified in advance.

Although data plays a critical role in RPA, this aspect is typically not expressed visually, but hidden in the configurations of the operations. Figure 2 shows a sample model of an RPA bot. This small example illustrates the need to visualize data and its flow through the process: What URL is the bot visiting? Which Excel file is being manipulated? Is there a relationship between the value extracted from the web page and the value inserted into the spreadsheet cell?

This problem multiplies as bots become more complex and handle multiple data sources. Data dependencies between operations are not visible, but can only be uncovered incrementally by examining the configuration of each operation.

The example exhibits another peculiarity of data access in RPA: The "Get Text From Element" and "Set Cell Value" operations are each preceded by operations that provide the appropriate data context for the operations to work in. These preparatory operations determine the data on which the operations will be performed, i.e., their input is not configured but determined by the context.

3   Conceptualizing Data in RPA Bots

To capture the dualism of data in RPA, the ontology of RPA operations and its data relationships are refined and extended in the following.

Foremost, `DataResource` is introduced as an intermediate class between `CSO:Data` and `File`, and `TransientData` as its sibling, representing internal data. The more abstract `DataResource` class is intended to reflect that there are more data sources than `Files`, like `Databases` or `WebResources`. `DataResources` exist independently of RPA bots and can also be accessed by other services or users. `TransientData`, on the other hand, only exists within the scope of the bot instance and will be discarded when the bot instance terminates. It can be further divided into `SimpleTransientData`, which represents data of primitive types like strings, and `ComplexTransientData`, such as `TabularData`.

The ORPAO already introduced the relations reads, writes, and transforms as specializations of the generic CSO:accesses, connecting RPAOperations and CSO:Data (cf. Sect. 2). With the newly introduced classes of DataResources and TransientData, we can refine them to now hold between AutomationOperations and DataResources. This complies with the definition of AutomationOperations being the class of operations that can access data outside the bot [11]. At the same time, focusing solely on read and write access does not encompass the full spectrum of data access that services can typically perform, such as *create*, *read*, *update*, and *delete* (CRUD), and that can also be implemented with RPA. Therefore, we first introduce two new relations, creates and deletes, to be able to express that an operation creates or destroys a DataResource.

Also, the different types of access to DataResources need to be extended and detailed further. First, there are operations that can directly modify DataResources in a persistent way, like AppendToFile. However, many operations, such as those related to office or the browser, do not directly operate on the data but on a working copy of it. For example, ExcelWriteCell requires that an Excel workbook has been opened before to which it can write content, as pointed out in Sect. 2. At the same time, only after an explicit save operation (SaveWorkbook) has been performed, the change is persisted. Consequently, we can observe additional subtypes of access related to these working copies:

provisions(New) describes that an operation provides a working copy of the related (newly created) DataResource for the subsequent operations, e.g., OpenNewExcelWorkbook provisionsNew ExcelWorkbook. persists describes that an operation saves the changes made to the provisioned DataResource, like SaveWorkbook persists ExcelWorkbook. Finally, closes describes that an operation destroys a working copy, such as CloseWorkbook closes ExcelWorkbook.

Furthermore, we can specialize the relations reads and writes: Operations that can access the resource directly without any preceding data provisioning are related to DataResources by directlyReadsFrom or directlyWritesTo. For example, AppendToFile directlyWritesTo TextFile. In contrast, the relations implicitlyReadsFrom and implicitlyWritesTo indicate that data provisioning is required and thus that the data access is not performed directly on the original resource. For example, ExcelWriteCell implicitlyWritesTo ExcelWorkbook. Such implicit changes will be lost if not followed by a persists operation.

As described in Sect. 2, the access relations in the ORPAO were already associated with the notion of inputs and outputs using roles. We retain this definition for the newly introduced specialized relations that reflect direct and implicit access. Thus, given an operation and its relation to a DataResource, we can deduce which data plays the role of an input for the operation and which data is considered an output of the operation.

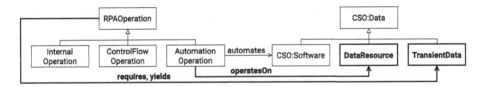

Fig. 3. Updated abstract of important elements in the ORPAO (cf. Figure 1), including the new main data classes and relations (depicted in black)

Next, the relations to `TransientData` are investigated. Similar to the read and write relations, we introduce `requires` and `yields` to express that certain `TransientData` plays the input/output role for a given `RPAOperation`.[1]

While `*ReadsFrom`/`*WritesTo` and `requires`/`yields` all represent the same idea of inputs and outputs, there are important differences. The former denote access of `AutomationOperations` to external data, i.e., they affect the state of the computer outside the RPA bot. The latter represent the use of bot-internal data, i.e., `TransientData`, by any `RPAOperation`. For example, `InternalOperations` like `MatchRegularExpression` operate on internal data and `ControlFlowOperations` may use them for decision-making.

The updated overview of the main concepts is shown in Fig. 3. The different relations between `AutomationOperations` and `DataResources` are subsumed under a generic relation `operatesOn`, which replaces the previously used `CSO:accesses`, since it now encompasses more concepts than just read and write.

Overall, using the new relations, we can express at a conceptual level what type of access an `AutomationOperation` performs on which `DataResources`, and if and how an `RPAOperation` works with `TransientData`, i.e., bot-internal data. For example, `ExcelReadCell implicitlyReadsFrom ExcelWorkbook` and `yields StringTransientData`. Consequently, it requires data in form of an Excel workbook as input, and produces data in form of a string to be used internally. As it performs an implicit access, it can be inferred that the operation reads the data from a working copy of the workbook which needs to be provisioned before.

4   Visualizing Data in RPA Bot Models

To be able to model RPA bots based on the ontology of RPA operations, it was extended in [12] by a mapping of its concepts to the meta-meta-model for business process model languages created by Heidari et al. [3]. In order to model and visualize the discussed data aspects, the newly introduced concepts must be mapped to the meta-meta-model as well.

In general, the introduced concept of `DataResources` matches the concept of *DataStores* in the meta-meta-model, since data can be read from or written to

---

[1] The naming is inspired by the relations `CSO:methodRequires` and `CSO:methodYields` that relate `CSO:Methods` with `CSO:Data` in the Core Software Ontology [6].

Table 1. Mapping of ORPAO relations between `AutomationOperations` and `Data-`
`Resources` to process model patterns.

Relation	Model Pattern
`creates`	Task with *DataStore* as output
`directly[ReadsFrom│WritesTo]`	Task with *DataStore* as [input│output]
`deletes`	*No model concept for destructing model elements*
`provisions`	Task with *DataStore* as input and *ProvisionedDataStore* as output
`implicitly[ReadsFrom│WritesTo]`	Task with *ProvisionedDataStore* as [input│output]
`persists`	Task with *ProvisionedDataStore* as input and *DataStore* as output
`closes`	*No model concept for destructing model elements*

it, and it stores data permanently beyond the scope of the bot. But the concepts
in the meta-meta-model do not allow expressing different types of data access
beyond inputs and outputs. Thus, the finer-grained access types discussed before
cannot be expressed directly, such as the implicit access via provisioned data. To
address this issue, we differentiate between *DataStores* that represent the actual
data and *ProvisionedDataStores*, the provisioned version of it. They represent a
working copy of the data, e.g., created by opening a file in a software program.

Table 1 details the mapping of relations in the ORPAO between
`DataResources` and `AutomationOperations` to model patterns based on the
meta-meta-model. Due to the lack of data associations besides read and write in
the meta-meta-model, the relations `creates` and `directlyWritesTo` share the
same pattern. Still, both relations should be modeled to ensure the data-flow

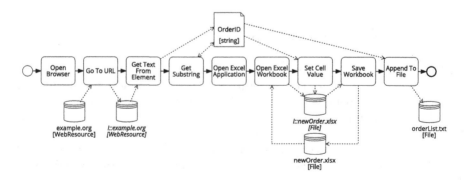

Fig. 4. Exemplary RPA bot model with data annotations

can be captured as detailed as possible and textual annotations could be used for clarification.

TransientData is mapped to *DataObjects*, more specifically, to a *DataObjectInput* if the TransientData is required by the operations and mapped to *DataObjectOutput* in case the operation yields the data. Data objects in general, also in the case of BPMN [7], represent data that only exists in the scope of the (bot) process instance and is lost at instance termination. This corresponds to the definition of TransientData as bot-internal, instance-specific data.

This definition also clarifies why the provisioned version of data is of type *DataStore* and not *DataObject*. Even though they are not persisted, they still exist outside the bot, such as an opened file in Excel that could remain open after the bot terminated, or could be accessed externally as well.

The extended mapping is applied to the example bot model given in Fig. 2. Figure 4 features the same process, now annotated with data information. As there is no concept for the *ProvisionedDataStores*, the difference is marked by italicizing the label. The model now shows which steps of the bot access external data, and whether it is a direct access, like for AppendToFile, or an indirect access, like SetCellValue. Moreover, it also visualizes the flow of data in the model: The data extracted from the website "example.org" is first internally manipulated by GetSubstring, further used to modify the Excel file "newOrder.xlsx", and later appended to the content of "orderList.txt".

To reduce the complexity of the model, the concept of ContextContainers introduced in [12] could be adapted, which allows subsuming operations that handle the context for indirect operations and could thus help reduce the overall model size and improve its clarity.[2]

5   Improving the Modeling of Bots by Considering Data

In the following, we outline possible applications of the introduced conceptualization and visualization.

Currently, the configuration of an operation in a bot is often hidden, e.g., in a sidebar. By using the semantic information provided by the ontology, the input and output configuration for an operation could be automatically derived from the visual bot model. For example, if an operation is connected to a data store using a read association, it can be concluded that the modeled DataResource is an input for the modeled operation. Consequently, the operation can be configured accordingly, given that the actual data resource is referenced in a defined way, such as using the label as in Fig. 4. However, it is important to note that associations to *ProvisionedDataStores* do not result in a configuration, as these operations depend on data provisioned before. Similarly, the model could be automatically updated as soon as the input/output configuration of an operation is modified.

---

[2] A model of the running example using these context containers and including data can be found here: https://github.com/bptlab/onto-rpa-platform/raw/main/components/data/figures/ContextContainerExample.svg.

By leveraging ontological knowledge about the inputs and outputs of operations, the bot model repository can be searched for a specific data usage, such as accessing a specific website or file, which can facilitate the maintenance of bots in case a web service or file structure changes.

It also enables the application of well-established techniques for data-flow analysis and error-detection in process models to RPA bot models, such as the data validation problems described in [8,10]. In particular, problems such as *redundant data*, where `TransientData` is written but never read; *missing data*; or *lost data*, where data is overwritten without being read in between, are relevant to RPA. Relevant in the context of RPA are also the problems of *mismatched data*, i.e., the (in)compatibility of data structures produced as output and later used as input, and *inconsistent data* due to concurrent data access.

In addition, RPA-specific data issues can be analyzed in the bot model. For example, related to the concept of "working copies", models can be checked for *missing context* or *lost changes*, i.e., an implicit data access that is not preceded by an appropriate provisioning step or that is not eventually persisted.

6   Conclusion

In this paper, we discussed the role of data in RPA services and their bot models, and presented a corresponding extension to the ontology of RPA operations along with a possible graphical representation for data in bot models. In addition to the improved representation, it enables vendor-agnostic data-flow analysis that can provide valuable insights and prevent errors. There are several aspects that can be further developed in the future. For example, differentiating between implicit and persisting accesses may help in error handling to determine which changes have already been persisted and thus need to be reverted or compensated for. Besides, the understandability and perceived usefulness of the approach by users should be investigated, especially since the additional elements increase the complexity of models. At the same time, different possible notations in addition to the one outlined in the paper could be assessed.

References

1. van der Aalst, W.M.P., Bichler, M., Heinzl, A.: Robotic process automation. Bus. Inf. Syst. Eng. **60**(4), 269–272 (2018). https://doi.org/10.1007/s12599-018-0542-4
2. Correia, C., Rodrigues da Silva, A.: Platform-independent specifications for robotic process automation applications. In: MODELSWARD 2022, pp. 379–386, SciTePress (2022). https://doi.org/10.5220/0010991200003119
3. Heidari, F., Loucopoulos, P., Brazier, F., Barjis, J.: A meta-meta-model for seven business process modeling languages. In: 2013 IEEE 15th Conference on Business Informatics, pp. 216–221, IEEE (2013), https://doi.org/10.1109/CBI.2013.38
4. Hofmann, P., Samp, C., Urbach, N.: Robotic process automation. Electron. Mark. **30**(1), 99–106 (2020). https://doi.org/10.1007/s12525-019-00365-8
5. Lacity, M., Willcocks, L., Craig, A.: Robotic process automation at telefonica O2. MIS Quart. Executive **15**(1) (2015)

6. Oberle, D., Grimm, S., Staab, S.: An Ontology for Software. In: Staab, S., Studer, R. (eds.) Handbook on Ontologies, pp. 383–402. Springer, Berlin, Heidelberg (2009). https://doi.org/10.1007/978-3-540-92673-3_17

7. Object Management Group: Business Process Model and Notation (BPMN) (2014). https://www.omg.org/spec/BPMN/

8. Sadiq, S., Orlowska, M., Sadiq, W., Foulger, C.: Data flow and validation in workflow modelling. In: Proceedings of the 15th Australasian Database Conference, pp. 207–214, Australian Computer Society (2004)

9. Syed, R., et al.: Robotic process automation: contemporary themes and challenges. Comput. Indust. **115**, 103162 (2020). https://doi.org/10.1016/j.compind.2019.103162

10. Trčka, N., van der Aalst, W.M.P., Sidorova, N.: Data-flow anti-patterns: discovering data-flow errors in workflows. In: van Eck, P., Gordijn, J., Wieringa, R. (eds.) CAiSE 2009. LNCS, vol. 5565, pp. 425–439. Springer, Heidelberg (2009). https://doi.org/10.1007/978-3-642-02144-2_34

11. Völker, M., Weske, M.: Conceptualizing bots in robotic process automation. In: Ghose, A., Horkoff, J., Silva Souza, V.E., Parsons, J., Evermann, J. (eds.) ER 2021. LNCS, vol. 13011, pp. 3–13. Springer, Cham (2021). https://doi.org/10.1007/978-3-030-89022-3_1

12. Völker, M., Weske, M.: Ontology-supported modeling of bots in robotic process automation. In: Ralyté, J., Chakravarthy, S., Mohania, M., Jeusfeld, M.A., Karlapalem, K. (eds.) ER 2022. LNCS, vol. 13607, pp. 239–254. Springer, Cham (2022). https://doi.org/10.1007/978-3-031-17995-2_17

Remaining Time Prediction for Collaborative Business Processes with Privacy Preservation

Jian Cao[1(✉)], Chi Wang[1], Wei Guan[1], Shiyou Qian[1], and Haiyan Zhao[2]

[1] Shanghai Jiaotong University, Shanghai, China
{cao-jian,guan-wei,qshiyou}@sjtu.edu.cn
[2] University of Shanghai for Science and Technology, Shanghai, China

Abstract. In collaborative business processes that involve multiple organizations, privacy concerns prevent organizations from sharing the raw data of their activities. This makes it challenging to predict remaining time without access to data on completed activities of other organizations. To address this challenge, this research proposes a strategy for predicting remaining time in collaborative business processes, which involve sequential sub-processes executed by different partners, while preserving the privacy of organizations. The proposed strategy involves transferring latent information from precedent sub-processes to the models of latter sub-processes, rather than raw data. Two models were designed to implement this strategy, and the experimental results indicate that the prediction accuracy of the models is comparable to that of models that use raw data.

Keywords: predictive business process monitoring · remaining time prediction · collaborative process · privacy preservation

1 Introduction

Predictive business process monitoring enables the assessment of future performance or reduction of possible violations [13,26]. Over the years, different methods have been proposed for various predictive business process monitoring tasks, such as compliance violation checks [7,32], anomaly detection [12], next activity prediction [17,24], and outcome prediction [27]. Remaining time prediction for business process cases is one of these tasks and can be used to facilitate remedial actions, such as resource allocation [33].

Various approaches have been proposed for remaining time prediction in recent years [30]. These approaches can be classified based on their process-awareness. Process-aware algorithms make predictions based on the process model, which is typically represented as a state transition system constructed from an event log [20]. Non-process aware approaches, on the other hand, rely on machine learning algorithms to make predictions. Features are selected and generated from completed activities and other information [15,18], which are then

F. Monti et al. (Eds.): ICSOC 2023, LNCS 14420, pp. 38–53, 2023.
https://doi.org/10.1007/978-3-031-48424-7_4

fed into regression models such as random forest [23] and XGBoost [22]. In recent years, deep learning models for remaining time prediction have gained popularity. These models obtain features automatically through end-to-end structures, making them particularly useful for event sequences that record the execution of business processes. Recurrent neural networks, especially those with a long short-term memory (LSTM) architecture, have been applied to solve predictive process monitoring problems due to their remarkable performance in sequence modeling tasks [14]. Furthermore, more complex deep learning models have also been proposed recently [33].

A typical collaborative business process structure consists of sequential sub-processes and each partner is responsible for a sub-process that is initiated after the completion of the preceding sub-process. As shown in Fig. 1, a simplified international shipping process can be divided into three sub-processes: *transportation from the seller to the domestic warehouse, international shipping between warehouses*, and *delivery from the overseas warehouse to the buyers*. The warehouses are responsible for packing, sorting, and picking the merchandise from different logistics channels. In scenarios where multiple organizations are involved, each responsible for a sub-process, predicting the remaining time during process execution is crucial. However, due to privacy concerns, these organizations may not want to share the raw data on activity execution for their respective sub-processes. Unfortunately, existing remaining time prediction models rely heavily on detailed information of the completed activities, making it challenging to predict the remaining time without access to such information.

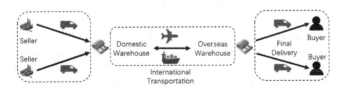

Fig. 1. A Collaborative Business Process Model for International Transportation

Currently, there is no research on how to undertake remaining time prediction for collaborative business processes while maintaining privacy. Federated learning (FL) [2] and split learning (SL) [21] are two popular privacy-preserving machine learning models in a distributed environment. In FL, the machine learning model generation takes place at the data owners' computers, and a coordinating server is used to generate a global model and share the knowledge among the distributed entities. In SL, a model is split between the client and the server. The client model is trained on the client using the local data and the outputs of the client model are sent to the server, which completes the rest of the training without looking at raw data from any client. Compared with FL, SL is more suitable for remaining time prediction for collaborative business processes since different partners only have data on their own sub- processes. However, in SL, only one final result is generated from the model of the server. For the remaining time prediction problem, each sub-process needs the remaining time prediction service, which means the partial model for the sub-process should output the remaining time prediction, and at the same time, it should provide information to the latter partial models.

In this paper, we propose a strategy for predicting remaining time in the collaborative business processes consisting of sequential sub-processes while preserving privacy. Our main contributions are:

- We formalize the problem of remaining time prediction in collaborative business processes with privacy preservation.
- We propose a strategy to share hidden state information between sub-models for remaining time prediction in collaborative business processes. Specifically, we design two models to implement this strategy.
- We conduct experiments on multiple datasets. The results show that our models have comparable prediction accuracy to models that use raw data.

2   Related Work

2.1   Remaining Time Prediction

Remaining time is the time needed to complete an instance process. Existing algorithms can be broadly classified into two categories based on whether the algorithm relies on a process model. Process-aware models predict remaining time based on statistical information derived from the process model, and two primary tools for process-aware prediction algorithms are state transition systems [1] and stochastic Petri nets [19]. For instance, in [20], a specific type of stochastic Petri net is utilized to capture arbitrary duration distributions for remaining time prediction, while in [29], remaining time prediction is based on stochastic Petri nets with generally distributed transitions using k-nearest neighbors. On the other hand, non-process aware approaches predict remaining time directly from event logs without explicitly constructing a process model. Several traditional machine learning algorithms, such as naive Bayes [18], SVR [18], random forest [23], and XGBoost [22], can be applied directly to the features obtained from event logs.

Neural networks can encode raw data into higher-level feature representations [4]. Given that events in business processes are similar to words in natural language processing, complex network structures like recurrent neural networks (RNNs) [9] have been explored. Particularly, RNNs with long short-term memory (LSTM) structures have been adopted by many studies. For instance, LSTM has been utilized to predict the cycle time of activities [24]. Researchers have extended the basic LSTM model to further improve prediction performance. For example, in [16], convolutional neural networks (CNNs) are combined with LSTMs to consider both spatial and temporal dependencies in underlying business processes. Deep learning models with more complex structures have also been explored [33]. For instance, in [31], a new deep learning model that utilizes two types of data representation based on a parallel-structure model is proposed, which consists of a CNN and a multi-layer perceptron (MLP) with an embedding layer, to predict the remaining time. A transformer-based model was proposed in [5] to learn high-level representations from event logs using an attention-based network. Additionally, adversarial learning techniques are used to boost prediction performance [25].

While numerous models for predicting remaining time have been developed, they typically assume that the model can access information about all completed activities, and prioritize improving prediction accuracy. In contrast, our focus is on the prediction of remaining time for collaborative business processes, where privacy concerns of the organizations responsible for executing sub-processes must be taken into account.

2.2   Privacy Preservation in Process Mining

The issue of preserving privacy is crucial in the field of process mining, as event logs may contain confidential information regarding the parties involved in the process. Therefore, it is necessary to pre-process the logs prior to their publication to ensure the privacy of individuals. An established approach to this problem is to anonymize the event log so that it becomes difficult for an attacker to identify any specific individual [8]. Additionally, context information is also taken into account, as it can potentially reveal private details [10].

Our approach differs from the current privacy preservation research in process mining, as we aim to protect the privacy of each organization during the training and inference of a remaining time prediction model.

3   Problem Formulation

3.1   Event Logs and Traces

Business process monitoring typically relies on event logs that record the events during process execution [28]. An *event log* is composed of sequences of events called *trace*. Each trace corresponds to a case of a business process. An *event* has various attributes, among which three attributes must appear: *activity name*, *timestamp* and *case id*. The *activity name* represents the activity the event executes, while the *timestamp* specifies when the event occurs. The *case id* indicates to which case the event belongs. With other event-wise or case-wise attributes, an event can be defined as follows:

$$e = (a, cid, t, (d_1, v_1), ..., (d_m, v_m)) \tag{1}$$

where e is the event, a is the activity name, cid is the case ID and t is the timestamp. Each tuple (d_i, v_i) represents an attribute and its corresponding value and m is the total number of attributes.

Events with the same case ID form a chronological sequence called a trace, which is defined as:

$$\sigma = [e_1, ...e_n], e_i.cid = e_j.cid, \forall i, j \in [1, ..., n] \tag{2}$$

where σ is the trace, e_i, e_j are the i-th and j-th events in the trace and $e_i.cid$ represents the case ID of e_i.

In predictive business process monitoring, the goal is to make predictions for ongoing traces based on a small set of events that have already occurred, which forms the prefix of the trace. The prefix can be defined as:

$$prefix(\sigma, l) = [e_1, ..., e_l], 0 \le l < |\sigma| \tag{3}$$

where l is the length of the prefix and $|\sigma|$ is the length of the complete trace.

The objective of the remaining time prediction problem is to develop a model capable of forecasting the remaining time of an active business process instance based on the given prefix:

$$\hat{y}_l = RTPM(prefix(\sigma, l), C) \tag{4}$$

where $\hat{y}_l$ is the predicted remaining time and C represents other information that can be used for prediction. $RTPM$ is the prediction model that can be trained on the historical traces.

3.2   Remaining Time Prediction with Privacy Preservation

In a collaborative business process, each participant is accountable for executing a sub-process, which refers to a segment of the overall process. The sub-processes may have complex relationships between them, such as parallel or exclusive relationships. In this paper, we focus on the most prevalent type of collaborative business process where sub-processes are executed sequentially. Nonetheless, activities within each sub-process may be organized into complex structures.

The trace of a business process instance executed by multiple participants can be seen as a collection of segments. Each segment of a trace represents a sub-process that is executed by one of the participants. Each participant has access only to the segments of its sub-process. Each sub-process has its own model for remaining time prediction. To improve the prediction accuracy, the models for later sub-processes require information from preceding segments. However, the participants of the preceding sub-processes do not wish to share detailed activity information. One possible solution to this conflict is to only share implicit information that does not reveal specific raw information about the activities performed in the preceding sub-processes.

For instance, a collaborative business process consists of two sub-processes as shown in Fig. 2. When the prefix P_2^1, which consists of two events e_1^1 and e_2^1, is available, the model for the first sub-process can make the prediction. After the first sub-process is completed and the second sub-process starts to execute, we have two prefixes, i.e., P_2^1 and P_2^2. The two models use h^{12} and h^{21} to share

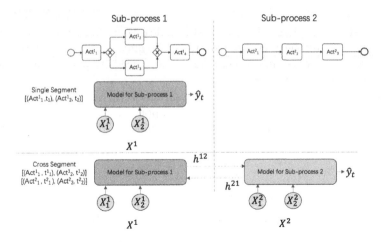

Fig. 2. Two stages of remaining time prediction for collaborative business process

the features of the segmented input they obtain. These features are processed information that do not include the raw information.

Therefore, the prediction of remaining time for the k-th sub-process is executed in the following manner:

$$\hat{y}_l^k = RTPM(\boldsymbol{P}_l^k, C, \boldsymbol{h}^{k-1}) \tag{5}$$

$$\boldsymbol{h}^k = HG(\boldsymbol{P}_l^k, C, \boldsymbol{h}^{k-1}) \tag{6}$$

where $\boldsymbol{h}^{k-1}$ is the latent information provided by the $k-1$-th sub-model, and HG is the model to generate the latent information for the prediction model of the next sub-process. Additionally, implicit information can also be provided to train the model for the precedent sub-process.

4   Remaining Time Prediction with Privacy Preservation

To train the remaining time prediction models for each sub-process, we adopt a strategy where the models are allowed to share hidden state information. This strategy ensures that the input cannot be recovered from the hidden state information even if the model structure is unknown. As LSTM has shown success in solving the remaining time prediction problem, we propose two LSTM-based models that implement this strategy.

4.1   Two-Way Information Sharing Model (TISM)

A potential solution is to adopt a split learning approach [3], which involves dividing the LSTM model into a set of interconnected sub-networks, where each sub-network corresponds to a sub-process. However, unlike the general split learning model, each sub-network in our approach not only provides implicit information to the next sub-network, but also directly outputs predictions. Each sub-network utilizes the final hidden state information and a fully connected layer to generate a remaining time prediction and needs to pass the final hidden state information of activation to the next sub-network. Additionally, gradients are returned to the immediate precedent sub-network, which updates its network weights during the training stage. This approach is depicted in Fig. 3 and referred to as the two-way information sharing model (TISM).

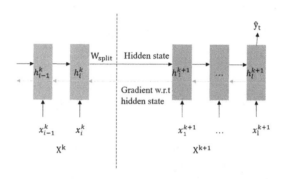

Fig. 3. Two-way Information Sharing Prediction Model

Let us consider a business process with two sub-processes as an example. The final hidden state of the sub-network for the first sub-process is:

$$h_k^1 = LSTM^1(e_1^1, ..., e_k^1, h_0) \tag{7}$$

where h_k^1 is the output of the sub-network at step k, where k is the sequence length of the prefix until the split point and $e_i^1, i \in 1, 2, ..., k$ represents the input events for the first segment. The randomly initialized hidden state h_0 is unique to the first sub-network. Recurrent neural networks for the first sub-process are represented by $LSTM^1()$.

The initial hidden state of the second sub-network is computed as follows:

$$h_1^2 = LSTM^2(e_1^2, Relu(W_{split}h_k^1)) \tag{8}$$

Here, h_1^2 denotes the first hidden state in the second sub-network, which immediately follows the first sub-network. The second sub-network uses $LSTM^2()$ to compute this state, with the input event e_1^2 and the activation of the hidden state from the first sub-network, h_k^1. $Relu$ represents the rectified linear activation function. Finally, the model predicts the remaining time at prefix length l:

$$h_l^2 = LSTM^2(e_1^2, ..., e_l^2, Relu(W_{split}h_k^1)) \tag{9}$$

$$\hat{y}_t = FC^2(h_l^2) \tag{10}$$

where $\hat{y}_t$ is the predicted remaining time and $FC^2()$ is the fully connected layer.

The network optimization within each sub-network is carried out through backpropagation through time (BPTT). Nevertheless, at the split layer, the gradient is transmitted from the back sub-network to the front sub-network as follows:

$$\frac{\partial L}{\partial W_{split}} = \frac{\partial L}{\partial h_1^2} \frac{\partial h_1^2}{\partial W_{split}} \tag{11}$$

where L is the mean absolute error loss function. Gradient-based collaborative models facilitate sufficient exchange of information between segments, enabling preceding sub-process models to provide more valuable implicit data.

4.2   One-Way Information Sharing Model (OISM)

The prediction task of a sub-network in TISM may be affected unpredictably as it needs to receive gradient information from the next sub-network to update its parameters.

Thus, we present an alternative approach called the one-way information sharing model (OISM) in which only the preceding sub-network shares information with the subsequent sub-network, while the subsequent sub-network does not provide any feedback to the preceding one. This approach ensures that each sub-network can concentrate solely on optimizing its own objective without any interference from the other sub-networks. The architecture of the OISM is depicted in Fig. 4.

In OISM, LSTM-based models, except the last one, encode the prefix into hidden states and produce D-dimensional vectors at every step. These vectors can be combined to form a matrix of size $k_i \times D$, where k_i is the sequence length of the i-th segment. Consider the first sub-network as an example:

$$\begin{aligned} H^1 &= [h_1^1, ..., h_{k_1}^1] \\ &= [LSTM^1(x_1^1, h_0^1), ..., LSTM^1(x_{k_1}^1, h_{k_1-1}^1)] \end{aligned} \tag{12}$$

where H^1 is the matrix produced by the first sub-network. h_0^1 is the initial hidden state of the first sub-network. $h_i^1, i \in 1, 2, ..., k_1$ is the hidden state of the first sub-network. $x_i^1, i \in 1, 2, ..., k_1$ form the prefix and k_1 is the length of the segmented prefix.

By performing maximum, minimum, and average pooling on the matrix, D-dimensional vectors can be obtained respectively. By concatenating the three pooled vectors with the final hidden state obtained by LSTM, a $4 \times D$ matrix is obtained as the representation of the segmented prefix.

$$S^1 = [Max(H^1), Min(H^1), Mean(H^1), h_{k_1}^1] \tag{13}$$

where S^1 is the representation of the first segment.

Assuming that there are $N-1$ sub-processes prior to the last one, the concatenation of the matrices yields a larger matrix with a size of $4(N-1) \times D$. This matrix integrates all implicit features from the previous segments.

$$S = [S^1, ..., S^{N-1}] \tag{14}$$

The final sub-network, which is also the N-th sub-network, receives the $4(N-1) \times D$ matrix, along with the final hidden state that is encoded in its own sub-network. An attention mechanism is employed to calculate a context vector using both the feature matrix and the hidden state information.

$$h_{l_N}^N = LSTM^N(x_1^N, ..., x_{l_N}^N, h_0^N) \tag{15}$$

The context vector is calculated as follows:

$$c_{l_N} = Attention^N(h_{l_N}^N, S) \tag{16}$$

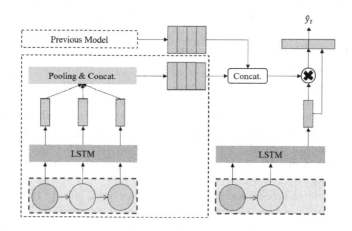

Fig. 4. One-way Information Sharing Prediction Model

where $Attention^N()$ is the attention mechanism in the N-th sub-network. This attention-based multi-segment model calculates the attention distribution of the feature matrix of the previous segments with respect to the final hidden state information to obtain the context vector. The context vector is obtained through a weighted sum of the feature matrix based on the learned correlation between the hidden state information and the matrix using an additive model with learnable parameters. This model not only extracts useful prefix information but also minimizes the effect on the optimization of the former sub-networks during training. Finally, the context vector and the final hidden state information is used to predict the remaining time.

$$\hat{y}_t = FC^N([c_l, h_l^N]) \tag{17}$$

where $FC^N()$ is the fully connected layer of the N-th sub-network.

4.3 Collaborative Model Training and Inference

The collaborative mechanisms for model training in TISM and OISM differ. In TISM, the former sub-networks must accept the returned gradient information when the latter sub-networks are trained, and they must remain online to participate in parameter updating based on the gradient. The convergence of each sub-network depends not only on its own training, but also on the optimization of the other networks. Therefore, the total training time is determined by the network that requires the most rounds of training.

In contrast, OISM provides more flexibility in model training. Each sub-network can have its own training schedule, as long as the preceding models have been trained completely. The preceding networks only need to participate in the inference task and are no longer involved in the training process for the subsequent networks. Therefore, the model can be trained sequentially according to the segment ID, which reduces the complexity of collaboration. However, the subsequent networks need to make necessary adjustments after the preceding networks have been updated to ensure the consistency of the model versions.

The inference procedure for both TISM and OISM is identical. The subsequent network waits for the information from the preceding network (either hidden state information or pooled features), performs inference using its model, and then forwards the information or outputs the remaining time prediction.

5 Experiments

5.1 Experiment Setup

Dataset. In order to address the challenge of obtaining real-world traces of collaborative business processes, we resort to simulating such traces by dividing each business process trace into multiple segments. In the following experiment, we use the following datasets:

- 2012w: This event log pertains to a loan application process of a Dutch financial institute.[1] In this dataset, in addition to activity names and timestamps, each trace is associated with a loan amount information and each activity also has the resource information.
- credit: This dataset contains information about a credit requirement process in a bank[2]. Specifically, in this dataset, the event sequences in the traces are consistent.
- PTC: The dataset contains events pertaining to two years of travel expense claims in a university[3]. In this process, after submission by the employee, the request is sent for approval to the travel administration.

---

[1] https://doi.org/10.4121/uuid:3926db30-f712-4394-aebc-75976070e91f.

[2] https://doi.org/10.4121/uuid:453e8ad1-4df0-4511-a916-93f46a37a1b5.

[3] https://doi.org/10.4121/uuid:52fb97d4-4588-43c9-9d04-3604d4613b51.

Sub-process Data Preparation. To divide the traces into segments based on sub-processes, it is important to understand the general execution pattern and semantic knowledge of the activities before segmenting the processes. We used PROM6.9[4] to process the event logs. A heuristic net plugin in PROM6.9 was used to analyze the processes and mine causal graphs. Based on the execution paths and activity names' semantics, we divided the processes into sub-processes.

After the trace segmentation, we created a total of five datasets whose statistical information is summarized in Table 1.

Table 1. Experiment Datasets

Name	#Case	#Activity Types	Sequence Length	Segment Time Span(days)
2012w_2	2043	{3,3}	{5.4 ± 2.8,4.1 ± 3.6}	{10.7 ± 6.5,4.1 ± 3.2}
credit_2	10035	{3,5}	{3,5}	{0.3 ± 0.5,0.7 ± 0.8}
credit_3	10035	{3,3,2}	{3,3,2}	{0.3 ± 0.5,0.5 ± 0.7,0.4 ± 0.7}
PTC_2	1392	{ 7,10}	{3.4 ± 0.7,5.2 ± 0.7}	{3.8 ± 5.5,37.7 ± 40.2}
PTC_3	1381	{7,6,4}	{3.4 ± 0.7,2.3 ± 0.6, 3}	{3.8 ± 5.6,28.9 ± 39.7,12.6 ± 8.6}

[a] Name: the first part is the name of the dataset and the second part is the number of sub-processes.
[b] # Case: the number of cases.
[c] # Activity Types: the number of activity types in each sub-process.
[d] Sequence Length: the average lengths of sub-processes respectively.
[e] Segment Time Span: the average duration of sub-processes.

Metrics. We use mean absolute error (MAE) to measure the prediction performance of a model, which is defined by:

$$MAE = \frac{1}{m} \sum_{i=1}^{m} | y_i - \hat{y}_i | \tag{18}$$

where m stands for the number of samples, and y_i, $\hat{y}_i$ stands for the real and predicted value of each sample.

Comparative Models. As there is currently no research on the topic of remaining time prediction for collaborative business process with privacy preservation, we have designed the following models for comparison:

- *Prediction with Complete Information (PCI)*: In this model, the privacy issue is not considered. Therefore, a typical LSTM model is applied to the complete traces.
- *Prediction with Key Events (PKE)* : In this model, in addition to the hidden state, the first and last events of the former segments can be shared with the sub-network of the next sub-process.

---

[4] https://www.promtools.org/.

– *Prediction with Own Data (POD)*: In this model, the sub-network can only use the data of its own sub-process for remaining time prediction, i.e., no information exchange takes place among the sub-networks.

Implementation. The PyTorch framework is used to implement all models, which consist of a two-layer LSTM network. The hidden state dimension is set to 64. The maximum input prefix length is determined based on the maximum length of each segment, and the remaining input is padded with zeros if a segment is shorter. The mean absolute error (MAE) is used as the loss function, and the optimization algorithm is NAdam with default parameter values.

5.2   Experimental Results

The MAEs for the remaining time prediction on each segment and overall are presented in Table 2. Generally, the models that share more raw data between sub-models have lower MAE and perform better in both single-segment and overall prediction. However, there is an exception on the 2012w_2 dataset, where POD performs the best, which could be due to the independence between sub-processes. Both TISM and OISM exhibit similar performance compared to models that can access full or partial raw data.

Table 2. Prediction Accuracy of Different Models

Dataset	Segment ID	TISM	OISM	PCI	PKE	POD
2012w_2	1	5.66 ± 0.12	4.62 ± 0.13	4.52 ± 0.08	4.56 ± 0.18	$\mathbf{4.52 \pm 0.05}$
	2	1.83 ± 0.02	1.76 ± 0.02	1.73 ± 0.08	1.71 ± 0.04	$\mathbf{1.69 \pm 0.03}$
	total	4.14 ± 0.07	3.48 ± 0.08	3.41 ± 0.01	3.42 ± 0.11	$\mathbf{3.40 \pm 0.04}$
credit_2	1	0.135	0.092	0.090	$\mathbf{0.088}$	0.089
	2	0.058	0.087	$\mathbf{0.053}$	0.055	0.054
	total	0.092	0.089	$\mathbf{0.068}$	0.069	0.070
credit_3	1	0.170	0.089	$\mathbf{0.088}$	0.089	0.090
	2	0.088	0.091	$\mathbf{0.065}$	0.066	0.076
	3	0.026	0.026	$\mathbf{0.025}$	0.026	0.026
	total	0.114	0.081	$\mathbf{0.069}$	0.070	0.075
PTC_2	1	$\mathbf{17.98 \pm 0.01}$	18.06 ± 0.03	18.03 ± 0.04	18.08 ± 0.19	18.05 ± 0.04
	2	3.02 ± 0.01	$\mathbf{2.99 \pm 0.01}$	3.00 ± 0.01	3.04 ± 0.03	3.08 ± 0.02
	total	9.76 ± 0.01	9.79 ± 0.02	$\mathbf{9.77 \pm 0.01}$	9.79 ± 0.05	9.83 ± 0.01
PTC_3	1	$\mathbf{18.03 \pm 0.02}$	18.06 ± 0.11	18.05 ± 0.01	18.10 ± 0.07	18.10 ± 0.03
	2	3.79 ± 0.08	3.78 ± 0.04	$\mathbf{3.73 \pm 0.03}$	3.79 ± 0.01	3.82 ± 0.02
	3	2.07 ± 0.01	1.99 ± 0.05	$\mathbf{1.97 \pm 0.03}$	2.05 ± 0.06	2.09 ± 0.01
	total	9.79 ± 0.03	9.76 ± 0.04	$\mathbf{9.73 \pm 0.01}$	9.79 ± 0.04	9.81 ± 0.01

The performance of TISM and OISM is highly comparable overall. However, when it comes to the *credit* dataset, where traces have identical activity sequences, the models only rely on temporal and resource information to make predictions. As a result, TISM experiences a drop in performance on the first sub-process. The reason for this is that the first sub-network receives gradient information and updates the network to improve the performance of other sub-networks, which can hinder its own performance.

5.3   Discussion on Privacy Preservation

TISM and OISM utilize the intermediate layer's output to transfer the hidden state of the sub-network instead of sharing the original prefix encoding directly. This approach ensures privacy preservation [34]. In federated deep learning, reconstruction attacks and membership attacks are two general methods to invade private information. These attacks restore the clients' data on the client side by deciphering gradients based on the model parameter updates on the server side [11]. However, the split learning framework used in our models adopts a segmentation approach where each sub-process can only possess a part of the overall prediction model. This approach eliminates the sharing of model parameters and enhances isolation among sub-processes [6]. Moreover, TISM and OISM incorporate non-linear activation and pooling layers, respectively, at the split layer, which makes data restoration more challenging.

In conclusion, the privacy-preserving models proposed in this paper can satisfy the requirements of data isolation and privacy protection while achieving the expected prediction accuracy.

6   Conclusion

This paper proposes a privacy-preserving strategy for remaining time prediction in collaborative business processes, where partners are reluctant to share their detailed activity information. Instead of raw data, the hidden state of the network is shared between sub-models to achieve privacy preservation. Two models, TISM and OISM, are designed to implement this strategy. The experimental results demonstrate that both models achieve comparable prediction performance to models that can access partners' raw data while preserving privacy. In the future, the authors plan to investigate the addition of noise to the information exchanged between sub-networks to enhance privacy protection.

Acknowledgment. This work is supported by China National Science Foundation (Granted Number 62072301) and the Program of Technology Innovation of the Science and Technology Commission of Shanghai Municipality (Granted No. 21511104700).

References

1. Van der Aalst, W.M., Rubin, V., Verbeek, H., van Dongen, B.F., Kindler, E., Gün-ther, C.W.: Process mining: a two-step approach to balance between underfitting and overfitting. Softw. Syst. Model. **9**(1), 87–111 (2010)
2. Abdulrahman, S., Tout, H., Ould-Slimane, H., Mourad, A., Talhi, C., Guizani, M.: A survey on federated learning: the journey from centralized to distributed on-site learning and beyond. IEEE Internet Things J. **8**(7), 5476–5497 (2021). https://doi.org/10.1109/JIOT.2020.3030072
3. Abedi, A., Khan, S.S.: FedSL: federated split learning on distributed sequential data in recurrent neural networks. CoRR abs/2011.03180 (2020). https://arxiv.org/abs/2011.03180
4. Bengio, Y., Courville, A., Vincent, P.: Representation learning: a review and new perspectives. IEEE Trans. Pattern Anal. Mach. Intell. **35**(8), 1798–1828 (2013)
5. Bukhsh, Z.A., Saeed, A., Dijkman, R.M.: Processtransformer: predictive business process monitoring with transformer network. arXiv abs/2104.00721 (2021)
6. Thapa, C., Arachchige, P.C.M., Camtepe, S., Sun, L.: Splitfed: when federated learning meets split learning. In: Proceedings of the AAAI Conference on Artificial Intelligence, pp. 8485–8493 (2022)
7. Conforti, R., de Leoni, M., La Rosa, M., van der Aalst, W.M., ter Hofstede, A.H.: A recommendation system for predicting risks across multiple business process instances. Decis. Support Syst. **69**, 1–19 (2015)
8. Elkoumy, G., Pankova, A., Dumas, M.: Mine me but don't single me out: differentially private event logs for process mining. In: 2021 3rd International Conference on Process Mining (ICPM), pp. 80–87 (2021)
9. Evermann, J., Rehse, J.-R., Fettke, P.: A deep learning approach for predicting process behaviour at runtime. In: Dumas, M., Fantinato, M. (eds.) BPM 2016. LNBIP, vol. 281, pp. 327–338. Springer, Cham (2017). https://doi.org/10.1007/978-3-319-58457-7_24
10. Fahrenkrog-Petersen, S.A., van der Aa, H., Weidlich, M.: PRIPEL: privacy-preserving event log publishing including contextual information. In: Fahland, D., Ghidini, C., Becker, J., Dumas, M. (eds.) BPM 2020. LNCS, vol. 12168, pp. 111–128. Springer, Cham (2020). https://doi.org/10.1007/978-3-030-58666-9_7
11. Fan, L., et al.: Rethinking privacy preserving deep learning: how to evaluate and thwart privacy attacks. arXiv abs/2006.11601 (2020)
12. Hamrouni, I., Lahdhiri, H., Ben Abdellafou, K., Aljuhani, A., Taouali, O.: Anomaly detection for process monitoring based on machine learning technique. Neural Comput. Appl. **35**(5), 4073–4097 (2022). https://doi.org/10.1007/s00521-022-07901-2
13. Márquez-Chamorro, A.E., Resinas, M., Ruiz-Cortés, A.: Predictive monitoring of business processes: a survey. IEEE Trans. Serv. Comput. **11**(6), 962–977 (2017)
14. Navarin, N., Vincenzi, B., Polato, M., Sperduti, A.: LSTM networks for data-aware remaining time prediction of business process instances. In: 2017 IEEE Symposium Series on Computational Intelligence (SSCI), pp. 1–7 (2017). https://doi.org/10.1109/SSCI.2017.8285184
15. Ogunbiyi, N., Basukoski, A., Chaussalet, T.: Investigating social contextual factors in remaining-time predictive process monitoring-a survival analysis approach. Algorithms **13**(11), 267 (2020). https://doi.org/10.3390/a13110267
16. Park, G., Song, M.: Predicting performances in business processes using deep neural networks. Decis. Support Syst. **129**, 113191 (2020). https://doi.org/10.1016/j.dss.2019.113191

17. Pauwels, S., Calders, T.: Incremental predictive process monitoring: the next activity case. In: Polyvyanyy, A., Wynn, M.T., Van Looy, A., Reichert, M. (eds.) BPM 2021. LNCS, vol. 12875, pp. 123–140. Springer, Cham (2021). https://doi.org/10.1007/978-3-030-85469-0_10

18. Polato, M., Sperduti, A., Burattin, A., de Leoni, M.: Data-aware remaining time prediction of business process instances. In: 2014 International Joint Conference on Neural Networks (IJCNN), pp. 816–823 (2014). https://doi.org/10.1109/IJCNN.2014.6889360

19. Rogge-Solti, A., Weske, M.: Prediction of remaining service execution time using stochastic petri nets with arbitrary firing delays. In: Basu, S., Pautasso, C., Zhang, L., Fu, X. (eds.) ICSOC 2013. LNCS, vol. 8274, pp. 389–403. Springer, Heidelberg (2013). https://doi.org/10.1007/978-3-642-45005-1_27

20. Rogge-Solti, A., Weske, M.: Prediction of business process durations using non-markovian stochastic petri nets. Inf. Syst. **54**(C), 1–14 (2015). https://doi.org/10.1016/j.is.2015.04.004

21. Ryu, J., Won, D., Lee, Y.: A study of split learning model. In: 2022 16th International Conference on Ubiquitous Information Management and Communication (IMCOM), pp. 1–4 (2022). https://doi.org/10.1109/IMCOM53663.2022.9721798

22. Senderovich, A., Di Francescomarino, C., Ghidini, C., Jorbina, K., Maggi, F.M.: Intra and inter-case features in predictive process monitoring: a tale of two dimensions. In: Carmona, J., Engels, G., Kumar, A. (eds.) BPM 2017. LNCS, vol. 10445, pp. 306–323. Springer, Cham (2017). https://doi.org/10.1007/978-3-319-65000-5_18

23. van der Spoel, S., van Keulen, M., Amrit, C.: Process prediction in noisy data sets: a case study in a Dutch hospital. In: Cudre-Mauroux, P., Ceravolo, P., Gašević, D. (eds.) SIMPDA 2012. LNBIP, vol. 162, pp. 60–83. Springer, Heidelberg (2013). https://doi.org/10.1007/978-3-642-40919-6_4

24. Tax, N., Verenich, I., La Rosa, M., Dumas, M.: Predictive business process monitoring with LSTM neural networks. In: Dubois, E., Pohl, K. (eds.) CAiSE 2017. LNCS, vol. 10253, pp. 477–492. Springer, Cham (2017). https://doi.org/10.1007/978-3-319-59536-8_30

25. Taymouri, F., La Rosa, M., Erfani, S.M.: A deep adversarial model for suffix and remaining time prediction of event sequences. In: Proceedings of the 2021 SIAM International Conference on Data Mining (SDM), pp. 522–530 (2021). https://doi.org/10.1137/1.9781611976700.59

26. Teinemaa, I., Dumas, M., Maggi, F.M., Di Francescomarino, C.: Predictive business process monitoring with structured and unstructured data. In: La Rosa, M., Loos, P., Pastor, O. (eds.) BPM 2016. LNCS, vol. 9850, pp. 401–417. Springer, Cham (2016). https://doi.org/10.1007/978-3-319-45348-4_23

27. Teinemaa, I., Dumas, M., Rosa, M.L., Maggi, F.M.: Outcome-oriented predictive process monitoring: review and benchmark. ACM Trans. Knowl. Discov. Data **13**(2), 1–57 (2019). https://doi.org/10.1145/3301300

28. Van Der Aalst, W.: Process mining. Commun. ACM **55**(8), 76–83 (2012)

29. Vandenabeele, J., Vermaut, G., Peeperkorn, J., Weerdt, J.D.: Enhancing stochastic petri net-based remaining time prediction using k-nearest neighbors. arXiv abs/2206.13109 (2022)

30. Verenich, I., Dumas, M., Rosa, M.L., Maggi, F.M., Teinemaa, I.: Survey and cross-benchmark comparison of remaining time prediction methods in business process monitoring. ACM Trans. Intell. Syst. Technol. (TIST) **10**(4), 1–34 (2019)

31. Wahid, N.A., Bae, H., Adi, T.N., Choi, Y., Iskandar, Y.A.: Parallel-structure deep learning for prediction of remaining time of process instances. Appl. Sci. **11**(21), 9848 (2021). https://doi.org/10.3390/app11219848
32. Wang, J., Chang, V., Yu, D., Liu, C., Ma, X., Yu, D.: Conformance-oriented predictive process monitoring in BPaaS based on combination of neural networks. J. Grid Comput. **20**(3), 25 (2022). https://doi.org/10.1007/s10723-022-09613-2
33. Xu, X., Liu, C., Li, T., Guo, N., Ren, C.G., Zeng, Q.T.: Business process remaining time prediction: an approach based on bidirectional quasi recurrent neural network with attention. Acta Electronica Sinica **50**(8), 1975–1984 (2022)
34. Yin, X., Zhu, Y., Hu, J.: A comprehensive survey of privacy-preserving federated learning: a taxonomy, review, and future directions. ACM Comput. Surv. **54**(6), 1–36 (2021). https://doi.org/10.1145/3460427

SWARM: A Scientific Workflow Fragments Recommendation Approach via Contrastive Learning and Semantic Matching

Yang Gu, Jian Cao$^{(\boxtimes)}$, Jinghua Tang, Shiyou Qian, and Wei Guan

Shanghai Jiao Tong University, Shanghai, China
{gu_yang,cao-jian,tang_tony,qshiyou,guan-wei}@sjtu.edu.cn

Abstract. Discovering and recommending scientific workflow fragments that can be reused or repurposed from public repositories is becoming increasingly significant in the scientific domain. Although popular fragment discovery strategies can identify frequent and similar fragments, they lack the ability to further mine pattern semantics. Moreover, current recommendation approaches are primarily based on text matching between natural language queries and the descriptions of candidate fragments, neglecting crucial structural information that conveys their functions. To address these challenges, this paper designs SWARM, a scientific workflow fragments recommendation approach via contrastive learning and semantic matching. SWARM consists of two phases: *fragment discovery* based on frequent subgraph mining and a contrastive semantics extraction model, and *fragment recommendation* based on a matching degree prediction model incorporating a pre-trained fragment encoder, which is used to predict and rank the degree of semantic matching between the user query and candidate fragments. SWARM aims to extract and integrate textual and structural semantics from fragments to discover and recommend them. The experimental results on commonly-used real-world datasets show that SWARM outperforms state-of-the-art methods with statistical significance.

Keywords: Scientific Workflow · Fragment Discovery · Fragment Recommendation · Contrastive Learning · Semantic Matching

1 Introduction

Scientific Workflows (SWs), represented as directed acyclic graphs (DAGs), can arrange a series of services in a specific order [1,2]. They are widely used to process complex data. By providing queries and retrieving shared scientific workflows with similar text or structure from online repositories like myExperiment [3], Pegasus [4], and Galaxy [5], researchers can save more time for data preparation and analysis. However, as the complexity of needs increases, a single workflow may not suffice, and combining fragments from multiple workflows becomes

© The Author(s), under exclusive license to Springer Nature Switzerland AG 2023
F. Monti et al. (Eds.): ICSOC 2023, LNCS 14420, pp. 54–71, 2023.
https://doi.org/10.1007/978-3-031-48424-7_5

necessary [6]. Consequently, discovering and recommending appropriate scientific workflow fragments efficiently is becoming an important research topic.

Most methods for discovering fragments are based on the idea that frequently occurring fragments in past service solutions are likely to appear in future ones [7]. In [1], frequent basic subfunctions are discovered using the frequent subgraph mining algorithm. Researchers in [6,8] develop a crossing-workflow fragments discovery mechanism for reusing fragments from diverse scientific workflows. In general, these methods can identify functionally similar fragments as service patterns but lack the mining of pattern semantics from a higher-level abstraction perspective, which is critical for downstream fragments recommendation.

Based on the format of user query, recommending scientific workflow fragments can be divided into two primary approaches: text-based and structure-based. Text-based approaches [9,10] involve users inputting relevant keywords or natural language text, which are then matched with candidate fragments using text similarity measures. These approaches are easy for users to put forward their requirements, but overlook the structure of fragments. Structure-based methods that use graph matching algorithms [8], such as subgraph isomorphism, can be utilized if the user query is specified in a fragment template [6,11]. However, it can be inconvenient and challenging for users to provide a fragment structure.

This paper focuses on the case when natural language is used to describe the user query, which is more user-friendly than drafts and can express users' needs more accurately than keywords. Existing fragments recommendation approaches for this case primarily rely on text matching [9], which neglects critical structural semantics of fragments. Meanwhile, frequently occurring fragments with similar functions exhibit internal structural invariance referring to the fact that two observations of the same concepts are identical [12], which can be captured by contrastive model and facilitate the subsequent semantic matching. Unfortunately, this aspect is often disregarded in the fragment discovery stage of existing approaches. To overcome these shortcomings, we propose a scientific workflow fragments recommendation approach via contrastive learning and semantic matching (SWARM). SWARM consists of two phases: *fragment discovery* based on frequent subgraph mining and a contrastive semantics extraction model, and *fragment recommendation* based on a matching degree prediction model incorporating a pre-trained fragment encoder.

SWARM attempts to extract and integrate textual and structural semantics from fragments in order to discover and recommend them. Specifically, it uses contrastive learning to extract the structural semantics of fragments through their **paths**. This is because scientific workflows are executed along the paths [13]. The major contributions of this paper are as follows:

- We propose a novel two-phase framework for recommending relevant scientific workflow fragments according to user queries.
- We design a contrastive model to extract the structural semantics of frequent and similar fragments from a high-level abstraction perspective, resulting in a pre-trained fragment encoder for facilitating the downstream semantic matching.

– We conduct comprehensive experiments on commonly-used real-world datasets. The results demonstrate that our proposed method consistently outperforms the state-of-the-art approaches in different metrics.

2   Related Work

2.1   Scientific Workflow Fragments Discovery

Frequent pattern mining techniques are the dominant approaches to discovering fragments. For instance, Cheng et al. [10] propose a multi-layer mining approach based on a hierarchical model to detect and abstract frequent workflow fragments. Other methods such as FragFlow [14], employ graph mining techniques to derive the most common usage patterns in a workflow repository. Furthermore, several researchers argue that fragments can be found across various workflows instead of just one. Hence, they develop an activity network model [8] and a knowledge graph [6] to capture invocation relations between activity pairs, aiming to construct crossing-workflow fragments.

In this paper, we use the dominating frequent subgraph mining algorithm to discover fragments and additionally extract their pattern semantics from an abstract perspective.

2.2   Scientific Workflow Fragments Recommendation

To leverage recommendation approaches for workflow fragments, users need to provide textual or structural features of their personalized requirements.

Textual queries are usually keywords or natural language texts describing the novel experiment [9]. TF-IDF (Term Frequency-Inverse Document Frequency) and topic modeling can be used to match the textual features of queries and discovered fragments [6]. Moreover, social information in the workflow repository can help find semantically similar fragments [15]. However, most text-based methods neglect the fragment structures that contain rich and important semantic information. Structure-based methods that use graph matching algorithms [8] can be utilized if the user query is specified in a fragment template or draft [6]. Zhang et al. [11] use the term "unit of work" (UoW) to represent the workflow fragment and present a service social network-based technique for recommending chained services. Additionally, some works introduce a fragment-index mechanism and coverage strategy [1] to identify semantically relevant fragments. Nevertheless, requiring users to provide the partial structure of their preferred fragments could be difficult for inexperienced users.

Our approach is a text-based recommendation strategy. Unlike traditional text-based methods that rely solely on the textual similarity, it recommends fragments by matching semantics from both textual and structural features.

3 Preliminaries

3.1 Definitions

Definition 1 (Scientific Workflow). *A scientific workflow* sw *is a tuple* $(title, des_{sw}, Act, Lnk)$, *where* $title$ *is the title of sw,* des_{sw} *is the textual description of sw in short-document,* Act *is a set of activities belonging to sw, and* Lnk *is a set of datalinks connecting activities in Act [3].*

Definition 2 (Activity). *An activity* act *is a tuple* $(name, type, des_{act})$, *where* $name$ *is the label of act reflecting the activity's functionality directly,* $type$ *is the operation type, and* des_{act} *is the textual description of act, which explains the function of this activity in detail.*

Definition 3 (Path). *A path* $path$ *is a sequence* $\langle act_1, act_2, ..., act_n \rangle$, *where* n *is a finite positive integer and* $act_i \neq act_j(i \neq j)$. *These n activities are connected by datalinks in Lnk. Paths are essential substructure of the workflow/fragment.*

Definition 4 (Fragment). *A scientific workflow fragment* $frag$ *is a tuple* $(Act_{frag}, Lnk_{frag}, Input_{frag}, Output_{frag})$, *where they are the frag's activity set, datalink set, inputs and outputs, respectively.*

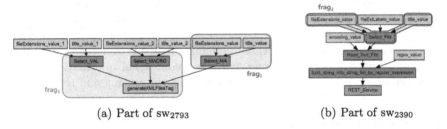

(a) Part of sw_{2793} (b) Part of sw_{2390}

Fig. 1. Two partial scientific workflows in myExperiment. (sw_{2793} (http://www.myexperiment.org/workflows/2793.html) and sw_{2390} (http://www.myexperiment.org/workflows/2390.html) are two whole workflows. $frag_1$, $frag_2$ and $frag_3$ are fragments mined from these workflows.)

Definition 5 (User Query). *A user query is a natural language text* T_r. *For instance, a scientist may provide* T_0: *"I want to create a framework configuration XML file based on user interaction." as the query.*

Figure 1(a) and Fig. 1(b) depict parts of scientific workflow sw_{2793} and sw_{2390} from myExperiment repository, respectively. Notably, the sample fragments $frag_1$ and $frag_2$ circled by the red curve are similar in structure and function.

3.2 Language Model

Since the majority users of scientific workflows are from the biomedical and bioinformatics fields [3], we choose BioLinkBERT[1] [16], achieving SOTA perfor-

---

[1] https://huggingface.co/michiyasunaga.

mance on several biomedical NLP benchmarks such as BLURB[2], as our basic embedding model. To enhance its capability for multi-domain adaptation, we unsupervisedly fine-tune the original BioLinkBERT using the workflow descriptions in experimental datasets. This fine-tuning process enables us to effectively embed different objects, such as description texts, paths and fragments. The effectiveness is demonstrated through the experiment presented in Sect. 6.3.

4   Problem Formulation and the Framework of SWARM

4.1   Problem Definition

We formally state the fragment recommendation problem to be investigated as follows: First, we build a repository of fragments mined from scientific workflows, with each fragment having a DAG structure G_c. Given a textual user query T_r, our goal is to recommend N workflow fragments by balancing the fragment scale and the semantic matching degree between the user query and candidate fragment, which is a value $y \in [0.0, 1.0]$ describing the extent to which the recommended fragment matches the user needs semantically. A higher semantic matching degree means greater satisfaction for the user.

Moreover, given that small-scale fragments (e.g., two activities) offer limited functionality and necessitate additional effort to be integrated with other fragments, we strive to recommend the largest N fragments (i.e., having the maximum number of activities) whose matching degree is over the threshold R. The recommended fragments, along with their contextual information (inputs and outputs), are provided to users for facilitating the reusing and repurposing.

4.2   Overall Framework

The framework of SWARM is seamlessly integrated into two parts: *Fragment Discovery Phase* and *Fragment Recommendation Phase*.

- In *Fragment Discovery Phase*, we employ a frequent subgraph mining algorithm to identify frequent fragments, which are stored in a dedicated repository. These frequent and similar fragments are combined into higher-level patterns, and their structural semantics are extracted using contrastive learning, resulting in a pre-trained fragment encoder.
- In *Fragment Recommendation Phase*, we first pre-select $5N$ scientific workflows based on the text similarity with the query, and the fragments contained in those workflows serve as candidate fragments. Next, we develop a prediction model based on the pre-trained fragment encoder for the degree of semantic matching y, which is used to rank candidate fragments precisely and select N fragments by balancing the fragment scale and y.

---

[2] https://microsoft.github.io/BLURB/leaderboard.html.

5 Method Design

5.1 Fragment Discovery Phase

The goal of *Fragment Discovery Phase* is to build a repository of workflow fragments in preparation for fragment recommendation. Given a workflow repository, we would like to mine frequent workflow fragments, i.e., fragments that occur across multiple workflows. This is because a novel user query tends to be related to various workflows, and frequent fragments are more likely to represent patterns that can be reused in a newly specified experiment [7].

1) Frequent Subgraph Mining: Before mining the workflows, it is necessary to homogenize the activity labels to avoid missing relevant fragments. The activity alignment approach, as introduced in [17] (using the finetuned BioLinkBERT instead), is adopted to identify and align functionally similar activities that can be represented by an abstract activity. Afterwards, workflows are rewritten in an abstract format by replacing activities with their abstract counterparts.

Subsequently, we employ the gSpan algorithm [18], the state-of-the-art subgraph mining technique for handling directed graphs, to identify frequent fragments from all workflow graphs. Those frequent subgraphs are named **abstract fragments**. For each abstract fragment, we find the workflows in which it appears and substitute the abstract activity name with the original activity name, finally generating many **concrete fragments** making up fragment repository.

2) Contrastive Learning-Based Semantics Extraction: The discovery of functionally similar fragments enables us to abstract and extract semantic patterns. Indeed, different concrete fragments from the same abstract fragment exhibit internal structural invariance [12]. For example, $frag_1$ and $frag_2$ in Fig. 1 belong to the same abstract fragment, and they share similarities in both structure and function.

Contrastive learning, on the other hand, is commonly used to capture the invariant signal of positive samples with similar semantic information [19]. Thus, our objective in this section is to leverage contrastive learning to extract the structural semantics of frequent and similar fragments. Analogous to two augmented views from an image in contrastive learning of visual representations [12], the two similar concrete fragments from the same abstract fragment can be viewed as a positive pair. These pairs are utilized as input to a contrastive learning-based semantics extraction model, as illustrated in Fig. 2.

This model adopts an online-target branch architecture based on *BYOL*, which is recognized as one of the leading contrastive methods and does not require negative pairs. In the following, we mainly focus on the introduction of **Fragment Encoder** in two branches, which consists of three parts, *Path Collector*, *Path Encoding*, and *Fragment Encoding based on PathAttention Net*.

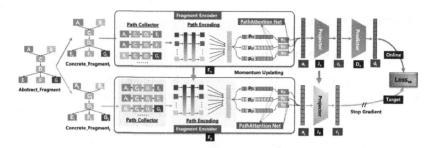

Fig. 2. Overview of Contrastive Learning-based Semantics Extraction Model.

A. Path Collector. Within the context of DAGs, paths serve as essential topo-
logical information and encapsulate the core execution semantics of the workflows [13]. Therefore, we first collect all paths of each concrete fragment using the
Depth-first search (DFS) algorithm. Then, these paths are sent to *Path Encoding*
for representing the path semantics.

B. Path Encoding. Suppose a set of paths $\{p_1, p_2, ..., p_e\}$ is collected by *Path
Collector* for each fragment, where p_i is a path consisting of L_i activities.
To begin with, we employ the finetuned BioLinkBERT model to generate D-
dimensional activity vectors. Then, each path p_i can be encoded by the average
pooling of L_i activity vectors within its sequence. Notably, we select the k most
important paths for encoding to ensure feature uniformity. If the number of
paths is less than k, zero vectors are used as padding. The importance of paths
is determined using BioLinkBERT by the average semantic similarity of their
activity sets to the workflow descriptions. The effect of different values of k on
recommendation effectiveness will be discussed in Sect. 6.5.

C. Fragment Encoding based on PathAttention Net. After *Path Encoding*,
we get two sets of top-k path vectors of a positive fragment-pair. In the following, we aim to build two fragment-level vectors from their path vectors using
the attention net, respectively. Taking one of the two fragments as an example,
the attention mechanism is utilized to extract the importance of different paths
and aggregate informative paths into fragment vectors. The attention score, representing the path importance, is computed using a *PathAttention Net*. First,
the top-k path vectors are passed through a one-layer MLP for feature fusion.
Then, the softmax function is applied to the convoluted features using a projection vector to obtain the attention score γ_i for each path. Finally, the concrete
fragment vector a is the weighted average sum of k D-dimensional path vectors.

Other components of semantics extraction model are basically consistent with
the original BYOL and refer to [19] for details. The training goal is to minimize
the distance between two positive fragments projected to the unit hypersphere:

$$Loss_{se} = \|d_i - c_j\|_2^2 + \left\|d_j' - c_i'\right\|_2^2 = 4 - 2 \cdot \left(\frac{\langle d_i, c_j \rangle}{\|d_i\|_2 \cdot \|c_j\|_2} + \frac{\langle d_j', c_i' \rangle}{\|d_j'\|_2 \cdot \|c_i'\|_2} \right) \quad (1)$$

where d_i, c_j are the outputs of the online and target branch for $frag_i$ and $frag_j$, respectively. d'_j, c'_i are the results of feeding $frag_j$ to the online branch and $frag_i$ to the target branch. At the end of training, we keep only the fragment encoder F_α for downstream recommendation.

5.2   Fragment Recommendation Phase

In this phase, we aim to recommend several "best" fragments from the fragment repository to satisfy the user requirement. To address the computational challenge of matching each fragment with the query using a complex model, we follow a two-step process: *Fragment Pre-Selection* and *Fragment Ranking*.

1) Fragment Pre-selection: Intuitively, the workflow's description text partially describes the function of its constituent fragments. Therefore, we utilize the fine-tuned BioLinkBERT model to embed the texts and select the top $5N$ workflows that exhibit the highest text similarity to the user query. Subsequently, the fragments found within these workflows (also in the fragment repository) are considered as candidate fragments.

For instance, given the scientist's query T_0 in Definition 5, we can pre-select $5N$ candidate workflows based on the text similarity as follows: $[sw_{2793}(0.707)$, $sw_{2873}(0.263)$, ..., $sw_{2390}(0.142)$, ...] (N is set to 10 in this case), where e.g., sw_{2793} refers to the most textually similar workflow with id 2793 (as shown in Fig. 1(a)) and 0.707 denotes the text similarity score between T_0 and T_{2793}.

2) Fragment Ranking: After the preliminary, we aim to recommend the largest N fragments whose matching degree is over the threshold R. Our *Matching Degree Prediction Model* illustrated in Fig. 3 comprises three parts: *Text Encoder*, *Fragment Encoder*, and *Matching Degree Prediction*.

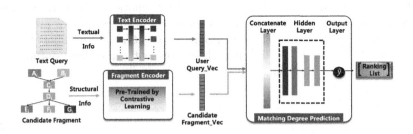

Fig. 3. Overview of Matching Degree Prediction Model.

A. Text Encoder. In this part, we also use the finetuned BioLinkBERT to acquire a D-dimensional vector of the user query for storing contextual semantics.

B. Fragment Encoder. We utilize the **pre-trained Fragment Encoder** to further capture the structural semantics of fragments and their semantic correlation with the query. The encoder's parameters are initialized with the pre-trained weights and are not frozen during the training. This encoding process generates a D-dimensional vector representing the features of the candidate fragment.

C. Matching Degree Prediction. After concatenating two D-dimensional vectors of the user query and candidate fragment, the fused features are passed through a four-layer MLP for deep feature fusion. We have experimented with alternative designs for feature integration, such as Bi-Interaction Pooling [20], but have not observed improved performance. In the output layer, we use a sigmoid function to ensure that the predicted score falls in the range [0, 1], representing the matching degree between the query and the candidate. Given training data of size I, $\hat{y}_i$ is the predicted score, and y_i is the label, the training aims to minimize the loss function:

$$Loss_{mdp} = \frac{1}{I} \sum_{i=1}^{I} (y_i - \hat{y}_i)^2 + \lambda \sum_{\omega \in \Omega} \omega^2 \tag{2}$$

where λ controls the strength of regularization and Ω represents the parameters of the neural network. Next, we discuss how to obtain the value of y_i.

D. Label Generation based on Improved-Path Similarity (PS). To train the matching degree prediction model, we select the description of a workflow sw_r whose structure is G_r as the user query T_r. Meanwhile, the candidate fragment G_c is also inputted into the model.

The workflow structure including the modules and their connections provides valuable insights into the functional semantics of the workflow [3]. Since the matching degree, the prediction model's output, represents the semantic similarity between G_c and T_r, and as G_r, the golden standard workflow structure corresponding to T_r, is known during the training process, we can utilize the functional semantic similarity between G_c and G_r as the training label in Eq. 2.

Paths contain both textual and structural information, reflecting the workflow(fragment)'s execution semantics. Therefore, based on [3], we propose an improved-path similarity of G_c and G_r, $Sim_{PS}(G_c, G_r)$, as the label of matching degree of G_c and T_r. To begin with, we present a matching optimization problem, abstracted from the calculation of path similarity:

$$\max \quad tot = \sum_{(q_1, q_2) \in M} sim(q_1, q_2)$$

$$s.t. \quad \begin{cases} q_1 \in Q_1, q_2 \in Q_2 \\ \forall v \in Q_1 \cup Q_2 \text{ , at most one edge in } M \text{ is incident upon } v \end{cases} \tag{3}$$

where Q_1 and Q_2 are two sets, $sim(q_1, q_2)$ is their similarity, and we try to find a matching $M \subseteq Q_1 \times Q_2$ to maximize tot. This problem can be solved by the *maximum weight matching (mw)* algorithm and the *maximum weight non-crossing matching (mwnc)* algorithm [13]. For our path similarity calculation, all pairwise activity (from G_c and G_r respectively) similarities are firstly computed by the alignment approach in Sect. 5.1. Then we collect path sets for fragment G_c and workflow G_r as PS_c and PS_r, respectively. The $mwnc$ algorithm considering the order of activities is used to compare all pairs (P_c, P_r) from PS_c and PS_r. We determine the similarity of each path-pair as follows:

$$nnSim(P_c, P_r) = \sum sim(act_1, act_2), \quad where \ (act_1, act_2) \in Matched(P_c, P_r)$$
$$Sim(P_c, P_r) = \frac{nnSim(P_c, P_r)}{|P_c|} \tag{4}$$

where $sim(act_1, act_2)$ is the similarity of two activities, $Matched(P_c, P_r)$ is the best matching solved by $mwnc$ between P_c and P_r, and $|P_c|$ is the size of P_c. In this way, all pairwise path similarities $Sim(P_c, P_r)$ are obtained. Following that, we can determine the similarity of the fragment and the workflow by computing and normalizing the maximum weight matching of PS_c and PS_r:

$$nnSim_{PS}(G_c, G_r) = \sum Sim(P_c, P_r), \quad where \ (P_c, P_r) \in Matched(PS_c, PS_r)$$
$$Sim_{PS}(G_c, G_r) = \frac{nnSim_{PS}(G_c, G_r)}{|PS_c|} \tag{5}$$

where $Matched(PS_c, PS_r)$ is the best matching solved by mw between PS_c and PS_r, and $|PS_c|$ is the size of PS_c.

E. Fragment Recommendation. After the matching degree prediction model has been successfully trained, it can determine how well each candidate fragment matches the user query. Then the largest N fragments with a matching degree higher than the threshold R are selected as the final result.

For instance, we input the features of the scientist's query T_0 and the candidate fragments contained in pre-selected workflows $sw_{2793}, sw_{2873}, sw_{2390}, \cdots$ to the trained model to predict the matching degree one by one. Based on that and fragment scale, the final top-$N(=10)$ fragments are recommended: [$frag_1(0.887)$, $frag_2(0.873)$, $frag_3(0.856)$, ...], where e.g., the first $frag_1$ as shown in Fig. 1(a) corresponds to the highest matching degree 0.887 with T_0.

6 Experiments

6.1 Experimental Settings

1) Datasets: We conduct experiments on two real-world datasets: (1) myExperiment: a collection of 2,012 Taverna workflows obtained from the well-known scientific workflow repository, *myExperiment* [1,11]; (2) Galaxy: a dataset comprising 627 Galaxy workflows sourced from the public *European Galaxy* repository[3], which adheres to the FAIR data principles [5]. The prototype of our SWARM is available at https://github.com/t-harden/SWARM.

Using frequent subgraph mining, we discovered abstract and concrete fragments from the two datasets, creating fragment repositories, respectively. Table 1 presents the dataset statistics.

---

[3] https://usegalaxy.eu/.

Table 1. Statistics of two datasets with their fragments.

Dataset	myExperiment	Galaxy
# Original workflows	2,012	627
# Abstract fragments	6,243	2,814
# Concrete fragments	57,253	22,046
# Workflows containing fragments	716	335

The distribution of #Concrete fragments w.r.t. #Contained activities and #Workflows containing fragments w.r.t. #Contained fragments are depicted in Fig. 4 for both datasets. Generally, more than half of the fragments are relatively large in scale (containing more than 16 activities), and most workflows have a small number of fragments (containing less than 7 fragments) for both datasets.

Moreover, for the myExperiment (Galaxy) dataset, 156,963(77,481) positive concrete fragment-pairs are selected from 6,243(2,814) abstract fragments to construct the training set for the semantics extraction model. Regarding the matching degree prediction model, 716*57,253(335*22,046) sample pairs of user query-candidate fragment are generated, of which 65% are used for training (not including sample queries), 15% for validation, and the remaining 20% for testing.

2) Evaluation Metrics: On the myExperiment (Galaxy) dataset, we select $S = 76(32)$ samples from 716(335) workflows, ensuring an even distribution of fragment scales within each sample. The descriptions of these sample workflows serve as testing queries. Given a sample user query T_s corresponding to the workflow graph G_s, our objective is to recommend the largest N fragments with a matching degree higher than the threshold R, as discussed in Sect. 4.1.

We evaluate the recommended fragments using three widely-used metrics [1,11,15]: *Path Similarity(PS)@N*, *Scale@N*, and *Recall@N*, and larger values of them indicate better performance. The statistical significance between SWARM and comparative approaches is tested using a Wilcoxon signed-rank test [21].

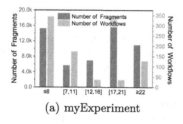

(a) myExperiment

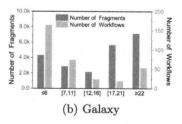

(b) Galaxy

Fig. 4. The distribution of #Concrete fragments w.r.t. #Contained activities and #Workflows containing fragments w.r.t. #Contained fragments for two datasets. The horizontal coordinate denotes #activities in a fragment and #fragments in a workflow.

(1)**PS@N**. Since G_s is the most desirable (golden standard) fragment for T_s, we can evaluate the performance by measuring improved-path similarity between the recommended fragment and G_s: $PS@N = \frac{1}{N} \sum_{i=1}^{N} Sim_{PS}(G_i, G_s)$, where G_i is the i_{th} fragment and Sim_{PS} denotes the structure similarity calculated by Eq. 4 and Eq. 5. (2)**Scale@N**. It measures the average scale of N recommended fragments: $Scale@N = \frac{1}{N} \sum_{i=1}^{N} Scale(G_i)$, where $Scale(G_i)$ is the number of G_i's activities. (3)**Recall@N**. It is the ratio between the number of N fragments' activities that cover G_s's activities and the total number of G_s's activities: $Recall@N = \frac{|(\bigcup_{i=1}^{N} Act_i) \cap Act_s|}{|Act_s|}$, where Act_i and Act_s are activity sets.

3) Implementation Details: In the frequent subgraph mining, $support(g)$ is set to 3. Consistent with BioLinkBERT, the vector dimension D is set to 768. We train the semantics extraction model and matching degree prediction model 10 times each on a machine with an NVIDIA GeForce-RTX-3090-Ti GPU.

For the semantics extraction model, k is set to 2 and one-layer MLP in *PathAttention Net* has $2*k$ hidden cells. The moving average decay is set to 0.99. The model is trained for a maximum of 100 epochs using the Adam optimizer with a learning rate of 5×10^{-4}. For the prediction model, *Matching Degree Prediction* part consists of a four-layer MLP with dimensions [512, 512, 256, 256]. The model runs for at most 200 epochs using the Adam optimizer with a learning rate, initially 5×10^{-4} and decreasing to 10^{-4} in the 50th epoch.

6.2   Comparative Methods

We compare SWARM with several state-of-the-art baselines:

1) Keyword-based Approach (KW) [9]: Homogenized activity labels are used to match with the user query using an improved TF-IDF similarity method.

2) Activity Description-based Approach (AD) [22]: This approach recommends fragments based on the similarity of user queries and activity descriptions.

3) Fragment Path Annotation-based Approach (FPA) [3]: Unlike KW, all activity labels in the paths of the fragments, as well as the workflow descriptions, are considered during similarity calculation and recommendation.

4) Topic Semantics-based Approach (TOPICS) [6]: Individual activities are selected based on a topic model, and candidate fragments are constructed using relations in the activity knowledge graph.

5) Unit of Work-based Approach (UOW) [11]: Workflow fragments are represented as Unit of Works (UoWs), and a service social network is developed for mining and retrieval of UoWs serving context-aware queries.

6) Social-aware Knowledge Graph-based Approach (SKG) [15]: Rules from a social-aware knowledge graph are extracted to estimate the viability of composing services and aid in locating and composing candidate services.

Generally, the first three baselines rely solely on textual descriptions, whereas the last three baselines focus primarily on the structural information of the fragments. In SWARM, textual and structural features are both utilized.

6.3   Overall Performance

Table 2. The overall recommendation performance with different N.

Method	myExperiment						Galaxy					
	N = 5			N = 10			N = 5			N = 10		
	PS	Scale	Recall	PS	Scale	Recall	PS	Scale	Recall	PS	Scale	Recall
KW	0.405⋆	8.425⋆	0.094⋆	0.395⋆	8.109⋆	0.113⋆	0.324⋆	12.403⋆	0.076⋆	0.312⋆	12.102⋆	0.091⋆
AD	0.437⋆	8.562⋆	0.099⋆	0.419⋆	8.284⋆	0.121⋆	0.358⋆	12.472⋆	0.080⋆	0.339⋆	12.144⋆	0.098⋆
FPA	0.483⋆	**10.847**⋆	0.122⋆	0.480⋆	**10.541**⋆	0.133⋆	0.403⋆	**14.865**⋆	0.115⋆	0.386⋆	**14.654**⋆	0.128⋆
TOPICS	0.683⋆	8.765⋆	0.367⋆	0.653⋆	8.610⋆	0.394⋆	0.653⋆	12.967⋆	0.369⋆	0.633⋆	12.815⋆	0.396⋆
UOW	0.707⋆	8.799⋆	0.363⋆	0.663⋆	8.607⋆	0.398⋆	0.677⋆	12.989⋆	0.383⋆	0.649⋆	12.837⋆	0.418⋆
SKG	0.734⋆	8.902⋆	0.405⋆	0.701⋆	8.725⋆	0.453⋆	0.692⋆	13.002⋆	0.416⋆	0.668⋆	12.941⋆	0.446⋆
SWARM	**0.951**	9.764	**0.538**	**0.945**	9.642	**0.601**	**0.901**	13.854	**0.525**	**0.893**	13.663	**0.593**

* The best results are highlighted in bold. ⋆ denotes statistical significance ($p < 0.05$) between the comparative method and SWARM.

We compare SWARM with various competitive methods as presented in Table 2, where the average results for each metric across S samples are reported when the threshold of matching degree R is 0.8. Below are our findings:

1) SWARM v.s. Baselines: SWARM almost consistently outperforms state-of-the-art baselines with a significance level on both datasets. For instance, it achieves significant improvements over six counterparts w.r.t. PS@5 and Recall@5 by 29.5%–134.6% and 32.7%–474.3%, respectively on the myExperiment dataset. While SWARM is slightly inferior to FPA by 10.0% in Scale@5, this slight difference is acceptable considering the substantial improvements in PS and Recall. Furthermore, FPA searches the entire fragment repository, which is much larger than SWARM's, resulting in longer recommendation time.

Overall, SWARM surpasses annotation-based methods (the first three), highlighting the importance of the fragment structure besides textual information. Although the last three baselines partially consider structural features, their performance still lags behind SWARM's, demonstrating the effectiveness of our method in extracting and integrating textual and structural semantics.

2) myExperiment v.s. Galaxy: Another interesting observation is that the performance of structure-based methods is significantly better than annotation-based methods on the Galaxy dataset compared to the myExperiment dataset. For instance, when comparing SKG and FPA as representatives of their respective methods, SKG demonstrates an average improvement of 49.0% and 236.3% in PS and Recall metrics, respectively, on the myExperiment dataset. However, this gap widens to 72.4% and 255.1% on the Galaxy dataset due to the lack of well-annotated titles or descriptions for Galaxy workflows. Given the varying quality of online repositories, our SWARM model, which effectively integrates textual and structural features simultaneously, is indispensable and offers greater generalization capabilities for different formats of workflow fragments.

Additionally, while myExperiment workflows are primarily from biomedical domains, Galaxy workflows support many scientific domains. However, SWARM performs impressively on both datasets, showing its high capability for multi-domain adaptation. This underscores the effectiveness of fine-tuning BioLinkBERT in enabling the model to effectively adapt to different scientific domains.

6.4   Ablation Study

We conduct ablation studies on the two datasets for different values of N (5,10), and the average results are presented in Table 3. Below are our observations:

Table 3. Ablation studies on the main components/mechanisms of our approach.

Method	myExperiment			Galaxy		
	PS	Scale	Recall	PS	Scale	Recall
SWARM	**0.948**	9.703	**0.570**	**0.897**	13.758	**0.559**
\PreEncoder	0.866	8.886	0.490	0.825	12.976	0.471
\PreSel	0.926	**10.387**	0.523	0.872	**14.059**	0.505
↻PathAtt	0.822	7.936	0.459	0.793	12.045	0.446

* The best results are highlighted in bold. \PreEncoder and \PreSel denote removing the pretraining of fragment encoder and the pre-selection step from SWARM. ↻PathAtt denotes replacing PathAttention Net with average pooling and one-layer MLP projection for paths in SWARM.

1) Removing the **pretraining of fragment encoder** causes severe performance degradation, dropping by an average of [8.3%, 7.1%, 14.9%] on the two datasets w.r.t. three metrics, respectively. Such striking differences highlight the necessity of using a contrastive model to extract structural semantics of frequent and similar fragments from a high-level abstraction perspective, resulting in a pre-trained fragment encoder for facilitating downstream semantic matching.

2) The two-step approach SWARM generally outperforms the direct ranking-based (one-step) approach, SWARM\PreSel. The **pre-selection** step that selects candidate workflows and fragments with higher text similarity is skipped in SWARM\PreSel, hence using the prediction model directly may return some noisy fragments with a high matching degree but low text similarity. These fragments may be slightly larger in scale but can harm the PS and Recall metrics, not to mention the increase in computing cost for the whole fragment repository.

3) Replacing average pooling with **PathAttention Net** obtains remarkable performance gains. We owe it to the attention mechanism's precise and selective learning of textual and structural semantics in candidate fragments' paths.

6.5   Further Investigation

To further evaluate the influence of key parameters or components in our framework, we compare our method to those replacing with other standard values or modules on the myExperiment dataset. The results are shown in Fig. 5.

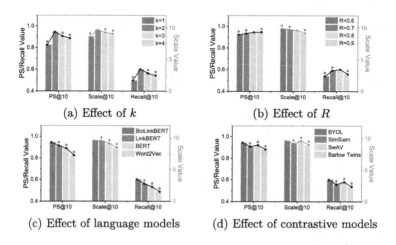

Fig. 5. Performance analysis of different parameters or components (k, R, language models, and contrastive models) when $N = 10$. $\star$ denotes statistical significance ($p < 0.05$) between the comparative method and SWARM.

1) Effect of k: In Fig. 5(a), it is evident that SWARM performs best when $k = 2$, whereas a single path is insufficient for effective encoding. Moreover, a larger k increases the training burden and introduces redundant or irrelevant activity noise, causing a performance degradation when $k = 3, 4$. Further analysis reveals that the selected two key paths can cover more than 87% of the activities in each fragment, indicating that they capture a significant portion of the critical information. With the assistance of the attention mechanism, these paths effectively represent the key semantics of the fragment. In short, k can be set to a relatively small and appropriate value based on the coverage rate of paths in fragments and the computational overhead.

2) Effect of R: Figure 5(b) shows the performance of SWARM when the threshold R varies from 0.6 to 0.9. As R increases from 0.6 to 0.8, PS@10 and Recall@10 raise steadily, proving that a higher matching degree can select valuable fragments. However, when R continues to grow to 0.9, Recall@10 drops obviously.

Through a case study, the reason is that the number of fragments with a matching degree higher than 0.9 is too small to cover the user needs. Furthermore, Scale@10 exhibits a slight downward trend, but the difference is minimal, within 0.75. Thus, an appropriate value of R can be identified, i.e., $R = 0.8$.

3) Effect of Language Models: Figure 5(c) demonstrates that replacing BioLinkBERT models with Word2Vec, BERT, and LinkBERT causes a consistent performance reduction. For instance, compared to SWARM, the approach with Word2Vec decreases by 12.65%, 11.10% and 18.49% on PS@10, Scale@10 and Recall@10. This confirms the effectiveness of finetuned large-scale domain-specific language models in extracting linguistic information and underlying semantics.

4) Effect of Contrastive Models: We compare different contrastive methods in the semantics extraction model. Figure 5(d) shows that the variants employing SimSiam, SwAV, or Barlow Twins all underperform SWARM with BYOL. These results align with findings in the contrastive learning field [12, 23].

6.6   Discussion

SWARM demonstrates encouraging overall performance in the experiment. However, the semantics-based approach is limited by the available information in users' text queries. To enhance the usability and compatibility of the recommended fragments, it would be beneficial to request users to provide more detailed fields such as intended inputs/outputs or structured specifications. By incorporating additional contextual semantics, the quality of results could be further improved. Nevertheless, it is important to strike a balance between user-friendliness and the usability of the obtained outcomes.

7   Conclusion

This paper puts forward SWARM, a two-phase approach for scientific workflow fragment recommendation based on contrastive learning and semantic matching. In *Fragment Discovery Phase*, SWARM first created a fragment repository using frequent subgraph mining. Then a contrastive learning-based semantics extraction model was used to pre-train the fragment encoder that captured the structural semantics of fragments. In *Fragment Recommendation Phase*, SWARM pre-selected candidate fragments using text similarity measures and used a matching degree prediction model based on the pre-trained fragment encoder to recommend fragments, considering both semantic matching and fragment scale. Comprehensive experiments on real-world datasets prove the superiority of SWARM over its counterparts with statistical significance. Future work will be dedicated to exploring the composition of fragments to generate novel and tailored workflows that further precisely meet user requirements.

Acknowledgements. This work is supported by China National Science Foundation (No. 62072301) and the Program of Technology Innovation of the Science and Technology Commission of Shanghai Municipality (No. 21511104700).

References

1. Wen, J., Zhou, Z., Lei, F., Zhang, J.: Basic and personalized pattern-based workflow fragments discovery. Pers. Ubiquit. Comput. **25**(6), 1091–1111 (2021)
2. Gu, Y., Cao, J., Qian, S., Guan, W.: SWORTS: a scientific workflow retrieval approach by learning textual and structural semantics. IEEE Trans. Serv. Comput. (2023)
3. Starlinger, J.: Similarity measures for scientific workflows. Ph.D. thesis, Humboldt-Universität zu Berlin, Mathematisch-Naturwissenschaftliche Fakultät (2016). http://dx.doi.org/10.18452/17406
4. Deelman, E., et al.: The evolution of the pegasus workflow management software. Comput. Sci. Eng. **21**(4), 22–36 (2019)
5. Blanchi, C., Gebre, B., Wittenburg, P.: Canonical workflow for machine learning tasks. Data Intell. **4**(2), 173–185 (2022)
6. Zhou, Z., Wen, J., Wang, Y., Xue, X., Hung, P.C., Nguyen, L.D.: Topic-based crossing-workflow fragment discovery. Futur. Gener. Comput. Syst. **112**, 1141–1155 (2020)
7. Wang, X., Niu, W., Li, G., Yang, X., Shi, Z.: Mining frequent agent action patterns for effective multi-agent-based web service composition. In: Cao, L., Bazzan, A.L.C., Symeonidis, A.L., Gorodetsky, V.I., Weiss, G., Yu, P.S. (eds.) ADMI 2011. LNCS (LNAI), vol. 7103, pp. 211–227. Springer, Heidelberg (2012). https://doi.org/10.1007/978-3-642-27609-5_14
8. Wen, J., Zhou, Z., Shi, Z., Wang, J., Duan, Y., Zhang, Y.: Crossing scientific workflow fragments discovery through activity abstraction in smart campus. IEEE Access **6**, 40530–40546 (2018)
9. Belhajjame, K., Grigori, D., Harmassi, M., Ben Yahia, M.: Keyword-based search of workflow fragments and their composition. In: Nguyen, N.T., Kowalczyk, R., Pinto, A.M., Cardoso, J. (eds.) Transactions on Computational Collective Intelligence XXVI. LNCS, vol. 10190, pp. 67–90. Springer, Cham (2017). https://doi.org/10.1007/978-3-319-59268-8_4
10. Cheng, Z., Zhou, Z.: Workflow fragments of layer hierarchy detection and recommendation. In: 2016 IEEE International Conference on Systems, Man, and Cybernetics (SMC), pp. 000695–000700. IEEE (2016)
11. Zhang, J., Pourreza, M., Lee, S., Nemani, R., Lee, T.J.: Unit of work supporting generative scientific workflow recommendation. In: Pahl, C., Vukovic, M., Yin, J., Yu, Q. (eds.) ICSOC 2018. LNCS, vol. 11236, pp. 446–462. Springer, Cham (2018). https://doi.org/10.1007/978-3-030-03596-9_32
12. Chen, X., He, K.: Exploring simple siamese representation learning. In: Proceedings of the IEEE/CVF Conference on Computer Vision and Pattern Recognition, pp. 15750–15758 (2021)
13. Starlinger, J., Brancotte, B., Cohen-Boulakia, S., Leser, U.: Similarity search for scientific workflows. Proc. VLDB Endow. (PVLDB) **7**(12), 1143–1154 (2014)
14. Garijo, D., et al.: Fragflow automated fragment detection in scientific workflows. In: 2014 IEEE 10th International Conference on e-Science, vol. 1, pp. 281–289. IEEE (2014)

15. Diao, J., Zhou, Z., Xue, X., Zhao, D., Chen, S.: Bioinformatic workflow fragment discovery leveraging the social-aware knowledge graph. In: Explainable, Trustworthy and Responsive Intelligent Processing of Biological Resources Integrating Data, Information, Knowledge, and Wisdom-Volume II, vol. 16648714, p. 88 (2023)
16. Yasunaga, M., Leskovec, J., Liang, P.: LinkBERT: Pretraining Language Models with Document Links. arXiv preprint arXiv:2203.15827 (2022)
17. Gu, Y., Cao, J., Qian, S., Zhu, N., Guan, W.: MANSOR: a module alignment method based on neighbor information for scientific workflow. Concurr. Comput. Pract. Exp. e7736 (2023)
18. Yan, X., Han, J.: gSpan: graph-based substructure pattern mining. In: Proceedings of 2002 IEEE International Conference on Data Mining, pp. 721–724. IEEE (2002)
19. Grill, J.B., et al.: Bootstrap your own latent-a new approach to self-supervised learning. Adv. Neural. Inf. Process. Syst. **33**, 21271–21284 (2020)
20. He, X., Chua, T.S.: Neural factorization machines for sparse predictive analytics. In: Proceedings of the 40th International ACM SIGIR Conference on Research and Development in Information Retrieval, pp. 355–364 (2017)
21. Woolson, R.F.: Wilcoxon signed-rank test. In: Wiley Encyclopedia of Clinical Trials, pp. 1–3 (2007)
22. Wang, H., Chi, X., Wang, Z., Xu, X., Chen, S.: Extracting fine-grained service value features and distributions for accurate service recommendation. In: 2017 IEEE International Conference on Web Services (ICWS), pp. 277–284. IEEE (2017)
23. Ericsson, L., Gouk, H., Hospedales, T.M.: How well do self-supervised models transfer? In: Proceedings of the IEEE/CVF Conference on Computer Vision and Pattern Recognition, pp. 5414–5423 (2021)

TCTV: Trace Clustering Considering Intra- and Inter-cluster Similarity Based on Trace Variants

Leilei Lin[1], Ying Di[1], Wenlong Chen[2(✉)], Yunuo Cao[1], Rui Zhu[3], and Yuan Zhang[1]

[1] School of Management, Capital Normal University, Beijing, China
{leilei_lin,Yunuo,zhangyuan}@cnu.edu.cn
[2] Information Engineering College, Capital Normal University, Beijing, China
chenwenlong@cnu.edu.cn
[3] School of Software, Yunnan University, Kunming, China
rzhu@ynu.edu.cn

Abstract. As we know that simply applying existing techniques in process mining will often yield a highly incomprehensible process model that called the spaghetti-like model, because real-life processes are typically less structured and more complex than expected by stakeholders. In order to address this issue, trace clustering is considered one of the most relevant pre-processing approaches as grouping similar event logs can radically reduce the complexity of the discovered models. Trace variants denote unique control-flow complete trajectories of a process model. The comparison of trace variants opens the door for a fine-grained analysis of the distinctive features inherent in the execution of a process. In this paper, we propose a split-merge clustering method based on trace variants for pre-processing event logs. Our method consists of three phases: (1) trace variants are filtered out from the event log, and the k-nearest neighbor graph is constructed based on all trace variants; (2) the graph would be partitioned into the initial sub-clusters by applying the coarsening and partitioning operations; (3) we dynamically merge two sub-clusters in the hierarchical clustering process with the relative inter-connectivity and the relative closeness. The experiments on real-life event logs confirmed the improvements of our method compared with the baselines.

Keywords: Process mining · Trace clustering · K-nearest neighborgraph · Hierarchical clustering

1 Introduction

Since web services are distributed over autonomous parties, it is vital to monitor the correct execution of service processes. Fortunately, massive event logs are collected in Information Systems (e.g., Process-Aware Information Systems), which can be fully analyzed to improve service quality. Process mining acts as a

F. Monti et al. (Eds.): ICSOC 2023, LNCS 14420, pp. 72–87, 2023.
https://doi.org/10.1007/978-3-031-48424-7_6

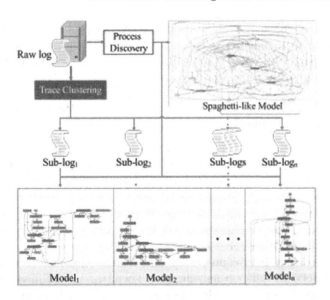

Fig. 1. Illustration of the basic trace clustering procedure in process mining

link between data mining and business process management, which can extract useful knowledge from event logs for setting and improving ongoing business processes [1]. The topics in process mining can be broadly classified into three categories [17]: process discovery (i.e. extracting one or several process models from an event log without using any apriori information), conformance checking (i.e. monitoring deviations by comparing a model and a log) and process model enhancement (i.e. extending or improving an existing model using additional information in a log). However, the challenge often faced in practical applications is that the process model mined from the raw log is extremely complex and unreadable, which is called the spaghetti-like model as shown in Fig. 1. To the best of our knowledge, trace clustering is one very interesting approach that can help limit this issue. As depicted in Fig. 1, the raw log would be partitioned into many sub-logs by trace clustering. Then, more accurate and comprehensible models would be mined by applying process discovery algorithms on sub-logs.

In the last years, many excellent trace clustering algorithms have been proposed and they provide good solutions for highly flexible environments. However, most trace clustering algorithms only consider distances between traces in event logs and do not take into account the internal relations among trace variants, where the internal relations reflect the same semantics of business processes. For example, imagine the process of purchasing a certain item in an online shop; the fragment of the process that considers filling out the form for the credit card number needs sometimes to be executed once, twice, three, ... several times. These traces would be partitioned into different groups if only computing distances, but all these different executions are not semantically different. A similar situation arises when certain fragments of a process can be executed concurrently. Boltenhagen et al. [4] tried to solve this problem based on already existing models, but in many scenarios, the process is not known in advance.

In this paper, we propose a radically different approach for Trace Clustering analysis based on Trace Variants, named TCTV. Utilizing relative interconnectivity and relative closeness, TCTV considers not only the distances between sub-clusters but also the internal relations in the clustering process. Specifically, the main contributions are summarized as follows:

- We use trace variant instead of trace as the minimum unit for trace clustering, which can improve the efficiency and accuracy of the technique. In addition, a kNN graph based on the trace variants is constructed to depict the global relationships among all variants in the log.
- Inspired by the METIS [15], which can efficiently partition the irregular graph into a multilevel scheme, we divide the kNN graph into multiple sub-clusters through two operations: coarsen and partition.
- We define relative inter-connectivity and relative closeness to compute the similarity between different sub-clusters. Then, the idea of hierarchical clustering is used to merge sub-clusters and the similarity between sub-clusters is calculated dynamically during the merging process.

In the experiments, we evaluate the performance of TCTV on different datasets. Empirical results show that the proposed method achieved state-of-the-art in trace clustering.

2   Related Work

Discovering models from logs is an important means of optimizing business processes. But logs originating from flexible environments contain many trace variants, which can significantly degrade the quality of the mined models. In the ideal case, the process would obviously be mitigated if few trace variants could be identified. Trace clustering provides a clever solution to address this issue. Over the past decade, trace clustering has been widely applied in process mining.

Greco et al. [12] employed n-gram to depict traces, but the activity sequences generated by n-gram are only locally constrained. Taking inspiration from the n-gram pattern, Bose et al. [22] introduced multiple feature sets for user selection (e.g., maximum, Super maximum, and Near Super maximum Repeats). These feature sets can be easily discovered in linear time, enabling real-time analysis of large datasets. However, this approach poses challenges when dealing with loop structures. Following a similar approach, Appice and Malerba [2] developed a joint training strategy for clustering traces based on multiple dimensions (i.e., activity, resource, sequence, and temporal). Similarity measures based on instance-level similarity, however, may be domain-specific depending on how similarity is extracted. In [10], the authors cleverly employed a multi-criteria non-compensatory logic for achieving global aggregation among conflicting criteria. To reduce the time complexity of trace clustering, [6] proposed a novel technique based on trace profiling.

Inspired by [5] in the area of web usage mining, Ferreira et al. [11] proposed clustering sequences by learning a mixture of first-order Markov models through the Expectation-Maximization (EM) algorithm. While this method can handle incomplete information in logs (e.g., missing trace IDs), it suffers from severe restrictions imposed by the order of trace selection. Weirdt et al. [9] identified a discrepancy between clustering and evaluation in methods that solely rely on distance-based clustering. To address this phenomenon, they proposed a model-driven clustering algorithm based on heuristic mining. However, this algorithm employs a greedy strategy for trace selection from logs, which may lead to local optimization. Furthermore, another drawback of this method is its time-consuming nature due to frequent mining algorithm usage. Yaguang et al. [23] improved the accuracy of trace clustering by utilizing Petri nets. Nonetheless, the problem of high-time complexity still persists. Chatain et al. [7] performed trace clustering using centroids, where centroids represent partial coverage in process models. However, it fails to handle concurrent structures in process models. Taymouri et al. [24] introduced activity duration as a novel discriminative feature and applied discrete wavelet transform on this feature, termed mutual fingerprints. However, constructing mutual fingerprints requires substantial domain expertise to ensure algorithm correctness.

As already remarked, many excellent researchers are working hard to promote the work of trace clustering, but the existing methods still have limitations with handling concurrent and loop structures. Therefore, we try to stand a new perspective to improve the performance of trace clustering by utilizing relative inter-connectivity and relative closeness between sub-clusters.

3   Preliminaries

In this section, a number of basic definitions will be introduced, and these definitions are borrowed from [8,20].

Definition 1 (Event log). *Let $\mathcal{T}$ be a finite set of activities. An event log $\mathcal{L}$ over $\mathcal{T}$ is defined as $\mathcal{L} = (\mathcal{E}, \mathcal{C}, \zeta, \tau, \succ)$, where $\mathcal{E}$ is a set of events, $\mathcal{C}$ is a set of case identifiers, $\zeta : \mathcal{E} \to \mathcal{C}$ a surjective function relating events to cases, $\tau : \mathcal{E} \to \mathcal{T}$ a function relating events to activities and $\succ \subseteq \mathcal{E} \times \mathcal{E}$ a total order on events.*

Definition 2 (Trace). *Let $\mathcal{T}$ be a finite set of activities and $\mathcal{L} = (\mathcal{E}, \mathcal{C}, \zeta, \tau, \succ)$ a log over $\mathcal{T}$. For all cases $c \in \mathcal{C}$, we define the trace $\sigma_c = \langle e_1, e_2, \cdots, e_n \rangle$ as an event sequence over the event set $\mathcal{E}(\sigma_c) = \{e \in \mathcal{E} | \zeta(e) = c\}$ as all events relating to case c, where n is the number of events in $\mathcal{E}(\sigma_c)$, $e_i \in \mathcal{E}(\sigma_c)$, $i \in \{1, 2, \cdots, n-1\}$ and if $1 \leq i < n$, it holds that $e_i \succ e_{i+1}$. The length of the trace σ_c is defined as the number of elements in $\mathcal{E}(\sigma_c)$, which is denoted as $|\sigma_c|$.*

Definition 3 (Trace Clustering). *A trace clustering $\mathcal{C}$ is a partition of an event log $\mathcal{L}$: a set of nonempty subsets of $\mathcal{L}$ such that the union of all clusters is equal to the event log, and none of the clusters overlap: $\bigcup_{\mathcal{A} \in \mathcal{C}} \mathcal{A} = \mathcal{L} \land \forall \mathcal{A}, \mathcal{B} \in \mathcal{C} : \mathcal{A} \cap \mathcal{B} \neq \emptyset \to \mathcal{A} = \mathcal{B}$.*

Definition 4 (Trace variant). *Let $\mathcal{T}$ be the universe of activities. The set of all finite sequences over $\mathcal{T}$ is denoted with $\mathcal{T}^*$. A trace variant $\gamma = \langle e_1, e_2, \cdots, e_n \rangle \in \mathcal{T}^*$ is a sequence of activities performed for a case.*

Definition 5 (Simple event log). *Let $B\left(\mathcal{T}^*\right)$ is the set of all multisets over $\mathcal{T}^*$. A simple event log L is defined as a multiset of trace variants $L \in B\left(\mathcal{T}^*\right)$. L denotes the universe of simple event logs.*

Definitions 1 and 2 state that an event log consists of a set of traces, each capturing the sequence of events for a given case of the process ordered by timestamp [1]. Definition 3 outlines the goal of trace clustering, which is to divide the raw log into sub-logs. Each sub-log contains at least one trace, and there is no overlap between traces. In Definition 4, a trace variant represents a specific instantiation or manifestation of a trace within the event log. In other words, if two traces belong to the same trace variant, they must have the same activities, events, and orders. The simple event log based on Definition 5 is a collection of trace variants.

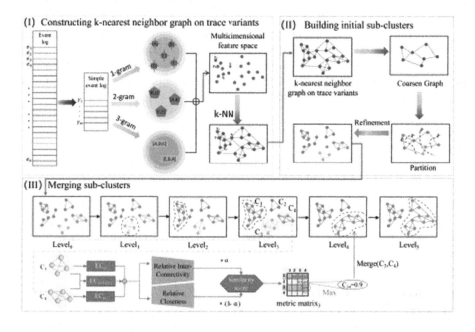

Fig. 2. Overview of our technique named TCTV for trace clustering

4   Methodology

In this section, we present TCTV (Trace Clustering based on Trace Variants), a new trace clustering algorithm that overcomes the limitations of existing trace clustering algorithms discussed in Sect. 2. Figure 2 shows an overview of our proposed method. Initially, we filter the event log to create a simple event log comprising trace variants. We employ n-gram patterns to construct the feature space of this simple event log and build a connected k-nearest neighbor (kNN) graph based on this space. Next, We perform multi-level coarsening and partitioning of the kNN graph to obtain initial sub-clusters. Subsequently, we dynamically merge two sub-clusters based on their relative inter-connectivity and relative closeness. Finally, the number of clusters required by the users is obtained through an upward-agglomerative hierarchical clustering process.

4.1 Constructing K-Nearest Neighbor Graph on Trace Variants

The first phase of TCTV involves constructing the k-nearest neighbor graph of trace variants, where these variants are derived from the raw event log, resulting in a simple event log. For instance, we assume that the raw event log $\mathcal{L} = \{\sigma_1, \sigma_2, \sigma_3, \sigma_4, ..., \sigma_n\} = \{\langle A, B, C, D, E\rangle, \langle A, B, C, E\rangle, \langle A, B, C, D, E\rangle, \langle A, B, C, E\rangle,$ ..., $\langle A, B, C, D, E, F\rangle\}$. After traversing $\mathcal{L}$ once, we can filter to get the simple event log $L = \{\gamma_1, \gamma_2, ..., \gamma_m\} = \{\langle A, B, C, D, E\rangle, \langle A, B, C, E\rangle, ..., \langle A, B, C, D, E, F\rangle\}$, where the value of m is much smaller than the value of n.

Next, we perform feature extraction on trace variants in the sample event log. The n-gram is an efficient feature extraction technique that has been well utilized in the field of process mining [13]. In this paper, we combine different lengths of n-gram patterns for clustering (i.e., 1-gram, 2-gram, and 3-gram), which can yield more comprehensive representation of trace variants in the log. Taking L above as an example, the trace variant is $\gamma_1 = \langle A, B, C, D, E\rangle$. The 1-gram set for this trace variant corresponds to$\{(A), (B), (C), (D), (E)\}$, the 2-gram set corresponds to$\{(A, B), (B, C), (C, D), (D, E)\}$, and the 3-gram set corresponds to $\{(A, B, C), (B, C, D), (C, D, E)\}$. Furthermore, we incorporate the frequency information of n-gram patterns to refine the trace variant features. At last, all the trace variants would be transformed into a multidimensional feature space.

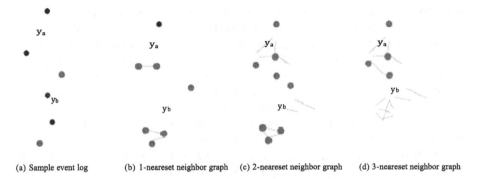

(a) Sample event log   (b) 1-neareset neighbor graph   (c) 2-neareset neighbor graph   (d) 3-neareset neighbor graph

Fig. 3. The k-nearest graph from a simple event log

Once the feature space is generated, we employ a k-nearest neighbor (kNN) graph to depict the simple event log L. Specifically, let $G = (V, E, w)$ be a kNN graph, $V = \{v_1, ..., v_n\}$ is a set of vertices and the number of vertices $n = |V|$, where each vertex v_i represents a trace variant γ_i, and $E = \{(u, v)\,|\,u, v \in V\}$ is a set of edges. The number of edges $m = |E|$. In this context, $w(u, v)$ is the positive weighting of the edges, which signifies the magnitude of affinity between trace variants γ_u and γ_v. Figure 3 illustrates the kNN graph for a simple event log with k set to 1, 2, and 3, respectively. It is important to note that the value of k is determined by whether the kNN graph is a connected graph or not. In other words, when $k = 1$, for $\forall a, b \in V$, if there is a path from a to b, then no iteration is performed. As shown in Fig. 3(b), when $k = 1$, trace variants γ_a and γ_b are not connected, so $k = 2$ iterations must be performed, and so on.

4.2   Building Initial Sub-clusters

In the second phase of TCTV, the kNN graph is partitioned into a large number of initial sub-clusters. By only considering the distance between trace variants, it is not possible to overcome the execution semantic gap caused by concurrency or loop structures. In addition, the performance of TCTV can be effectively improved by using sub-clusters as the minimum unit for clustering.

Before the partitioning operation, we will perform a coarsening operation. Because in the real-life logs, the number of trace variants is very large, directly dividing the kNN graph will seriously affect its efficiency. The coarsening process, as illustrated in Fig. 3, involves obtaining a coarser version of the kNN graph $G = (V, E, w)$ by finding the maximal matching. For any vertex v_i, its matching value is the sum of the weights of all the edges connected to it. We define the matching weight as $w(M)$, and the computation formula is as follows:

$$w(M_i) = \sum_{v_j \in V, i \neq j} (w(v_i, v_j) \cdot \mathbb{I}(v_i, v_j)) \tag{1}$$

where $w(v_i, v_j)$ represents the weight of the edge (v_i, v_j), $\mathbb{I}(v_i, v_j)$ is the indicator function that represents if the edge (v_i, v_j) exists, the value of $\mathbb{I}(v_i, v_j)$ is 1, otherwise 0. For example, shown in Fig. 4, after traversing all vertices, we obtain a matrix of matching weights and find that $w(M_p) = 4.1$ is the maximum matching weight in G. Therefore, the set of vertices γ_x, γ_y, γ_z, γ_p in G are abstracted to form a single vertex p^1 in the next coarser level graph. To preserve the connectivity information in the coarser graph, the edges that were originally connected to all four vertices γ_x, γ_y, γ_z, γ_p are reconnected to p^1. Note that if there exist multiple edges from a vertex to these four vertices, then the weight of the reconnected edge to p^1 is cumulative. As shown in Fig. 4, γ_m has two edges (γ_m, γ_y), (γ_m, γ_z) before coarsening operation, so the weight $w(\gamma_m, p^1) = w(\gamma_m, \gamma_y) + w(\gamma_m, \gamma_z) = 0.3 + 0.1 = 0.4$.

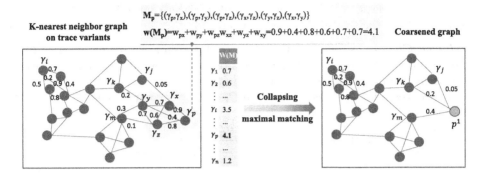

Fig. 4. An example for illustrating the process of graph coarsening

After obtaining the coarsened graph, we utilize the spectral bisection (SB) method [25] to compute a high-quality bipartition (i.e., small edge cut) of the graph, ensuring that each partition contains approximately half of the total weights of the original graph. We will iterate the partitioning process until the number of sub-clusters equals *NUM*, where *NUM* is a hyperparameter in TCTV and its value is much larger than the number obtained from the final trace clustering. For most of the data sets that we encountered, setting *NUM* to 100 in TCTV which provides a good trade-off between efficiency and accuracy. It should be noted that after the partitioning is completed, all abstract vertices in the coarsened graph will be reverted to their original state in the kNN graph.

4.3   Merging Sub-clusters

As soon as the initial sub-clusters are generated in the second phase, TCTV then switches to agglomerative hierarchical clustering, where these small sub-clusters are merged together. In this phase, we define the relative inter-connectivity and relative closeness to measure the similarity between two sub-clusters inspired by the Chameleon algorithm [14].

Relative Inter-connectivit. The relative inter-connectivity between C_i and C_j is defined as the absolute inter-connectivity C_i and C_j normalized by the internal inter-connectivity of both C_i and C_j.

The relative inter-connectivity between C_i and C_j is given by

$$RI\left(C_i, C_j\right) = \frac{\left|EC_{|C_i, C_j|}\right|}{\frac{\left|EC_{C_i}\right| + \left|EC_{C_j}\right|}{2}} \tag{2}$$

here, $\left|EC_{|C_i, C_j|}\right|$ represents the sum of edge weights that connect C_i and C_j, which indicates the absolute inter-connectivity between C_i and C_j. $\left|EC_{C_i}\right|$ denotes the size of its min-cut bisector (i.e., the weighted sum of edges that divide the fine-grained graph formed by the trace variants within C_i into two roughly equal parts), which reflects the internal inter-connectivity of C_i. Similarly, $\left|EC_{C_j}\right|$ is the size of its min-cut bisector for C_j.

Relative Closeness. The relative closeness between a pair of sub-clusters C_i and C_j is defined as the absolute closeness between C_j and C_j normalized with respect to the internal closeness of C_j and C_j.

Hence, the relative closeness between C_i and C_j is computed as,

$$RC\left(C_i, C_j\right) = \frac{\bar{S}_{EC_{|C_i,C_j|}}}{\frac{|C_i|}{|C_i|+|C_j|}\bar{S}_{EC_{C_i}} + \frac{|C_j|}{|C_i|+|C_j|}\bar{S}_{EC_{C_j}}} \tag{3}$$

where $|C_i|$ and $|C_j|$ represent the number of trace variants contained in C_j and C_j, respectively. $\bar{S}_{EC_{|C_i,C_j|}}$ denotes the average weight of all edges connecting C_j and C_j, which reflects the average edge weight between these two sub-clusters. $\bar{S}_{EC_{C_i}}$ and $\bar{S}_{EC_{C_j}}$ are the average weights of the edges that belong in the min-cut bisector of C_j C_j. Also note that a weighted average of the internal closeness of C_j and C_j is used to normalize the absolute closeness of the two sub-clusters, that favors the absolute closeness of sub-cluster that contains the larger number of trace variant vertices.

Next, we define a similarity score function S to combine the relative inter-connectivity and relative closeness, and then each merging in the hierarchical clustering would select the sub-cluster pairs of maximize similarity score.

$$S\left(C_i, C_j\right) = \alpha * RI\left(C_i, C_j\right) + (1 - \alpha) * RC\left(C_i, C_j\right) \tag{4}$$

where α is a trade-off factor with a range of values between $[0, 1]$. When the value of α is greater than 0.5, it indicates that the similarity score takes more account of RI, otherwise it considers the RC more. In this paper, $\alpha = 0.5$.

As shown in Fig. 5, the process of merging sub-clusters using agglomerative hierarchical clustering is detailed. At the first level, there are a total of 7 sub-clusters. By computing the similarity score function defined in Eq. 4, we obtain a 7×7 metric matrix, where matrix(i, j) represents the similarity score $S(C_i, C_j)$ between sub-clusters C_i and C_j. At the first level, the maximum similarity score in the matrix is $S(C_2, C_3) = 0.9$, leading us to merge C_2 and C_3 to form a new sub-cluster C_{23}. Moving on to the second level, we recalculate the similarity scores between clusters and update the metric matrix to a 6×6 dimension, enabling dynamic modeling of cluster similarities. We iteratively repeat the above steps until the number of clusters reaches the desired value specified by the users. This allows us to dynamically adjust and refine the clustering based on the evolving similarities between clusters at each level of the hierarchy.

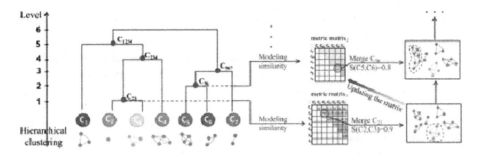

Fig. 5. The details of merging sub-clusters in hierarchical clustering

5 Experiments

The proposed method (i.e., TCTV) is implemented as a stand-alone Python application, and all the code is publicly-available1[1].

5.1 Datasets

We conducted all experiments using three publicly available datasets: BPIC13[2], BPIC17[3] and BPIC20[4], which we refer to as event logs. BPIC is open real-world data provided by IEEE Task Force on Process Mining, which has become an important benchmark in process mining. These three datasets originate from diverse domains and exhibit substantial disparities, providing robust validation for the trace clustering algorithm's capabilities: (i) BPIC13 is provided by the Ghent University, contains the event log for the Volvo IT incident and problem management with 819 traces and 2351 events; (ii) BPIC17 is generated by the loan application process of Dutch financial institutions, includes all applications submitted through the online system in 2016. This dataset has 31,504 traces and 1,202,267 events; (iii) BPIC20 covers events related to travel permits, including all relevant events associated with the declaration of prepaid travel expenses and travel declarations. It has 7,065 traces and 86,581 events.

5.2 Baselines and Metrics

Baselines. In order to comprehensively demonstrate the effectiveness of the TCTV algorithm, in this section, we compare TCTV with three algorithms (**MR** [22], **ActiTraC** [9] and **TraCluSI** [8]). The reasons for selecting these three algorithms are: (i) the methods commonly applied in data mining and trace clustering literature and their implementations are publicly accessible; (ii) if there are many extended versions of a method, only the best one is selected; (iii)

---

[1] https://anonymous.4open.science/r/TCTV.

[2] https://data.4tu.nl/collections/789491a1-2b09-4ed6-af75-8a5aadada5ac.

[3] https://data.4tu.nl/articles/dataset/BPI_Challenge_2017/12696884.

[4] https://data.4tu.nl/collections/BPI_Challenge_2020/5065541.

the input of the method is the set of traces and the smallest unit is a trace, while the output is the set of trace clustering.

Metrics. There are many methods to measure the quality of trace clustering [8,11,16,18], and in this paper, the silhouette coefficient [21], fitness [3] and precision [19] are chosen to evaluate the performance of trace clustering algorithm, respectively:

1) Silhouette Coefficient: As we know, silhouette coefficient is the most commonly used to evaluate the effect of clustering. In Eq. 5, $a(i)$ represents the average distance between trace σ_i and the other traces in the same cluster, $b(i)$ represents the average distance between trace σ_i and the traces in the nearest neighboring cluster. The calculation process of the silhouette coefficient s(i) for trace σ_i is as follows:

$$s(i) = \frac{b(i) - a(i)}{max\{a(i), b(i)\}} \tag{5}$$

The silhouette coefficient $\mathcal{S}$ for event log $\mathcal{L}$ is the average of silhouette scores for all traces (total number of traces N) of $\mathcal{L}$, as shown in Eq. 6. The silhouette coefficient ranges from -1 (worst) to 1 (best).

$$\mathcal{S}_{\mathcal{L}} = \frac{1}{N} \sum_{i=1}^{N} s(i) \tag{6}$$

2) Fitness: The ultimate goal of trace clustering is to improve the quality of the model by dividing the event log. However, the silhouette coefficient cannot measure clustering results from the perspective of the process model, leading to the divergence between the clustering bias and the evaluation bias. Therefore, we also choose fitness to measure the performance of trace clustering by replying to the traces on process models. For each trace σ_i of the event log $\mathcal{L}$, let c_i be the number of consumed tokens, p_i the number of produced tokens, m_i the number of missing tokens and r_i the number of remaining tokens. Then, the following equation calculates the fitness of $\mathcal{L}$.

$$f_{\mathcal{L}} = \frac{1}{2}\left(1 - \frac{\sum_{\sigma_i \in \mathcal{L}} m_i}{\sum_{\sigma_i \in \mathcal{L}} c_i}\right) + \frac{1}{2}\left(1 - \frac{\sum_{\sigma_i \in \mathcal{L}} r_i}{\sum_{\sigma_i \in \mathcal{L}} p_i}\right) \tag{7}$$

As shown in Eq. 7, the range of fitness is $[0, 1]$, where 0 is the worst value and 1 is the best value.

3) Precision: The aim of precision in process mining is to prefer the model with minimal behavior to represent as closely as possible the log, thus avoiding the overly general model. Let $\mathcal{L} = \{\sigma_i, ..., \sigma_{|\mathcal{L}|}\}$ and $PN = (P, T, W, M_0)$ be an event log and a petri net, respectively. For each trace σ_i ($1 \leq i \leq |\mathcal{L}|$), state s_j^i ($1 \leq j \leq |\sigma_i| + 1$) denotes the j-th state of σ_i. $A_T(s)$ represents the allowed tasks of the PN under state s, while R_T represents the reflected tasks of $\mathcal{L}$ under state s. The escaping edges (E_E) of s is defined as $E_E(s) = A_T(s) \setminus R_T(s)$. The precision is defined as follows:

$$p(\mathcal{L}, PN) = 1 - \frac{\sum_{i=1}^{|\mathcal{L}|}\sum_{j=1}^{|\sigma_i|+1}|E_E(s_j^i)|}{\sum_{i=1}^{|\mathcal{L}|}\sum_{j=1}^{|\sigma_i|+1}|A_T(s_j^i)|} \tag{8}$$

It's worth noting that we use the Inductive Miner algorithm to discover the process model, in order to evaluate the performance of trace clustering in terms of fitness and precision.

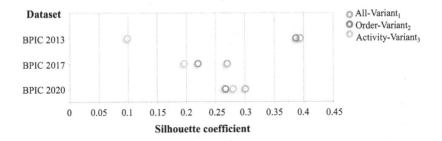

Fig. 6. The silhouette coefficient under three types of trace variants

5.3 Evaluation on Different Trace Variants

Different trace variants can have a significant impact on the clustering results. Therefore, for our first experiment, we select three common trace variants to evaluate the performance of TCTV: (a) "All-Variant$_1$", which considers all information in trace (i.e., activities, events, and orders); (b) "Order-Variant$_2$", which considers whether some orders appear or not; (c) "Activity-Variant$_3$", which considers some activities appear or not. As shown in Fig. 6, on the BPIC2013 dataset, the silhouette coefficient of "Activity-Variant$_3$" is significantly lower than the other two trace variant types, while on the BPIC2020 dataset, the silhouette coefficient of "Activity-Variant$_3$" is higher than that of "Order-Variant$_2$". However, the silhouette coefficient scores of "All-Variant$_1$" are consistently higher than the other two trace variant types on all datesets. Therefore, in TCTV, we default to using the "All-Variant$_1$".

5.4 Comparing with the Baselines

In the second experiment, the performance of our proposed method (TCTV) and the baselines (MR, ActiTraC, and TraCluSI) are compared in silhouette coefficient, fitness and precision.

Firstly, the performance of the silhouette coefficient is shown in Fig. 7(a)–(c). We can see that ActiTraC and TraCluSI have significantly lower silhouette coefficients than TCTV and MR. For example, as shown in Fig. 7a, TCTV and MR can achieve an accuracy of about 0.4, while the average scores of ActiTraC and TraCluSI are only about 0.3. Similar observations can also be made from Fig. 7b and Fig. 7c. In addition, we can find that the silhouette coefficient score

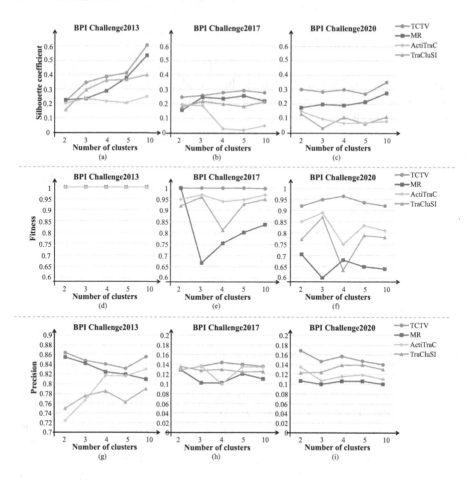

Fig. 7. Comparisons of four algorithms on three metrics.

of TCTV is generally higher than that of MR. Specifically, although TCTV outperformed MR slightly in both BPIC2013 and BPIC2017, its average silhouette coefficient score in BPIC2020 was higher than that of MR by 0.1.

Secondly, we use the fitness evaluation metric to measure the clustering effect of the four algorithms. As shown in Fig. 7(d)–(f), TCTV outperforms the other algorithms in terms of fitness. In comparison, although ActiTraC and TraCluSI also take into account the structural information of sub-clusters, their fitness scores are still lower than TCTV. This can be attributed to ActiTraC's frequent use of greedy strategies during the clustering process, which can lead to local optima. Additionally, TraCluSI's utilization of Super-Instances may result in information loss. What's worse, due to the uncertainty in Super-Instance selection, the clustering results exhibit evident instability. For instance, as shown in Fig. 7(f), the distance between the best and worst fitness scores of the TraCluSI algorithm can reach 0.2. On the other hand, MR appears to be ineffective on the BPIC2017 and BPIC2020 datasets. This is because MR solely considers distance information between traces and neglects the structural information of sub-clusters, leading to lower fitness scores. It is noteworthy that in Fig. 7(d), the fitness scores of all four algorithms are exceptionally high, reaching 1. This is due to the BPIC2013 dataset containing only three activities, resulting in a limited number of possible permutations.

Thirdly, Fig. 7(g)–(i) show the precision scores under three datasets. TCTV outperforms the other algorithms on all three datasets, indicating that the models obtained from TCTV clustering results do not suffer from overgeneralization problems. The performance of MR on three datasets are extremely unstable, mainly due to the neglect of concurrency and loop structures. ActiTraC also has low precision scores after weighted average due to the use of a greedy strategy.

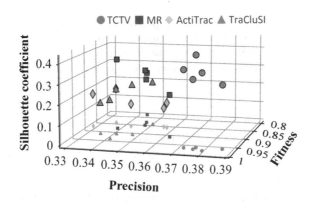

Fig. 8. Results of evaluation on three-dimensional scatter plot.

Overall, as illustrated in Fig. 8, each point in the scatter plot represents the average score of the three datasets under the same number of clusters. We find that MR performs well in terms of silhouette coefficient, but the performance on fitness and precision is lower than ActiTraC and TraCluSI. In contrast, although ActiTrac and TraCluSI have high fitness and precision, their silhouette coefficient scores are very low. However, the proposed method (i.e., TCTV) in this paper performed well in all aspects.

On the aspect of software and hardware, we conduct all experiments on an AMD Ryzen i7-6800HQ@3.20 GHZ with 16 GB RAM (64 bit), running Windows 11 and Python3.7. Based on the test results, it is evident that TCTV demonstrates the highest efficiency, with an average runtime of 141.37 s. In comparison, TraCluSI has an average running time of 157.31 s, MR's average running time is 374.2 s, and ActiTraC's execution time is significantly longer, with an average running time of 2235.2 s.

6   Conclusion and Future Work

Trace clustering is a highly relevant topic in process mining, because it can reduce the complexity of the model mined from event logs in a flexible environment. In this article, we present a novel technique of trace clustering, called TCTV, which considers the intra-cluster and inter-cluster similarity based on trace variants. Our approach consists of three phases: constructing the kNN graph, building (hundreds of) initial sub-clusters, and merging sub-clusters. We choose three metrics (i.e., silhouette coefficient, fitness, and precision) to evaluate the performance of TCTV. The experimental results show that our method outperforms state-of-the-art baselines with real-life logs.

In the future, we plan to extend our method to support multiple view clustering, while TCTV only considers the control-flow perspective.

Acknowledgements. The work was supported by the general project numbered KM202310028003 of Beijing Municipal Education Commission, the National Natural Science Foundation of China (61872252), the National Natural Science Foundation of China under Grant 62362067, Yunnan Xing Dian Talents Support Plan.

References

1. van der Aalst, W.: Process Mining: Discovery, Conformance and Enhancement of Business Processes. Springer, Heidelberg (2011). https://doi.org/10.1007/978-3-662-49851-4
2. Appice, A., Malerba, D.: A co-training strategy for multiple view clustering in process mining. IEEE Trans. Serv. Comput. **9**(6), 832–845 (2015)
3. Berti, A., van der Aalst, W.M.: Reviving token-based replay: increasing speed while improving diagnostics. In: Algorithms and Theories for the Analysis of Event Data, vol. 2371, pp. 87–103 (2019)
4. Boltenhagen, M., Carmona, J., Chatain, T.: Model-based trace variant analysis of event logs. Inf. Syst. **102**, 101675 (2020)
5. Cadez, I., Heckerman, D., Meek, C., Smyth, P., White, S.: Model-based clustering and visualization of navigation patterns on a web site. Data Min. Knowl. Disc. **7**, 399–424 (2003)
6. Ceravolo, P., Damiani, E., Torabi, M., Barbon, S.: Toward a new generation of log pre-processing methods for process mining. In: Carmona, J., Engels, G., Kumar, A. (eds.) BPM 2017. LNBIP, vol. 297, pp. 55–70. Springer, Cham (2017). https://doi.org/10.1007/978-3-319-65015-9_4
7. Chatain, T., Carmona, J., van Dongen, B.: Alignment-based trace clustering. In: Mayr, H.C., Guizzardi, G., Ma, H., Pastor, O. (eds.) ER 2017. LNCS, vol. 10650, pp. 295–308. Springer, Cham (2017). https://doi.org/10.1007/978-3-319-69904-2_24
8. De Koninck, P., De Weerdt, J.: Scalable mixed-paradigm trace clustering using super-instances. In: International Conference on Process Mining, pp. 17–24 (2019)
9. De Weerdt, J., vanden Broucke, S., Vanthienen, J., Baesens, B.: Active trace clustering for improved process discovery. IEEE Trans. Knowl. Data Eng. **25**(12), 2708–2720 (2013)

10. Delias, P., Doumpos, M., Grigoroudis, E., Matsatsinis, N.: A non-compensatory approach for trace clustering. Int. Trans. Oper. Res. **26**(5), 1828–1846 (2017)
11. Ferreira, D., Zacarias, M., Malheiros, M., Ferreira, P.: Approaching process mining with sequence clustering: experiments and findings. In: Alonso, G., Dadam, P., Rosemann, M. (eds.) BPM 2007. LNCS, vol. 4714, pp. 360–374. Springer, Heidelberg (2007). https://doi.org/10.1007/978-3-540-75183-0_26
12. Greco, G., Guzzo, A., Pontieri, L., Saccà, D.: Mining expressive process models by clustering workflow traces. In: Dai, H., Srikant, R., Zhang, C. (eds.) PAKDD 2004. LNCS (LNAI), vol. 3056, pp. 52–62. Springer, Heidelberg (2004). https://doi.org/10.1007/978-3-540-24775-3_8
13. Greco, G., Guzzo, A., Pontieri, L., Saccà, D.: Discovering expressive process models by clustering log traces. IEEE Trans. Knowl. Data Eng. **18**, 1010–1027 (2006)
14. Karypis, G., Han, E.H., Kumar, V.: Chameleon a hierarchical clustering algorithm using dynamic modeling. Computer **32**, 68–75 (1999)
15. Karypis, G., Kumar, V., Comput, S.: A fast and high quality multilevel scheme for partitioning irregular graphs. SIAM J. Sci. Comput. **20**(1), 359–392 (1998)
16. Lee, D., Park, J., Pulshashi, I.R., Bae, H.: Clustering and operation analysis for assembly blocks using process mining in shipbuilding industry. In: Song, M., Wynn, M.T., Liu, J. (eds.) AP-BPM 2013. LNBIP, vol. 159, pp. 67–80. Springer, Cham (2013). https://doi.org/10.1007/978-3-319-02922-1_5
17. Lin, L., Wen, L., Lin, L., Pei, J., Yang, H.: LCDD: detecting business process drifts based on local completeness. IEEE Trans. Serv. Comput. **15**(4), 2086–2099 (2022)
18. Lu, X., Tabatabaei, S.A., Hoogendoorn, M., Reijers, H.A.: Trace clustering on very large event data in healthcare using frequent sequence patterns. In: Hildebrandt, T., van Dongen, B.F., Röglinger, M., Mendling, J. (eds.) BPM 2019. LNCS, vol. 11675, pp. 198–215. Springer, Cham (2019). https://doi.org/10.1007/978-3-030-26619-6_14
19. Muñoz-Gama, J., Carmona, J.: A fresh look at precision in process conformance. In: Hull, R., Mendling, J., Tai, S. (eds.) BPM 2010. LNCS, vol. 6336, pp. 211–226. Springer, Heidelberg (2010). https://doi.org/10.1007/978-3-642-15618-2_16
20. Rafiei, M., Wangelik, F., Aalst, W.: TraVaS: differentially private trace variant selection for process mining. In: Montali, M., Senderovich, A., Weidlich, M. (eds.) ICPM 2022. LNBIP, vol. 468, pp. 114–126. Springer, Cham (2022). https://doi.org/10.1007/978-3-031-27815-0_9
21. Rousseeuw, P.: Silhouettes: a graphical aid to the interpretation and validation of cluster analysis. Comput. Appl. Math. **20**, 53–65 (1987)
22. Bose, R.P.J.C., van der Aalst, W.M.P.: Trace clustering based on conserved patterns: towards achieving better process models. In: Rinderle-Ma, S., Sadiq, S., Leymann, F. (eds.) BPM 2009. LNBIP, vol. 43, pp. 170–181. Springer, Heidelberg (2010). https://doi.org/10.1007/978-3-642-12186-9_16
23. Sun, Y., Bauer, B.: A novel top-down approach for clustering traces. In: Zdravkovic, J., Kirikova, M., Johannesson, P. (eds.) CAiSE 2015. LNCS, vol. 9097, pp. 331–345. Springer, Cham (2015). https://doi.org/10.1007/978-3-319-19069-3_21
24. Taymouri, F., La Rosa, M., Carmona, J.: Business process variant analysis based on mutual fingerprints of event logs. In: Dustdar, S., Yu, E., Salinesi, C., Rieu, D., Pant, V. (eds.) CAiSE 2020. LNCS, vol. 12127, pp. 299–318. Springer, Cham (2020). https://doi.org/10.1007/978-3-030-49435-3_19
25. Urschel, J.C., Zikatanov, L.T.: Spectral bisection of graphs and connectedness. Linear Algebra Appl. **449**, 1–16 (2014)

Service Descriptions, Tags, Discovery and Recommendation

Influence-Guided Data Augmentation in Graph Contrastive Learning for Recommendation

Qi Zhang, Heran Xi, and Jinghua Zhu[✉]

School of Computer Science and Technology, HeilongJiang University, Harbin, China
zhujinghua@hlju.edu.cn

Abstract. The graph contrastive learning approach, which combines graph convolutional networks (GCNs) with contrastive learning, has been widely applied in recommender systems and achieved tremendous success. Most graph contrastive learning (GCL) methods for recommendation perform random data augmentation operations on the user-item interaction graph to generate subgraphs, learn node embeddings through graph convolutional networks, and finally maximize the consistency of node embeddings in different subgraphs using contrastive loss. GCL improves the recommendation performance while slowing down the rate at which node embeddings tend to be similar, alleviating the over-smoothing problem to some extent. However, random data augmentation (e.g., random node dropout or edge dropout) will destroy the structure of the original input graph and change the original semantic information, leading to performance degradation. In this paper, we propose a novel graph contrastive learning model, IG-GCL, which uses the influence of elements in a graph to achieve guided data augmentation. Specifically, the model uses the mutual reinforcement network and node degree to calculate the importance scores of nodes and edges in the graph, respectively, thereby creating a more powerful data augmentation method to improve the performance of contrastive learning. We conduct extensive experiments on three real-world benchmark datasets. Experimental results demonstrate that IG-GCL can obtain performance improvements by stacking multi-layer neural networks, has the ability to mitigate the over-smoothing problem, and consistently outperforms the baseline, validating the effectiveness of the proposed influence-guided data augmentation method.

Keywords: Recommendation · Contrastive Learning · Graph Convolution Network · Data Augmentation

1 Introduction

Graph Convolutional Networks (GCNs) [7] can aggregate neighborhood information to enhance node representation learning and provide a flexible and convenient way to model multi-hop information. Therefore, GCN-based models

F. Monti et al. (Eds.): ICSOC 2023, LNCS 14420, pp. 91–99, 2023.
https://doi.org/10.1007/978-3-031-48424-7_7

have gained more and more attention in recent years and achieve state-of-the-art performance in recommendation [1,4,9,11]. Most GCN-based models follow the supervised learning paradigm, where the supervised signals come from observed user-item interactions. However, in practical recommendation scenarios, the observed interactions are very limited, leading to data sparsity issues. Therefore, researchers want to introduce unsupervised learning in recommendation.

Contrastive learning is an important unsupervised learning method that maximizes the mutual information between positive pairs while pushing away negative pairs. Researchers have applied contrastive learning to recommendation and proposed many GCL strategies that show good results in scenarios such as dat-sparse and cold start [8,10,12,13]. SGL [10] is a popular contrastive learning recommendation method that uses randomized data augmentation (node/edge drop, etc.). However, random augmentation may remove many influential nodes or edges. Thus, the subgraphs may not align well with the semantic information of the original graph, ultimately impacting model performance.

Besides, most GCN models achieve optimal performance when stacked with two or three layers. If the depth increases, the performance decreases dramatically. This is because stacking multiple layers can lead to over-smoothing, where the embedding becomes increasingly similar and eventually indistinguishable.

To address the above problem, we propose IG-GCL. We introduce an importance calculation method to identify key elements, thus realize an influence-guided graph contrastive learning process that maximally preserves the structural and semantic information of the original graph. Furthermore, in each training cycle, the data augmentation method removes some non-critical nodes or edges from the input graph. This disrupts the message propagation that should take place through these nodes or edges, causing certain nodes to not participate in the neighborhood aggregation process, slowing down the rate at which nodes embedding become similar, and thus mitigates the over-smoothing problem.

To summarize, the major contributions of this work are as follows:

- We propose an influence-guided data augmentation: node importance is calculated by the mutual augmentation network, and edge importance is calculated by node degree. Then, use these to guide data augmentation.
- We propose IG-GCL, a recommendation model that utilizes influence-guided data augmentation. IG-GCL consists of supervised and self-supervised tasks.
- Experimental results on three real-world datasets show that IG-GCL improves recommendation performance and effectively mitigates over-smoothing.

2   Methods

2.1   Preliminaries

Let $G = (V, E)$ represent user-item interaction graph, $V = \{U \cup I | u \in U, i \in I\}$ consists of user nodes $u \in U$ and item nodes $i \in I$, where the number of user nodes is N and the number of item nodes is M. $E = \{e_{ij}\}_{1 \leq i < j \leq |V|}$ is the set of user-item interaction edges in the graph. Let N_u and N_i denote the set of neighbor nodes of the user and the item, respectively. Let $\boldsymbol{R} \in \mathbb{R}^{N \times M}$ denote the user-item interaction matrix, where $\boldsymbol{R}_{ij} = \boldsymbol{R}_{ji} = 1$ if $e_{ij} \in E$, and 0 elsewhere.

2.2   Motivation and Framework

In recommendation, using random data augmentation causes the subgraph to lose semantic information and fail to reflect real-world scenarios. To solve this problem, we propose an influence-guided data augmentation method, IG-GCL.

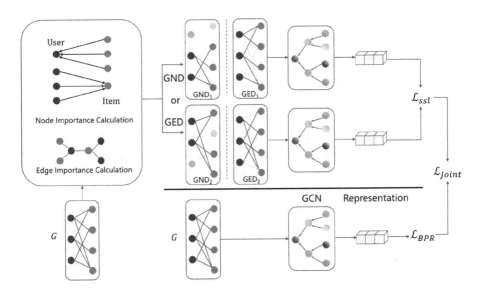

Fig. 1. An illustration of IG-GCL model architecture.

Figure 1 shows the model framework. First, calculate the importance of nodes and edges using the mutual augmentation network and node degree information. Next, use the importance to guide the data augmentation so as to better retain the key nodes. Node embeddings are then learned using the GCN model and jointly optimized using supervised and self-supervised tasks.

2.3   Influence-Guided Data Augmentation Strategy

Importance Score Calculation. We argue that the influence of users and items go hand in hand; the importance of items depends not only on the number of users interacting with them but also on the influence of those users; similarly, for users, if a user interacts with multiple cold items, then that user's importance will be somewhat affected.

Therefore, in this paper, we use the mutually reinforcing relationship between user and item nodes according to the idea in HITS [14] to calculate the node

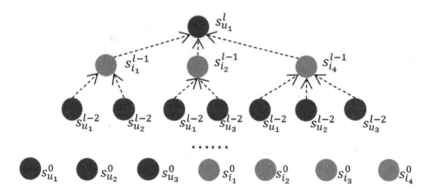

Fig. 2. Take node u_1 as an example to show the importance calculation process.

importance in the graph in a circular iteration. As shown in Fig 2, we take u_1 as an example to introduce how to calculate node importance in a mutual reinforcement network. We calculate the l layer score $s_{u_1}^{(l)}$ of u_1 based on the $(l-1)$ layer score $s_i^{(l-1)}$ of the item interacting with u_1. Similarly, we calculate $s_i^{(l-1)}$ based on the importance score $s_u^{(l-2)}$ of the user interacting with the item. So the importance scores of nodes are as follows:

$$s_u^{(l)} = \sum_{i \in N_u} s_i^{(l-1)}, \qquad s_i^{(l)} = \sum_{u \in N_i} s_u^{(l-1)} \tag{1}$$

We take the initial importance score $s_v^{(0)} = 1$ for node $v \in V$. We calculate the importance of all user nodes and item nodes in the graph by iterating through Eqs. (1) layer by layer until convergence. However, there are a large number of nodes in the dataset, and the values of $s_u^{(l)}$ and $s_i^{(l)}$ are large when the importance scores of user and item nodes are calculated after one layer. After a few cycles, the amount of computation increases dramatically. Therefore, after we calculate one layer, we normalize the current node importance scores as follows:

$$sum_1 = \sum_{u \in U} s_u^{(l)} \qquad s_u^{(l)} = \frac{s_u^{(l)}}{sum_1}, \qquad sum_2 = \sum_{i \in I} s_i^{(l)} \qquad s_i^{(l)} = \frac{s_i^{(l)}}{sum_2} \tag{2}$$

Convergence is reached when the loop iterations are computed L times, and we take the L-th level score as the importance parameter of the nodes: $s_u = s_u^{(L)}$ and $s_i = s_i^{(L)}$. Writing in matrix form, we use $s_u \in \mathbb{R}^N$ and $s_i \in \mathbb{R}^M$ to denote the importance scores of user nodes and item nodes, respectively. The importance scores of users and items are mutually reinforcing represented as follows:

$$s_u^{(l)} = \partial(\boldsymbol{R} \cdot s_i^{(l-1)}), \qquad s_i^{(l)} = \partial(\boldsymbol{R^T} \cdot s_u^{(l-1)}) \tag{3}$$

Which $\boldsymbol{s}_u^{(0)} = (1, 1, \ldots, 1)$ and $\boldsymbol{s}_i^{(0)} = (1, 1, \ldots, 1)$, ∂ represents normalized operation, take the L-th result as the final importance score: $\boldsymbol{s}_u = \boldsymbol{s}_u^{(L)}$, $\boldsymbol{s}_i = \boldsymbol{s}_i^{(L)}$.

We introduce the degree information method [5] to calculate the edge importance score based on the degrees of the nodes at both ends. If there is an interaction between user u and item i, the importance score of edge e_{ui} is:

$$e_{ui} = d_u \times d_i \tag{4}$$

where d_u and d_i represent the degree of user u and item i, respectively. After calculating the importance of all edges we also do a normalization operation:

$$sum_3 = \sum_{u \in U} \sum_{i \in I} e_{ui} \quad and \quad e_{ui} = \frac{e_{ui}}{sum_3} \tag{5}$$

writing in matrix form:

$$\boldsymbol{S}_E = \partial(\boldsymbol{d}_u \cdot \boldsymbol{R} \cdot \boldsymbol{d}_i) \tag{6}$$

where $\boldsymbol{d}_u \in \mathbb{R}^N$, $\boldsymbol{d}_i \in \mathbb{R}^M$ are the degree vectors of user and item nodes, respectively, and $\boldsymbol{S}_E \in \mathbb{R}^{N \times M}$ is the edge importance score matrix.

Guided Data Augmentation. We devised two methods of data augmentation based on importance scores: Guided node dropping and Guided edge dropping.

Guided node dropping (GND): Based on the importance scores s_u and s_i of the nodes, guided deletion of nodes and their connecting edges is performed to maximize the retention of critical nodes. G_1 and G_2 can be modeled as:

$$G_1 = GND(\boldsymbol{s}_u, \boldsymbol{s}_i, \rho, G), \quad G_2 = GND(\boldsymbol{s}_u, \boldsymbol{s}_i, \rho, G), \tag{7}$$

where ρ is the node loss rate, the number of nodes to be removed is $\rho|V|$.

Guided edge dropping (GED): Guided deletion operations are performed on the edges in the interaction graph according to the edge importance matrix $\boldsymbol{S}_E$. The method to generate two subgraphs is expressed as:

$$G'_1 = GED(\boldsymbol{S}_E, G, \rho), \quad G'_2 = GED(\boldsymbol{S}_E, G, \rho), \tag{8}$$

where ρ is the edge loss rate and the number of edges to be retained is $(1-\rho)|E|$.

IG-GCL can slow down the rate at which node embeddings converge to similarity by removing the non-critical elements during neighborhood aggregation. Thus, our model mitigates the problem of over-smoothing while retaining key elements. After generating subgraphs through influence-guided data augmentation, we use the same GCN model (LightGCN) and loss function as the SGL to learn node embeddings and optimize the model. The loss function is as follows:

$$\mathcal{L} = \mathcal{L}_{BPR} + \lambda \mathcal{L}_{ssl} + \mu \|\Theta\|_2^2 \tag{9}$$

3 Experiments

3.1 Experimental Settings

Datasets and Evaluation Metrics. We conduct experiments on three datasets: Yelp2018, Amazon-book and MovieLens-1M. We use top-K recommendation evaluation metrics: Recall and NDCG [3] where $K = 20$.

Hyper-Parameter Settings. In this paper, the models are implemented in the PyTorch environment, the embedding size is 64. We optimized our method with Adam [6], with a learning rate of $1e^{-3}$, a training batch size of 2048, and a discard rate ρ of 0.1.

Baselines. NGCF [9], LR-GCCF [2], LightGCN [4], SGL [10].

Table 1. Effect of the guided data augmentation strategy.

Datasets		Yelp2018		Amazon-Book	
Layer	Method	Recall	NDCG	Recall	NDCG
1	SGL-ND	0.0643	0.0529	0.0432	0.0334
	IG-GCL-GND	0.0654(+1.71%)	0.0542(+2.46%)	0.0451(+4.4%)	0.0351(+5.09%)
	SGL-ED	0.0637	0.0526	0.0451	0.0353
	IG-GCL-GED	0.064(+0.47%)	0.0532(+1.14%)	0.0455(+0.89%)	0.0354(+0.28%)
2	SGL-ND	0.0658	0.0538	0.0427	0.0335
	IG-GCL-GND	0.0665(+1.06%)	0.0547(+1.67%)	0.044(+3.04%)	0.0352(+5.07%)
	SGL-ED	0.0668	0.0549	0.0468	0.0371
	IG-GCL-GED	0.0675(+1.05%)	0.0554(+0.91%)	0.0475(+1.5%)	0.0373(+0.54%)
3	SGL-ND	0.0644	0.0528	0.044	0.0346
	IG-GCL-GND	0.0657(+2.02%)	0.0539(+2.08%)	0.0456(+3.64%)	0.0363(+4.91%)
	SGL-ED	0.0675	0.0555	0.0478	0.0379
	IG-GCL-GED	0.0684(+1.33%)	0.0559(+0.72%)	0.0486(+1.67%)	0.0382(+0.79%)

3.2 Effect of Data Augmentation Strategies

To verify the effectiveness of the data augmentation approach proposed in this paper, we perform a detailed comparison with SGL.

Through Table 1, we can see that the results of IG-GCL outperform SGL, proving the effectiveness of the influence-guided data augmentation strategy.

In addition, on average, GND improved recall by 2.65% and NDCG by 3.55% on both datasets; GED improved recall by 1.15% and NDCG by 0.73%. GND gets higher performance improvements than GED. This is because when the node dropping operation is performed, all the interactions of the node are also deleted, which is equivalent to doing multiple edge dropping operations. Therefore, through GND, we can avoid dropping many important interactions while retaining important nodes, so that the model's performance can be improved more.

3.3 Comparison Baseline

Table 2 shows the results of the model IG-GCL compared with the baseline.

Firstly, we can see that the combined contrastive learning model outperforms the traditional GCN-based model, further demonstrating the need to combine self-supervised learning with recommender systems.

Secondly, IG-GCL outperforms all baseline models, which validates the effectiveness of our proposed influence-guided data augmentation approach.

Table 2. Performance comparison of IG-GCL and baseline.

Datasets	yelp2018		Amazon-book		Movielens-1M	
Method	Recall	NDCG	Recall	NDCG	Recall	NDCG
NGCF	0.0579	0.0477	0.0337	0.0261	0.2513	0.2511
LR-GCCF	0.0561	0.0343	0.03407	0.0204	0.2231	0.2124
LightGCN	0.0649	0.053	0.0411	0.0315	0.2576	0.2427
SGL-ND	0.0658	0.0538	0.044	0.0346	0.2849	0.3163
GND	0.0682	0.0562	0.0483	0.0378	0.2901	0.3239
SGL-ED	0.0675	0.0555	0.0506	0.0384	0.2829	0.3156
GED	**0.0697**	**0.057**	**0.0514**	**0.0402**	**0.2915**	**0.3268**

In addition, unlike previous recommendation models that achieve the best performance at around the third layer, IG-GCL still achieves improved performance when stacking more than three layers, as shown in Fig. 3. IG-GCL achieves the best performance when stacking five layers on the Yelp2018 dataset and six layers on the Amazon-Book dataset. This indicates that the model can be made to mitigate the over-smoothing problem through guided data augmentation operations.

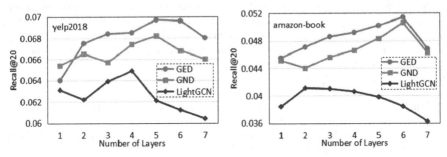

Fig. 3. Performance comparison of IG-GCL with different layers.

4   Conclusion

In this work, we propose a novel graph contrastive learning model called IG-GCL. The model addresses the problem that random data augmentation operations destroy the original graph structure and lose semantic information when generating contrastive views, resulting in degraded model performance, through influence-based data augmentation operations. IG-GCL leverages mutual enhancement networks to compute the importance of nodes in the graph and uses degree information to calculate the importance of edges. Then, data augmentation is performed guided by the calculated influence to increase the probability that unimportant nodes or edges are removed and to maximize the retention of high-impact elements to improve the quality of the generated subgraphs. Influence-guided data augmentation can slow down the rate at which nodes tend to be similar in embedding learning, making the model somewhat resistant to over-smoothing. Experimental results on the benchmark datasets show that IG-GCL consistently outperforms the baseline model under the same experimental setup, thus demonstrating the effectiveness of our proposed method.

Acknowledgements. This work was supported by the Natural Science Foundation of China [grant numbers 82374626].

References

1. Berg, R.v.d., Kipf, T.N., Welling, M.: Graph convolutional matrix completion. arXiv preprint arXiv:1706.02263 (2017)
2. Chen, L., Wu, L., Hong, R., Zhang, K., Wang, M.: Revisiting graph based collaborative filtering: a linear residual graph convolutional network approach. In: Proceedings of the AAAI Conference on Artificial Intelligence, vol. 34, pp. 27–34 (2020)
3. He, X., Chen, T., Kan, M.Y., Chen, X.: TriRank: review-aware explainable recommendation by modeling aspects. In: Proceedings of the 24th ACM International on Conference on Information and Knowledge Management, pp. 1661–1670 (2015)
4. He, X., Deng, K., Wang, X., Li, Y., Zhang, Y., Wang, M.: LightGCN: simplifying and powering graph convolution network for recommendation. In: Proceedings of the 43rd International ACM SIGIR Conference on Research and Development in Information Retrieval, pp. 639–648 (2020)
5. Holme, P., Kim, B.J., Yoon, C.N., Han, S.K.: Attack vulnerability of complex networks. Phys. Rev. E **65**(5), 056109 (2002)
6. Kingma, D.P., Ba, J.: Adam: a method for stochastic optimization. arXiv preprint arXiv:1412.6980 (2014)
7. Kipf, T.N., Welling, M.: Semi-supervised classification with graph convolutional networks. arXiv preprint arXiv:1609.02907 (2016)
8. Velickovic, P., Fedus, W., Hamilton, W.L., Liò, P., Bengio, Y., Hjelm, R.D.: Deep graph infomax. ICLR (Poster) **2**(3), 4 (2019)
9. Wang, X., He, X., Wang, M., Feng, F., Chua, T.S.: Neural graph collaborative filtering. In: Proceedings of the 42nd International ACM SIGIR Conference on Research and Development in Information Retrieval, pp. 165–174 (2019)
10. Wu, J., et al.: Self-supervised graph learning for recommendation. In: Proceedings of the 44th International ACM SIGIR Conference on Research and Development in Information Retrieval, pp. 726–735 (2021)
11. Ying, R., He, R., Chen, K., Eksombatchai, P., Hamilton, W.L., Leskovec, J.: Graph convolutional neural networks for web-scale recommender systems. In: Proceedings of the 24th ACM SIGKDD International Conference on Knowledge Discovery & Data Mining, pp. 974–983 (2018)
12. You, Y., Chen, T., Sui, Y., Chen, T., Wang, Z., Shen, Y.: Graph contrastive learning with augmentations. Adv. Neural. Inf. Process. Syst. **33**, 5812–5823 (2020)

13. Yu, J., Yin, H., Li, J., Wang, Q., Hung, N.Q.V., Zhang, X.: Self-supervised multi-channel hypergraph convolutional network for social recommendation. In: Proceedings of the Web Conference 2021, pp. 413–424 (2021)
14. Zheng, Y., Zhang, L., Xie, X., Ma, W.Y.: Mining interesting locations and travel sequences from GPS trajectories. In: Proceedings of the 18th International Conference on World Wide Web, pp. 791–800 (2009)

Observation Is Reality? A Graph Diffusion-Based Approach for Service Tags Recommendation

Shuang Yu, Qingfeng Li, Mingyi Liu, and Zhongjie Wang[✉]

Faculty of Computing, Harbin Institute of Technology, Harbin, China
{yushuang,liumy,rainy}@hit.edu.cn, 23S003090@stu.hit.edu.cn

Abstract. Accurate service tags recommendation plays a crucial role in classifying, searching, managing, composing, and expanding services. However, many service tags recommendation studies fail to consider real-world scenarios, greatly limiting their performance and capability of handling complex situations. First, the simplification of service tags recommendation to single-tag classification or clustering overlooks the complexity and diversity of crossover services, as well as the intricate interactions between services or their tags. Second, inadequate or ambiguous descriptions of many services result in insufficient information for accurate recommendations. Third, the observation is not always reality due to the presence of unseen data or noise. To address these issues, a new graph diffusion-based graph neural network framework is proposed for multi-tags recommendation, named SpiderTags. It considers both the textual description of services and explicit relationships between services or their tags to enhance performance. Moreover, considering that the observed explicit graph may not be reality and not optimal for downstream tasks, SpiderTags introduces a graph diffusion mechanism to search for a more optimal graph for downstream tasks. A series of experiments conducted on the real-world ProgrammableWeb dataset demonstrate the effectiveness of SpiderTags in service tags recommendation task. Our code is available on https://github.com/gplinked/SpiderTags.

Keywords: Web service · Service tags recommendation · Graph diffusion · Graph neural network

1 Introduction

Service tags are crucial for users and managers to classify, retrieve, manage, and expand services. Tagging services was initially done manually based on the description of services. However, there are some problems with manual tagging. First, it is difficult to standardize annotation due to the different understandings of annotators. Second, with the explosion of the number of services, the cost of manual annotation increases significantly. To ensure the objectivity of annotation and reduce the annotation cost, the service tags recommendation task, which

F. Monti et al. (Eds.): ICSOC 2023, LNCS 14420, pp. 100–114, 2023.
https://doi.org/10.1007/978-3-031-48424-7_8

utilizes machine learning technology to automatically tag services, come into being and become a research hotspot in the service computing community.

Currently, many researches have been proposed and achieved competitive performance on the service tags recommendation task, such as WTLearning [10], ServeNet [27], Dual-GCN [21], PICF-LDA [14], and BGNN [2]. However, these researches fail to fully consider the real scenarios of service tags recommendation, greatly limiting the recommendation performance and the ability to handle complex scenarios. More specifically,

(1) Most of the previous studies assumed that a service was only attached with one tag or cluster [14,27,31]. These studies simplify the problem but have some shortcomings. Firstly, most real-world services involve multiple aspects, making a single tag insufficient to accurately describe the complexity and diversity of crossover services (e.g., e-health, e-commerce, social media). The absence of tags suppresses the search methods of services. Secondly, a single tag cannot accurately express the complex interactions between services. In reality, different services form an ecosystem where they depend on and interact with each other. Attaching multiple representative tags to services based on actual context would better depict the diverse interactions within the service ecosystem, improving recommendation outcomes to match users' needs and preferences.

(2) Due to inadequate or ambiguous descriptions of many services, it is challenging to provide sufficient information for accurate service tags recommendation. Researchers have confirmed that the graph-based information, such as the service social network (SSN) [31] that captures the inherent invocation and dependency relationships between services, and the tag collaboration network (TCN) [4] that represents the correlations between tags assigned to these services, can offer valuable insights for category inference that text alone lacks. Therefore, it is necessary to introduce such graph-based information into the service tags recommendation task to improve the performance.

(3) Notably, the algorithms such as those in (2) usually make assumption that the observed explicit relationships are ideal enough to provide sufficient and effective information for training graph neural networks (GNNs) when considering the social relationships among services or the mutual influences between tags [20]. However, this assumption is inconsistent with the reality, as there are many unobserved data in the real-world scenarios or the real-world graphs are often noisy due to the inevitably error-prone data measurement or collection. As a result, the observed explicit relationships from complex service systems are not always reality or optimal for downstream tasks [6,30], limiting the performance of GNNs in service tags recommendation [8].

For the first issue, this paper no longer regards the service tags recommendation as a simple single-tag classification or clustering problem. Instead, it focuses on the multi-tags recommendation problem of associating services with one or multiple tags. To address this, a novel GNN-based service tags recommendation approach called **SpiderTags** is proposed. For the second issue, inspired by [4,31], SpiderTags considers both the textual description of services and the explicit structural relationships formed by the mutual influences between services or service tags to learn feature representation. By incorporating these factors, the performance of the service tags recommendation is enhanced. For the third issue, this paper introduces a graph diffusion mechanism into SpiderTags backbone to extract hidden valuable information from the original explicit graph structure, thereby obtaining a more optimized graph structure for training SpiderTags and achieving superior performance in service tags recommendation.

In summary, the main contributions of this paper are as follows:

1. A new graph diffusion-based GNN approach, **SpiderTags**, is proposed for service tags recommendation. It incorporates both the textual description of services and explicit relationships between services/tags to enhance the performance. Considering that the observed explicit structure may not be optimal for downstream tasks, SpiderTags introduces a graph diffusion mechanism to search for a more optimal graph structure for better results.
2. Through SpiderTags, a new graph is obtained to capture the associations between services/tags. Compared to the original graph, the new graph has a more optimized structure (i.e. is more in line with reality) and contains valuable implicit information for service tags recommendation.
3. A series of experiments conducted on the real-world ProgrammableWeb dataset demonstrate the effectiveness of SpiderTags with graph diffusion module in the service tags recommendation task.

2   Related Works

Service tags are primarily used for concise and clear descriptions and categorization of services, enabling users to quickly search and select services of interest. Service tags recommendation involves automatically finding the most suitable tags for a given service, aiding in personalized service recommendations for users.

Researchers often consider service tags recommendation as a simple text classification problem, where each service description is treated as a textual unit, and efforts are made to assign appropriate tags to them. Text classification is a classic natural language processing (NLP) problem, and text feature extraction is the core of solving the problem. In the early days, only one-hot encoding was used to represent word vectors. Until 2013, the word2vec tool was proposed by Google, which revolutionized word representation in NLP. However, word2vec can only assign a static vector to represent each word regardless of its context, making it challenging to handle polysemous words effectively. In 2018, ELMO [16] and GPT [13] came out one after another. In the same year, Google developed a transformer-based model, named Bidirectional Encoder Representations from Transformers (BERT) [5,19]. These models employ more advanced techniques to capture the contextual meaning of words within sentences or entire documents. BERT stands out due to its transformer architecture enable efficiently process and understand long-range dependencies between words in a sentence.

Recently, many deep learning-based models use the extracted features from service descriptions to predict relevant tags for service recommendation, such as Recurrent Neural Network (RNN) [25], Long and short term memory neural network (LSTM) [22,29], Convolutional Neural Network (CNN) [28], hybrid networks PSO-Bi-LSTM-CNN [12], and ServeNet [27]. However, relying solely on textual information makes these methods ignore the dependencies and interactions between services.

To further enhance the performance of the service tags recommendation, researchers have proposed incorporating graph-based service interaction network [4,31]. Recently, due to its unique information propagation mechanism and remarkable abilities in modeling graphs, GNNs have attracted increasing attention [11,15,24], especially for solving service tags recommendation tasks with graph-based information [3,18,26]. For example, Chen et al. [3] proposed a novel tag-aware recommendation model based on graph convolutional network (GCN), called TGCN. TGCN leverages the contextual semantics of multi-hop neighbors in the user-tag-item graph to alleviate the issues of sparsity, ambiguity, and redundancy in the existing feature-based tag-aware recommendation systems. Wang et al. [18] presented a novel approach for web service recommendation using a motif-based graph attentional network, allowing for the simultaneous learning of unique node weights across multiple motifs. Note that these methods usually assume that the observed relationships are ideal enough for service recommendation. Nevertheless, this assumption is inconsistent with the reality due to the presence of unseen data and noise, which hinders the model performance to some extent.

3   Methods

In this section, we detail the framework of the proposed SpiserTags model, before which we need to introduce several preliminaries closely related to this study.

3.1   Preliminaries

Definition 1. *A Service Set*, *denoted as $S = \{s_1, s_2, s_3, \ldots, s_n\}$, consists of atomic APIs or mashups that provide multiple functionalities to satisfy users' need. Each service $s_i \in S$ is defined as $s_i = \{d_i, T_i\}$, where d_i is the textual description of the service and T_i is the set of labels associated with the service s_i. $1 \leq |T_i| \leq |T|$, where T is the pre-defined labels set.*

Definition 2. *Tag Collaboration Network (TCN)* *is an undirected graph, denoted as $G_t = \{T, E_t\}$, where T is a set of tags in TCN, defined as $T = \{t_1, t_2, \ldots, t_n\}$. E_t is an edge set in TCN, denoted as $E_t = \{(t_i, t_j, \omega) \mid t_i \in T, t_j \in T\}$, where ω represents the weight of co-occurrences of tags t_i, t_j.*

Definition 3. *Service Social Network (SNN)* *is an undirected graph, denoted as $G_s = \{S, E_s\}$, where S is a service set in SNN, $E_s = \{(s_i, s_j, \omega) \mid s_i \in S, s_j \in S\}$ is an edge set in SNN, ω is the weight denoting the times of co-occurrence of APIs s_i, s_j or the number of common APIs of mashups s_i, s_j.*

Definition 4. *Service Tags Recommendation* *is a task for training a model* R_p *to predict the tag collection* $T_i \in T$ *of the given service* $s_i \in S$. *The process can be formally represented as* $T_i = R_p (s_i \mid T)$.

3.2   Structure of SpiderTags

Figure 1 illustrates the structure of SpiderTags proposed in this paper. SpiderTags takes both the service text description and the service interaction network as input, and outputs multiple tags that can fully describe the input service. The model consists of two parts: encoder and decoder. The encoder comprises three components: service network encoding, service description encoding and feature integration. The first two components primarily focus on transforming service text information and service network graph information into feature vectors. The feature integration component concatenates the text feature and the graph feature into a new feature vector as the input of the decoder. The decoder's role is to map the encoded feature vector to the tag space $\mathcal{T}$. Next, we will provide a detailed description of the three components in the encoder and the decoder of SpiderTags model.

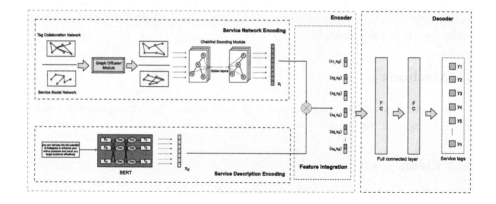

Fig. 1. Structure of SpiderTags.

A. Service Network Encoding

The service network encoding consists of two modules: graph diffusion module and ChebNet encoding module.

Graph diffusion module. The graph diffusion module is used to improve the structure of the service interaction network by combining the kernel-based diffusion mapping with machine learning technique. Specifically, it uses a kernel function $K : \Omega \times \Omega \rightarrow R$ (such as Gaussian kernel, polynomial kernel, etc.) to compute the pairwise similarity between points in the data space Ω, and leverage this similarity information to construct a mapping to a lower-dimensional space.

Assuming an undirected graph $G = (V, E)$, with $N = |V|$ representing the number of nodes and $A \in R^{N \times N}$ representing the adjacency matrix of the graph G, the generalized graph diffusion based on the diffusion matrix is denoted as follows [7]:

$$S = \sum_{k=0}^{\infty} \theta_k T^k \tag{1}$$

where T is the generalized transition matrix defined as $T = D^{-1/2}AD^{-1/2}$, with D is the diagonal degree matrix, and θ_k is a non-negative scaling coefficient that control the diffusion process. Here, the selection of θ_k and T should satisfy the convergence condition in Eq. (1).

Generalized graph diffusion propagates signals through iterative application of the diffusion operator (such as symmetric normalized Laplacian operator, exponential operator), enabling smooth diffusion on the graph for effective information transmission. In this paper, the graph diffusion module applies the generalized graph diffusion in Eq. (1) to the service interaction network, including TCN and SSN, for capturing the associations between services or service tags. This results in an optimized graph $\tilde{G}$ for downstream tasks, which improves the accuracy and robustness of information processing. Figure 2 illustrates the partial original graph from SSN and its new graph after graph diffusion.

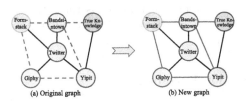

(a) Original graph   (b) New graph

Fig. 2. Example of partial original graph of SSN and new graph after diffusion.

ChebNet Encoding. SpiderTags uses ChebNet to extract feature representations of the service network. ChebNet is an improved version of GCN that addresses two major shortcomings of the original spectral graph convolution. First, the original convolution kernel is designed to capture global graph structure and has a large number of parameters. Second, the convolution operation itself is computationally complex. To overcome these issues, ChebNet employs Chebyshev polynomials to define the convolution kernel in GCN as follows:

$$g_{\theta'}(\Lambda) \approx \sum_{k=0}^{K} \theta_k' T_k(\tilde{\Lambda}) \; \tilde{\Lambda}$$

$$= \frac{2}{\lambda_{max}} \Lambda - I_N \tag{2}$$

Here, K denotes the order of the polynomial, and Λ represents the eigenvalues of the Laplacian matrix. $\lambda_{\max}$ is the largest eigenvalue of the Laplacian matrix. The Chebyshev polynomial T_k is recursively defined as follows:

$$T_0(\mathrm{x}) = 1 \tag{3}$$

$$T_1(\mathrm{x}) = \mathrm{x} \tag{4}$$

$$T_{n+1}(\mathrm{x}) = 2\mathrm{x}T_n(\mathrm{x}) - T_{n-1}(\mathrm{x}) \tag{5}$$

The message-passing mechanism of ChebNet is a crucial step for transmitting and aggregating information in graph structure data. Each node v has an initial feature representation x_v. In each message-passing step, node v aggregates and combines information from its neighboring nodes , the update of feature representation is as follows:

$$x_v' = (p_\omega(L))\, vx_v = \sum_{i=0}^{d} \omega_i \sum_{u \in G} L_{vu}^i x_u \tag{6}$$

After several rounds of message-passing, ChebNet learns the node features from the diffused graph $\tilde{G}$ and finally outputs a fixed-length feature vector:

$$x_i = f_{\mathrm{mean\_pool}}\left(\sigma\left(T_k H_{k-1} W_k\right)\right) \tag{7}$$

where f_{mean_pool} is the pooling function, H_k is the output of the k-th layer ChebConv, σ is the activation function, T_k is the k-th order Chebyshev polynomial of the symmetric normalized Laplacian matrix, and W_k is the weight matrix of the k-th layer.

B. Service Description Encoding

This section is primarily responsible for converting the input service description text into fixed-length feature vectors x_d. For this purpose, we use a transformer-based embedding model BERT to convert the service text description into a d-dimensional vector x_d using a tokenizer:

$$x_d = f_{\mathrm{BERT}}\left(\mathrm{tokenizer}(r)\right) \tag{8}$$

$$\mathrm{tokenizer}(r) = (TokenEmbedding \oplus SegmentEmbedding \oplus PositionEmbedding) \tag{9}$$

C. Feature Integration

In this component, the obtained service description feature encoding x_d and service network feature encoding x_i are concatenated to fuse as follows:

$$x_{\mathrm{merge}} = (x_i, x_d) \tag{10}$$

D. Decoder

The fused feature vector (x_{merge}) from encoder part is input into the decoder to obtain the category probability. In decoder, SpiderTags employs two fully connected layers followed by a sigmoid layer to convert the fused feature x_{merge} into the probability $\tilde{y}_i$ indicating whether each tag t_i can describe the target service. The decoder part can be expressed formally as follows:

$$f_1 = \sum_{v=1}^{d+i} \omega_v x_{\text{merge}} + b_1 \qquad (11)$$

$$f_2 = \sum_{v=1}^{d+i} \omega_v f_1 + b_2 \qquad (12)$$

$$\tilde{y}_i = \text{sigmoid}\,(f_2) \qquad (13)$$

E. Optimization Object

The proposed SpiderTags utilizes the cross-entropy function as the loss function, which is defined as follows:

$$L = -\frac{1}{N} \sum_i y_i \log(\tilde{y}_i) \qquad (14)$$

where N is the number of tags, y_i is the true tag, $\tilde{y}_i$ is the predicted probability.

4   Experiments

In this section, the experimental setup and experimental results will be introduced and discussed in detail.

4.1   Experiment Setup

Dataset. The previous research has confirmed that the observed explicit service network is helpful for service tags recommendation task. In this paper, we introduce two service networks under different scenarios to validate the effectiveness and applicability of the proposed SpiderTags model, i.e. TCN [4] and SSN [31], both of which are extracted from the real-world data of ProgrammableWeb. The two service networks are both weighted undirected graphs that describe the interactions between service tags and the ones between atomic APIs (or mashups [1]), respectively. Moreover, the dataset used for multi-tags recommendation in this paper is obtained from [4], which is named MtR. Referring to the dataset setting in reference [4], this dataset remove all services without related service descriptions or tags, and selects the 50 most common tags, covering a total of 10,000 services. Furthermore, to validate the applicability of the SpiderTags model for the classic single-tag recommendation task, the single-tag recommendation dataset denoted as StR is obtained from [31], in which the dataset is filtered to obtain 4,099 services with 3,380 mashups and 719 APIs, covering a total of 255 tags.

Baselines. In this paper, we conduct a series of experiments to analyze and validate the effectiveness of our proposed SpiderTags model. TagTag [4] and SRaSLR [31] have already demonstrated that using graph data is more effective for service tag recommendation. Therefore, this paper utilizes four graph-related baseline models for comparison and ablation studies, including GAT [17], SGC [23], APPNP [9], and TagTag [4]. These four methods adopt the same TCN, MtR dataset, and feature fusion process. Moreover, we also compare the proposed SpiderTags model with a single-tag recommendation model called SRaSLR [31] on the StR dataset, in order to validate the applicability of SpiderTags model for the single-tag recommendation task.

Experimental Settings. To reduce the randomness during the experimental process, we conduct five independent repeated experiments for each method, and calculate the averaged results and corresponding standard deviation (Std.) over 5 trials. All experiments are run on a RTX GPU server with Ubuntu 20.04 and Pytorch 1.10.0. The dataset is randomly divided into a training set, a validation set, a test set, in a ratio of 7:2:1, with batch sizes of 16, 8, and 4, respectively. Moreover, all models utilize 128-dimensional word vectors obtained from training with BERT and Node2Vec, including service description encoding, tags collaboration network encoding and social network encoding. The Adam optimizer is adopted to automatically update weights during learning. The learning rate is set to 0.0001, and the weight decay is set to 0.00001.

Evaluation Metrics. In experiments, five metrics are used to evaluate the performance of the models comprehensively, including F1-score (F1), Precision, Recall, and Loss. F1-score is the harmonic mean of precision and recall, which is defined as follows:

$$F1 = \frac{2 * Precision * Recall}{Precision + Recall} \tag{15}$$

For the applicability analysis experiment (i.e. single-tag recommendation), the Top-k Accuracy is additionally introduced to measure whether the correct tag is included in the Top-k recommended tags for single-label recommendation. The calculation for Top-k Accuracy (denoted as Acc@k) is given as follows:

$$Acc@k = \frac{|\{s|s \in S, t_s \in y_s\}|}{|S|} \tag{16}$$

Here, s denotes the given service, t_s represents the tag for s, and y_s refers to the Top-k predicted results obtained by the learning models.

4.2   Performance Comparison

In this subsection, we compare the SpiderTags model with four other baselines on the TCN-attached StR dataset. The results (in percent±standard deviation) are shown in Table 1. It can be seen from Table 1 that the SpiderTags model achieves the best performance in terms of the Recall, F1, and Loss metrics, and the second-best performance in terms of Precision. Compared to the second-best model TagTag, the SpiderTags model improves by 15.9% and 7.3% in Recall and F1, respectively. Compared to the third-place model APPNP, the SpiderTags improves by 136.1% and 58.4% in Recall and F1, respectively.

Table 1. Performance comparison of different methods on the MtR dataset. The best and second-best results are respectively addressed in bold and underline.

Models	Precision	Recall	F1	Loss
GAT	21.04(±0.03)	6.89(±0.30)	11.45(±0.16)	26.02(±0.91)
SGC	17.11(±0.02)	2.98(±0.05)	4.92(±0.08)	27.41(±0.19)
APPNP	**31.16(±0.29)**	16.76(±0.31)	21.00(±0.14)	25.36(±0.22)
TagTag	29.85(±0.61)	33.09(±3.07)	31.00(±0.52)	30.87(±0.24)
SpiderTags	30.50(±0.22)	**39.77(±0.23)**	**33.27(±0.23)**	**20.70(±0.31)**

Note that the TagTag also achieves significant improvements in Recall and F1 compared to the other three baseline models, indicating that the TagTag model has a strong ability to recognize positive samples so achieving better Recall. In terms of Loss, our proposed SpiderTags model reduces by 18.3% compared with the APPNP model that ranks second, indicating that the prediction results of the SpiderTags model are truly more superior. On the basis of ordinary GCN, SpiderTags makes structural improvements to the upstream graph data, so achieving significant improvement on the Recall, F1 and Loss metrics.

4.3 Ablation Study

To validate the effectiveness of the graph diffusion module for the service tags recommendation task, Table 2 illustrates the effect of graph diffusion module on the four baseline models including GAT, SGC, APPNP, and TagTag.

It can be seen from Table 2 that after adding the graph diffusion module, there are significant improvements on the performance of Recall, F1, and Loss. More specifically, in Recall, the SGC achieves the largest increase with 616.89%, and the TagTag achieves the smallest increase with 10.9%. Moreover, as for the F1 metric, the largest performance improvement is obtained by the SGC, reaching 334.6%; and the smallest performance improvement is obtained by TagTag, namely 1.8%. In addition, the TagTag algorithm achieves the most reduction in the Loss metric, namely 222%; and the APPNP model achieves the least reduction in the same metric, namely 5.8%. In terms of Precision, the APPNP and TagTag models present slight changes after incorporating the graph diffusion module, while the GAT and SGC exhibited significant improvements of 43.5% and 57.46% respectively.

From the above results, it can be found that after incorporating the graph diffusion module, the baseline models show varying degrees of improvements in Precision, Recall, F1, and Loss. This indicates that the graph diffusion module utilized by the proposed SpiderTags model indeed effectively enhances the upstream graph structure and achieves superior recommendation performance.

Table 2. Results of four baseline models with/without graph diffusion (GD) module (in percent±standard deviation) on the MtR dataset. The best results for each baseline are respectively addressed in bold.

Models	Precision	Recall	F1	Loss
GAT	21.04(±0.39)	6.89(±3.02)	11.45(±0.16)	26.02(±0.09)
GAT+GD	**30.32(±0.79)**	**21.61(±0.31)**	**23.72(±0.35)**	**24.42(±0.12)**
SGC	17.11(±0.02)	2.98(±0.05)	4.92(±0.08)	27.41(±0.19)
SGC+GD	**26.58(±0.89)**	**21.50(±0.27)**	**22.17(±0.23)**	**0.2420(±0.82)**
APPNP	**31.16(±0.04)**	16.76(±0.06)	21.00(±0.02)	25.36(±0.22)
APPNP+GD	29.90(±0.11)	**26.73(±0.10)**	**26.90(±0.07)**	**23.89(±0.50)**
TagTag	29.85(±0.61)	33.09(±3.07)	31.00(±0.52)	30.87(±0.24)
TagTag+GD	**31.31(±0.24)**	**38.06(±0.18)**	**32.89(±0.12)**	**20.93(±0.05)**

4.4   Adaptability Analysis

To verify the adaptability of the proposed SpiderTags model to the classic single-tag recommendation task, we modify the output of SpiderTags for adapting to the single-classification scenario. Since the SRaSLR model is just a single-tag recommendation method, we regard it as a comparable method of the SpiderTags under single-tag task. The results are shown in Fig. 3.

As shown in Fig. 3, there are significant improvements in Acc@1, Precision, Recall, and F1. Although the improvement in the Acc@5 accuracy is minimal compared with other four metrics, it has still increased by 7.1%, which demonstrates that the SpiderTags model not only improves the performance on the multi-tags recommendation scenarios, but also applies to the single-tag classification scenarios.

4.5   Noise and Incomplete Problem Analysis

Table 3 intuitively shows the changes of the graph structure after introducing the graph diffusion into the TCN and SSN respectively.The chosen form of graph diffusion in this article is based on the heat kernel, with the parameters α represents the diffusion speed parameter in the heat kernel function, and ϵ represents the convergence threshold of the algorithm.

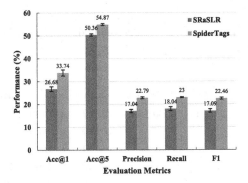

Fig. 3. Adaptability results of SpiderTags on the MsR dataset for the classic single-tag recommendation task.

It can be observed from Table 3 that in the denser TCN graph, the graph diffusion removes the less important edges through neighborhood filtering, effectively eliminating the noise from the graph and improving the recommendation performance. In addition, in the sparser SSN graph where each node has fewer edges, the graph diffusion significantly spreads the limited edge information to more nodes through neighborhood expansion, thus increasing the average node degree. Next, the effects of graph diffusion module will be intuitively analyzed in detail based on the characteristics of TCN and SSN graph, respectively.

As shown in Fig. 4, we display the graph structure changes of some nodes on the SSN graph before and after graph diffusion. Taking nodes 6 and 10 as examples, they have smaller node degrees in the original graph, while their adjacent node 12 has a larger node degree. During the diffusion process, node 12 shares its abundant edge information through diffusion with its adjacent nodes 6 and 10, giving them more adjacent nodes. A careful observation reveals that after diffusion, node 12 (Twitter API) loses its adjacent node 11 (Google Map API), but instead connects to node 11 through node 6 (Formstack API) and 10 (Giphy API), which improves structure of the graph by suggesting that the Twitter API can be associated to the Google Map API through Formstack and Giphy, rather than directly binding with Google Map. The transformation rectifies the redundant correlation in original graph, demonstrating that the graph diffusion enhances the graph structure without blind expansion, as it also takes into account the removal of noisy edges (such as the edge (10,11)).

As shown in Fig. 5, we illustrate the graph structure changes of some nodes on the TCN graph before and after graph diffusion. Taking nodes 4 and 5 as examples, node 4 removes noisy edges such as (4,13), (4,1), (4,10), (4,6) after graph diffusion, while incorporating additional edge information such as (4,11). Node 5 removes the noisy edge (4,5), while incorporating additional edge information such as (5,2) and (5,3).

Due to the diffusion of useful information through the neighborhood and the removal of irrelevant noise during graph diffusion, the diffusion models can solve the problem of fully connectedness with minor edges and incomplete capture of global information.

Table 3. Changes of the graph structure on TCN and SSN after graph diffusion. |Nodes|, and |Edges| is the number of nodes and edges respectively, |Degree| denotes the average node degree.

Graph data	Original graph			New graph after graph diffuison			
	|Nodes|	|Edges|	|Degree|	Parameters		|Edges|	|Degree|
TCN	50	2014	80.56	$\alpha=10$	$\epsilon=0.001$	1,275	51
				$\alpha=10$	$\epsilon=0.005$	600	24.04
				$\alpha=10$	$\epsilon=0.100$	596	23.84
				$\alpha= 5$	$\epsilon=0.001$	319	12.76
				$\alpha= 2$	$\epsilon=0.001$	293	11.72
				$\alpha=0.5$	$\epsilon=0.001$	1,275	51
				$\alpha=0.1$	$\epsilon=0.001$	1,275	51
				$\alpha=0.05$	$\epsilon=0.001$	1,275	51
SSN	720	3,431	9.53	$\alpha=10$	$\epsilon=0.001$	127,521	354.20
				$\alpha=10$	$\epsilon=0.010$	126,431	351.10
				$\alpha=10$	$\epsilon=0.100$	116,835	324.50
				$\alpha= 5$	$\epsilon=0.001$	126,783	352.10
				$\alpha= 2$	$\epsilon=0.001$	27,225	75.60
				$\alpha=0.5$	$\epsilon=0.001$	10,324	28.60
				$\alpha=0.1$	$\epsilon=0.001$	35,328	98.10
				$\alpha=0.05$	$\epsilon=0.001$	41,196	114.43

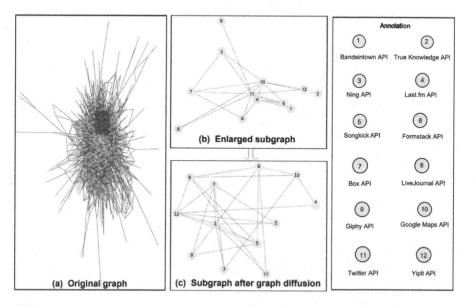

Fig. 4. Illustration of graph diffusion on the SSN graph. (a) the original SSN graph; (b) a subgraph from (a); (c) the novel graph of (b) after graph diffusion.

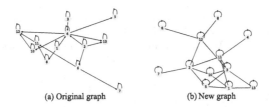

(a) Original graph   (b) New graph

Fig. 5. Illustration of graph diffusion on the TCN graph.

5   Conclusion

In this paper, a new graph diffusion-based GNN approach for service tags recommendation is proposed, named SpiderTags. It considers both the textual description of services and the explicit relationships between services or their tags to enhance performance. Since the observed explicit structure may not be optimal for downstream tasks, SpiderTags introduces a graph diffusion mechanism to search for a more optimal graph structure for service tags recommendation. A series of experimental results demonstrate the effectiveness and adaptability of SpiderTags for service tags recommendation, as well as the effectiveness of graph diffusion module in improving graph structure. In the future, we will focus on more effective graph diffusion mechanisms to optimize the graph structure, so as to further improve the service tags recommendation performance.

Acknowledgement. The research in this paper is partially supported by the National Key Research and Development Program of China (No.2022YFF0903301), the Natural Science Foundation of China (No. 62372140), and the Natural Science Foundation of Heilongjiang Province (No.LH2023F016).

References

1. Benslimane, D., Dustdar, S., et al.: Services mashups: the new generation of web applications. IEEE Internet Comput. **12**(5), 13–15 (2008)
2. Cao, B., Zhang, L., et al.: Web service recommendation via combining bilinear graph representation and xdeepfm quality prediction. IEEE Trans. Netw. Serv. Manage. **20**(2), 1078–1092 (2023)
3. Chen, B., Guo, W., et al.: TGCN: tag graph convolutional network for tag-aware recommendation. In: CIKM 2020, pp. 155–164 (2020)
4. Chen, W., Liu, M., et al.: Tagtag: a novel framework for service tags recommendation and missing tag prediction. In: ICSOC 2022, vol. 13740, pp. 340–348 (2022)
5. Devlin, J., Chang, M., et al.: BERT: pre-training of deep bidirectional transformers for language understanding. In: NAACL-HLT 2019, pp. 4171–4186 (2019)
6. Ding, K., Xu, Z., et al.: Data augmentation for deep graph learning: a survey. SIGKDD Explor. **24**(2), 61–77 (2022)
7. Gasteiger, J., Weißenberger, S., et al.: Diffusion improves graph learning. In: Advances in Neural Information Processing Systems 32 (2019)
8. Jin, W., Ma, Y., et al.: Graph structure learning for robust graph neural networks. In: SIGKDD 2020, pp. 66–74 (2020)

9. Klicpera, J., Bojchevski, A., et al.: Predict then propagate: graph neural networks meet personalized pagerank. In: ICLR 2019 (2019)
10. Lo, W., Yin, J., et al.: Accelerated sparse learning on tag annotation for web service discovery. In: ICWS 2015, pp. 265–272 (2015)
11. Luo, L., Haffari, G., et al.: Graph sequential neural ODE process for link prediction on dynamic and sparse graphs. In: WSDM 2023, pp. 778–786 (2023)
12. Punitha, K.: A novel mixed wide and PSO-BI-LSTM-CNN model for the effective web services classification. Webology **17**(2), 218–237 (2020)
13. Radford, A., Narasimhan, K.: Improving language understanding by generative pre-training (2018)
14. Shen, J., Huang, W., et al.: PICF-ldDA a topic enhanced lDA with probability incremental correction factor for web API service clustering. J. Cloud Comput. **11**(1), 1–13 (2022)
15. Tan, Y., Liu, Y., et al.: Federated learning on non-iid graphs via structural knowledge sharing. CoRR abs/2211.13009 (2022)
16. Tseng, S., Georgiou, P.G., et al.: Multimodal embeddings from language models. CoRR abs/1909.04302 (2019)
17. Velickovic, P., Cucurull, G., et al.: Graph attention networks. In: ICLR 2018 (2018)
18. Wang, G., Yu, J., et al.: Motif-based graph attentional neural network for web service recommendation. Knowl.-Based Syst. **269**, 110512 (2023)
19. Wang, R., Chen, D., et al.: Bevt: bert pretraining of video transformers. In: CVPR 2022, pp. 14733–14743 (2022)
20. Wang, R., Mou, S., et al.: Graph structure estimation neural networks. In: The Web Conference 2021, pp. 342–353 (2021)
21. Wang, X., Liu, J., et al.: A novel dual-graph convolutional network based web service classification framework. In: ICWS 2020, pp. 281–288 (2020)
22. Wang, X., Zhou, P., et al.: Servicebert: a pre-trained model for web service tagging and recommendation. In: International Conference on Service-Oriented Computing, pp. 464–478 (2021)
23. Wu, F., Jr., A.H.S., et al.: Simplifying graph convolutional networks. In: ICML 2019. vol. 97, pp. 6861–6871 (2019)
24. Wu, Z., Pan, S., et al.: A comprehensive survey on graph neural networks. IEEE Trans. Neural Networks Learn. Syst. **32**(1), 4–24 (2021)
25. Xu, Y., Xiao, W., et al.: Towards effective semantic annotation for mobile and edge services for internet-of-things ecosystems. Futur. Gener. Comput. Syst. **139**, 64–73 (2023)
26. Yang, M., Cao, S., et al.: Intellitag: an intelligent cloud customer service system based on tag recommendation. In: ICDE 2021, pp. 2559–2570 (2021)
27. Yang, Y., Qamar, N., et al.: Servenet: a deep neural network for web services classification. In: ICWS 2020, pp. 168–175 (2020)
28. Yang, Z., Feng, J.: Explainable multi-task convolutional neural network framework for electronic petition tag recommendation. Electron. Commer. Res. Appl. **59**, 101263 (2023)
29. Ye, H., Cao, B., et al.: Web services classification based on wide & BI-LSTM model. IEEE Access **7**, 43697–43706 (2019)
30. You, J., Ma, X., et al.: Handling missing data with graph representation learning. In: NeurIPS 2020 (2020)
31. Zhu, Y., Liu, M., et al.: Sraslr: a novel social relation aware service label recommendation model. In: ICWS 2021, pp. 87–96 (2021)

Uncovering Implicit Bundling Constraints: Empowering Cloud Network Service Discovery

Hayet Brabra[1]([✉])(iD), Imen Jerbi[1,2,3](iD), Mohamed Sellami[1](iD),
Walid Gaaloul[1](iD), and Djamal Zeghlache[1](iD)

[1] SAMOVAR, Telecom SudParis, Institut Polytechnique de Paris, Palaiseau, France
hayet.brabra@telecom-sudparis.eu
[2] ISITCom Hammam Sousse, University of Sousse, Sousse, Tunisia
[3] OASIS, National Engineering School of Tunis, University of Tunis, Tunis, Tunisia

Abstract. Cloud service providers (CSPs) offer their networking services (NSs) in the form of service bundles containing underlying services, not necessarily requested by the users. While service bundling is a common practice in the cloud providing multiple components as a single service, unawareness of this hidden structure of services at design time may limit their portability, compatibility, and interoperability across multiple providers. This calls for service discovery solutions that can identify and reveal such hidden bundling to cloud users so they become aware of the consequences of existing bundling before any deployment stage. This paper presents a new NSs discovery approach that takes into account and makes transparent network services bundling for cloud users.

Keywords: Service discovery · Service matching · Bundling Constraints

1 Introduction

The expansion of published cloud network services (NSs) calls for efficient service discovery solutions [1]. These latter aim to assist users in selecting the most appropriate NSs for their distributed cloud applications. Most existing works [3, 5] focus on the description and discovery of services operating at the application layer, i.e., the last layer of the Open Systems Interconnection (OSI) model [2]. Some efforts have also been proposed to adapt existing solutions to the network layer [7,8], i.e., the third layer of the OSI model. While these approaches are valuable, the discovery problem remains particularly more challenging in the context of NSs due to the *pure bundling* strategy often employed by NS providers. *Pure bundling* is a cloud provider purchase strategy in which only a bundle of services is available to buy (i.e. component service from the bundles could not be bought separately) [4]. From a service discovery perspective, this strategy complicates the analysis of the offerings [10] especially since the bundling details

F. Monti et al. (Eds.): ICSOC 2023, LNCS 14420, pp. 115–123, 2023.
https://doi.org/10.1007/978-3-031-48424-7_9

are currently embedded in the textual descriptions published by existing CSPs. Without a transparent description of the offer, service discovery algorithms are likely to fall short in exploring this information and selecting the appropriate services. What makes the discovery problem also challenging for cloud NSs is their variation, between providers, areas, regions, and zones. For instance, the same service may be available in some regions but restricted in others.

In this paper, we argue that user requests and advertised NSs should be represented in a unified CSP-independent way. This description should take into account the bundling and variation details of NSs as well. This allows cloud users to observe all the resources that are bundled by each offered service and to predict the bundling consequences at the design phase. As graph structures are a natural choice to represent the dependency relationships between services and resources, we describe both user requests and NS offers using a graph model. Thus, we reformulate NS discovery as a matching problem between the NS request graph and a Cloud NS offer graph. Our contributions can be summarized as follows: (i) We propose a graph-based model that represents NS user requests and cloud provider NS offers w.r.t the OSI principles and in a provider-agnostic way. (ii) We leverage the advances in graph embedding and clustering techniques to enable efficient service discovery. (iii) We propose a discovery algorithm that takes a requested NS as input and locates the advertised NSs that best match it. The algorithm's innovation resides in its capacity to deliver precise service matching, identifying subgraphs within the cloud NS offer that can be completely matched with a requested NS, while also highlighting the unmatched portions. These latter represent service bundles that were not explicitly requested by the users.

2   Approach Overview

Our approach for cloud NSs discovery consists of two parts: Offline and Online, as in Fig. 1. During the "Offline" part, we create the service index for published cloud NSs that serves later as one of the main inputs of the service discovery task in the Online part. During the "Online" part, we handle the user's request and identify the most appropriate cloud NSs satisfying it. Specifically, the "Offline" part relies on three tasks: OSI-compliant service description, vectorization, and clustering. OSI-compliant service description (Of.1 in Fig. 1) takes two inputs: a catalog of NSs defined by a network expert[1] and textual descriptions of Cloud NSs extracted from CSPs' NS documentations. During (Of.1), we analyze the textual descriptions of cloud NSs and map them into services from the catalog of NSs to produce their OSI-compliant service description graphs (Cloud NS graphs for short) defined according to our graph-based model[2]. Furthermore, the vectorization task (Of.2) takes cloud NS graphs and transforms them into low-dimensional vector representations. Precisely, we propose to vectorize the cloud NSs using graph embedding vectors (embedding vectors for short) and location vectors.

---

[1] The catalog describes high-level functionalities of NSs w.r.t to OSI principles, independently from the CSPs vocabulary and implementation.

[2] Details on the OSI-compliant service description task are at Supplementary-material-1.

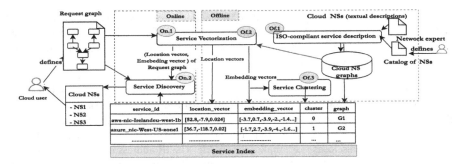

Fig. 1. Hidden bundles-aware discovery architecture overview

Embedding vectors provide numerical representations that capture the properties of the entire graph, including node features (i.e., properties of the underlying services/resources) and graph connectivity edges (i.e., services/resources
dependencies). The aim is to represent cloud NSs from a purely functional view
independently of their location. **Location vectors**, capture location constraints
related to cloud NSs in terms of regions and availability zones where they operate. The **clustering** task (Of.3) uses the **embedding vectors** to group the cloud
NSs into clusters to reduce the discovery cost during the online part. The offline
part ends with building the **service index** structuring cloud NSs based on their
embedding vectors, location vectors, clusters, and graph-based descriptions.

The "Online" part consists of two key tasks: **vectorization** and **service discovery**.
First, the **vectorization** task (On.1) takes a user request defined as a graph (**request
graph**) and produces its corresponding **embedding** and **location** vectors. Then,
the **service discovery** task (On.2) uses the **request graph**, its associated **vectors**,
and the **service index** to find the appropriate cloud NSs that best match the
user request and respect the associated location constraints, while providing a
transparent description of the hidden bundles embodied in the cloud NSs.

3   OSI-Based Network Service Description

We introduce our model for describing users' requests and cloud NSs as graphs.
The model, in Fig. 2, defines a service in terms of (a) its locations, (b) its composing services and (c) the resources that it discloses or needs to realize its
functionality. The model represents NSs as a Directed Acyclic Labeled Property
Graph NLDAG=(V,E), where V represents a set of three types of nodes: Service,
for network services; Location, defining where services are situated; and Resource,
denoting service needs or disclosures. Both Service and Resource nodes hold a
single property, ID, marking their identifier. Location nodes possess three more
properties: region, AZ, and provider. E is a set of directed edges denoting the nodes'
dependencies. We consider only four labels for edges (Fig. 2): needs, disclose, com-
posed_by, located_in, each with its own semantic. Let e = (n,n') ∈ E, if e is labeled
needs means n requires n' to operate; disclose means n makes n' accessible; located_in
means n is located in n'; composed_by means n is made up of n'.

Values of services, resources, and locations nodes' properties are defined based on the OSI model vocabulary. As an example, we illustrate in Fig. 3 the description of the Elastic Network Interface (ENI) service provided by AWS in the Ireland region and specifically in the eu-west-1a availability zone. Because this service's identifier varies between providers (e.g., called Network Interface Card (NIC) in Azure vocabulary), we represent it with a CSP-independent name and we identify it with NetworkEndPoint as in the OSI model vocabulary. To be consistent with on-premise solutions, AWS (and all CSPs) provide the NetworkEndPoint service as a logical network component to be executed on a VM so it can connect to a network. Thus, the NetworkEndPoint is offered as a Cloud NS that discloses (i.e., makes accessible) the IP address of the VM on which it runs. To realize its functionality, a NetworkEndPoint service needs the DLConnectivity service, that operates at the Data Link layer and establishes connectivity between VMs of the same network via their MAC addresses. The DLConnectivity service is delivered by all CSPs as a composition of two services: a DLSwitching to bridge packets between VMs of the same network and a DLEndPoint that discloses the MACaddresses of the communicating VMs to make them accessible within the network.

Fig. 2. Graph-based model for requests and Cloud NSs description

Fig. 3. Description of the AWS NetworkEndPoint service w.r.t our model

4   Service Vectorization and Clustering

We first present the adopted graph embedding model to learn the embedding vectors in Subsect. 4.1. Then, we present our proposed method to generate the location vectors in Subsect. 4.2. Finally, we detail our clustering algorithm to group the cloud NSs in Subsect. 4.3.

4.1   Learning NS Embedding Vectors

To "learn embedding vectors" for the user request and cloud NS graphs, we propose a Graph Neural Network (GNN) based model. GNN is a type of neural network that operates on graph structures [12]. Motivated by the GNN promising results, we trained a GNN-based model for a graph classification task to learn embedding vectors. This task maps the input graphs to either cloud NS labels (e.g., aws-NIC, azure-NIC, etc.) or labels of services in our NS catalog (e.g., DL connectivity, Network connectivity, etc.). As in Fig. 4, the pipeline of the proposed GNN model is composed of an encoding layer, L GNN layers, a pooling layer, and a classification layer. It takes graphs representing Cloud NSs and user requests as inputs (e.g., G_0, G_j) and outputs the corresponding embedding vectors (H_{G_0}, H_{G_j}) and a probability distribution over service labels (y_0, y_1,...).

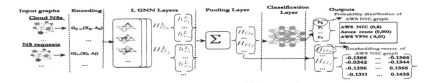

Fig. 4. The general pipeline of the GNN model for learning *embedding* vectors

4.2 Generating NS Location Vectors

Location vectors capture geographic location constraints related to network services in terms of the region(s) and availability zone(s) in which they operate. For instance, in Fig. 3, the location node through its region and az attributes: {region: "Ireland", az: "eu-west-1a" } represents a geographic location constraint for both NetworkEnd-Point and DLConnectivity services. To capture this location constraint from a spatial perspective, we encode it using 3 dimensions: region latitude, region longitude, and az code. Latitude and longitude for regions can be obtained since they correspond to precise locations. However, cloud providers do not provide precise locations for their azs. Thus, we generate a code for each az reflecting its geographic location, using formula (1):

$$\text{az}_{\text{code}}(i,j) = (i+j) \cdot \beta \qquad (\forall i \in [1, |R_p|], j \in [0, Z_{ri} - 1]) \qquad (1)$$

where i is the number attributed to a region after sorting, $|R_p|$ is the total number of regions for a provider p, Z_{ri} is the number of azs within the region r_i and j is the number attributed to az based on the default provider azs' sorting (i.e., eu-west-1a $\rightarrow$ 0). The factor $(i + j)$ ensures that the code for each az within a region is unique. While β is a normalization factor. Thus, given the above geographic location constraint {region: "Ireland", az: "eu-west-1a" }, the corresponding location vector would be $[52.865196, -7.9794599, 0.0024]$.

4.3 Clustering Cloud NSs

The clustering task uses only embedding vectors to group cloud NSs into clusters regardless of their location constraints to reduce the discovery cost. The intuition is to create clusters that have similar services from the same provider. As a clustering algorithm, we use K-means due to its simplicity and wide adoption for Web service clustering [11]. Precisely, given the number of clusters K to form and a data set $H = H_1, ..., H_n$ of n cloud NSs, with H_i a d-dimensional embedding vector. The K-means algorithm partitions the cloud NSs into K clusters $C = C_1, ..., C_K$ and identifies the adequate centroids that minimize the sum of the distances between each embedding vector and its assigned centroid.

5 Service Discovery

The service discovery (On.2 in Fig. 1) involves finding the best match for the requested NS while, eventually, providing a clear description of any unrequested bundled service. To achieve this, we propose a matching technique that combines vector-based similarity (e.g., cosine similarity between two embedding vectors) and subgraph isomorphism

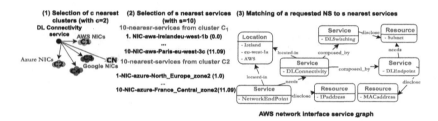

Fig. 5. Execution of Algorithm 1

methods [6]. We used a subgraph isomorphism method to identify the subgraph within the cloud NS offer that is isomorphic to the requested NS graph. Simultaneously, the vector-based similarity is computed to check whether the identified subgraph is also semantically similar to the requested NS graph. However, directly applying this matching method to the initial number of cloud NS offers is time-consuming. Therefore, we leverage the clustering we performed offline to limit the NS search space and benefit from nearest-neighbor search (NNS) strategies [9] to first select the nearest cloud NSs to the requested NS. Subsequently, we apply our matching technique to the selected nearest cloud NSs. Concretely, our matching technique, as illustrated in Algorithm 1, takes five inputs: a requested NS U_s, the set of centroids of cloud NS clusters S_c, the cloud NSs index S_{ind}, c the number of the nearest clusters to the requested NS, and finally s the number of the nearest cloud NSs to the requested NS. The algorithm returns the most suitable cloud NSs (i.e. $S^{candidates}$), matching the requested NS. In doing so, it relies on three main steps: selection of c nearest clusters (line 1), selection of s nearest services (line 2), and service matching (line 3). As illustrated in Fig. 5, the service discovery algorithm first selects the c nearest clusters to the requested DL Connectivity service by applying a linear search (Line 1 in Algorithm 1). This search matches the embedding vector of the requested DL connectivity service to those of the k cluster centers (i.e., C_1, C_2, ..., C_N). Moreover, from each c ($c=2$ in this example) selected cluster, the algorithm selects the s (e.g., $s=10$) nearest cloud NSs to the requested NS by applying a KD-tree search [9] over their location vectors.

Algorithm 1 Service discovery algorithm

Input: $U_s = <U_s^g, U_s^{ev}, U_s^{lv}>$: requested NS, with U_s^g the NS graph, U^{ev} the NS embedding vector, U_s^{lv} the NS location vector
S_c : Service clusters centroids
S_{ind} : The cloud NSs index
c : The number of cluster neighbors
s : The number of service neighbors
Output: $S^{candidates}$: The most suitable cloud NSs matching the requested NS
1: $\mathcal{N}^{clusters} \leftarrow getNC(U_s^{ev}, S_c)$ /* select the nearest clusters */
2: $\mathcal{N}^{services} \leftarrow getNS(U_s^{lv}, S_{ind}, \mathcal{N}^{clusters})$ /* select the nearest services */
3: $S^{candidates} \leftarrow match(U_s, \mathcal{N}^{services})$ /* apply service matching */

From the selected s nearest cloud NSs ($\mathcal{N}^{services}$), the algorithm selects the most appropriate cloud NSs for the requested NS by applying our service matching technique whose algorithm is depicted in Algorithm 2. While its in-depth details are available at[3], note that it relies on two main functions: (i) get_isomorphic_subgraph which

---

[3] Supplementary-material-1.

identifies the sub-graph (C_{sb}) in the NS candidate graph $(\mathcal{N}^{services}[C][0]^g)$ that is isomorphic and semantically equivalent to the requested NS graph (U_s^g) (line 5); (ii) `get_hidden_bundles` (line 7) that identifies the hidden bundle subgraphs (H_{sb}) in the NS candidate graph(C^g) that are not present in the requested NS graph (U_s^g). As illustrated in Fig. 5, the subgraph in green from the graph of *aws-nic-Ireland-eu-west-1b* is isomorphic and semantically similar to the requested DLConnectivity graph, while the subgraph in red represents the hidden bundle subgraph. From this match, we can reveal that *aws-nic-Ireland-eu-west-1b* from C_1 is an appropriate candidate for the requested DLConnectivity service, but it bundles the unrequested NetworkEndPoint service.

Algorithm 2 Service matching operation: $\mathcal{S}^{candidates} \leftarrow match(U_s, \mathcal{N}^{services})$

Input: $U_s =< U_s^g, U_s^{ev}, U_s^{lv} >$): user requested NS with U_s^g the NS graph, U_s^{ev} the NS embedding vector, and U_s^{lv} the NS location vector
$\mathcal{N}^{clusters}$: selected c nearest clusters
$\mathcal{N}^{services}$: selected s nearest cloud NSs
Output: $\mathcal{S}^{candidates}$: The most suitable cloud NSs matching the requested NS

1: **for** cluster C in $\mathcal{N}^{clusters}$ **do**
2:     **if** similarity $(U_s^{ev}, \mathcal{N}^{services}[C][0]^{ev}) == 1$ **then**
3:         $\mathcal{S}^{candidates}.append(\mathcal{N}^{services}[C][0], \emptyset)$;
4:     **else**
5:         $C_{sb} \leftarrow$ get_isomorphic_subgraph$(U_s^g, \mathcal{N}^{services}[C][0]^g)$ such that similarity $(U_s^{ev}, \mathcal{N}^{services}[C][0]_{sb}^{ev}) == 1$
6:         **if** C_{sb} != $\emptyset$ **then**
7:             $H_{sb} \leftarrow$ get_hidden_bundles$(U_s^g, \mathcal{N}^{services}[C][0]^g, C_{sb})$
8:             $\mathcal{S}^{candidates}.append(\mathcal{N}^{services}[C][0], H_{sb})$
9:         **end if**
10:     **end if**
11: **end forreturn** sort$(\mathcal{S}^{candidates})$

6   Experimental Study

We evaluate the effectiveness of our discovery approach by studying its accuracy and completeness in: (Q1) matching user requests with the most appropriate cloud NSs; (Q2) identifying the hidden bundles included in cloud NS offers. To do so, we developed our discovery approach in Python using several standard packages: PyG (PyTorch Geometric) was used for GNN, Scikit-Learn for clustering and nearest-neighbor search (NNS) algorithms, etc. As for the dataset, it was built upon the graphs of (1) two cloud NS services, namely Network Card Interface and Peering, from two major cloud providers (AWS and Azure), and (2) six NS services from NS catalog. This allowed us to gather a total of 1843 real NS candidates. As for user requests, we relied on the DL Connectivity service but with 12 different location constraints, as illustrated in Table 1.

6.1   Experimental Results

Table 2 present the results of the experiments conducted to evaluate Q1, and Q2. Both number of the nearest clusters (c) and the number of the nearest cloud NSs (s) are fixed for each request. s is fixed to 1 if the AZ is provided within the requested service. Otherwise, if the AZ is not provided, s takes the product of the number of provider regions in the given location and the maximal number of provider AZs. We report the

Table 1. User requests used for evaluating Q1 and Q2

Request	Location constraints
DLC1	Location (Paris, eu-west-3a, AWS)
DLC2	Location (North Virginia, us-east-1c, AWS)
DLC3	Location (Mumbai, ap-south-1b, AWS)
DLC4	Location (France, not provided, AWS)
DLC5	Location (Germany, not provided, AWS)
DLC6	Location (USA, not provided, AWS)

Request	Location constraints
DLC7	Location (Virginia, Zone 3, Azure)
DLC8	Location (Ireland, Zone 1, Azure)
DLC9	Location (Victoria (Australia), Zone 2, Azure)
DLC10	Location (France, not provided, Azure)
DLC11	Location (Germany, not provided, Azure)
DLC12	Location (USA, not provided, Azure)

Table 2. Q1 and Q2 evaluation results

Request	N. of neighbors	Q1 evaluation results			Q2 evaluation results		
		Precision	Recall	F-Score	Precision	Recall	F-Score
DLC1	c=1; s=1	100%	100%	100%	100%	100%	100%
DLC2	c=1; s=1	100%	100%	100%	100%	100%	100%
DLC3	c=1; s=1	100%	100%	100%	100%	100%	100%
DLC4	c=1; s=6 (1*6)	**50 %**	100%	**66.66 %**	100%	100%	100%
DLC5	c=1; s=6 (1*6)	**50%**	100%	**66.66%**	100%	100%	100%
DLC6	c=1; s=24 (4*6)	100%	100%	100%	100%	100%	100%
DLC7	c=1; s=1	100%	100%	100%	100%	100%	100%
DLC8	c=1; s=1	100%	100%	100%	100%	100%	100%
DLC9	c=1; s=1	100%	100%	100%	100%	100%	100%
DLC10	s=6 (2*3)	100%	100%	100%	100%	100%	100%
DLC11	s=6 (2*3)	100%	100%	100%	100 %	100%	100%
DLC12	c=1; s=45 (15*3)	93 %	93 %	93 %	100 %	100 %	100 %
Average		**91%**	**99,41 %**	**93,86 %**	**100 %**	**100 %**	**100 %**

Q1 and Q2 evaluation in terms of Precision, Recall, and F-Score. Q1's evaluation results reveal that for the majority of user requests (DLC1-3 and DLC 6-11), both precision and recall achieved a perfect score of 100%. This signifies that all the matched cloud NSs were relevant and suitable for these requests. In contrast, we observe a low precision (50 %) for DLC4 and DLC5. This is due to that both Germany and France have only 3 AZs, while the number of returned nearest cloud NSs is fixed to 6. As a result, in addition to the 3 relevant services, 3 irrelevant ones are also included, leading to lower precision. AS for Q2 evaluation, the precision values demonstrate the accuracy of the NS discovery approach in identifying hidden bundles within cloud NS offers. The results exhibit a consistent precision of 100% for all user requests, signifying that all the identified hidden bundles were relevant and correctly identified. Furthermore, the recall values indicate that the NS discovery approach successfully identified all the hidden bundles for all user requests. As a result, the F-scores for Q2 are also 100%, reflecting the high accuracy achieved in both precision and recall.

7   Conclusion

We proposed a bundles-aware NS discovery approach that takes into account and makes transparent network services bundling for cloud users. Our approach performs well in accurately matching user requests with the most appropriate cloud NSs and identifying hidden bundles. Evaluation results suggest adjusting parameters (c and s) dynamically for future work. We also plan to expand evaluations with more user requests and additional cloud NSs in the dataset.

References

1. Al-Sayed, M.M., Hassan, H.A., Omara, F.A.: An intelligent cloud service discovery framework. Future Gener. Comput. Syst. **106**, 438–466 (2020)
2. Day, J.D., Zimmermann, H.: The OSI reference model. Proc. IEEE **71**, 1334–1340 (1983)
3. Ghazouani, S., Slimani, Y.: A survey on cloud service description. J. Netw. Comput. Appl. **91**, 61–74 (2017)
4. Guidon, S., et al.: Transportation service bundling–for whose benefit? Consumer valuation of pure bundling in the passenger transportation market. Transp. Res. Part A: Policy Pract. **131**, 91–106 (2020)
5. Heidari, A., Navimipour, N.J.: Service discovery mechanisms in cloud computing: a comprehensive and systematic literature review. Kybernetes **51**, 952–981 (2021)
6. Jüttner, A., Madarasi, P.: Vf2++-an improved subgraph isomorphism algorithm. Discr. Appl. Math. **242**, 69–81 (2018)
7. Kim, S.I., Kim, H.S.: Ontology-based NSD modeling for NFV service management. In: 2022 International Conference on Information Networking (ICOIN) (2022)
8. el houda Nouar, N., et al.: A semantic virtualized network functions description and discovery model. Comput. Netw. **195**, 108152 (2021)
9. Ram, P., Sinha, K.: Revisiting kd-tree for nearest neighbor search. In: 25th ACM SIGKDD. Association for Computing Machinery (2019)
10. Wu, C., Jin, C., Chen, Y.J.: Managing customer search via bundling. Manuf. Serv. Oper. Manage. **24**, 1906–1925 (2022)
11. Wu, J., Chen, L., Zheng, Z., Lyu, M., Wu, Z.: Clustering web services to facilitate service discovery. Knowl. Inf. Syst. **38**, 207–229 (2014)
12. Zhou, J., et al.: Graph neural networks: a review of methods and applications. AI Open **1**, 57–81 (2020)

Service Frameworks for IoT, Mobile and Smart Environments

A Deep Reinforcement Learning Approach to Online Microservice Deployment in Mobile Edge Computing

Yuqi Zhao[1], Jian Wang[1,4(✉)], and Bing Li[1,2,3(✉)]

[1] School of Computer Science, Wuhan University, Wuhan, People's Republic of China
{yuqizhao,jianwang,bingli}@whu.edu.cn
[2] Complex Network Research Center, Wuhan University, Wuhan,
People's Republic of China
[3] Hubei Luojia Laboratory, Wuhan, People's Republic of China
[4] Yunnan Key Laboratory of Service Computing, Yunnan, People's Republic of China

Abstract. Mobile edge computing (MEC) is receiving growing attention. In MEC environments, application requests (i.e., a set of consecutive microservice requests) of users are first sent to nearby edge servers, which can significantly reduce the latency compared to sending requests to the cloud center. Therefore, it is vital to deploy suitable microservices on edge servers considering the resource and coverage limitations of edge servers and the movement of users. However, existing deployment approaches focus on offline scenarios, where a service vacuum may occur between two offline deployments due to the long deployment time. Online microservice deployment is thus becoming an urgent need to satisfy user requirements better. This paper proposes DDQN, a deep reinforcement learning approach to online microservice deployment. Specifically, DDQN leverages the Dueling DQN (Deep Q-Network) model to generate real-time microservice deployment plans. Experiments show that the proposed method can effectively improve the success rate of microservice deployment in online scenarios without losing timeliness.

Keywords: Mobile Edge Computing · Microservice Deployment · Deep Reinforcement Learning

1 Introduction

With the rapid advancement of mobile applications and devices, MEC has emerged as a promising computing paradigm. MEC aims to extend the capabilities of cloud centers by bringing computing power and network capacity closer to the users. By deploying applications in proximity to users, MEC offers significant reductions in request latency and improved service experiences. However, edge servers typically have limited computational resources and coverage capabilities [6], making it feasible to deploy only a restricted number of applications and serve a limited user range. Considering these limitations, deploying applications

F. Monti et al. (Eds.): ICSOC 2023, LNCS 14420, pp. 127–142, 2023.
https://doi.org/10.1007/978-3-031-48424-7_10

with smaller footprints and composable components on edge servers proves more suitable than deploying single applications with larger footprints.

The microservice architecture, as a novel software architecture paradigm, offers greater flexibility and adaptability to change compared to traditional monolithic architecture. In the realm of MEC applications, the adoption of microservice architecture has become widespread. This is primarily because it enhances the resource utilization of edge servers and enables the realization of complex user requests through the flexible composition of multiple microservices [13]. For instance, a voice navigation request can be fulfilled by composing three microservices: data loading, voice recognition, and path planning. In line with this trend, user application requests are typically divided into a sequence of microservice requests. Consequently, mobile users will request different microservices at various locations, thereby sending corresponding requests to different edge servers. However, two challenges arise in ensuring the successful delivery of requested microservices to users.

The first challenge is the limited resources of edge servers, which can hinder microservice deployment, causing unfulfilled user requests [14]. The second one arises when users move while microservices are processing, potentially moving out of the edge server's coverage area before getting the result, leading to retrieval failures. These challenges emphasize the crucial problem of microservice deployment in MEC environments.

Existing approaches to microservice deployment [2,4,8] primarily focus on offline scenarios, where they utilize known information about microservice requests to deploy appropriate microservices on suitable edge servers. However, the time required for offline pre-deployment processes can create a service vacuum, where certain service requests remain unattended. In other words, these approaches may fail to respond to some service requests during the service vacuum period. This highlights the challenge of online microservice deployment, where microservices need to be dynamically deployed in response to incoming requests without prior knowledge of users' microservice requests. Therefore, the online scenario serves as a complement to the offline scenario. To address this challenge, this paper proposes an online microservice deployment approach based on deep reinforcement learning.

In our work, we transform the online microservice deployment problem into an online bin packing problem to optimize resource utilization and success rates. We propose DDQN, a solution based on Dueling Deep Q-Network (DQN) [17], to enhance deployment success without compromising efficiency. Extensive experiments validate the effectiveness of this approach in online and dynamic scenarios.

2   Problem Description

2.1   Scenario Analysis

A typical microservice online deployment scenario is illustrated in Fig. 1. The scenario contains two main actors: a queue of microservices to be deployed Q

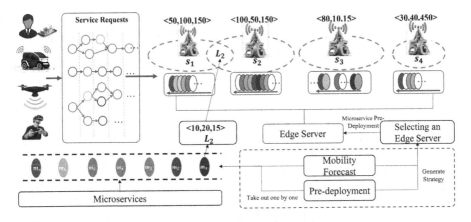

Fig. 1. A typical microservice online deployment scenario.

and a number of edge servers S. The microservices in the queue of microservices to be deployed need to be deployed to one of the edge servers one by one. Each edge server has four main attributes: server id, remaining resources, coverage, and location information. There are three remaining resources, including CPU, memory, and bandwidth, and these attributes can be represented by a multi-dimensional vector $< C, M, B >$. The coverage $cov(s_j)$ represents the range of services the edge server can provide, and this edge server can process only requests within this coverage. Each microservice to be deployed has three key attributes: microservice id, resource requirement, and possible requested location L. Resource requirement refers to the number of resources needed to deploy the microservice in the same form as the remaining resources of the edge server, which is also a multi-dimensional vector. The possible requested location refers to the location where the microservice is likely to be requested by users in the future. Considering the limited coverage of edge servers, this information will impact which edge server is selected.

2.2 Problem Modeling

This section presents formal modeling of the online deployment problem of microservices in mobile edge environments.

Definition 1: Coverage restriction. Coverage restriction refers to the fact that a user can only initiate a microservice request to an edge server that covers its current geographical location. Let d_{ij} denote the distance between a user u_i and a particular edge server s_j and let $cov(s_j)$ represent the edge server the coverage of s_j. The coverage limit can then be expressed as:

$$d_{ij} \le cov\left(s_j\right), \forall i, j \in \{1, 2, \ldots, n\}. \tag{1}$$

Definition 2: Resource constraint. It means an edge server can only deploy a microservice that requires no more resources than what is currently available.

Since the required resources for a microservice are a multidimensional vector, the edge server can deploy the microservice only if all needed resources are satisfied. Let $Need(m_i)$ denote the resource requirement of microservice m_i and $Remain(s_j)$ denote the remaining resources of edge server s_j. The resource limitation can be expressed as:

$$Need(m_i) \leq Remain\,(s_j)\,, \forall i, j \in \{1, 2, \ldots, n\}\,. \tag{2}$$

Definition 3: Image pulling limitation. In a realistic scenario, if an edge server is requested for a microservice that has never been deployed before, it needs to pull and deploy the image of the microservice, which will take up a large number of bandwidth resources during the pull. Let $Size(m_i)$ denote the size of microservice m_i and $bandwidth_{remain}(s_j)$ denote the remaining bandwidth resources of edge server s_j. During the pull process, the bandwidth of s_j and the duration time will be occupied as:

$$Temp_{bandwidth}(s_j) = Random(image) * Bandwidth_{remain}(s_j), \tag{3}$$

$$T_{temp} = \frac{Size(m_i)}{Bandwidth_{remain}(s_j) - Temp_{bandwidth}(s_j)}. \tag{4}$$

If a service is requested again after a successful pull and deployment, there is no need to pull the image again. If a microservice is requested during an image pull, the request will also be considered a failure.

Definition 4: Deployment success rate. The success rate γ is a key indicator of microservice deployment. Let n_p be the number of successfully deployed microservices. Let n_m be the total number of microservices to be deployed. Then we have

$$\gamma = \frac{n_p}{n_m}. \tag{5}$$

Definition 5: Microservice deployment problem. The optimization objective of microservice deployment is to improve the success rate of microservice deployment γ, with the restrictions of both resource and coverage conditions. This problem can be regarded as a multi-constrained single-objective optimization problem, which can be formally expressed as:

$$maximize_\gamma = \frac{n_p}{n_m},$$
$$subject\ to:$$
$$d_{ij} \leq cov\,(s_j)\,, \forall i, j \in \{1, \ldots, n\}$$
$$Need\,(m_i) \leq Remain\,(s_j)\,, \forall i, j \in \{1, \ldots, n\}. \tag{6}$$

3   Proposed Model

To address the problem of online microservice deployment, the paper proposes an optimization approach based on deep reinforcement learning, as shown in

Fig. 2. As stated before, the core difficulty of this problem lies in the decision selection of each edge server. First, we use the mobility prediction model and the user's historical trajectory information to predict the user's future trajectory. The expected future trajectory is then combined with the known knowledge of the user's service combinations to be requested to obtain the user's microservice pre-deployment information. The microservice pre-deployment information consists of a series of key-value pairs, each consisting of two elements $< L, CM >$, where L represents the location of the request to be initiated, and CM represents the corresponding microservice candidate set.

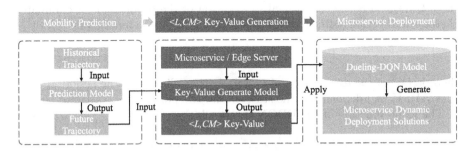

Fig. 2. Framework for Edge Microservice Deployment.

3.1 Mobility Prediction

The mobility prediction model primarily aims to predict future trajectories from historical data. The revolution in this section is a collection of positions consisting of some columns of latitude and longitude, with the same time interval between each place and no additional reference information beyond that. Considering that the accuracy of using latitude and longitude as coordinates is too low, i.e., a slight deviation of latitude and longitude will lead to a significant gap in physical distance, to improve the final prediction accuracy, the means of converting the trajectory information from latitude and longitude information into velocity variation information and normalizing it is adopted. The overall prediction process uses the first seven trajectory points to predict the last trajectory point and iterates one by one to predict the future trajectory containing multiple locations.

3.2 The Proposed DDQN Model

The proposed DDQN is a direct action selection reinforcement learning method. In this method, a value function uses an ϵ-greedy strategy to select the appropriate action by outputting the probability distribution of each action. The output of the network has two parts: one predicts the gain value of each action, and the other predicts the value of the current environment. The two parts are weighted and summed to obtain the action advantage value of each action. The network structure is shown in Fig. 3. The equation of DDQN is expressed as follows.

$$U_t = Reward_t + \gamma Reward_{t+1} + \gamma^2 Reward_{t+2} + \cdots, \tag{7}$$

where U_t denotes the weighted summation of all future rewards starting from moment t. At moment t, U_t is unknown and depends on all future states and actions. The action value function of DQN is:

$$Q_\pi (s_t, a_t) = E \left[U_t \mid S_t = s_t, A_t = a_t \right], \tag{8}$$

where $Q_\pi(s_t, a_t)$ is the conditional expectation of the payoff U_t that eliminates all states and actions after moment $t + 1$. The state value function is:

$$V_\pi (s_t) = E \left[Q_\pi (s_t, A) \right], \tag{9}$$

where $V_\pi(s_t)$ is the expectation of $Q_\pi(s_t, A)$ that eliminates the action a_t from $Q_\pi(s_t, A)$. $V_\pi(s_t)$ depends on the state s_t and the policy π.

The value function of the DDQN can be obtained as:

$$Q^*(s, a) = V^*(s) + A^*(s, a) - mean_a A^*(s, a). \tag{10}$$

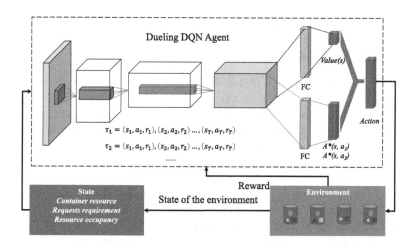

Fig. 3. DDQN model structure.

3.3   Module Configuration

Since DDQN adds the calculation for action gain to the network structure, it not only evaluates the value of the current environment but also takes into account the impact of each action on the environment, making it possible to give better actions in the face of complex environmental states.

However, in the dueling network, we use the neural network $A(s, a; w^A)$ to approximate the optimal dominance function $A^*(s, a)$ and the neural network $V(s; w^V)$ to approximate the optimal state value function $V^*(s)$, where both w^A and w^V are network parameters.

$$Q(s, a; w) = V(s; w^V) + a(s, a; w^A) - mean_a A(s, a; w^A). \tag{11}$$

In this problem, a round refers to a microservice deployment process, where state s refers to the edge server state information and the microservice to be deployed, action a refers to the selected edge server, and the *reward* is the benefit of a deployment action. Finally, the network is updated by calculating the overall reward value.

Action Design. The action in this problem is a server ID constructed using the one-hot coding. With the edge server number, an attempt is made to deploy the current microservice on that edge server, and then a reward value is generated based on the result of the deployment.

Reward Design. In addressing this problem, three factors are critical for calculating the reward value. The initial factor, denoted by Y, concerns the success of the deployment. The deployment can be deemed successful only when two constraints are satisfied. This factor is calculated as follows.

$$Y = \begin{cases} 1, d_{ij} \leq cov(s_i) \& Need(m_i) \leq Remain(s_j), \forall i, j \in \{1, \dots, n\} \\ -1, otherwise. \end{cases} \tag{12}$$

Proceeding further, we consider a factor given by the current deployment success rate γ_c, as described in Eq. 5. The current deployment success rate signifies the proportion of microservices successfully deployed when the current microservice is rolled out. It is computed by dividing the number of successfully deployed microservices n_p by the total number of microservices currently processed n_c.

Finally, we evaluate the factor encapsulated by the current resource utilization rate β_c. The current resource utilization rate represents the calculated resource usage of the edge server following the deployment of the current microservice. It is determined by dividing the total resources of the successfully deployed microservice $Need_{sum}$ by the total initial resources of the currently selected edge servers $Initial_{sum}$. The equation is defined as follows:

$$\beta_c = \frac{Need_{sum}}{Initial_{sum}}. \tag{13}$$

The final *Reward* is calculated as:

$$Reward = \begin{cases} \lambda * \gamma_c + (1 - \lambda) * \beta_c, & Y = 1, \\ -1, & Y = -1. \end{cases} \tag{14}$$

A constant value λ greater than zero is introduced in the reward equation to balance the deployment success rate with resource utilization. To enhance the impact of deployment failure on the decision, the reward for the deployment failure is set to -1.

4   Experiments

This section reports the experiments to analyze the effectiveness of the proposed approach. All code was written in Python and ran on a Macbook Pro laptop with 16 GB RAM and the macOS 12.4 operating system. The experiments were designed to answer the following research questions:

- RQ1: Can the proposed deep reinforcement learning approach improve the deployment success rate and resource utilization?
- RQ2: Is it possible to achieve model convergence with the proposed deep reinforcement learning approach?
- RQ3: What is the time consumption of the proposed deep reinforcement learning method?

Table 1. Experimental parameter setting.

Parameter Name	Default Value	Change Range	Change Step
λ	0.5	None	None
n_s	10	None	None
R_s	$(500, 500, 500)$	None	None
n_m	30	$30 \rightarrow 70$	5
M_r	1.0	$1.0 \rightarrow 2.0$	0.1
C_r	1.0	$0.5 \rightarrow 1.0$	0.05

4.1   Datasets

We experimented with two publicly accessible datasets: **EUA-dataset** [7], which furnishes the geographical positions of 816 mobile users and 125 base stations, and **Telecom Dataset** [16], which consists of more than 7.2 million Internet access records over six months from 9,481 mobile phones of 3,233 base stations.

In this experiment, edge servers are randomly selected from the available data, and the number of servers selected varies for each trial. Each edge server has three attributes: location, coverage, and computational resources. For the microservice data, this experiment requires constructing a large number of microservice queues for the reinforcement learning model to be trained, with each queue serving as one training round. Each microservice queue has n_m microservices, which are randomly drawn from the microservice data. To meet the requirements of this experiment, we added one attribute to each microservice: the possible requested location.

4.2   Comparison Approaches

We compared the proposed Dueling-DQN with eight comparison approaches, which are mainly divided into three types: optimal algorithms [9], quick algorithms [1], and deep reinforcement learning-based algorithms [3,10]. The optimal algorithms consist of optimized random and optimized greedy algorithms. The quick algorithms include quick randomized algorithms and quick greedy algorithms. The main difference between optimal algorithms and quick algorithms is that quick algorithms do not perform edge server selection and directly select one from all edge servers for microservice deployment, while the optimal ones perform the selection process twice. We also performed different optimization strategies based on the underlying deep reinforcement learning algorithm for comparison.

4.3   Experiment Setup

In this experiment, six parameters are involved. Among them, the number of edge servers (n_s) and the total number of resources of edge servers (R_s) are fixed because the prerequisite to apply the reinforcement learning method is that the initial state information of all edge servers must be known. The constant λ in the reward equation (Eq. 14) is determined by pre-testing and will not change subsequently. Finally, the following three parameters will change **the number**

Table 2. Comparison of the deployment success rate over M_r.

Dataset	Method	Microservice Resource Ratio									
		1	1.1	1.2	1.3	1.4	1.5	1.6	1.7	1.8	1.9
EUA Dataset	QG	50.12	51.87	41.77	40.4	54.67	45.91	59.56	46.97	55.6	51.99
	OR	49.21	52.42	42.41	39.78	53.66	47.38	60	46.94	55.67	52.9
	QR	53.95	55.62	54.91	56.5	56.24	56.3	56.2	54.09	58.56	54.04
	OG	49.16	52.25	41.78	40.59	52.89	46.37	61.57	47.28	56.61	54.27
	PG-no-req	57.49	58.66	65.46	52.04	62.62	64.76	50.72	52.6	64.03	63.24
	PG-req	48.8	59.52	63.48	61.26	68.39	72.04	68.1	64.68	63.03	68.16
	PG-eG	61.92	64.65	63.47	63.24	61.58	61.82	61.91	61.38	67.56	67.86
	PG-req+eG	65.87	**69.54**	58.68	**68.48**	68	45.12	59.6	44.52	38.35	70.56
	RSDQL	64.14	67.15	68.51	66.12	67.12	64.13	66.34	62.71	65.43	70.15
	DDQN	**71.46**	68.09	**70.94**	66.46	**69.67**	**72.05**	**69.85**	64.92	**67.67**	**73.68**
Telecom Dataset	QG	52.97	54.76	44.31	42.78	58.05	49.46	63.68	50.58	59.88	55.45
	OR	52.46	56.58	45.78	42.22	57.35	50.75	63.76	49.54	58.99	57.02
	QR	58.27	58.70	58.77	59.68	59.75	60.19	59.22	58.40	63.21	56.81
	OG	52.66	55.64	44.25	42.92	56.55	49.59	64.98	50.78	59.75	57.26
	PG-req	52.20	64.15	67.18	64.42	72.17	77.72	74.07	68.39	67.75	69.42
	PG-no-req	60.61	63.33	69.98	55.75	65.91	69.43	53.31	55.89	68.86	66.76
	PG-eG	66.08	68.78	67.35	67.72	65.87	66.61	66.36	64.62	**72.25**	71.36
	PG-req+eG	70.28	72.10	62.04	**72.60**	72.49	48.69	64.00	47.57	41.11	75.98
	RSDQL	67.87	70.59	71.98	70.61	71.61	68.61	71.42	65.96	69.31	74.07
	DDQN	**76.68**	**73.35**	**75.97**	70.81	**74.97**	**77.85**	**74.67**	**68.48**	71.34	**77.44**

of microservices (n_m), the microservice resource ratio (M_r) and the location coverage (C_r). Specifically, M_r represents the microservice's resource allocation relative to the total resources available on a specific edge server.

Default values were used for all parameters in each group of control experiments, except for the varied parameters. To improve the accuracy of the results, we conducted 100 iterations of each method and averaged the final results. The configuration of all parameters involved in the experiments is shown in Table 1.

4.4 Model Performance Comparative Analysis(RQ1)

Deployment Success Rate. This part explores the effect of the deep reinforcement learning model, primarily to ascertain whether it can enhance the deployment success rate (γ) when compared to alternative methods. Three experiments were conducted to explore the effectiveness of the deep reinforcement learning models by changing three parameters: the number of microservices, the proportion of microservice resources, and location coverage, respectively. The overall deployment success rate of the DDQN model is the highest, which indicates the effectiveness of the proposed deep reinforcement learning method.

Analysis of the change of the microservice resource ratio: As shown in Table 2, with the increase of the microservice resource ratio, it can be found that the

Table 3. Comparison of the deployment success rate over n_m.

Dataset	Method	Number of Requests								
		30	35	40	45	50	55	60	65	70
EUA Dataset	OG	52.28	58.71	48.82	54.95	57.96	55.74	54.83	48.88	49.16
	OR	53.86	59.83	48.46	55.53	57.59	55.36	55.56	51.02	49.21
	QG	53.33	57.32	47.66	55.18	58.54	55.59	54.92	51.98	50.12
	QR	46.96	49.64	49.1	48.8	49.99	52.96	53.36	55.19	53.95
	PG-no-req	46.19	44.72	27.77	55.4	46.66	58.36	64.74	64.7	57.49
	PG-eG	62.31	64.44	64.69	67.66	67.44	63.76	63.55	66.75	61.92
	PG-req	57.92	26.17	50.46	32.14	57.52	61.62	37.57	53.89	63.71
	PG-req+eG	52.13	53.34	58.3	57.53	56.42	63.04	66.47	61.47	65.87
	RSDQL	63.16	65.23	64.23	68.12	67.12	64.13	66.23	67.91	65.43
	DDQN	**66.3**	**67.29**	**68.55**	**70.67**	**70.43**	**69.2**	**70.84**	**71.44**	**71.46**
Telecom Dataset	OG	56.69	61.82	51.74	57.77	62.72	58.86	59.43	53.14	53.19
	OR	57.62	64.61	51.68	60.00	62.31	60.08	59.74	53.69	52.03
	QG	56.11	61.95	51.92	58.50	63.55	60.18	58.03	55.91	52.82
	QR	50.00	52.32	53.01	52.76	53.11	57.21	58.12	60.07	57.90
	PG-no-req	50.31	48.39	29.19	58.60	50.77	61.29	68.58	69.46	62.65
	PG-eG	66.44	68.63	70.12	72.46	71.32	67.42	68.20	70.48	66.74
	PG-req	61.35	27.68	54.54	33.76	60.94	66.93	40.32	58.63	69.30
	PG-req+eG	56.05	57.92	62.16	60.70	60.31	67.31	70.13	65.04	69.50
	RSDQL	67.03	69.23	70.84	73.75	72.73	68.45	71.47	72.40	69.16
	DDQN	**71.12**	**72.60**	**74.01**	**76.28**	**75.73**	**73.80**	**74.79**	**75.56**	**76.82**

deployment success rate of all three algorithms decreases. This is because when the number of microservices remains unchanged, the increase of the microservice resource ratio increases the average resource requirement of a single microservice.

Analysis of the change in the number of microservices: As shown in Table 3, the success rate of microservice deployment increases for deep reinforcement learning and random methods as the number of microservices increases. In contrast, the success rate for greedy methods shows an initial increase followed by a subsequent decrease. When the number of microservices increases, the average resource request of a single microservice decreases, and vice versa.

Analysis of the location coverage variation: As shown in Table 4, the deployment success rate of all three algorithms increases as the location coverage increases. This is because the location coverage is one of the aspects of edge server screening. When the location coverage increases, an edge server is more likely to cover the location of the current microservice request, which can further improve the deployment success rate of microservices.

Resource Utilization. This part explores the effect of the deep reinforcement learning model. In other words, it investigates whether this model can improve the resource utilization β compared with the competing methods. As shown in Fig. 4, the overall resource utilization of the DDQN model is the highest, which shows the effectiveness of the proposed method.

Table 4. Comparison of the deployment success rate over C_r.

Dataset	Method	Location Coverage									
		0.5	0.55	0.6	0.65	0.7	0.75	0.8	0.85	0.9	0.95
EUA Dataset	OG	47.39	54.79	51.82	48.19	49.19	55.65	54.87	51.18	42.58	42.99
	OR	47.39	54.63	52.29	49.46	47.66	54.7	54.15	51.12	42.95	43.78
	QG	46.92	54.88	51.94	49.45	47.72	53.97	54.79	51.98	42.54	43.86
	QR	53.49	53.85	52.96	54.79	52.97	53.67	52.23	52.92	55.6	55.66
	PG-no-req	58.22	56.88	54.9	64.47	59.26	57.52	60.45	54.96	52.68	53.8
	PG-eG	61.21	60.82	62.84	59.89	64.94	67.54	60.06	61.42	64.32	63.1
	PG-req	61.4	56.17	61.66	42.18	50.47	47.96	59.3	59.48	60.48	55.28
	PG-req+eG	57.69	**67.9**	54.76	61.02	63.27	63.98	67.53	57.54	66.21	**67.22**
	RSDQL	65.23	66.32	63.51	63.12	67.33	65.76	65.32	63.61	65.43	63.25
	DDQN	**69.51**	67.25	**65.46**	**64.49**	**70.66**	**69.21**	**70.25**	**66.75**	**68.01**	63.13
Telecom Dataset	OG	50.43	59.87	55.62	53.49	54.81	61.24	60.21	55.67	46.97	46.31
	OR	51.12	59.61	57.87	53.55	51.96	60.85	57.93	55.80	47.07	46.88
	QG	51.59	60.40	56.96	55.28	52.78	59.93	58.30	57.77	47.20	48.74
	QR	58.33	59.87	56.98	61.10	59.05	59.26	56.55	58.98	60.89	59.20
	PG-no-req	64.16	62.47	59.54	70.14	64.57	63.00	65.82	60.38	58.87	57.25
	PG-eG	68.03	65.55	69.21	65.26	69.70	73.73	66.69	65.83	70.27	**69.28**
	PG-req	67.79	62.43	66.10	46.07	53.69	51.04	63.73	66.26	66.96	61.09
	PG-req+eG	62.16	72.39	59.36	66.28	69.67	68.53	72.30	64.23	71.21	74.88
	RSDQL	72.21	70.46	**71.08**	70.14	74.85	69.84	70.51	67.79	71.36	68.78
	DDQN	**75.17**	**73.44**	69.46	**70.37**	**75.79**	**74.92**	**75.93**	**72.58**	**73.63**	68.22

Impact of the microservice resource ratio change: As shown in Fig. 4(a), with the increase of the microservice resource ratio, it can be found that the resource utilization of all algorithms decreases. This is because when the number of microservices remains unchanged, an increase in the microservice resource ratio results in a higher average resource demand for an individual microservice.

Impact of the number of microservices change: As shown in Fig. 4(b), when the number of microservices reaches a certain threshold, there is a tendency to consistently select the edge server with the highest total resources. This can result in a concentration of resource allocation on a single edge server, potentially leading to resource bottlenecks and an increased likelihood of subsequent microservice deployment failures. Impact of the location coverage variation: As shown in Fig. 4(c), the resource utilization of all three algorithms increases as the location coverage increases. This is because the location coverage is one of the aspects of edge server screening. When the location coverage increases, an edge server is more likely to cover the location of the current microservice request, which can further improve the resource utilization of edge serves.

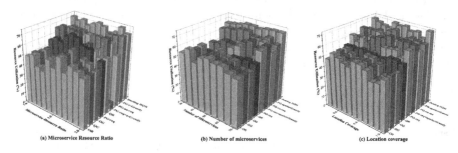

Fig. 4. (a) Microservice resource ratio, (b) number of microservice, and (c) location coverage vs. resource utilization.

4.5   Model Convergence Analysis (RQ2)

This part explores the convergence of deep reinforcement learning models. We conducted experiments on five algorithms, including RSDQL, PG, PG-req, PG-eg, and PG-req-eg, in an environment with a location coverage of 1, a microservice resource rate of 1, and a total of 70 service requests. As shown in Fig. 5, in the training rounds between 0 and 100, the model performance rises rapidly; the model performance rises slowly between rounds 100 and 200; and finally, the model can almost converge after 200 rounds. The results verify the convergence of the models in terms of the optimal deployment success rate and resource utilization.

Because the parameter λ plays the role of balancing the weights of the two optimization goals, namely deployment success rate and resource utilization, adjusting λ allows the model to align more effectively with the optimization

Fig. 5. Deployment success rate under different training rounds.

goal that has the most significant overall impact. We subsequently fine-tuned the model when $\lambda = 0.5$ and 0.7, and performed three experiments to de-average each parameter, and the results indicate that the model performs the best when Lambda = 0.5.

4.6   Time Consumption Analysis(RQ3)

This section delves into the timeliness aspect of the proposed deep reinforcement learning model. When conducting time statistics, the duration of model training is not considered. Instead, only the time taken for the model to make the edge server selection decision is calculated, as the model in this scenario is trained well in advance. The training concept behind the model is to generate various queues for microservice deployment and continually carry out deployment operations, enabling the reinforcement model to make improved decisions.

Table 5. Time consumption analysis at different data densities

Method	Data Density					Average
	20%	40%	60%	80%	100%	
QR	1.31	1.58	1.62	1.63	1.7	1.57
OR	1.36	1.56	1.67	1.67	1.68	1.59
QG	1.37	1.46	1.48	1.48	1.53	1.46
OG	1.55	1.88	1.96	1.98	2.22	1.92
PG	64.77	65.08	65.18	65.42	65.77	65.24
RSDQL	35.08	36.61	43.23	44.41	44.56	40.78
DDQN	14.86	17.08	17.88	17.91	18.31	17.21
Improvement	57.64%	53.35%	58.64%	59.67%	58.91%	57.80%

Table 5 demonstrates the time required for different decision-making methods. The DDQN method takes approximately 17.21 ms per decision, while the quick and random methods take around one to two ms. Among them, the fast random method exhibits the shortest decision time. This is attributed to the fact that the fast random method does not involve two screenings and only relies on random decisions. Although the deep reinforcement learning methods take more time, they still fall within the range of 20 ms. Considering that the deployment time of microservices on the edge server exceeds 100 ms, the proposed deep reinforcement learning model can be considered to have better timeliness.

5   Related Work

In response to the limitations imposed by edge server resources and coverage, research on microservice deployment in mobile edge computing has typically been classified into two main categories: static and dynamic service deployment.

Static service deployment assumes user stability during service requests [2, 5, 15, 18]. For example, Chen *et al.* [2] and Tonini *et al.* [15] proposed strategies taking into account factors such as server coverage, adjacency characteristics, and budget constraints, successfully addressing deployment in static edge scenarios. However, these studies fail to consider the impact of user mobility.

Dynamic service deployment incorporates user mobility. For example, Xiong *et al.* [19] used a learning-based approach for predicting service quality based on multidimensional context, while Lv *et al.* [10] implemented a Reward Sharing Deep Q Learning approach for multi-objective microservice deployment. Many studies [11, 12, 16, 20–22] have limited their scope to single service or single mobile user scenarios or have assumed known user mobility without necessary computational predictions. These approaches often oversimplify problem scenarios or overlook key factors like resource constraints and coverage limitations.

Present research frequently omits crucial factors related to service deployment, failing to fully incorporate user mobility and service portfolio flexibility. In response, this paper suggests a deep reinforcement learning approach for dynamic deployment, aiming to elevate the success rate of microservice deployment while maintaining timeliness.

6   Conclusion

This paper presents an approach to online microservice deployment in mobile edge environments, modeling the problem and proposing a solution using DDQN. Experiments demonstrate the method's efficacy in enhancing deployment success rate without compromising decision speed. In our future endeavors, we strive to enhance the practicality of the algorithm through a targeted reduction of assumptions. This will be achieved by explicitly identifying and quantifying these assumptions, allowing us to establish clear benchmarks and metrics for improvement.

Acknowledgment. This work is supported by the National Natural Science Foundation of China (Nos. 62032016, 61832014, and 61972292), the Key Research and Development Program of Hubei Province (No. 2021BAA031), and the Foundation of Yunnan Key Lab of Service Computing (No. YNSC23102). Bing Li and Jian Wang are corresponding authors of the paper.

References

1. Bhandarkar, A.B., Jayaweera, S.K.: Optimal trajectory learning for UAV-mounted mobile base stations using RL and greedy algorithms. In: 17th International Conference on Wireless and Mobile Computing, Networking and Communications, WiMob 2021, Bologna, Italy, 11–13 October 2021, pp. 13–18. IEEE (2021)
2. Chen, F., Zhou, J., Xia, X., Jin, H., He, Q.: Optimal application deployment in mobile edge computing environment. In: 13th IEEE International Conference on Cloud Computing, CLOUD 2020, Virtual Event, 18–24 October 2020, pp. 184–192. IEEE (2020)
3. Chen, L.: IoT microservice deployment in edge-cloud hybrid environment using reinforcement learning. IEEE Internet Things J. **8**(16), 12610–12622 (2021)
4. Deng, J., Li, B., Wang, J., Zhao, Y.: Microservice pre-deployment based on mobility prediction and service composition in edge. In: 2021 IEEE International Conference on Web Services, ICWS 2021, Chicago, IL, USA, 5–10 September 2021, pp. 569–578. IEEE (2021)
5. Farhadi, V., et al.: Service placement and request scheduling for data-intensive applications in edge clouds. IEEE/ACM Trans. Netw. **29**(2), 779–792 (2021)
6. He, Q., et al.: A game-theoretical approach for user allocation in edge computing environment. IEEE Trans. Parallel Distrib. Syst. **31**(3), 515–529 (2020)
7. Lai, P., et al.: Optimal edge user allocation in edge computing with variable sized vector bin packing. In: Service-Oriented Computing - 16th International Conference, ICSOC, vol. 11236, pp. 230–245 (2018)
8. Li, B., He, Q., Cui, G., Xia, X., Yang, Y.: READ: robustness-oriented edge application deployment in edge computing environment. IEEE Trans. Serv. Comput. **15**, 1746–1759 (2020)
9. Luo, W., Liang, J., Wang, T.: Randomized and optimal algorithms for k-lifetime dominating set in wireless sensor networks. IEEE Access **10**, 23774–23784 (2022)
10. Lv, W., et al.: Microservice deployment in edge computing based on deep q learning. IEEE Trans. Parallel Distrib. Syst. **33**(11), 2968–2978 (2022)
11. Ma, H., Zhou, Z., Chen, X.: Predictive service placement in mobile edge computing. In: 2019 IEEE/CIC International Conference on Communications in China (ICCC), pp. 792–797. IEEE (2019)
12. Mudam, R., Bhartia, S., Chattopadhyay, S., Bhattacharya, A.: Mobility-aware service placement for vehicular users in edge-cloud environment. In: Kafeza, E., Benatallah, B., Martinelli, F., Hacid, H., Bouguettaya, A., Motahari, H. (eds.) ICSOC 2020. LNCS, vol. 12571, pp. 248–265. Springer, Cham (2020). https://doi.org/10.1007/978-3-030-65310-1_19
13. Rababah, O.: A survey of automated web service composition methods (2018)
14. Raponi, S., Caprolu, M., Pietro, R.D.: Intrusion detection at the network edge: Solutions, limitations, and future directions - slides. In: International Conference on Edge Computing (2019)

15. Tonini, F., Khorsandi, B.M., Amato, E., Raffaelli, C.: Scalable edge computing deployment for reliable service provisioning in vehicular networks. J. Sens. Actuator Netw. **8**(4), 51 (2019)
16. Wang, S., Guo, Y., Zhang, N., Yang, P., Zhou, A., Shen, X.: Delay-aware microservice coordination in mobile edge computing: a reinforcement learning approach. IEEE Trans. Mob. Comput. **20**(3), 939–951 (2019)
17. Wang, Z., Schaul, T., Hessel, M., Hasselt, H., Lanctot, M., Freitas, N.: Dueling network architectures for deep reinforcement learning. In: International Conference on Machine Learning, pp. 1995–2003. PMLR (2016)
18. Xiang, Z., Deng, S., Taheri, J., Zomaya, A.: Dynamical service deployment and replacement in resource-constrained edges. Mob. Netw. Appl. **25**(2), 674–689 (2020)
19. Xiong, W., et al.: A self-adaptive approach to service deployment under mobile edge computing for autonomous driving. Eng. Appl. Artif. Intell. **81**, 397–407 (2019)
20. Zhao, X., Shi, Y., Chen, S.: MAESP: mobility aware edge service placement in mobile edge networks. Comput. Netw. **182**, 107435 (2020)
21. Zhao, Y., Li, B., Wang, J., Jiang, D., Li, D.: Integrating deep reinforcement learning with pointer networks for service request scheduling in edge computing. Knowl. Based Syst. **258**, 109983 (2022)
22. Zhou, J., Fan, J., Wang, J., Jia, J.: Dynamic service deployment for budget-constrained mobile edge computing. Concurr. Pract. Exp. **31**(24), e5436.1–e5436.16 (2019)

CET-AoTM: Cloud-Edge-Terminal Collaborative Trust Evaluation Scheme for AIoT Networks

Chaodong Yu, Geming Xia$^{(\boxtimes)}$, Linxuan Song, Wei Peng, Jian Chen, Danlei Zhang, and Hongfeng Li

National University of Defense Technology, Changsha 410003, China
`xiageming@163.com`

Abstract. With the emergence of 5G (5th Generation mobile communication technology), the integration of AI (Artificial Intelligence) and IoT (Internet of Things) has gained momentum, facilitating the rapid development of AIoT (Artificial Intelligence of Things). Through sensor-enabled data collection, smart terminals are able to analyze, forecast, and make decisions based on data using AI technology. However, smart terminals may inadvertently contribute corrupted and forged data, or malicious terminals may intentionally spread false data, which poses a significant threat to the credibility of AIoT services. Therefore, evaluating the trustworthiness of smart terminals plays a crucial role in ensuring high-quality sensing data and reducing the risk of AIoT. To address this issue, we propose a novel cloud-edge-terminal collaborative AIoT trust model (CET-AoTM). CET-AoTM aggregates the cumulative experience attribute of smart terminals in AIoT and evaluates their credibility by leveraging the collaborative architecture of cloud-edge-terminal. In order to solve the challenge that a large number of new smart terminals lack historical interaction due to the high dynamic nature of AIoT, CET-AoTM evaluates the credibility of the terminals based on the fuzzy attributes such as location attribute, propagation attribute and communication attribute of the smart terminals as a supplement to the trust framework. And a demand-driven cloud-edge-terminal collaboration mechanism is designed to flexibly adapt to different service requirements. The experimental results show that the proposed method has high detection rate under low historical interaction scenario, which is not inferior to popular approaches at prensent.

Keywords: Cloud-Edge-Terminal · AIoT · Trust · Neural Network · Fuzzy Logic

1 Introduction

The Internet of Things (IoT) [20] is a revolutionary network model that enables connectivity and information exchange between physical objects via terminal

---

First Author and Second Author contribute equally to this work.

F. Monti et al. (Eds.): ICSOC 2023, LNCS 14420, pp. 143–158, 2023.
https://doi.org/10.1007/978-3-031-48424-7_11

sensors and specific communication media. As 5G, 6G (5th and 6th Generation mobile communication technology), and other mobile technologies continue to advance, the immense volume of data generated by IoT poses significant challenges in terms of data screening, storage, processing and analysis. Fortunately, Artificial Intelligence (AI) technology holds great promise in addressing these challenges by facilitating data analysis, prediction, and decision-making. In 2017, the concept of Artificial Intelligence of Things (AIoT) [3] was proposed, which is a research model aiming to seamlessly integrate AI with IoT. Moreover, AIoT enables intelligent control of terminal devices and achieves deep semantic understanding and value extraction from IoT information through natural language interactions, including voice and video. Currently, AIoT has been extensively researched in various fields, including biometric recognition, smart home [19], smart agriculture [11], smart industry [8], and smart city [4,21]. These advancements highlight the immense potential of AIoT in transforming and revolutionizing numerous industries by leveraging the power of combined AI and IoT technologies. While AIoT brings convenience and efficiency to data awareness and decision-making, it also poses significant challenges. One of the key challenges is evaluating the credibility of smart terminals. In the AIoT environment, any IoT smart terminal can provide sensing data. However, due to limitations in performance, smart terminals may provide low-quality or incorrect sensing data. Moreover, some smart terminals may intentionally provide false sensing data for malicious purposes [18], thereby undermining the credibility of entire data ecosystem. The ultimate risk would be a breach of the collaboration environment in AIoT. Therefore, it is imperative to establish a credible trust framework in AIoT, which includes evaluating the credibility of smart terminals. Some research [2,9,10,12–15,17,18] has been dedicated to the evaluation of trust in terminal devices.

Based on recent research, we have identified two significant shortcomings that the AIoT ecosystem still faces when it comes to building a robust and reliable trust framework. Firstly, the AIoT environment is highly dynamic and new smart terminals lack historical interaction and feedback ratings, making it difficult to establish prior trust. Traditional trust frameworks used in the past work are based on Jøsang's trust model [9]. In the absence of prior trust, evaluating the credibility of smart terminals is a challenge. Secondly, AIoT is demand-oriented. For delay-sensitive services, trust evaluation in smart terminals needs to be performed promptly. On the other hand, for precision-sensitive services, high requirements are placed on the accuracy of trust evaluation in smart terminals. Amidst the high integration of massive sensor data and AI technology, designing and configuring a trust framework that meets the AIoT service requirements is quite challenging.

In this paper, a novel cloud-edge-terminal collaborative AIoT trust evaluation model (CET-AoTM) is proposed to evaluate the trust relationship of smart terminals. At the terminal layer, the CET-AoTM extracts and analyzes records of direct and "virtual" interactions between smart terminals to derive experience attributes such as interaction state, accuracy, and response time. These attributes are then aggregated and iterated to obtain cumulative experience attributes for each smart terminal. The trust evaluation of smart terminals is achieved using machine learning algorithms based on these cumulative experience attributes. To overcome the challenge of evaluating trust in new smart terminals, the CET-AoTM incorporates the edge and cloud layers. These layers indirectly influence the trust attributes of the AIoT network services by utilizing fuzzy attributes such as location, propagation, and communication. This approach provides a supplementary means of trust evaluation at the terminal layer. Additionally, to address the demand-oriented nature of AIoT, a demand-driven cloud-edge-terminal collaboration mechanism is designed within the CET-AoTM. This mechanism allows for flexible trust evaluation among the cloud, edge, and terminal layers, enabling the system to meet different computing service requirements.

The contribution of our work is as follows:

1) A novel cloud-edge-terminal collaborative AIoT trust evaluation model for evaluating the trust value of smart terminals.
2) A fuzzy-logic based trust attribute for realizing trust evaluation in the absence of historical interaction in AIoT.
3) A demand-driven cloud-edge-terminal collaborative mechanism for solving the flexible trust needs in AIoT.

The rest of the paper is organized as follows. Section 2 presents the related work. Section 3 introduces the proposed cloud-edge-terminal collaborative AIoT trust evaluation model. Section 4 discusses the experimental results. Section 5 concludes the paper.

2 Related Work

A variety of trust mechanism of the Internet of Things has been investigated. Behrouz Pourghebleh [14] et al. reviewed trust management technologies in the Internet of Things. They classified the literature based on recommendations, predictions, strategies, and reputation. And they summarized various indicators of trust. Nguyen Binh Truong et al. [18] proposed an E-R trust evaluation model, constructed virtual interactions with crowdsourcing users of the Internet of Things based on experience and reputation And they realized high-quality recruitment schemes based on trust values. Gour Karmakar [10] et al. considered time dependence by introducing discrete cosine transform coefficient in trust evaluation. They trained the trust model with deep neural networks and tested it on real data sets. Junbin Liang [12] et al. realized trust evaluation of sensors through multi-source feedback. In the trust evaluation, they used multidimensional aggregation and dynamically adjusted different trust factor weights to adapt to the highly dynamic nature of the Internet of Things. Kashif Naseer Qureshi [15] et al. proposed cumulative trust under the scenario of edge intelligence. They realize the trust management of the edge intelligent IoT through the combination of direct trust and indirect trust. They implemented a trust management system based on omnet++ experimental platform. Ahmad Almogren [13] et al. built a trust management model based on fuzzy logic in the medical Internet of Things to prevent sybil attacks. They take the integrity and compatibility of the edge nodes as fuzzy inputs, and set the five-level fuzzy outputs as the reliability of the nodes. They have verified the good performance of the algorithm through sufficient experiments. Serin V. Simpson [17] et al. proposed two layers of trust for collusion attacks. They build a credible environment through fuzzy logic and a collective reputation to counter collusion attacks. The aggregation trust value is calculated at the edge node so that the damaged node in the network cannot attack its neighbors by providing false internal trust values. Mohammed Bahutair [2] et al. extracted multi-perspective trust attributes of crowdsourcing users in the Internet of Things, including social relationship, location, device attributes and business reliability. And they trained feedforward neural networks based on real data sets to obtain a trust evaluation model.

Most of the existing work is based on historical interactions and historical data sets for trust evaluation. However, the emergence of new smart terminals that either lack historical interaction with neighboring terminals or lack of data sets because they have not yet participated in the service in AIoT. Therefore, the existing work cannot accurately evaluate the trust value of these smart terminals in AIoT. Since AIoT is service demand-oriented, it's essential to balance the time and precision of the trust evaluation based on the service requirements of AIoT. Therefore, the existing work can't meet the demand-oriented requirement of trust in AIoT. Based on these considerations, this paper proposes a cloud-edge-terminal collaborative AIoT trust evaluation model that fully addresses the lack of interaction in AIoT and its service-oriented needs.

3   Cloud-Edge-Terminal Collaborative AIoT Trust Evaluation Model

This section explores the cloud-edge-terminal cooperative architecture and scenario of CET-AoTM, then introduces the cumulative experience trust algorithm and fuzzy attribute trust algorithm.

3.1   Cloud-Edge-Terminal Cooperative Architecture and Scenario

In CET-AoTM, the cloud-edge-terminal collaborative [3] scenario of AIoT is illustrated in Fig. 1. The scenario is composed of three layers: cloud layer, edge layer and terminal layer. The terminal layer is responsible for collecting sensor data and making early decisions with low computing requirements. The edge layer on the other hand, handles the aggregation of sensor data from the terminal layer and carries out advanced processing. Lastly, the cloud layer coordinates the collaboration between the edge layer and the terminal layer. Additionally, the cloud or edge layer can provide support for heavy calculations and high-precision decisions. The specific description of each layer is as follows

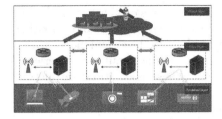

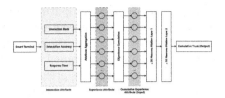

Fig. 1. AIoT cloud-edge-terminal collaborative scenario.

Fig. 2. The Neural Network architecture for cumulatvie experience trust algorithm.

In CET-AoTM, trust evaluation of smart terminals in AIoT is achieved through cloud-edge-terminal collaboration. Smart terminals interact directly with neighboring terminals and engage in "virtual interaction" [1] through the edge server. By analyzing these interactions, smart terminals gain cumulative experience attributes and evaluate trust using small machine learning algorithms. However, the dynamic nature of AIoT presents a challenge, as new smart terminals lack historical interactions. To address this, the edge or cloud layer fuzzifies the trust attribute to complement the trust framework. Trust evaluation varies based on computing tasks and delay requirements. For low-delay scenarios like autonomous driving or industrial manufacturing, edge-terminal collaboration minimizes time consumption. For high-accuracy tasks with relaxed delay constraints, the cloud layer enhances evaluation accuracy. CET-AoTM establishes a trusted AIoT environment.

3.2 Cumulative Experience Trust Algorithm

This paper proposed a cumulative experience trust algorithm for evaluating the trust value of smart terminals at the terminal layer. A smart terminal in AIoT can act as a requestor or consumer of a service. After the service is completed, direct interaction or "virtual interaction" will be generated between smart terminals as the prior experience attribute. The accumulated experience obtained by aggregating prior experience attribute can reflect the trust level of smart terminals to some extent. For constructing the terminal-layer trust evaluation algorithm, this paper employs a small machine learning algorithm - neural network (NN) [16]. We chose neural network for two reasons: scarce computing resources of smart terminals can be effectively utilized by small neural network to perform operations at the terminal; the neural network can construct the non-linear functional relationship between accumulated experience and trust value of smart terminals.

The trust evaluation algorithm of the terminal layer includes two key steps: the preprocessing of trust model and the trust evaluation of smart terminals.

The preprocessing of the trust model is an off-line process established before the smart terminal starts computing service (due to the consumption of computing resources, most of the execution is handled by the edge layer and cloud layer). The aim here is to explore the relationship between the accumulative experience attribute of the smart terminal and its trust value. These associations are inferred from the smart terminal's previous direct interactions and "virtual interactions" to form a trust model that is used to evaluate the trust value of the smart terminal in the subsequent trust evaluation phase. Specifically, smart terminals can use established trust models for decentralized trust evaluation on other smart terminals.

Figure 2 illustrates how cumulative experience can be used to evaluate trust values in a neural network. The diagram comprises an input layer of N_σ neurons, two hidden layers (with 30 and 10 neurons, respectively), and a one-neuron output layer. The neurons in the input layer correspond to the accumulative experience attribute of the smart terminal. The neurons in the output layer represent the trust values of the smart terminal. In this paper, the trust value of the smart terminal is between 0 and 1, and the smart terminal is regarded as either trustworthy or untrustworthy based on the trust threshold τ_{ts}.

The steps to train the trust evaluation algorithm is shown as follow. The algorithm takes the cumulative experience attribute E_Ψ of the smart terminals as the input. A cost threshold δ_n is set in the algorithm. In each training iteration of neural network, the trust value of smart terminal is calculated by input and weight. The calculated trust value is compared with the ground-truth (the label of the training data set), and the cost difference between them is calculated. If the cost difference exceeds δ_n, the iterative training is continued. If the cost difference is less than δ_n, the neural network stops training. E_Ψ of intelligent terminals is used in Algorithm 1 to train the trust model. The calculation of E_Ψ is discussed in detail in the following paragraphs. In this paper, the Gradient Descent Optimizer [7] is used to adjust the weight of neural networks. Finally, the algorithm returns the trained trust model, which can be used to evaluate the trust value of the smart terminal.

In this paper, the terminal layer realizes trust evaluation of smart terminals in AIoT by capturing their cumulative experience attributes. In AIoT, the smart terminals at the terminal layer will participate in the cooperation of the task as the initiator and executor of the computing task. And they generate the direct interaction and "virtual interaction" of the cooperation. The terminal layer will measure the interactions between smart terminals to gain their experiences and their impact on trust. With the continuous execution of computing tasks in AIoT, the experience of smart terminals will be continuously updated to form cumulative experience. Smart terminals with good interaction in collaborative computing tasks will enhance their trust value as their cumulative experience increases. On the contrary, the trust value of smart terminal will be reduced if it has bad interaction in the cooperation of computing task, because its cumulative experience (bad cooperative interaction will make the cumulative experience of smart terminal negative growth) will be reduced. In this paper, the cumulative experience attribute is proposed from the perspective of collaborative computing tasks.

The experience attributes of smart terminals will affect the overall reliability of AIoT computing task. Smart terminals with high experience attributes will result in higher reliability and less vulnerability to aggression. The terminal layer obtains its experience attribute by extracting the influence of the interaction record among smart terminals on trust. The interaction record set between smart terminals is described as Ξ_Π, where $\xi \in \Xi_\Pi$ corresponds to an attribute in the interaction record. Ξ_Π mainly includes interaction state ξ_s, interaction accuracy ξ_a, response time ξ_t, etc. The interaction state $\xi_s \in [0,1]$ indicates whether the collaborative computing task of smart terminals is successfully completed. The interactive accuracy $\xi_a \in [0,1]$ represents the accuracy degree of collaborative computing task completion of smart terminals. The response time ξ_t represents the time from the receiving of the computing task to the completion of the task. The response time ξ_t is calculated as shown in Eq. 1.

$$\xi_t = 1 - \frac{T_{N_i} - T_\sigma}{T_{N_i}} \tag{1}$$

where, T_{N_i} is the time for the smart terminal to complete the computing task, T_σ is the time threshold for a computing task response. Through Eq. 2, the response time of the smart terminal is normalized, making $\xi_t \in [-1, 1]$.

$$\xi_t = 2 * \frac{\xi_t - \xi_{tmin}}{\xi_{tmax} - \xi_{tmin}} - 1 \tag{2}$$

where ξ_{tmax} is the maximum of response time, ξ_{tmin} is the minimum of response time.

The terminal layer obtains the experience attribute of smart terminals by aggregating the attributes recorded by the interaction between smart terminals. For the aggregation of all attributes of interactive records, the average value can't be used to accurately obtain the accurate experience attributes of smart terminals. For example, for delay-sensitive computing tasks, the task initiator is most concerned about the response time of smart terminals, and can tolerate the accuracy of task completion (the task initiator can make up for the accuracy of task completion by recruiting more task completers). In addition, for accuracy-sensitive computing tasks, the task initiator will be most concerned about ξ_s and ξ_a, while the response time can be tolerated. Therefore, the experience attributes of smart terminals are shown in Eq. 3.

$$E_\psi = \frac{1}{\sum_{p_{\xi_i} \in P} p_{\xi_i}} \cdot \sum_{\xi_i \in P}^{\xi_i \in \Xi_\Pi} \xi_i \cdot p_{\xi_i} \tag{3}$$

where ξ_i is the attribute of the interaction record, p_{ξ_i} is the service requirement factor of the interactive record attribute (which refers to the weight of interactive record attributes in service demand-oriented computing tasks).

With the frequent computing tasks in AIoT, the experience attributes among smart terminals will be continuously accumulated and updated iteratively to obtain the cumulative experience attributes, thus summarizing the actual situation of smart terminals in the interaction of computing tasks. The cumulative experience attribute of smart terminal is calculated as shown in Eq. 4.

$$E_\Psi = \gamma \cdot E_{\Psi-1} + (1 - \gamma) \cdot E_\psi \tag{4}$$

where $\gamma \in [0,1]$, higher value of γ favor the accumulation of experiential attributes generated from the interaction record of the smart terminal, rather than the concentration of experiente attributes generated from the current interaction record.

Because of the lack of computing and storage capacity of smart terminals at the terminal layer, this paper constructs a small neural network to realize the trust evaluation of smart terminals. The neural network has four layers, one input layer, one output layer and two hidden layers. The input layer of the neural network is N_σ neurons, a hidden layer is 30 neurons, a hidden layer is 10 neurons, and the output layer is 1 neurons.

3.3   Fuzzy Attribute Trust Algorithm

In CET-AoTM, a small trust evaluation algorithm based on neural network is deployed at the terminal layer to realize the trust evaluation between smart terminals in AIoT. However, due to the high dynamic nature of AIoT environment, many new smart terminals lack interaction records. The cumulative experience trust algorithm is unable to realize the trust evaluation of smart terminals due to the lack of interaction records. Additionaly, due to the limited computing resources of smart terminals, the accuracy of trust evaluation will be reduced to some extent. Therefore, this paper establishes a trust evaluation algorithm based on fuzzy logic as a supplement.

In AIoT, uncertainty is introduced into trust evaluation due to the complexity of environment, unreliability of wireless communication transmission and unpredictability of smart terminal behavior. Any slight change in AIoT will result in a mismatch between the trust value of the smart terminals and their real-time state. In this paper, fuzzy logic is used to fuzzifier the factors that affect the trust value of smart terminals in AIoT to alleviate this mismatch. Secondly, the trust evaluation algorithm based on fuzzy logic is scalable. Different application scenarios in AIoT may have different requirements for smart terminals. The new requirements can be fuzzifiered into additional fuzzy factors, so as to realize the adjustment of trust evaluation algorithm. These are the reasons why this paper uses fuzzy logic as a supplementary trust evaluation algorithm.

The process of fuzzy attribute trust algorithm is shown as follow. After receiving a request from a smart terminal, the edge server (or cloud server) evaluates its trust value before providing a specific service to the terminal. The trust value of smart terminal is evaluated by the trust attributes, namely the location attribute, propagation attribute and communication attribute of smart terminals in AIoT. In order to manage the relationship between trust values and trust attributes among smart terminals, if-then fuzzy rules [5] are adopted. According to the predefined trust attributes, the server performs fuzzy logic processing to obtain the final trust value of the smart terminal.

In order to evaluate the trust value of smart terminal, this paper defines three trust attributes of the smart terminal: location attribute ϱ_{loc}, propagation attribute $\varrho_{p}ro$ and communication attribute $\varrho_{c}om$ as shown in Table 1. ϱ_{loc} represents the interactive distance between smart terminals. The terminal density and environment of AIoT will change with time. As the interaction distance between intelligent terminals increases, the uncertainty of trust relationship will also increase. ϱ_{pro} represents the recommendation trust transitivity between smart terminals. Trust is propagative, and the uncertainty of trust will increase with the increase of the propagation hops of trust between smart terminals. ϱ_{com} represents the medium for wireless communication between smart terminals. As the reliability of communication media between smart terminals decreases, the uncertainty of trust will increase. By applying these inputs to the inference engine and applying fuzzy logic, the fuzzy trust T_{fuz} of the smart terminal shown in Table 1 is obtained. And the final trust value of an smart terminal is the aggregation of T_{cum} and T_{fuz}.

Table 1. The performance of our CET-AOTM under different rounds

Type	Categories	Location Attribute Ratings	Symbols
Location Attribute	Short	0 to 100	S
	Medium	100 to 200	M
	Long	200 to 300	L
Propagation Attribute	Low	0 to 33	L
	Medium	33 to 66	M
	High	66 to 100	H
Communication Attribute	Wire Link	0 to 20	wire
	Wifi	20 to 40	wifi
	Bluetooth	40 to 60	bluetooth
	Zigbee	60 to 80	zigbee
	Lora	80 to 100	lora
Fuzzy Trust	Untrust	0 to 0.3	U-T
	Trust-3	0.3 to 0.6	T-3
	Trust-2	0.6 to 0.8	T-2
	Trust-1	0.8 to 1	T-1

3.4   Demand-Driven Cloud-Edge-Terminal Collaboration Mechanism

To enhance the task demand-oriented of the trust algorithm, this paper adopts a demand-driven cloud-edge-terminal collaboration mechanism. The service-oriented nature of AIoT means that different computing tasks have varying requirements for the trust values of smart terminals. For example, when dealing with delay-sensitive computing tasks, it is important to evaluate the trust value of smart terminals quickly to minimize delays caused by the trust evaluation process. Conversely, with accuracy-sensitive tasks, it is critical to accurately evaluate the trust value of smart terminals after initiation. Therefore, this paper focuses on time-delay sensitive and accuracy-sensitive computing tasks, and adopts different trust evaluation mechanisms for each type of computing task. For delay-sensitive computing tasks, the trust evaluation of smart terminals is mainly conducted at the edge layer. This effectively reduces the data transmission delay, thereby minimizing any delay caused by the trust evaluation process. With accuracy-sensitive computing tasks, trust evaluation of the smart terminals is primarily carried out at the cloud layer. The powerful computing power of the cloud server is utilized to fully collect and process trust attributes of terminals, ensuring an improved accuracy of trust evaluation. Additionally, the demand-driven mechanism is scalable, with computing tasks able to consider other requirements such as privacy protection and propose new requirements for the trust evaluation of the smart terminals.

4   Experiments

4.1   Dataset

Some statistics and analysis were carried out a real-time data stream collected from traffic sensors an parking sensors deployed in the city of Santander, Spain [18]. And we have observed that the performance distribution from any sensor nicely fits to the Beta probability distribution family. Therefore in this paper, smart terminals in AIOT are divided into two groups by using a Beta parameter estimation mechanism according to their behavior as shown in Fig. 3. On this basis, we also configure the same distribution of communication capabilities for these smart terminals. High-quality smart terminals have good performance in most computing tasks. They have lower packet loss rates and transmission errors. Based on the statistical information, performance of a high-quality smart terminal distribute in the interval (0, 1) but the highest distribution is in the range (0.75–0.85). Performance from a high-quality smart terminal follows a unimodal Beta distribution with two positive shape parameters $\text{Beta}(\alpha_h, \beta_h)$ satisfying $10 < \alpha_h < 15$ and $3 < \beta_h < 5$. Malicious smart terminals usually perform well on tasks, but can be unpredictable and intentionally malicious during computational tasks. Thus malicious smart terminal model follows a bi-modal Beta distribution. We define two Beta distribution models, one for very high performance $\text{Beta}(\alpha_{mh}, \beta_{mh})$, satisfying $18 < \alpha_{mh} < 22$ and $2.5 < \beta_{mh} < 3.5$. And another for very low performance Beta(α_{ml}, β_{ml}), satisfying $4 < \alpha_{ml} < 6$ and $25 < \beta_{ml} < 35$.

4.2   Experimental Settings

We evaluated the performance of the trust model by calculating the values of precision (pre), accuracy (acc), recall (rec) [6] and F1 score.

The experimental test was implemented in Matlab containing a set of smart terminals composed of a group of high-quality terminals and malicious terminals. In the experiment, we set the number of smart terminals N_σ to 100, and the trust threshold τ_{ts} to 0.5. In calculating the response time of the computing task, we set the response threshold T_σ to 25. In the aggregation of interactive record attributes, we set demand-oriented factor p_{ξ_i} to $1/3$. In the calculation of cumulative experience attribute, we set the cumulative factor γ to 0.7. In the calculation of F1 score, we set the degree of precision and recall of important factor v to 0.5. Note that the parameter settings will be adjusted for different use cases.

4.3   Comparison Methods

To demonstrate the effectiveness, we compared our proposed CET-AoTM with FTM-IoMT [13] and MUTI-T (Multi-Perspective Trust Management Framework for Crowdsourced IoT Services) [2], including the method based on neural network and the method based on fuzzy logic. And below we will detail them.

FTM-IoMT [13]: This method uses fuzzy logic to model the pairwise trustworthiness. In order to establish trust relationships between nodes in the medical IoT, it evaluates the integrity and compatibility of the nodes as trust attributes. In particular, it adopts the dual evaluation detection model based on fuzzy logic processing and fuzzy filtering.

MUTI-T [2]: This method divides the inherent characteristics of services in crowdsourcing IoT into multiple perspectives, including three perspectives: device owner, device and service. It constructs a neural network based on social relationship attributes, location attributes, reputation attributes and reliability attributes as trust attributes to evaluate workers in the crowdsourced IoT.

4.4   Results and Discussion

Performance. Fig. 4 depicts the precision of CET-AoTM at different epochs with low rounds of smart terminal interactive data training in AIoT. The precision steadily increases as the epoch progresses and eventually stabilizes around 95.5%. This indicates that even without interactive records, CET-AoTM can achieve high evaluating accuracy and meet the trust requirements of new intelligent terminals in AIoT. In our study, we considered scenarios with varying percentages of malicious smart terminals, as shown in Fig. 5. As the percentage of malicious terminals increased from 0% to 40%, both the accuracy and recall decreased. This means that even with an increase in the number of malicious terminals, high-quality smart terminals can still be accurately identified, ensuring that AIoT can recruit dependable workers for computing tasks.

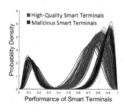

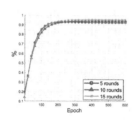

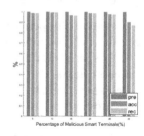

Fig. 3. Terminal models in CET-AoTM.

Fig. 4. Precision of different epochs.

Fig. 5. Precision, accuracy, and recall of different percentages of malicious smart terminals.

Table 2. The Performance of Our CET-AoTM under Different Rounds

Our CET-AoTM	Rounds									
	50	100	150	200	250	300	350	400	450	500
Accuracy	99.00	98.53	97.99	90.54	99.86	94.86	99.96	99.54	91.56	89.77
Recall	98.94	98.45	97.89	90.00	99.85	94.55	99.96	99.51	91.06	89.17
Precision	1.00	1.00	1.00	1.00	1.00	1.00	1.00	1.00	1.00	1.00
F1 score	99.79	99.69	99.57	97.83	99.97	98.86	99.99	99.90	98.07	97.63

Scalability. In this experiment, we tested the performance of our CET-AoTM in different rounds, as shown in Table 2. We observed that as the interaction scale of smart terminals increased, the accuracy and recall of the algorithm exhibited slight fluctuations, with a range of 10.19% and 10.79%, respectively. However, the algorithm maintained an overall high accuracy of 96.16% and recall of 95.94%. Only when the interaction scale reached 450 and 500 rounds did we observe a decline in the accuracy and recall of the algorithm. This decline can be attributed to the increasing complexity of the interaction environment in AIoT. Nevertheless, the algorithm continued to demonstrate good performance. Thus, our proposed CET-AoTM exhibited excellent scalability and adapted well to the large-scale frequent interaction environment in AIoT.

Comparison. In the experiment, we simulated different network environments in AIoT by varying the proportion of malicious smart terminals. We evaluated the performance of three algorithms based on their F1 score. The experiments were conducted over different rounds ranging from 80 to 100, as displayed in Fig. 6. The results showed that as the proportion of malicious smart terminals increased in AIoT, the F1 scores of all three algorithms declined to varying degrees. However, the CET-AoTM consistently achieved the highest F1 score, outperforming the other two algorithms. Notably, the F1 score of the scheme proposed in MUTI-T was consistently lower than the other two algorithms, with a significant drop when the proportion of malicious smart terminals reached 40%. Our CET-AoTM, as a supplementary trust framework, extracts attributes using the fuzzy attribute trust algorithm, which indirectly improves the performance of smart terminal trust evaluation in AIoT networks. Therefore, among the three methods, our CET-AoTM is the most accurate and reliable method for evaluating the trustworthiness of smart terminals in AIoT networks. Furthermore, we analyzed the precision, accuracy, and recall (shown in Fig. 7). Additionally, we observed that the precision of our CET-AoTM was consistently higher than that of the other two algorithms. As the proportion of malicious terminals increased, the interaction records of neighboring smart terminals were affected. However, CET-AoTM's trust augmentation through the fuzzy attribute trust algorithm improved the detection ability of trustworthy smart terminals.

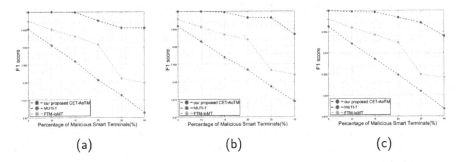

Fig. 6. F1 score of different schemes with different percentages of malicious smart terminal and different rounds. (a) 80 rounds (b) 90 rounds (c) 100 rounds.

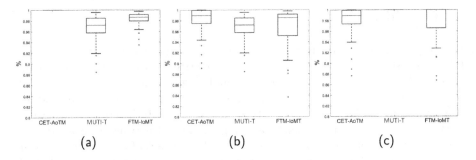

Fig. 7. Three evaluation indexes in accordance with percentage of malicious smart terminals. (a) precision (b) accuracy (c) recall.

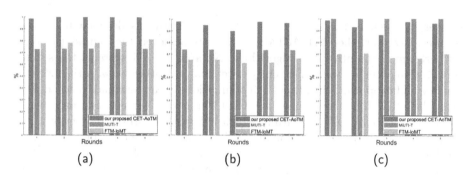

Fig. 8. Comparison of the performance of different schemes under low interaction (1–5 rounds). (a) precision (b) accuracy (c) recall.

Low Interaction Scenarios. In order to simulate the lack of interaction record of the new smart terminals in AIoT environment, we conducted the experiments of low interaction rounds as shown in Fig. 8. Through analysis, we found that the precision of our CET-AoTM was 98.57% in the 1 round due to the extremely low interactive scale of smart terminals (that the algorithm had 5 false evaluations in the detection of untrustworthy smart terminals). However, in subsequent rounds of low interaction scenarios, our CET-AoTM could still show superior performance for detecting trustworthy smart terminals. By analyzing the accuracy of the three schemes, it could be seen that in the low interaction scenario, FTM-IoMT and MUTI-T proposed scheme presented poor performance due to the lack of interaction with smart terminals (that the accuracy decreased by 27.40% compared with that in the normal interaction scenario). In low interaction scenarios, the accuracy of our CET-AoTM also fluctuated to a certain extent (17.47%), and could still maintain at 91.25 %. This indicated the superior detection performance of our CET-AoTM in the low interaction environment of AIoT.

5   Conclusion

We propose a cloud-edge-terminal collaborative AIoT trust evaluation model (CET-AoTM) to try to determine the level of trust between smart terminals. Specifically, our method is based on the cumulative experience trust algorithm at the terminal layer, and obtains the cumulative experience attribute by extracting and analyzing the interaction records of smart terminals. Then the trust value of the smart terminal is obtained by using the neural network to evaluate the cumulative experience attribute. In order to solve the lack of terminal interaction records, we adopt fuzzy attribute trust algorithm to supplement the trust framework by fuzzifier indirect trust attribute in AIoT. We also use a demand-driven cloud-edge collaborative mechanism to meet the different trust requirements of computing tasks in AIoT. We proved the superiority of our proposed method by experiment. In future work, we will further study the adaptive mechanism of cloud-edge-termianl collaboration in trust evaluation. Additionaly, the focus of our future work is to design a privacy protection framework to enable the data exchange of smart terminals in AIoT.

Acknowledgements. This work is supported by the National Natural Science Foundation of China under Grant 61972407.

References

1. Bhattacharjee, S., Ghosh, N., Shah, V.K., Das, S.K.: QnQ: quality and quantity based unified approach for secure and trustworthy mobile crowdsensing. IEEE Trans. Mob. Comput. **19**, 200–216 (2018)
2. Bouguettaya, A., Neiat, A.G., Bahutair, M.: Multi-perspective trust management framework for crowdsourced IoT services. IEEE Trans. Serv. Comput. **15**, 2396–2409 (2021)
3. Chang, Z., Liu, S., Xiong, X., Cai, Z., Tu, G.: A survey of recent advances in edge-computing-powered artificial intelligence of things. IEEE Internet Things J. **8**, 13849–13875 (2021)
4. Yu, C., Chen, J., Xia, G.: Coordinated control of intelligent fuzzy traffic signal based on edge computing distribution. Sensors (Basel, Switzerland) **22**, 5953 (2022)
5. Chien, C.: Fuzzy logic in control systems: fuzzy logic controller. IEEE Trans. Syst. Man Cybern. **20**, 404–418 (1990)
6. Olson, D.L., Delen, D.: Advanced Data Mining Techniques. Springer, Heidelberg (2008). https://doi.org/10.1007/978-3-540-76917-0
7. Duchi, J., Hazan, E., Singer, Y.: Adaptive subgradient methods for online learning and stochastic optimization. J. Mach. Learn. Res. **12**, 257–269 (2011)
8. Hu, L., Miao, Y., Wu, G., Hassan, M.M., Humar, I.: iRobot-factory: an intelligent robot factory based on cognitive manufacturing and edge computing. Future Gener. Comput. Syst. **90**, 569–577 (2019)
9. Jsang, A.: An algebra for assessing trust in certification chains. J. Acoust. Soc. Am. (1999)
10. Kamruzzaman, G.C.K.D.: IoT sensor numerical data trust model using temporal correlation. IEEE Internet Things J. **7**, 2573–2581 (2020)
11. Krintz, C., Wolski, R., Golubovic, N., Bakir, F.: Estimating outdoor temperature from CPU temperature for IoT applications in agriculture. In: The Internet of Things (2018)
12. Liang, J., Zhang, M., Leung, V.C.M.: A reliable trust computing mechanism based on multi-source feedback and fog computing in social sensor cloud. IEEE Internet Things J. **7**, 5481–5490 (2020)
13. Mohiuddin, I., Almajed, H.N., Guizani, N., Din, I.U., Al-Mogren, A.S.: FTM-IoMT: fuzzy-based trust management for preventing Sybil attacks in internet of medical things. IEEE Internet Things J. **8**(6), 4485–4497 (2020)
14. Pourghebleh, B., Wakil, K., Navimipour, N.J.: A comprehensive study on the trust management techniques in the internet of things. IEEE Internet Things J. **6**, 9326–9337 (2019)
15. Qureshi, K.N., Iftikhar, A., Bhatti, S.N., Piccialli, F., Jeon, G.: Trust management and evaluation for edge intelligence in the internet of things. Eng. Appl. Artif. Intell. **94**, 103756 (2020)
16. Haykin, S., Network, N.: A comprehensive foundation. Neural Netw. **2**, 41 (2004)

17. Simpson, S.V., Nagarajan, G.: A fuzzy based co-operative blackmailing attack detection scheme for edge computing nodes in MANET-IoT environment. Futur. Gener. Comput. Syst. **125**(11), 544–563 (2021)
18. Truong, N.B., Lee, G.M., Um, T.W., Mackay, M.: Trust evaluation mechanism for user recruitment in mobile crowd-sensing in the internet of things. IEEE Trans. Inf. Forensics Secur. **14**, 2705–2719 (2019)
19. Wang, F., Gong, W., Liu, J.: On spatial diversity in WiFi-based human activity recognition: a deep learning-based approach. IEEE Internet Things J. **6**(2), 2035–2047 (2018)
20. Wei, L., Yang, Y., Wu, J., Long, C., Li, B.: Trust management for internet of things: a comprehensive study. IEEE Internet Things J. **9**, 7664–7679 (2022)
21. Yu, C., Xia, G., Wang, Z.: Trust evaluation of computing power network based on improved particle swarm neural network. In: 2021 17th International Conference on Mobility, Sensing and Networking (MSN)

Context-Aware Service Delegation
for Opportunistic Pervasive Computing

Juan Luis Herrera[1]([✉])[ID], Hsiao-Yuan Chen[3][ID], Javier Berrocal[2][ID],
Juan M. Murillo[3][ID], and Christine Julien[3][ID]

[1] University of Bologna, Bologna, Italy
`juanluis.herrera@unibo.it`
[2] University of Extremadura, Cáceres, Spain
`{jberolm,juanmamu}@unex.es`
[3] University of Texas at Austin, Austin, USA
`{littlecircle0730,c.julien}@utexas.edu`

Abstract. The growth of capabilities of mobile devices allows them to
host increasingly sophisticated application services. Emerging paradigms
within the Cloud Continuum are based on the concept of running services closer to users, even on their own devices. Nonetheless, running
collaborative services on these devices requires attention to constraints
that differentiate the devices from cloud servers, such as limited battery
or constrained data plans. New techniques are required to empower users
to, first, execute services locally and, second, allow services to migrate
to other available devices. We define *Pervasive Delegation Of Services*
(PODS), a framework to opportunistically select the best candidate to
run a service from among those in a local network, as well as to delegate
it to others whenever the contextual circumstances change.

Keywords: Service Offloading · Service Delegation · Pervasive
Computing · Opportunistic Computing · Mobile Computing

1 Introduction

Computing capabilities of end devices have increased enormously, with new
paradigms in the *cloud continuum* and *mist computing* [1] bringing computation closer to users. Increasingly, services are deployed on nodes closer to or
even owned by end users, increasing privacy and decreasing application response
time. The development of new, more collaborative applications with the potential
to leverage these paradigms is also growing. Liveboard [2] allows multiple people
to edit whiteboards locally and have them shared and synchronized with others
when connectivity allows. Such applications still often make use of the cloud, or
the furthest parts of the cloud continuum, to enable data integration, processing,
and communication between users. This may result in a loss of privacy and a
delay in response time, metrics that can be critical to the user experience.

The increasing capabilities of devices allow them to be used not only as a user
interface to applications, but also as communication mediators that can manage

© The Author(s), under exclusive license to Springer Nature Switzerland AG 2023
F. Monti et al. (Eds.): ICSOC 2023, LNCS 14420, pp. 159–166, 2023.
https://doi.org/10.1007/978-3-031-48424-7_12

exchanges with peers (e.g., through device-to-device communication or opportunistic networks [3]). Shared whiteboards can be locally hosted and aggregated among co-located devices, without the need to relegate such services to the cloud or even an intermediate edge node. Applications like HTC Power to Give [4] allow mobile users to host services that can be consumed using BOINC [5]. Games like Minecraft [6] also leverage users' mobile devices to host multiplayer servers.

While such services can be supported using various levels of the cloud continuum, we examine what is necessary to support service execution on devices that are completely separated from the cloud. In some sense, this is extreme—we are rarely completely disconnected from the Internet. However, from a research perspective, such an approach allows us to examine what is feasible and to determine the degree to which the approach increases user privacy by providing local data isolation, decreases response time by reducing round-trips to the cloud, and lessens bandwidth demands on networks that connect users to the cloud.

We focus on *collaborative services* and in particular on services that facilitate digital collaboration among co-located users. Our end devices like smartphones are always with us and seem a natural conduit for facilitating these services. However, these devices have several limitations: they are resource constrained in terms of energy and computation; they are mobile, resulting in changing connectivity over time; and they have other workloads and are not dedicated solely to the service.

Therefore, while there is promise for delegating locally available services to end devices, new techniques are required to support delegation that is: locally facilitated among the participating devices themselves; context-dependent, using the state of the devices to decide delegations; and dynamic, periodically adjusting the configuration as the context changes. We characterize the use of a completely decentralized architecture for such services as the *collaborative mist* and place it in the context of other paradigms in Sect. 2, where we also examine existing approaches to service delegation, off-loading, and on-loading. We then present the *Pervasive Delegation Of Services* (PODS) framework in Sect. 3; PODS provides dynamic, context-dependent service delegation that is coordinated entirely among a set of co-located nodes using only device-to-device interactions. The use of PODS is likely to be highly applicable for services such as collaborative multimedia sharing and processing, collaborative office automation suites, or applications deployed in intermittent connectivity scenarios. The key novelty of PODS is the delegation of services to available nearby devices based on the context of the situation, automatically adapting the collaborative services' deployment characteristics to the dynamic scenario over time, in an entirely peer-to-peer manner.

2   Motivation

We next provide an introduction of aspects of the cloud continuum, and place the *collaborative mist* in this context. We then examine work related dynamic placement of services and motivate the gap that we seek to fill with PODS. We close this section with a detailed motivating application example for PODS.

The Cloud Continuum (and Beyond). The *cloud continuum* characterizes a design space that moves from completely centralized services in a pure cloud approach, through *fog computing*, which pushes infrastructure resources nearer the edge devices and *mist computing*, which starts to leverage the computational resources of the end devices themselves [1]. As the services become increasingly decentralized, end devices take on more responsibility and ownership of user data, increasing privacy. To leverage the capabilities of these architectures and better utilize end devices, conceptual frameworks for organizing applications and services have also emerged [7,8]. However, these applications and paradigms still require a central coordinator, usually the cloud, to at least make decisions about where services should be placed and distributed.

These paradigms have made great strides to improve user privacy, leverage the rich capabilities of end devices, and reduce the load on the infrastructure. However, the feasibility and implementation of such approaches depend on the computing capacity and available resources of the mobile end-user devices. Deciding which device or devices should host each service should account for the capabilities and situations of nearby devices. Hence, closing the gap remaining in realizing the collaborative mist requires higher-level yet completely distributed coordination system.

A Motivating Application. Consider an application to generate and compose video collaboratively among people at a party. From a computational perspective, such a video composition application can be easily executed on a mobile device. Collaboratively created videos can also be shared among the attendees in an opportunistic way, increasing the privacy of the attendees and reducing the network load. A service running on the mobile phone of the video organizer would be responsible for composing videos received from party-goers. Architecturally, the application could be composed of a single service whose API would have, as input, images from attendees, and as output, the generated video.

There are several barriers to implementing such an application. First, smartphones have limited resources: during video generation, the device hosting the video composition service could run out of battery, or have its user launch applications that compete for its resources. Moreover, the user running the collaborative service may move or even leave the party. Finally, there may be more powerful nodes available in the surroundings, able to host the service. The collaborative mist can bring the computation to the end devices themselves. End devices should also be supported in determining whether the service to be executed can be hosted locally, or whether it needs to be migrated to another node. In this application, the collaborative video organizer device itself can check if it ought to delegate the video composition service to another device. To empower users to manage their own information and applications in collaborative communities, we present PODS, a framework to perform service delegation in opportunistic and pervasive environments.

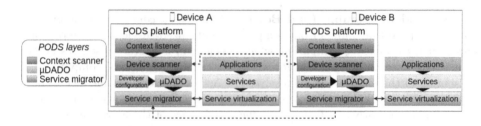

Fig. 1. Strawman architecture of the delegation system

3   Proposed Architecture

We next introduce the PODS architecture (Fig. 1). PODS provides services in the collaborative mist. Each service may be hosted by more than one device and may receive requests from more than one device. In this context, we identify two roles: *delegatee*, i.e., a device that is currently running an instance of the service, and *consumer*, i.e., a device that requests to use the service's functionality. These roles are not mutually exclusive: a delegatee may also be a consumer of the same service. A service of a collaborative application executing on a delegatee may have been started by that device, or the instance of the service may have been assigned to it at some point during the execution of the application.

PODS consists of three high-level functionalities. First, PODS monitors the resources and contextual attributes of nearby computing nodes, including those devices participating in a collaborative session (context scanner in Fig. 1). Second, PODS analyzes which device(s) in the near surroundings should host each collaborative service based on their context, optimizing application-specific Key Performance Indicators (KPIs) to obtain a good user experience (μDADO in Fig. 1). Third, in response to detected changes and updated analyses, PODS migrates services among co-located nodes (service migrator in Fig. 1). This allows running collaborative applications in a more reliable way when multiple devices make their resources available to support service execution.

3.1   Context Scanner

To enable PODS to detect the best suitable delegatees based on their context, as well as to adjust the number of replicas used, there are two key requirements that must be fulfilled. On the one hand, PODS requires information about a device's context to evaluate the device's suitability as a delegatee, as well as to determine if the number of executed replicas is appropriate. On the other hand, PODS needs to know about the context, not only of the device itself but also of other nearby devices. The context scanner fulfills both of these roles in PODS, through the use of two submodules, the *context listener* and the *device scanner*.

The context listener runs on every PODS device; its objective is to obtain a view of the current context of its device. PODS relies on a generic representation of context, using a simple ⟨*key, value*⟩ pair for each context attribute. This allows the use of context to be flexible and extensible for different applications to use diverse attributes. In our implementation, we rely on measurements of the device's *battery level, available RAM*, and *network connection to other devices*. The context listener updates the *snapshot* within PODS when triggered, either by a timer or by a change in a sensed value that directly impacts the availability of a service on the device, e.g., low battery warning or a network disconnection or connection event, which is notified through a publish-subscribe mechanism.

For the service migrator to make delegation decisions, it needs the context of the local device and the context of other connected devices. The device scanner queries other nearby devices for their context attributes. Once the context listener updates the local context, it triggers the device scanner to solicit the other devices' contexts. This allows each PODS device to maintain an up-to-date view of the status of the local network: current delegatees for each service, context status of each device, and, implicitly, the availability of services (e.g., if the only delegatee of a service has disconnected from the network, the service is unavailable for all its consumers in the local network). Possible interruptions of a delegation process are also handled by the device scanner. If, during the delegation of a service (described in Sect. 3.3), either the current or target delegatees disconnect, the device scanner re-triggers the context listener to update the context information. Once new context information is available, the context scanner feeds it into the next subsystem: μDADO.

3.2 μDADO

The next step is for PODS to decide which devices are the most suitable delegatee(s) for each service, as well as how many replicas should be instantiated. In environments with centralized coordination, similar problems have been addressed, for instance using the DADO framework [9]. DADO can optimize the number of replicas of each service, the device each replica should be deployed on, and the network configuration. However, DADO is unsuitable for the collaborative mist scenarios. First, while DADO can *output* the desired replica configuration, it is unable to instantiate the replicas directly. Moreover, DADO operates over a centrally controlled software-defined network, rather than an entirely opportunistic one. Third, although DADO automatically optimizes KPIs such as response time, services in the collaborative mist may want to optimize other (service-specific) KPIs, for instance, to minimize their effects on user activity (e.g., energy usage, relative RAM consumption). Finally, in situations with large numbers of devices, DADO can take several hours to generate a deployment plan [9]. This is not acceptable in opportunistic situations, which are highly dynamic and require quickly reaction to environmental changes.

Thus, we propose μDADO, a decision subsystem for PODS, adapted to opportunistic environments to execute in a fast and lightweight way. Given the input from the context scanner, μDADO outputs the number of replicas and optimal placement for a service. For flexibility, μDADO allows developers to configure and define the KPIs that their services should optimize. μDADO uses

Mixed-Integer Linear Programming (MILP) to model the mathematical optimization problem, with a set of parameters (i.e., inputs of the system), decision variables (i.e., expected outputs the system will optimize), an objective function (i.e., metrics to be optimized), and a set of constraints (i.e., rules of validity).

We first model the information obtained from the context scanner as an input to the problem. Let D be the set of devices detected by the context scanner. Let K be the set of needed KPIs that μDADO obtains from all neighboring devices based on their context snapshots. We define the matrix V, of dimensions $|K| \times |D|$, which contains the values of each KPI in each device. Hence, $V_{kd}, k \in K, d \in D$, is the value of KPI k in the device d, as obtained by the device scanner. We assume that each group of users is strongly connected, i.e., that all the devices are neighbors of each other. If a user loses connection with devices in a group, it is considered to be its own group. If the device is able to connect to the devices in the group again, it will *rejoin* the group. Each device independently computes its own V, but, the computation of V_{kd} is deterministic, i.e., any two devices will compute the same value of V_{kd} because they receive the same context information from d. Nonetheless, the local decision taken by μDADO is only considered if either the device is a delegatee, or if there are no available delegatees.

Continuing with the developer-defined configuration, let O be a vector of integer values of size $|O| = |K|$. Each element $O_k, k \in K$ takes the value of 1 if the KPI should be minimized, -1 if the KPI should be maximized, and 0 otherwise. This lets the developer decide which metrics are to be optimized for each service. Similarly, the developer can define constraints over these KPIs that should be met by delegatees. Let EQ be a binary vector, of size $|EQ| = |K|$, and an additional vector of real numbers, $EQ^v, |EQ^v| = |K|$. A binary element $EQ_k, k \in K$ will take the value of 1 if a valid delegatee d must have a value on their KPI k equal to EQ_k^v. Analogously, the vectors GT and GT^v are defined to require a KPI of delegatees to be *greater than* a given value, and LT, LT^v to require them to be *less than* a value. These can be combined to constrain KPIs to be within a given range using GT and LT, or to create constraints such as "greater than or equal to" combining GT and EQ. For a given service, the vectors O, EQ, LT, and GT are identical for all of the devices.

Next, we define the problem's decision variables. To perform delegatee selection we define a binary vector, X, of size $|X| = |D|$. Each binary element in the vector, $X_d, d \in D$, will take the value of 1 if the device d is selected to host a replica of the service. Moreover, it is important to consider whether each device can or cannot access the service. Thus, we define a binary vector $A, |A| = |D|$, where $A_d, d \in D$ will take the value of 1 if the device d can access the service.

There are three essential elements that the objective function must optimize: the KPIs the developer configured, the service's availability (i.e., the number of devices that can communicate with at least one delegatee), and the number of instantiated replicas. The term of the objective function handling the developer-configured KPIs is calculated as the summation of the KPIs in a delegatee; the KPIs used are limited to those that are indicated by the O vector. The term handling the service's availability calculates and minimizes the number of devices that cannot access the service. The third term, the number of replicas, simply counts the number of delegatees. Thus, the objective function (Eq. 1) is the minimization of the summation of these three terms:

$$\min \sum_{k \in K} \sum_{d \in D} (O_k V_{kd} X_d) + \sum_{d \in D} (1 - A_d) + \sum_{d \in D} X_d \tag{1}$$

To account for the developer-defined constraints on the KPIs, we include:

$$X_d V_{kd} EQ_k = EQ_k EQ_k^v \forall d \in D, k \in K \tag{2}$$

$$X_d V_{kd} GT_k \geq GT_k^v \forall d \in D, k \in K \tag{3}$$

$$X_d V_{kd} LT_k \leq LT_k^v \forall d \in D, k \in K \tag{4}$$

Formally, we can declare the problem μDADO solves as optimizing Eq. 1, subject to Eqs. 2–4. The developer provides μDADO with a configuration file , specifying their KPIs and constraints of interest. This configuration is then passed to a solver for this MILP formulation. In terms of temporal complexity, there are a total of $2^{2|D|}$ solutions for any given scenario, and hence, the problem has exponential complexity. On the other hand, in terms of memory, the total memory required for a problem instance of μDADO grows as a second-degree polynomial function of the number of devices and KPIs ($2|D| + 8|K| + |K||D| + |D|^2$).

3.3   Service Migrator and Virtualization Platform

The service migrator takes on the task of executing the migration to achieve the configurations that μDADO identifies. To do so, the service migrator first checks if a migration must be performed, as the target delegatee(s) may be the current delegatee(s). In case a delegatee differs, the migrator must know the number of currently executing replicas and the target number of replicas, creating or removing as many replicas as necessary. Finally, because many services are stateful, to move a service to another delegatee, the service migrator must take care to transfer the state along with the service. In particular, the service migrator packages the state of the service, including an data, files, or databases it accesses or modifies, and shares these with the target delegatee, which must reinstate the service in the same state as the previous delegatee. To maintain a coherent system of services across devices using PODS, these services should be provided as self-contained, self-provisioning, and ideally cross-platform packages containing the service, as well as its dependencies, if they exist. To have self-contained and self-provisioning packages that run in a cross-platform manner and have their status saved on one machine and loaded in another, PODS relies on an underlying service virtualization platform. The role of such a platform is to minimize the friction in service delegation, allowing services to run *machine-agnostically*, i.e., not needing to control the operating system they are running on or the dependencies and programs installed within the device. To maintain service availability continuously, the migration process first stands up the service on any new delegatees. Once these new instances are running, the PODS instance on the delegatee device notifies the PODS instance on the device that previously hosted the service, notifying it that the service can be shut down.

4   Conclusion and Future Work

The advent of paradigms in the *Cloud Continuum* motivates research focused on moving services closer to users. However, most approaches currently focus on moving services from the cloud to the mist layers, rather than into peer-to-peer delegation. This paper presents PODS, a platform for the management and delegation of services for opportunistic pervasive computing environments. In the future, we expect to perform experiments over multiple changing conditions.

Acknowledgment. This work has been partially funded by the projects TED2021-130913B-I00 and PDC2022-133465-I00, funded by MCIN/AEI/10.13039/501100011033 and by the European Union "Next GenerationEU/PRTR", by the Department of Economy, Science, and Digital Agenda of the Government of Extremadura (GR21133), and by the European Regional Development Fund. This work was also partially supported by the European Union under the Italian National Recovery and Resilience Plan (NRRP) of NextGenerationEU, partnership on "Telecommunications of the Future" (PE00000001 - program "RESTART"). CUP: J33C22 002880001 and by the *Whole Communities–Whole Health* Research Grand Challenge at the University of Texas at Austin.

References

1. Bittencourt, L., et al.: The internet of things, fog and cloud continuum: integration and challenges. Internet Things **3**, 134–155 (2018)
2. LiveBoard Inc., "LiveBoard - Online Interactive Whiteboard App For Educators (2022). https://www.liveboard.online/
3. Fu, X., Yao, H., Postolache, O., Yang, Y.: Message forwarding for WSN-assisted opportunistic network in disaster scenarios. J. Netw. Comput. Appl. **137**, 11–24 (2019)
4. HTC: HTC Power To Give, p. 1 (2015). https://www.htc.com/us/go/power-to-give/
5. Anderson, D.P.: Boinc: a platform for volunteer computing. J. Grid Comput. **18**(1), 99–122 (2020)
6. Mojang: Minecraft - Applications in Google Play (2023). https://play.google.com/store/apps/details?id=com.mojang.minecraftpe
7. Laso, S., et al.: Human microservices: a framework for turning humans into service providers. Softw. Pract. Exp. **51**(9), 1910–1935 (2021)
8. Villari, M., et al.: Osmosis: the osmotic computing platform for microelements in the cloud, edge, and internet of things. Computer **52**(8), 14–26 (2019)
9. Herrera, J.L., Galán-Jiménez, J., Berrocal, J., Murillo, J.M.: Optimizing the response time in SDN-fog environments for time-strict IoT applications. IEEE Internet Things J. **8**(23), 17 172–185 (2021)

Context-Aware Trustworthy IoT Energy Services Provisioning

Amani Abusafia[1]([✉])(iD), Athman Bouguettaya[1](iD), Abdallah Lakhdari[1](iD), and Sami Yangui[2](iD)

[1] The University of Sydney, Sydney, NSW 2000, Australia
{amani.abusafia,abdallah.lakhdari}@sydney.edu.au
[2] LAAS-CNRS, Université de Toulouse, INSA, 31400 Toulouse, France
yangui@laas.fr

Abstract. We propose an IoT energy service provisioning framework to ensure consumers' *Quality of Experience (QoE)*. A novel *context-aware trust assessment* model is proposed to evaluate the trustworthiness of providers. Our model adapts to the dynamic nature of energy service providers to maintain QoE by selecting trustworthy providers. The proposed model evaluates providers' trustworthiness in various contexts, considering their behavior and energy provisioning history. Additionally, a trust-adaptive composition technique is presented for optimal energy allocation. Experimental results demonstrate the effectiveness and efficiency of the proposed approaches.

Keywords: Energy-as-a-Service (EaaS) · Internet of Things (IoT) · Quality of Experience (QoE) · Trust Assessment · wireless power transfer

1 Introduction

Energy-as-a-Service (EaaS) refers to the wireless delivery of energy from an energy provider (e.g., a smart shoe) to a nearby energy consumer (e.g., a smartphone) [1]. Energy service may enable an eco-friendly self-sustained environment by exchanging *spare* or *harvested* energy [2,3]. For instance, an energy provider may offer their harvested energy to a nearby IoT device. Energy may be harvested from natural resources, e.g., physical movement [3]. For example, wearing a PowerWalk harvester may produce energy from an hourly walk at a comfortable speed to charge up to four smartphones [4]. Moreover, energy services offer a *convenient* and *ubiquitous* power access for IoT users without using cords or power banks [5]. Energy services may be deployed through the newly developed "Over-the-Air" wireless charging technologies [6,7]. Several companies are developing charging technologies that enable IoT devices to charge wirelessly over a distance, such as Xiaomi, Energous, and Cota [4,8]. For instance, Energous developed a device that can charge up to 3 W of power within a 5-meter distance. Although current technology may not provide efficient energy delivery [9], technological advances are expected to enable devices to exchange larger amounts of energy [6].

We propose a dynamic energy service ecosystem that consists of energy providers and consumers in *microcells* (see Fig. 1(A)). A microcell is any confined

F. Monti et al. (Eds.): ICSOC 2023, LNCS 14420, pp. 167–185, 2023.
https://doi.org/10.1007/978-3-031-48424-7_13

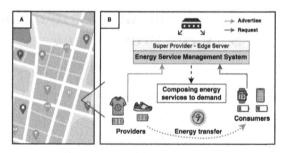

Fig. 1. (A) Microcells in a smart city (B) IoT energy services environment in a microcell

space where people may gather, e.g., cafes and restaurants. In this environment, IoT devices may share energy with nearby devices. The energy Service Oriented Architecture; SOA-based business model has three main actors: energy *provider*[1], energy *consumer*, and *super-provider* [6]. According to this business model, providers advertise their services, consumers submit their requests, and the super-provider (i.e., the microcell's owner) manages the exchange of energy services between providers and consumers in the microcell. This paper focuses on energy services sharing from the super-provider perspective.

Recent research suggests that super-providers may use energy services to *enhance consumers' Quality of Experience (QoE)* [4,10]. Studies show that businesses providing wireless energy services, like "air-charge", positively affect customer experiences[2]. In energy services, *Quality of Experience (QoE)* refer to the *aggregated satisfaction* of consumers with energy services *over time* [4,10]. Consumers' satisfaction is measured by the fulfillment of their energy needs [4,10]. This paper focuses on energy services provisioning as a key ingredient to provide customers with the best QoE.

A key challenge in QoE-based energy service provisioning is to *assess providers' commitment* to sharing energy [6,8]. For example, a provider may terminate the energy transfer by leaving the transfer range. They may also stop the transfer due to excessive device usage. Such service disruptions may reduce the expected amount of shared energy, thereby impacting the consumer's QoE. In such cases, real-time service replacement may not be guaranteed [11]. Thus, a super-provider needs to assess providers' trustworthiness before allocating services to consumers. Hence, a *trust assessment framework is necessary to evaluate the uncertainty in a provider's commitment.*

Trust refers to the belief that providers will adhere to agreements and maintain the quality of service as advertised [6,8]. Existing trust frameworks are hardly applicable to crowdsourced IoT energy services environments [2,6]. This is mainly due to the highly dynamic and fluctuating energy provisioning and usage behavior of IoT users [12]. Consequently, energy fluctuations directly result from the uncertainty around crowdsourced IoT energy providers meeting their energy commitments. As indicated, IoT users' commitment may fluctuate due

---

[1] We used interchangeably the terms energy provider and provider to refer to the energy provider.

[2] air-charge.com.

to the mobility and usage patterns of IoT users [6,12]. For instance, an IoT user may consume their advertised service due to unexpected heavy device usage [11]. Given IoT users' energy fluctuation and dynamic behavior, using existing trust frameworks may often lead to low trust scores for most providers. If most providers have low trust scores, the super-provider may not find enough trustworthy services to allocate. For example, existing trust frameworks would typically give a low trust score to a provider who consistently offers only 50 mAh, regardless of the advertised services. However, if the super-provider only needs 50mAh, assessing the provider based on this specific requirement would result in a higher trust score, making them a suitable candidate for allocation. Therefore, the same IoT energy provider's trust will vary according to the super-providers' requirements. Therefore, a new trust assessment framework is needed [6,8]. In this respect, we propose a context-aware trust assessment framework tailored specifically to energy services.

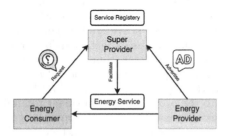

Fig. 2. IoT energy services business model

We propose a context-aware trust assessment framework to accurately assess and effectively allocate trustworthy providers. The framework assesses providers' trustworthiness based on the super-provider context-aware constraints. The providers' trust scores are then used to *select* and *compose* the best set of energy services to fulfill the super-provider requirements. Our framework enables utilizing providers that may appear untrustworthy but can make valuable contributions while maintaining commitment. In addition, we propose a heuristic-based approach that ensures a higher QoE. Our approach composes additional services, based on the trust scores of providers, as a backup in the case of service cancellation. The main contributions of this paper are:

- A novel trust-aware framework to compose energy services and ensure QoE.
- A context-aware trust assessment model to evaluate energy providers.
- A context model for defining super-provider constraints in evaluating provider trust.
- A heuristic-based approach to compose trustworthy energy services.

Motivating Scenario: We describe a scenario in a confined place (i.e., microcell) where people congregate, e.g., cafes and restaurants (see Fig. 1 (A)). Each microcell may have several IoT devices acting as energy providers or consumers (see Fig. 1 (B)). The super-provider aims to leverage the crowdsourced energy services to enhance the consumers' *experience*. We assume that all energy services and requests are sent to the *edge* (e.g., a microcell router, Fig. 1(B)) and managed by the super-provider (Fig. 2). We assume that the super-provider has prior knowledge of the *energy demand distribution* in the microcell over a given time window. Additionally, the super-provider adopts a QoE-based approach, such as [4,10], to select optimal providers to fulfill the microcell's energy demand. We assume that the super-provider offers incentives to encourage energy sharing in the form of credits [10,13]. The credits would be used to receive more energy when the providers act as consumers in the future [4]. However, rewards do not guarantee providers' commitment [13]. The *uncertainty* in providers' behavior may adversely affect consumers' QoE if a service fails and no other nearby services are available [11]. Thus, a trust framework is required to evaluate providers' commitment. While there are several trust frameworks for IoT services, they are not applicable to energy services as they do not accommodate the nature of energy services. An inaccurate trust assessment may lead to misjudgment of a service. This could lead to either not using it due to a low score or using an untrustworthy service that disappoints consumers. Given energy scarcity, it is paramount to assess trust in order to efficiently utilize all available services correctly. Furthermore, super-providers typically may vary in their service expectations and requirements. These expectations may result in different trustworthiness scores for the same provider. Hence, it is challenging to find the right trust assessment that meets super-provider expectations.

Figure 3 shows a provider's advertised service and history. Let us assume we limit the trust metrics to the provider's commitment to fulfill an energy request. Using a traditional trust framework where a provider is assessed based on all its available history, the provider trust score will be 67% without estimating the provided amount. This score is computed based on the ratio of the total provided energy to the total requested energy. However, using a more context-aware trust framework, where a super-provider defines their minimum requirements as a threshold, may result in a different score. For example, if a super-provider has a 60 mAh threshold, they will look at the provider's history and how often they fulfill 60 mAh requests. Based on this, they rated the provider's service to 60 mAh with a 93% trust score. In another example, if the threshold is set to evaluate the rate of providing 70mAh services in microcell B, the trust framework will consider the provider's history within microcell B to understand their performance in that area. As a result, the super-provider will rate the provider's services as 70mAh with a 100% trust score.

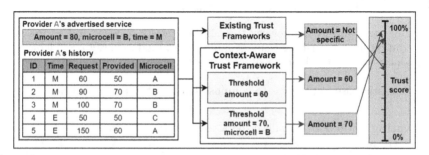

Fig. 3. Example of how different trust assessments yield different trust scores.

Allocating the *limited* available energy amid the *uncertainty* of providers' commitment presents a critical challenge for the efficient and QoE-aware provisioning of IoT energy services [6]. We propose a context-aware trust-assessment framework for energy services. Our framework assesses provider trust based on the expectations and requirements of super-providers, which may lead to varying trust scores for the same service. The framework composes the most trustworthy energy services, ensuring consumer QoE and leveraging super-providers' expectations to assess and adhere to their standards. Moreover, our composition approach accounts for the natural untrustworthiness in the energy crowdsourcing environment by selecting additional services as a backup. The selection of these services relies on the trustworthiness of the available services.

2   System Model

We focus on assessing the trust of energy services in microcells during a single time slot t. We use the below definitions to formalize the problem.

2.1   Energy Service Model

Definition 1. *Energy Service (S)*. We adopt the definition of EaaS introduced in [1]. An energy service S is defined as a tuple of $< s_{id}, p_{id}, F, Q >$, where:

- s_{id} is a unique service identifier,
- p_{id} is a unique provider identifier,
- F is the function of delivering wireless energy,
- Q is a tuple of $< q_1, q_2, ..., q_n >$, where each q_i denotes the Quality of Service (QoS), e.g., energy amount and geographical location.

Definition 2. *Energy Quality of Service (QoS)*. QoS attributes enable users to differentiate between energy services [8]. We extend the definition of QoS attributes from [1]. QoS is presented as a tuple of $< a, l, d, b >$ [1], where:

- a is the amount of energy offered by the provider,
- l is the geographical location of the provider,
- d is a tuple of $< st, et >$ that represents the service's start and end time,
- tr is the provider's trust score to offer their service,

Definition 3. *Energy Service Provider (P)*. P is an IoT device with spare energy to be shared as a service. P is defined as a tuple of $< p_{id}, \mathcal{H} >$, where:

- p_{id} is a unique provider identifier,
- $\mathcal{H}$ is the set of historical records of the provider's previous provisioning. We assume that all providers have a history, and dealing with newcomers is not the focus of this paper. We also assume that the edge will retrieve the history of providers from the cloud (see Fig. 1(B)). $\mathcal{H}$ is a tuple of $< h_1, h_2, ..., h_m >$, where each h_i represent the record of previous energy transfer as $< s, de, m, t >$ where:
  - s is the advertised energy service,
  - de is the amount of delivered energy,
  - m is the microcell where the energy sharing occurred,
  - t is the time interval $< st, et >$ of the energy sharing.

2.2 Super-Provider Preferences

Definition 4. *Energy Demand Distribution (ED). The super-provider uses the traffic history of the microcell to define the Energy Demand distribution (ED).*

We adopt the definition of ED from [4]. ED is the predicted consumers' energy demand distribution in the service time window W. Therefore, the demand for a single time slot is defined as a tuple $< d, t >$ where d is the aggregation of the predicted energy requests at time interval t. The prediction of energy requests may be obtained using prediction techniques applied to the historical records $\mathcal{H}$ for all IoT users who visited the microcell at time interval t [14,15]. Energy requests may be aggregated according to their spatio-temporal features [11]. Given a set of predicted energy requests, the super-provider aggregates the energy requests using the composition approach proposed by [1]. The approach considers the time interval of each request to define a composite energy request that includes all available requests. The super-provider sums the requested energy by all the available requests at that time interval using:

$$Ed.d(t) = \sum_{j=0}^{m} f(\mathcal{H}_j, t) \tag{1}$$

where d is the aggregated energy demand at time slot t, $\mathcal{H}_j$ is the provider's j history of energy requests at time t, m is the number of consumers who have visited the microcell at t in the past and f is the prediction function.

Definition 5. *Quality of Experience (QoE). QoE measures the aggregated satisfaction of energy consumers in a microcell at time slot t.*

The consumers' satisfaction is determined by the allocated services to the energy demand ED. We adopt the definition of QoE from [10], which measures QoE across time slots and adjusts it to assess a single time slot. Therefore, QoE is computed as:

$$QoE = \sum_{i=1}^{n} S_i.a/Ed.d(t) \tag{2}$$

Where n is the number of selected services, a is energy service i's amount, $Ed.d(t)$ is the aggregated energy demand at time slot t computed using Eq. 1, m is the number of aggregated requests, and re is energy request size.

2.3 Problem Definition

Given a super-provider in a microcell m who wants to fulfill their consumer's expected energy demand $Ed.d(t)$ at a time slot t. The super-provider has a set of n candidate providers $\mathcal{P} = \{p_1, p_2, ..., p_n\}$ who expressed their interest in offering their service $\mathcal{S} = \{s_1, s_2, ..., s_n\}$ at that time and location. Each provider has a history $\mathcal{H} =< h_1, h_2, ..., h_m >$ of sharing energy. The super-provider aims to ensure QoE by maximizing the fulfillment of energy demand. This will be achieved by allocating the most trustworthy providers. *We reformulate the service provision problem as a time-constrained optimization problem as follows:*

– Maximize QoE as $\sum_{i=1}^{n} S_i.a * \mathcal{P}_{Trust_i}/Ed.d(t)$

Subject to:

– $Ed.d(t) > 0$,
– $S_i.d \subset t$ for each $S_i \in \mathcal{S}$.

Where QoE is computed based on the allocated energy multiplied by the corresponding provider trust score, $\mathcal{P}_{Trust_i}$ is provider i trust score, $S_j.d$ is the time interval $< st, et >$ a provider of S_i may offer their energy, t is the duration of a time interval, and $Ed.d$ is the aggregated energy demand at time slot t.
We use the following assumptions to formulate the problem:

– Providers' energy size is fixed during composition.
– Providers and consumers are static during energy sharing.
– The super-provider context model is given as input, and determining the constraints is out of the scope of this paper.
– There is no energy loss in sharing. As the technology matures, we anticipate that the devices will share more energy, and the sharing energy loss will become minimal [4].
– The super-provider uses credits as incentives for energy sharing, which providers can later redeem for more energy when they become consumers [10].
– All providers have a history of energy provisioning and are willing to share them.
– The energy demand distribution ED is deterministic.
– A secure framework has been implemented to preserve the integrity and the privacy of the IoT devices [16].

3   Trust Assessment Model

We define the provider trust level assessment to determine the trustworthiness score ($\mathcal{P}_{Trust}$) of an energy service. The trust level assessment considers the behavior of providers and their history in delivering energy. We compute the trustworthiness of a provider using the following attributes:

– **Success Rate:** This attribute measures the reliability of a provider based on their past performance. We argue that providers with a high success rate are likely to be more reliable in the future, making this an important attribute in trust evaluation. The *success rate* ($\mathcal{SR}_P$) of a provider is the ratio of *completed energy services* to the total number of *initiated services* by that provider. Here, completed services refer to full energy delivery as advertised, while initiated services count all, regardless of completion. We compute $\mathcal{SR}_P$ of provider P as follows:

$$\mathcal{SR}_P = \frac{|\{S \in \mathcal{E}_P \mid S \text{ is completed}\}|}{|\mathcal{E}_P|} \qquad (3)$$

where $\mathcal{E}_P$ is all services initiated by provider P and $|.|$ is the cardinality of the set.

– **Delivery Size:** This attribute gauges the consistency of a provider in terms of the quantity of energy they deliver. The Delivery Size rate $(\mathcal{DS}_P)$ may be calculated as the ratio of successful energy deliveries' total size to all attempted deliveries' total size by a provider. $\mathcal{DS}_P$ is computed using:

$$\mathcal{DS}_P = \frac{\sum_{i=1}^{n} h_i.de}{\sum_{i=1}^{n} S_i.a} \tag{4}$$

where n represents the number of previous services delivered by the provider, $h_i.de$ represents the actual delivered energy retrieved from the history record h_i, and $S_i.a$ represents the advertised amount of the i-th energy service.

– **Timeliness Score:** This attribute measures a provider's adherence to the service schedule. Disconnections in the transfer process may sometimes occur due to the provider's indoor movement, leading to energy transfer delays [12]. These delays, increasing consumer wait times, can negatively impact their QoE. Hence, the Timeliness score $\mathcal{TL}_P$ is crucial in the trust model. $\mathcal{TL}_P$ is calculated using the following formula:

$$\mathcal{TL}_P \begin{cases} 1 & \text{if } \sum_{i=1}^{n} (h_i.t.et - S_i.et) <= 0 \\ \frac{1}{\sum_{i=1}^{n} (h_i.t.et - S_i.et)/n} & \text{otherwise} \end{cases} \tag{5}$$

where n is the provider's number of previously delivered energy services, $h_i.t.et$ represents the actual end time of delivering a service i retrieved from the provider's history record h_i, and $S_i.et$ represents the advertised end time of the i-th energy service.

– **Impact Score:** A provider's service cancellation may affect consumers' QoE. As a single service may be fulfilling multiple requests [11], the impact of canceling service on the consumers may be used to evaluate the providers' trustworthiness. We compute the service failure's impact $\mathcal{F}_S$ based on the number of affected consumers. We compute the failure impact $\mathcal{F}_S$ of a *canceled* energy service as follows:

$$\mathcal{F}_S = \frac{|\{C \in c \mid C \text{ is receiving from } S}{|C|} \tag{6}$$

where C is the set of all consumers in the microcell within the duration of the service $[S_{st} - S_{et}]$ and $|.|$ is the cardinality of a set.

We define the provider impact as the cumulative effect of all their services on consumers. Typically, a trustworthy provider will have minimal impact on consumers when a failure occurs. In other words, the provider's impact is calculated as the complementary value to the failure impact. Therefore, We compute the provider impact score $\mathcal{I}_P$ as follows:

$$\mathcal{I}_P = \left(\sum_{i=1}^{n} (1 - \mathcal{F}_{S_i}) \right) /n \tag{7}$$

where n represents the number of previous energy services delivered by the provider.

– **Mobility Pattern:** A provider's mobility pattern may influence their energy service provision. For example, if a provider's mobility pattern shows their staying time at a microcell is 5 min, and they advertised a service that requires 30 min, this might indicate the probability of not committing to the request. Therefore, we consider the staying duration pattern as an attribute in the trust assessment. We use the history of the provider's previous services to compute their duration patterns [17]. The number of previous services should be greater than a predefined threshold α to be considered. We compute the staying duration pattern $\mathcal{SD}_P$ as:

$$\mathcal{SD}_P = \left(\sum_{i=1}^{k} (S_i.et - S_i.st) \right) /k \mid k > \alpha \qquad (8)$$

where $S_i.st$ is the provider's previous service i start time, $S_i.et$ is the provider's previous service i end time, and k is the number of previous services. We compute the provider Duration trust factor $\mathcal{D}_P$ using the staying duration pattern $\mathcal{SD}_P$ as follows:

$$\mathcal{D}_P = \begin{cases} 1 & \text{if } (S.et - S.st) <= \mathcal{SD}_P \\ \frac{SD_C}{(S.et - S.st)} & \text{otherwise} \end{cases} \qquad (9)$$

where $S.st$ is the provider's current service start time, $S.et$ is the provider's current service end time.

Providers Trustworthiness

The provider trust score ($\mathcal{P}_{Trust}$) combines all the aforementioned trust attributes to offer a holistic assessment of a provider's trustworthiness. While each attribute reflects different aspects of a provider's service delivery, their significance varies depending on the super-provider-specific requirements. For example, a super-provider may ignore the timeliness score if they have customers who stay for a long time. Hence, we added a component in the trust-assessment constraints for the super-provider to determine attribute weights. $\mathcal{P}_{Trust}$ is calculated using the following formula:

$$\mathcal{P}_{Trust} = \sum_{J \in l} w_J \times \mathcal{L}_P \qquad (10)$$

where $\mathcal{L} = \{SR, TL, DS, I, D\}$ and w represents the weights of each trust attribute based on its importance, with the constraint that $\sum w_i = 1$ to normalize the impact of each factor on the overall trustworthiness score. Multiple methods exist for calculating the weight of each attribute, depending on the preference of the super-provider [18].

4   Energy Service Composition Framework

We introduce our energy service composition framework for allocating trustworthy energy services to provide consumers with the best QoE (see Fig. 4). The framework ensures QoE by allocating trustworthy services based on the super-provider context. The framework is divided into two phases: (1) context-aware

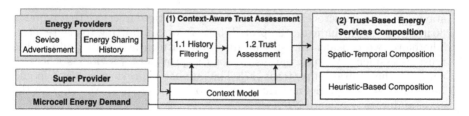

Fig. 4. Trust-based energy service composition framework

Algorithm 1 Trust-Based Energy Services Composition

Input: $Energy\ Providers(P), Energy\ Demand(ED), Context\ Model(CM)$
Output: ES_{comp}, QoE

    Phase 1: Context-Aware Trust Assessment

1: **for** $p\ in\ P$ **do**
2:    **if** $[p.st, p.et] \subseteq Ed.t$ **then**
3:       $p.h = History\_Filtering(p.\mathcal{H}, CM)$
4:       $\mathcal{P}_{Trust} = Trust\_Assessment(p.h, CM)$
5:       $newE = p.s.a * \mathcal{P}_{Trust}$
6:       $SelectedP.add(p, \mathcal{P}_{Trust}, newE)$

    Phase 2: Composition of Energy Services

7: $ES_{comp} = Energy\_Allocation(SelectedP, ED)$
8: $QoE = QoE\_Assessment(ES_{comp}, ED)$
9: **return** ES_{comp}, QoE

---

trust assessment and (2) trust-based energy service composition. The general steps of the framework are present in Algorthim 1. In what follows, we discuss each phase in detail:

4.1 Context-Aware Trust Assessment

In this phase, the proposed framework evaluates the historical performance of each provider to assess their trustworthiness. This framework uses our proposed trust model to evaluate a provider's trust. It further incorporates a context model, which represents the constraints set by the super-provider regarding the attributes and data used for the trust assessment. The context model consists of two main components: (1) history constraints and (2) trust assessment constraints. This model is then used in the trust assessment phase (see Fig. 4). In the following subsections, we will present the context model and discuss each step of the framework in detail.

Context Model. As mentioned, the context model establishes the constraints set by the super-provider concerning the attributes and data used in evaluating providers' trustworthiness. The context model consists of two sets of constraints. The first set pertains to the provider's history, addressing aspects such as considering their entire history or focusing solely on their behavior within a specific microcell. The second set defines the super-provider's constraints on trust assessment attributes, which may include using all trust model attributes or only a subset, adjusting the weights of trust model attributes, or evaluating particular attributes. While we provide a comprehensive model to represent the possible constraints of super-providers, we assume that the selection of which constraints to apply and the values of the variables in these constraints will be provided as input to our framework. These values will be determined based on the business context and requirements of the super-provider. In what follows, we discuss each constraint.

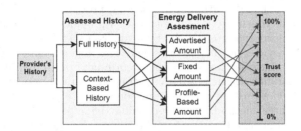

Fig. 5. Context-aware trust assessment model

- **History Constraints:** As previously mentioned, trust assessment can employ the provider's entire history or part of it, depending on the super-provider history constraints (see Fig. 5). For instance, a super-provider may assess providers' trust based on their history within a specific microcell. Another example would be evaluating the provider's energy-sharing history for larger requests, such as those exceeding 100 units. Therefore, we formulate the history constraints as a constraint satisfaction problem (CSP) [19]. Consequently, the super-provider history constraints are represented as a triple $< X, D, C >$, where X is a set of variables, D is a set of corresponding domains of values, and C is the super-provider's constraint set. The formulation of the super-provider history constraints is as follows:

X : y_i : A variable that equals 1 if provider i meets the constraints, and 0 otherwise.

D : The domain of y_i is binary, i.e.,0, 1.

C : Location constraint (c_L) : $\forall S \in P.\mathcal{H} : c_L = 1 \Rightarrow S.l = L$, where L is a specific microcell.

Time constraint (c_T) : $\forall S \in P.\mathcal{H} : c_T = 1 \Rightarrow S.d = D$, where D is a specific time interval.

Energy constraint (c_E) : $\forall S \in P.\mathcal{H} : c_S = 1 \Rightarrow S.a >= A$, where A is a specific energy service size.

$$(11)$$

The goal is to find an assignment for the variable y_i that satisfies all the constraints, effectively identifying the providers' history that meets the super-provider's specific constraints. Our CSP formulation is designed to be highly flexible and adaptable to various super-provider preferences. By allowing the super-provider to select any combination of constraints, we provide a tailored trust assessment that meets their specific requirements.

- **Trust Assessment Constraints:** The super-provider's trust constraints are related to the trust assessment attributes and the overall trust score. These constraints are formulated as a tuple of $< W, \alpha, ae >$ where:
  - w represents the weight assigned to each trust attribute based on its importance, with the constraint that $\sum w_i = 1$ to normalize the impact of each factor on the overall trustworthiness score,

- α is a threshold for the provider trust score. α is determined based on the super-provider preference. The super-provider might adopt a greedy approach, aiming to maximize energy without considering the providers' trustworthiness. Conversely, they could be risk-averse, prioritizing trust over the amount of provided energy. Alternatively, the super-provider may take a neutral stance, striking a balance between trustworthiness and the energy provided,
- ae is the adjusted expectations of a super-provider. Super-providers may have different expectations for assessing provider trustworthiness based on their microcell needs. For instance, a provider with a low trust score may be considered trustworthy by a super-provider if they need 50 units, and the provider has historically delivered that amount. Super-providers can determine their expectations according to their requirements, with various parameters such as delivery time and failure impact. In this work, we focus on adjusting expectations concerning energy. Consequently, we propose three methods for determining the super-provider expectations in terms of energy (see Fig. 5). This allows the super-provider to choose what best fits their needs:
  * Advertised amount: In this setting, a super-provider will assess providers based on the amount of delivered energy against what they advertised using Eq. 4,
  * Capped amount: In this setting, a super-provider will assess providers based on the amount of delivered energy against what the super-provider needs (*expected Amount*). For instance, assessing them on delivering 30 units regardless of their service advertisement. The needed amount will be fixed for all providers and may depend on the energy demand of the microcell, the available providers, and their trust score. For instance, if a super-provider needs 100 mAh and has five providers, and their trust score is low, then a possible solution is to assess them by looking into their history and the rate of them delivering 20 units,
  * Customized amount: In this setting, the super-provider assesses providers using an energy size extracted from their pattern of delivered energy from their history. The reason for adjusting the energy is that sometimes IoT users may overestimate what they can deliver [11]. The customized amount may be computed using statistical values such as mean, mode, and median, and it will be unique to each provider based on their profile.

If the super-provider wants to assess the providers on delivering a fixed amount or a profile-based amount as *expectedAmount* regardless of their service advertisement. In such a scenario, the denominator in Eq. 4 will be *expectedAmount*, and the $\mathcal{DS}_P$ score will be one if what is provided is larger than *expectedAmount*.

Recall that the context model is used in the context-aware trust assessment phase of the framework (see Fig. 4). This phase consists of two steps: history filtering and trust assessment. In the following subsections, we will discuss each step of the phase in detail.

History Filtering: As previously mentioned, the first step of the trust assessment involves filtering the providers' history. We employ the history constraints of the context model as a filter to refine the providers' history. The selection of which constraints to apply and the values of the variables will be determined based on the business context and requirements of the super-provider. Recall that the selection of which constraints to apply and the values of the variables in these constraints will be provided as input to our framework and are not the focus of our work. If a provider lacks sufficient history after applying the constraints, we can gather their history from microcells with similar contexts to our microcell. However, this approach is beyond the scope of this paper. In cases where there is insufficient history (i.e., the number of historical records is less than a predefined threshold), we use the provider's original history for assessment.

Trust Assessment: The next step uses the proposed trust model to assess the trust of the providers after refining their history in the previous step. The input for this step is the trust constraints from the context model. Note that the super-provider determines any combination of history and energy constraints (see Fig. 5). For example, a super-provider may require to use the full history and a fixed amount assessment. The output is each provider's trust score $Ptrust$, calculated using Eq. 10, and the weights of the equation are defined in the context model W. $Ptrust$ is then employed to identify the most trustworthy providers exceeding the super-provider's trust score threshold α.

4.2   Trust-Based Energy Services Composition

This phase aims to compose the most trustworthy energy services to ensure QoE. Given a set of providers and their trust score, we may utilize any priority-based spatio-temporal composition [1,4,13] or other resource allocation algorithms for service provisioning such as Max-Min, knapsack, and genetic algorithms. However, due to the scarcity of energy, a super-provider may end up having a pool of providers with lower trust scores. Intuitively, a super-provider may allocate extra providers as a backup. Hence, we propose a trust-priority heuristic approach that selects additional services to ensure sufficient energy services. Our approach reduces providers' services based on their trust scores and identifies complementary services as backups if the original providers do not fulfill their commitments. In other words, our approach will downsize the providers' energy service size based on their trust score (See Algorithm 1, Lines 5–6). There are other possible ways to over-provision by increasing the amount of energy demand based on the available providers and their trust score. We leave it for future work to estimate the optimal increase in energy demand using other techniques. Moreover, Moreover, our proposed approach operates on a 'best effort' basis. That is, if the demand is larger than the supply, it will compose the best available set of providers. Lastly, the super-provider assesses the QoE of the resulting composition using the model discussed in Sec. 2.3. The assessment of QoE gives an indicator of consumers' satisfaction in the microcell.

5   Evaluation

We investigate the effectiveness and efficiency of the proposed composition approaches based on a comprehensive set of experiments. This section presents a description of the dataset used in the experiments, followed by a description of the experiment setup and a discussion of the findings.

5.1   Dataset Description

We used a real dataset generated from an app developed in [20, 21]. The app monitors the wireless energy-sharing process that occurs by using coils connected to two smartphones. The consumer determines the granularity of the monitoring time. The app allows users to request energy from nearby smartphones by size, e.g.,1000 mAh, or by time, e.g., to charge for 5 min. The dataset consists of energy transfer records between a provider (smartphone) and a consumer (smartphone). The records include attributes such as provider ID, consumer ID, transaction date, time, energy service amount, request amount, and transfer duration. We used the energy dataset to generate QoS parameters for the energy services and requests. For example, the amount of wireless charging transfer in mAh defines the amount of requested/advertised/provided energy. Additionally, the energy dataset records of the wireless charging transfer duration were used to define the end time of each request/service.

We augmented the energy sharing dataset to mimic the behavior of the crowd within microcells by leveraging a dataset published by IBM for a coffee shop chain with three branches in New York City[3]. The dataset consists of transaction records of customer purchases in each coffee shop over one month. On average, each coffee shop has 560 transactional records per day and 16,500 transaction records in total. We used the IBM dataset to simulate the spatio-temporal features of energy services and requests. Our experiment employs the consumer ID, transaction date, time, location, and coffee shop ID from each record in the dataset to define the spatio-temporal features of energy services and requests, e.g., the start and location of an energy service or a request. We randomly generate service cancellations to create untrustworthy providers. Table 1 presents the experiment parameters and statistics.

5.2   Evaluation of the Composition Framework

We compare the proposed heuristic-based composition approached with a baseline traditional resource allocation algorithms, namely, first come first served allocation (*Greedy*), and a priority-based allocation algorithm (*Priority-based*) [22]. In Greedy, services are processed based on their start time regardless of their trust score. In Priority-based, services are processed based on the trust score We also compared our approach with the knapsack-inspired service composition method (*knapsack-based*) proposed by [1]. The approach selects services that maximize the minimum trust value of the participating providers. We also attempted to implement a brute force approach; nonetheless, its substantial computational and memory requirements made effective execution impossible. We conducted an ablation analysis to assess the impact of different factors, including

---

[3] https://ibm.co/2O7IvxJ.

Table 1. Experiments Variables

Variables	Values
Total energy service records for all coffee shops	49894
Energy providers	2248
Duration of all energy services	10–30 min
Energy services amount	150–300 mAh
Energy demand amount	500–2500 mAh
Time window	2 h

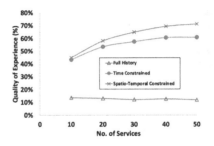

Fig. 6. The average of QoE using different history

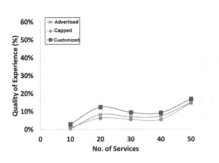

Fig. 7. The average of QoE using different trust assessments

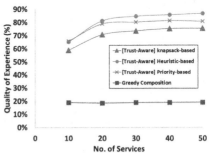

Fig. 8. The average of QoE in trustworthy environment

QoE with different: history constraints, energy delivery assessment constraints, and allocation strategies in different environments. We also examined the cost of incentives and compared the execution time for each method. As mentioned in Sect. 3, multiple methods exist for calculating the weight of the trust assessment attributes, depending on the preference of the super-provider [18]. We assigned all w in Eq. 10 to 0.2 for equal impact on the trust score. We ran the approaches in different settings by fixing the energy demand and gradually changing the number of services over the time interval T. We repeated the experiment 1000 times at each point and considered the average value for each approach.

Quality of Experience Evaluation. The first experiment evaluates the impact of the context model's history constraints on QoE. As mentioned earlier, QoE reflects consumer satisfaction over time, and a high QoE for a composition indicates a greater degree of consumer satisfaction. Figure 6 displays the average QoE using the *knapsack-based* approach with different constraints, i.e., full history, time-constraints representing the history filtered based on the energy demand's time interval, and spatio-temporal constraints assessing trust using the history at the time interval and the given microcell location. We set the energy demand in this experiment to 1000 mAh. Figure 6 shows that using providers' full history yielded the lowest QoE compared to the context-aware filtered history. This is because assessing trust based on the full history results in many low-trust providers not being used. However, the context-aware trust assessment

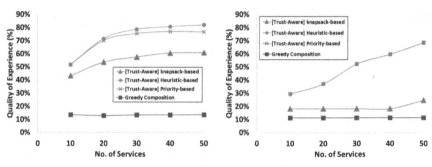

Fig. 9. The average of QoE in neutral environment

Fig. 10. The average of QoE in untrustworthy environment

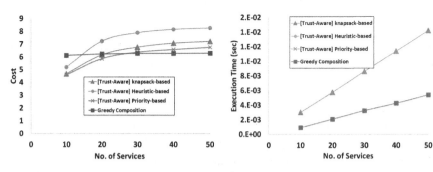

Fig. 11. The average of cost

Fig. 12. The average of computation cost

focuses on their behavior in the microcell. This leads to better assessment and thereby provides more services to allocate, which ensures a higher QoE.

The second experiment examines the impact of the context model's trust assessment constraints on QoE. Figure 7 displays the average QoE using the *knapsack-based* approach with different expected energy assessments: "advertised" assesses providers based on the service amount advertised in their history record, "capped" assesses them based on a fixed amount determined by the super-provider (e.g., 50 units), and "customized" is a profile-based assessment. In the customized assessment, we evaluated providers based on the median of their historical records. Figure 7 shows a slight QoE improvement when assessing providers based on the median; further experiments are needed to understand the consistency in providers' patterns and the sufficient number of records for profiling a user. We plan to explore the provider's patterns in the future.

The third experiment evaluates the effectiveness of our proposed heuristic-based composition. We compare our approach with the aforementioned approaches in three environment settings: a trustworthy environment where most of the provider's trust score is high, i.e., above 80% (see Fig. 8); a neutral environment where providers' trustworthiness follows a random distribution (see Fig. 9); and an untrustworthy environment where most of the provider's trust score is low, i.e., below 20% (see Fig. 10). Overall, our proposed approach performs better than the rest of the approaches due to its over-provisioning strategy. However, the over-provisioning comes with a higher cost of rewards (See Fig. 11). We compute the cost as the price per energy unit multiplied by the amount of provided energy [13]. Another observation is that QoE increases for all approaches except greedy in all settings. This is intuitive, as with the increase in services, there is more energy to fulfill the energy demand and thereby increase QoE.

Computation Efficiency Evaluation In the fourth experiment, we assessed the computational cost of all approaches. The execution time for all approaches increases with the increase in services' availability (see Fig. 12). This is due to the increase in processing time to assign these services.

6   Related Work

The background of our work comes from energy services and trust assessment in IoT services. We present the related work to our research in each domain.

Crowdsourcing Energy Services: Energy exchange services have emerged as alternative solutions for charging IoT devices [2,8]. Several studies have addressed challenges related to meeting the demands of energy consumers [1,11,12]. A time-based composition algorithm was introduced to compose energy services to satisfy consumers' energy needs [1]. The algorithm suggests using partial services and a fractional knapsack to maximize the provided energy. The intermittent nature of energy services has been addressed using a fluid approach [12]. Other research has addressed challenges from the provider's perspective [6,13]. A context-aware incentive model was suggested to address the resistance to offering energy services [13]. Another study proposed a model to estimate the energy loss in sharing energy services [23]. Recent studies have addressed these challenges from a super-provider's perspective [4,10,24]. A QoE model was suggested as a key indicator for allocating services to requests [4,10]. Neither QoE-based composition approach considers providers' uncertain availability. To the best of our knowledge, challenges related to the uncertainty of providers' provisioning remain unaddressed.

Trust Assessment in IoT Services: Trust assessment in crowdsourced IoT service environments is fairly new. Most of the proposed trust approaches rely on either previous experiences [25] or social relations [26] to assess trust. The work in [25] proposed a framework that assesses service providers based on their reputations by a central authority. A framework was proposed in [26] to eliminate the privacy risks associated with public Wi-Fi hotspots. The proposed framework lacks generality as it can only be used for Wi-Fi hotspot services. Another study proposed a QoE-based trustable framework for managing services in mobile edge computing (MEC) [27]. However, its focus on MEC system layers and lack of clear trust definition or experimental validation limits its applicability in our context. Another study proposes a trusted resource allocation mechanism for fog computing where a fog-to-fog offloading scheme balances the load on the fog layer [28]. However, the approaches mentioned above may not be ideal for IoT crowdsourcing environments. Trust assessment in such environments presents unique challenges due to characteristics like the diversity and anonymity of IoT users and devices and the lack of a central managing authority [18]. These characteristics make it more difficult to acquire an accurate measure of trust. A recent study proposed to assess trust in crowdsourcing IoT environments from multiple perspectives, such as device, owner, and service [18]. Other solutions proposed to assess trust from a usage-based perspective [29]. A trust assessment method is proposed to evaluate services based on their usage. For example, a user streaming a video may have lower trust requirements than another user engaged in online banking activities [29]. These frameworks are not applicable in IoT energy environments due to the energy scarcity, fluctuating behavior of IoT users, and influence of super-provider expectations on trust scores [12]. To the best of our knowledge, no solution assesses the trustworthiness of providers' provisioning while considering the super-providers' expectations and requirements.

7 Conclusion

The allocation of energy services has been proposed as a tool to assure consumers' Quality of Experience (QoE). However, the existing frameworks assume that providers will always deliver the advertised service. In contrast, the dynamic nature of the energy services environment may result in uncertainty in providers' commitment. Therefore, a trust assessment is required to evaluate the trustworthiness of providers. Existing trust assessments are not applicable due to the energy scarcity and the dynamic behavior of IoT users. Consequently, this paper proposes a novel context-aware trust assessment model. The proposed model assesses providers' trustworthiness in various contexts, considering their behavior and energy provisioning history. Moreover, a trust-adaptive composition technique is proposed for optimal energy allocation, ensuring efficient energy service provisioning. We conducted a set of experiments to assess the performance of the proposed framework. Experiments showed that filtering history based on the microcell context and adjusting expectations based on the super-provider's needs resulted in better trust assessment and improved QoE. The future direction is to consider the probability of change in the energy demand.

Acknowledgment. This research was partly made possible by LE220100078 and DP220101823 grants from the Australian Research Council. The statements made herein are solely the responsibility of the authors.

References

1. Lakhdari, A., et al.: Composing energy services in a crowdsourced IoT environment. IEEE Trans. Serv. Comput. **15**(3), 1280–1294 (2020)
2. Dhungana, A., et al.: Peer-to-peer energy sharing in mobile networks: applications, challenges, and open problems. Ad Hoc Netw. **97**, 102029 (2020)
3. Li, J., et al.: Activity-based profiling for energy harvesting estimation. In: IPSN, pp. 326–327 (2023)
4. Abusafia, A., Bouguettaya, A., Lakhdari, A.: Maximizing consumer satisfaction of IoT energy services. In: Troya, J., Medjahed, B., Piattini, M., Yao, L., Fernández, P., Ruiz-Cortés, A. (eds.) Service-Oriented Computing. ICSOC 2022. Lecture Notes in Computer Science, vol. 13740, pp. 395–412. Springer, Cham (2022). https://doi.org/10.1007/978-3-031-20984-0_28

5. Fang, W., et al.: Fair scheduling in resonant beam charging for IoT devices. IEEE IoT **6**(1), 641–653 (2018)
6. Abusafia, A., Lakhdari, A., Bouguettaya, A.: Service-based wireless energy crowdsourcing. In: Troya, J., Medjahed, B., Piattini, M., Yao, L., Fernández, P., Ruiz-Cortés, A. (eds.) Service-Oriented Computing. ICSOC 2022, LNCS, vol. 13740, pp. 653–668. Springer, Cham (2022). https://doi.org/10.1007/978-3-031-20984-0_47
7. Dolcourt, J.: Over-the-air wireless charging will come to smartphones (2019)
8. Lakhdari, A., et al.: Crowdsharing wireless energy services. In: CIC, pp. 18–24. IEEE (2020)
9. Feng, H., et al.: Advances in high-power wireless charging systems: overview and design considerations. TTE **6**(3), 886–919 (2020)
10. Abusafia, A., et al.: Quality of experience optimization in IoT energy services. In: ICWS, IEEE (2022)
11. Lakhdari, A., et al.: Elastic composition of crowdsourced IoT energy services. In: EAI Mobiquitous (2020)
12. Lakhdari, A., Bouguettaya, A.: Fluid composition of intermittent IoT energy services. In: SCC, pp. 329–336. IEEE (2020)
13. Abusafia, A., et al.: Incentive-based selection and composition of IoT energy services. In: IEEE SCC, pp. 304–311. IEEE (2020)
14. Mach, P., Becvar, Z.: Mobile edge computing: a survey on architecture and computation offloading. Comm. Surv. Tut. **19**(3), 1628–1656 (2017)
15. Abrishami, S., Kumar, P.: Using real-world store data for foot traffic forecasting. In: Big Data, pp. 1885–1890. IEEE (2018)
16. Zhang, J., et al.: Who is charging my phone? identifying wireless chargers via fingerprinting. IEEE Internet Things J. **8**(4), 2992–2999 (2020)
17. Gonzalez, M.C., Hidalgo, C.A., Barabasi, A.-L.: Understanding individual human mobility patterns. Nature **453**(7196), 779–782 (2008)
18. Bahutair, M., et al.: Multi-perspective trust management framework for crowdsourced IoT services. TSC **15**(4), 2396–2409 (2021)
19. Kumar, V.: Algorithms for constraint-satisfaction problems: a survey. AI Mag. **13**(1), 32–32 (1992)
20. Yang, P., et al.: Monitoring efficiency of IoT wireless charging. In: IEEE Percom (2023)
21. Yang, P., Abusafia, A., Lakhdari, A., Bouguettaya, A.: Towards peer-to-peer sharing of wireless energy services. In: Troya, J., et al. Service-Oriented Computing - ICSOC 2022 Workshops. ICSOC 2022. LNCS, vol. 13821, pp 388–392. Springer, Cham (2023). https://doi.org/10.1007/978-3-031-26507-5_38
22. Kruse, R., et al.: Data Structures and Program Design in C. Pearson, London (2007)
23. Yang, P., et al.: Energy loss prediction in IoT energy services. In: ICWS, IEEE (2023)
24. Abusafia, A., et al.: Flow-based energy services composition. In: TSC, IEEE (2023)
25. Kantarci, B., Mouftah, H.T.: Mobility-aware trustworthy crowdsourcing in cloud-centric internet of things. In: ISCC, pp. 1–6. IEEE (2014)
26. Cao, Z., et al.: Social Wi-Fi: Hotspot sharing with online friends. In: PIMRC, vol. 2015-Decem, pp. 2132–2137. IEEE, August 2015
27. Tahaei, H., Ko, K., Seo, W., Joo, S.: A QoE based trustable SDN framework for IoT devices in mobile edge computing. In: Park, J.J., Loia, V., Yi, G., Sung, Y. (eds.) CUTE/CSA -2017. LNEE, vol. 474, pp. 1147–1152. Springer, Singapore (2018). https://doi.org/10.1007/978-981-10-7605-3_183
28. Jain, V., Kumar, B.: A trusted resource allocation scheme in fog environment to satisfy high network demand. In: AJSE, pp. 1–18 (2022)
29. Ba-hutair, M.N., et al.: Multi-use trust in crowdsourced IoT services. IEEE Trans. Serv. Comput. **16**(2), 1268–1281 (2022)

Data-Driven Generation of Services for IoT-Based Online Activity Detection

Ronny Seiger[✉][iD], Marco Franceschetti[iD], and Barbara Weber[iD]

Institute of Computer Science, University of St.Gallen, St. Gallen, Switzerland
{ronny.seiger,marco.franceschetti,barbara.weber}@unisg.ch

Abstract. Business process management (BPM) technologies are increasingly adopted in the Internet of Things (IoT) to analyze processes executed in the physical world. Process mining is a mature discipline for analyzing business process executions from digital traces recorded by information systems. In typical IoT environments there is no central information system available to create homogeneous execution traces. Instead, many distributed devices including sensors and actuators produce low-level IoT data related to their operations, interactions and surroundings. We leverage this data to monitor the execution of activities and to create events suitable for process mining. We propose a framework to generate activity detection services from IoT data and a software architecture to execute these services. Our proof-of-concept implementation is based on an extensible complex event processing platform enabling the online detection of activities from IoT data. We use a running example from smart manufacturing to showcase the framework.

Keywords: Internet of Things · Business Process Management · Activity Detection Service · Complex Event Processing · Process Mining

1 Introduction

The Internet of Things (IoT) emerged as new paradigm to foster the interaction of software systems with the physical world through connected devices and objects [3]. Thereby, sensors act as new data sources providing real-time information about the execution of activities, interactions and states of devices and objects and their surroundings. In a Business Process Management (BPM) context, a Process-aware Information System (PAIS) is used to execute and monitor process and activity executions, creating digital traces in *event logs* that can be used for *process mining* [21]. In IoT, there is no central PAIS available to create event logs suitable for process mining [4,12]. Instead, we are faced with a heterogeneous set of IoT devices that are controlled by different software applications providing data on different levels of abstraction [3–5]. In this work we present a data-driven framework for generating activity detection services from IoT data. From an *Activity Signature*, which represents the sensor readings associated with

© The Author(s), under exclusive license to Springer Nature Switzerland AG 2023
F. Monti et al. (Eds.): ICSOC 2023, LNCS 14420, pp. 186–194, 2023.
https://doi.org/10.1007/978-3-031-48424-7_14

an activity, we generate services that are able to detect the occurrence of this activity using Complex Event Processing (CEP). These services are deployed to a CEP platform to generate process and activity-related events from IoT data. These high-level events serve as basis for process mining. We demonstrate and discuss the framework as a proof-of-concept from service generation to deployment and detection using examples from smart manufacturing. The approach promises to be generalizable to less automated IoT domains for analysis of manual activities, which are tracked through IoT devices (e.g., in smart healthcare). The contribution of this paper is 1) a framework for transforming IoT sensor readings into CEP-based activity detection services; and 2) an extensible software architecture enabling the use and composition of these services at runtime.

Section 2 recalls fundamentals and requirements. Section 3 presents the framework and software architecture. Section 4 discusses our approach. Section 5 elaborates on related work. Section 6 concludes the paper and presents future work.

2   Fundamentals and Requirements

Activities and Events: An *activity* is considered to be an atomic unit of work in a business process, which is executed by a (non-)human process performer [21]. *Events* are used to capture the occurrence of something of relevance that has happened in the process execution (e.g., the start of an activity). We refer to these events as *process-level events*. In contrast, events are also used to capture the state of IoT components and their surroundings *sensed* at a certain point in time [3]. We denote these as *low-level IoT events*. Moving between these levels requires event aggregation, event transformation, and event correlation [7,20].

IoT Setup: In this work, we use a smart factory model as a typical IoT environment [18]. The model simulates the execution of production activities in discrete manufacturing processes. It features different IoT components (production machines) that act as performers of process activities. Each IoT component is equipped with sensors $i_1, .., i_n$, motors $m_1, .., m_m$, output devices $o_1, .., o_o$, and machine-specific sensors (e.g., representing positions) [18]. Real-time access to the time-stamped values of these sensors and actuators (low-level IoT events) is enabled via a message broker [19]. A PAIS to record event logs is not available.

Requirements: We follow design science [16] in developing the activity detection framework. The following non-exhaustive list of non-functional requirements was derived based on the authors' experience in the field of BPM and IoT and on relevant characteristics of IoT/Cyber-physical Systems (CPS).

R1 Non-invasiveness: The approach should work non-invasively with existing IoT systems assuming they provide at least one interface to emit low-level events from their IoT components. It shall not be necessary to introduce a heavy-weight software component (e.g., a PAIS) to the IoT environment.

R2 No-code services: Activity detection services shall be added to IoT environments at runtime to be used by other components. These services shall require no implementation effort for service providers, enabling domain experts to create and deploy services for new types of activities (*extensibility*).

R3 Runtime capabilities: Components in IoT and CPS are interacting with the physical world when executing activities. Here activity detection is crucial to provide (near) real-time feedback [14]. Activity detection must work at runtime, possibly already considering partial activity occurrences.

R4 Robustness: IoT components interact with the physical world. They are subject to various (context) factors [14], which influence the activity executions regarding execution times and involved sensors/actuators. The activity detection shall be robust to a certain degree against these variations.

3   Generation of Activity Detection Services

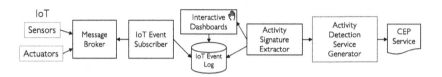

Fig. 1. Framework for generation of activity detection services from IoT data

Figure 1 presents the framework for generating activity detection services from IoT data. Low-level IoT events are published via a Message Broker. They are retrieved by an IoT Event Subscriber and persisted in an IoT Event Log. We rely on the domain expert applying an interactive method to identify and label activity executions observed in the IoT data from the IoT Event Log [18].

Activity Signatures: In [18] we introduce *Activity Signatures* to represent the IoT data associated with the execution of an activity. We assume the domain expert to identify **one** representative instance for each type of activity in the

Table 1. Activity signature for activity prototype of *Burn*

Sensor/Actuator	t_0	t_1	t_2	t_3	t_4	t_5	t_6	t_7	t_8	t_9	t_{10}	t_{11}	t_{12}
i1_pos_switch	0	0	1	1	1	1	1	1	1	0	0	0	0
i2_pos_switch	0	0	0	0	0	0	0	0	0	0	0	1	0
i5_light_barrier	1	1	1	1	1	1	1	1	1	1	1	1	1
m1_speed	0	-512	0	0	0	0	0	0	0	512	512	0	0
o7_valve	0	512	512	512	0	0	0	0	0	512	512	512	0
o8_compressor	0	0	0	0	0	0	0	0	0	0	0	0	0

Table 2. Changes in the activity signature for Burn

	Timestamps (t_i, t_{i+1})	Changes
1	(t_0, t_1)	m1_speed: $0 \to -512$; o7_valve: $0 \to 512$
2	(t_1, t_2)	i1_pos_switch: $0 \to 1$; m1_speed: $-512 \to 0$
3	(t_3, t_4)	o7_valve: $512 \to 0$
4	(t_8, t_9)	i1_pos_switch: $1 \to 0$; m1_speed: $0 \to 512$; o7_valve: $0 \to 512$
5	(t_{10}, t_{11})	i2_pos_switch: $0 \to 1$; m1_speed: $512 \to 0$
6	(t_{11}, t_{12})	i2_pos_switch: $1 \to 0$; o7_valve: $512 \to 0$

Listing 1. Query for change detection in the event sequences for timestamps (t_0, t_1)

```
@info(name="Detect-LowLevel-Pattern-1")                                    1
from every e1 = OV_1Stream, e2 = OV_1Stream[(e1.m1_speed==0 and            2
    e2.m1_speed==-512) and (e1.o7_valve==0 and e2.o7_valve==512)]
select "LowLevelPat-1" as name, "burn" as activity, "(t0,t1)" as time      3
insert into DetectedLowLevelPatterns;                                      4
```

IoT data–denoted as *Activity Prototype*–from which the signature is extracted. Table 1 contains the low-level IoT events for all sampled timestamps $t_0..t_{12}$ associated with the prototype of the *Burn* activity executed by *Oven*. The domain expert identified timestamps t_0 as start of this activity and t_{12} as its end.

Service Generation: The signature of an activity prototype including the activity-related data (start and end time, label) and low-level IoT events are retrieved from the interactive dashboards and from the IoT event log by an *Activity Signature Extractor*. This component forwards the signature into the core component of the framework, the *Activity Detection Service Generator*. We have decided to use CEP as the basic technology here as it is designed for processing high amounts of events in multiple streams in online settings (cf. 2) [6,8]. Typical CEP platforms feature an event processing language (EPL), which simplifies the development of CEP-based applications–*CEP apps* (cf. 2). We generate a CEP app for activity detection based on a given activity signature as follows.

1) Change Detection: For each pair of consecutive timestamps (t_i, t_{i+1}) the changes among the values of all sensors and actuators are derived. Table 2 shows the result for the signature of the activity prototype for *Burn*.

2) Change Translation: For each pair of consecutive timestamps, the change in the event attributes is translated into the syntax of the EPL for the *Event Sequence Pattern*, which considers changes in the attributes of consecutive events within one or multiple event streams [8]. Listing 1 shows the exemplary translation for (t_0, t_1) (Table 2, row 1) into a query of *Streaming SQL* used within *Siddhi* [6]. The attributes of two events $(e1, e2)$ on the stream related to the Oven are analyzed for the occurrence of the derived changes (line 2). We denote changes that relate to the low-level IoT events as *low-level patterns*. When one of these patterns is detected, a new event is created (line 3) and emitted on a stream for the occurrence of low-level patterns (line 4).

3) Change Sequence Detection: The low-level patterns refer to changes in an activity signature between two points in time (i.e., *one* row in Table 2). An activity is represented by the sequence of these patterns (i.e., *all* rows in Table 2). We use a *hierarchy* of events as CEP feature: the detection of the first low-level pattern (cf. Table 2, row 1) leads to a high-level event e_{H1}. The detection of the second low-level pattern (cf. Table 2, row 2) leads to a high-level event e_{H2} only if e_{H1} occurred before. This is continued by emitting e_{H3} only if e_{H2} occurred before, etc. The sequence of e_{H1} to e_{H6} represents the entire activity with e_{H1} and e_{H6} denoting its *start* and *end*. This allows us to work with *partial* activity detection (cf. 2), e.g., we can specify that 50 % of the high-level events or only e_{H1} are sufficient to identify an activity–trading off completeness and latency.

4) Activity Detection Service: The CEP app serves as event subscriber to receive low-level IoT events and as event publisher to emit process-level events to other subscribers following the publish-subscribe pattern. Additionally, we add service-based interfaces for request-response communication, transforming the CEP apps into CEP-based activity detection services. One service corresponds to one type of activity to be detected. We query the current status of tracking the activity detection as one service method. Additionally, we keep a log of detected activity executions and expose it via another method of the service API.

Service Deployment: Fig. 2 shows the software architecture for the online detection of process activities from IoT data streams. We use the CEP platform *Siddhi* as technological basis to run the activity detection services. Siddhi is itself a service providing an API for deploying and running CEP apps at runtime [6]. By using this API we are able to fully automate the generation of the activity detection services and their deployment to the CEP platform (cf. 2). The activity detection services may also be composed to create *Process Detection Services*. Assuming that either the control flow (i.e., sequence of activities) or the *Process Signature* (i.e., composition of activity signatures [18]) is known, a new CEP-based service can be generated to detect process executions in a similar way.

Online Activity Detection: Upon deployment to the CEP platform, the activ-

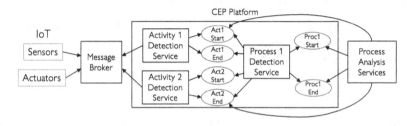

Fig. 2. Service-based software architecture for activity detection at runtime

ity detection services can be activated using the platform's API. When activated, a service establishes the connections to the external event sources (here: the IoT components) and the interfaces to be used by external event and service consumers. Low-level IoT events are processed based on the CEP queries in the services. The detected process-level events are published via the message-based interfaces to be used, e.g., for online process discovery or conformance checking.

4   Discussion

We implemented the framework as a proof-of-concept prototype. We generated 6 services to detect activities executed in our smart factory and recorded the associated low-level IoT data (cf. https://doi.org/10.5281/zenodo.8087219). We discuss how the framework fulfills requirements **R1–R4** and its limitations:

R1 (Non-invasiveness): The integration with existing IoT environments is achieved using *Siddhi* as a light-weight service that integrates seamlessly with other services using standard protocols [6]. Nevertheless, activity detection highly depends on the quality of the low-level data that the IoT components provide. Here, additional sensors and semantic knowledge about IoT components can help to increase data quality through more advanced CEP queries [18].

R2 (No-code services): The activity detection services are automatically generated and deployed to the CEP platform. The domain expert only needs to identify an activity prototype [18]. In contrast to machine learning models, the CEP apps show the patterns used in activity detection–fostering *explainability*. Extensibility is ensured as new services can be added via the CEP platform API.

R3 (Runtime capabilities): CEP platforms process high volumes of event streams at runtime [6,8]. The CEP-based activity detection services allow processing IoT event streams in near real-time and emit process-level events with CAIRO properties [9] for further process analysis. Relying on sequences of patterns in the low-level IoT events, we can also detect partial activity executions.

R4 (Robustness): External factors and different execution parameters might lead to variations in the low-level IoT events and the corresponding changes for the same activities [14]. Detecting the sequence of changes is robust against varying execution *durations* as time is not factored in. Activities of the same type showing different *change sequences* might lead to incorrect activity detections. One approach to address variations is to limit the detection to only the *low-level start* and *end patterns*. The domain expert might also resort to an underfitting approach, selecting the activity prototype that is most common for all instances.

5   Related Work

A general discussion of opportunities, challenges and an architecture for CEP as a service are presented in [11]. Prior works studied the integration of IoT with BPM, with the BPM-meets-IoT manifesto [12] at the forefront. Related works addressing process activity detection and monitoring are [13,17]. The framework proposed in this paper involves event extraction, abstraction, and correlation: Diba et al. in [7] give a general overview on existing approaches to these tasks. Related to the processing of IoT data is the work in [5], which proposes an architecture combining CEP with stream processing to realize a system able to process heterogeneous IoT data in real time. The proposed architecture, however, does not integrate automatically generated services: we aim at bridging this gap and alleviating analysts' workload. A similar intent is found in [10], with a visual framework for programming CEP apps for processing IoT data; an approach for developing IoT-based monitoring systems is also presented in [2]. While the goal of these works is to support developers by abstracting low-level design aspects, they still involve manual work in a visual programming environment. In contrast, we provide an approach for a fully automated generation of CEP apps as services. In [1], the authors propose a method to automatically generate CEP queries associated with the lifecycle transitions of control flow elements for process monitoring. The method is based on the annotation of a process model with *Monitoring Points*, and therefore assumes formalized, structured knowledge of a process. We relax this assumption and allow unstructured process knowledge, requiring only domain knowledge for recognizing an activity prototype. The approach in [15] allows automatically learning and generating CEP rules for activity detection from historical traces. However, it requires a corpus of training data for the learning phase, which might not always be available. Our approach is applicable also in cases where only one trace is available.

6   Conclusion and Future Work

Novel IoT data sources foster process analysis and decision making at runtime, even in the absence of a PAIS. However, IoT data can be too heterogeneous and too fine-grained to be suitable for process mining [4]. We propose a framework to generate services capable of detecting activity executions from IoT data at runtime. The framework relies on the domain expert to identify an activity execution in the IoT data, from which we generate and deploy an activity detection service based on CEP. The CEP platform provides means for near real-time event processing and extension mechanisms for service composition at runtime.

In future work we will apply semantic knowledge about IoT components and activities to integrate additional CEP patterns for increased robustness of the approach. We will apply the framework in larger scale manufacturing and healthcare settings to prove its feasibility and generalizability in other IoT domains.

Acknowledgments. This work has received funding from the Swiss National Science Foundation under Grant No. IZSTZ0_208497 (*ProAmbitIon* project).

References

1. Backmann, M., Baumgrass, A., Herzberg, N., Meyer, A., Weske, M.: Model-driven event query generation for business process monitoring. In: Lomuscio, A.R., Nepal, S., Patrizi, F., Benatallah, B., Brandić, I. (eds.) ICSOC 2013. LNCS, vol. 8377, pp. 406–418. Springer, Cham (2014). https://doi.org/10.1007/978-3-319-06859-6_36
2. Barricelli, B.R., Valtolina, S.: A visual language and interactive system for end-user development of internet of things ecosystems. J. Vis. Lang. Comput. **40**, 1–19 (2017)
3. Bauer, M., et al.: IoT reference model. Enabling things to talk: designing IoT solutions with the IoT architectural reference model, pp. 113–162 (2013)
4. Beerepoot, I., Di Ciccio, C., Reijers, H.A., Rinderle-Ma, S., Bandara, W., et al.: The biggest business process management problems to solve before we die. Comput. Ind. **146**, 103837 (2023)
5. Corral-Plaza, D., Medina-Bulo, I., Ortiz, G., Boubeta-Puig, J.: A stream processing architecture for heterogeneous data sources in the internet of things. Comput. Stand. Interfaces **70**, 103426 (2020)
6. Dayarathna, M., Perera, S.: Recent advancements in event processing. ACM Comput. Surv. **51**(2), 1–36 (2018)
7. Diba, K., Batoulis, K., Weidlich, M., Weske, M.: Extraction, correlation, and abstraction of event data for process mining. Wiley Interdisciplinary Rev. Data Min. Knowl. Disc. **10**(3), e1346 (2020)
8. Etzion, O., Niblett, P.: Event Processing in Action. Manning Publications, Shelter Island (2010)
9. Franceschetti, M., Seiger, R., Weber, B.: An event-centric metamodel for IoT-driven process monitoring and conformance checking. In: Business Process Management Workshops. Springer International Publishing (2023)
10. Gökalp, M.O., Koçyiğit, A., Eren, P.E.: A visual programming framework for distributed internet of things centric complex event processing. Comput. Electr. Eng. **74**, 581–604 (2019)
11. Higashino, W.A., Capretz, M.A., Bittencourt, L.F.: CEPaaS: complex event processing as a service. In: International Congress on Big Data, pp. 169–176. IEEE (2017)
12. Janiesch, C., et al.: The internet of things meets business process management: a manifesto. IEEE Syst. Man. Cybern. Mag. **6**(4), 34–44 (2020)
13. Janssen, D., Mannhardt, F., Koschmider, A., van Zelst, S.J.: Process model discovery from sensor event data. In: Leemans, S., Leopold, H. (eds.) ICPM 2020. LNBIP, vol. 406, pp. 69–81. Springer, Cham (2021). https://doi.org/10.1007/978-3-030-72693-5_6
14. Lee, E.A.: Cyber physical systems: design challenges. In: 2008 11th IEEE International Symposium on Object and Component-Oriented Real-Time Distributed Computing (ISORC), pp. 363–369. IEEE (2008)
15. Mousheimish, R., Taher, Y., Zeitouni, K.: autoCEP: automatic learning of predictive rules for complex event processing. In: Sheng, Q.Z., Stroulia, E., Tata, S., Bhiri, S. (eds.) ICSOC 2016. LNCS, vol. 9936, pp. 586–593. Springer, Cham (2016). https://doi.org/10.1007/978-3-319-46295-0_38
16. Peffers, K., Tuunanen, T., Rothenberger, M.A., Chatterjee, S.: A design science research methodology for information systems research. J. Manag. Inf. Syst. **24**(3), 45–77 (2007)

17. Rebmann, A., Emrich, A., Fettke, P.: Enabling the discovery of manual processes using a multi-modal activity recognition approach. In: Di Francescomarino, C., Dijkman, R., Zdun, U. (eds.) BPM 2019. LNBIP, vol. 362, pp. 130–141. Springer, Cham (2019). https://doi.org/10.1007/978-3-030-37453-2_12
18. Seiger, R., Franceschetti, M., Weber, B.: An interactive method for detection of process activity executions from IoT data. Fut. Internet **15**(2), 77 (2023)
19. Seiger, R., Malburg, L., Weber, B., Bergmann, R.: Integrating process management and event processing in smart factories: a systems architecture and use cases. J. Manuf. Syst. **63**, 575–592 (2022)
20. Soffer, P., et al.: From event streams to process models and back: challenges and opportunities. Inf. Sys. **81**, 181–200 (2019)
21. van der Aalst, W., et al.: Process mining manifesto. In: Daniel, F., Barkaoui, K., Dustdar, S. (eds.) BPM 2011. LNBIP, vol. 99, pp. 169–194. Springer, Heidelberg (2012). https://doi.org/10.1007/978-3-642-28108-2_19

Detecting Changes in Crowdsourced Social Media Images

Muhammad Umair$^{(\boxtimes)}$ ⓘ, Athman Bouguettaya ⓘ, and Abdallah Lakhdari ⓘ

The University of Sydney, Sydney, NSW 2006, Australia
{muhammad.umair,athman.bouguettaya,abdallah.lakhdari}@sydney.edu.au

Abstract. We propose a novel service framework to detect changes in crowdsourced images. We use a service-oriented approach to model and represent crowdsourced images as *image services*. *Non-functional attributes* of an image service are leveraged to detect changes in an image. The changes are reported in form of a *version tree*. The version tree is constructed in a way that it reflects the extent of changes introduced in different versions. Afterwards, we find semantic differences in between different versions to determine the extent of changes introduced in a specific version. Preliminary experimental results demonstrate the effectiveness of the proposed approach.

Keywords: Image as a service · Modified images · Version tree · Fake images · Fake news · Trust · Image provenance · Social media · Big data

1 Introduction

Social media has become a key platform to share news and information related to public incidents [5]. There are more than 5 billion active users on social media [10]. Social media users publish a large amount of data related to public events [12]. These social media images may contain critical information about public incidents i.e., road accidents, crime scenes, violent scenes, etc. The images related to a particular incident may have different versions uploaded on social media. Utilizing these versions can significantly facilitate the task of scene reconstruction to explore unfolding situations which might have led to the incident.

Existing work on scene reconstruction is based on image processing that is usually computationally intensive [7]. A novel technique has recently been proposed to reconstruct scenes using images' metadata [2]. It leverages the service paradigm to represent social media images and related posted information as *services*. It abstracts social media users as *social-sensors* and an image as a *social-sensor service*, abbreviated as *SocSen*. Henceforth, we use the term '*image service*' to refer to '*social-sensor service*'. The only difference between an image service and a SocSen service is that an image service comparatively contains a vast set of non-functional attributes. An image service is defined to have *functional* and *non-functional* properties. Functional attributes are the parameters

F. Monti et al. (Eds.): ICSOC 2023, LNCS 14420, pp. 195–211, 2023.
https://doi.org/10.1007/978-3-031-48424-7_15

related to the actions pertaining to the capture of an image service. Examples of functional attributes are switching picture/video modes, pressing on/off button, delayed/timed picture taking, taking panoramic shots, etc. Non-functional attributes facilitate the delivery of the purpose of taking a picture. Examples of non-functional attributes are *subject distance, camera elevation angle, resolution, location* etc. The non-functional attributes are usually available in form of different *metadata* tags. An image service can also have different versions.

Most existing work on image services is related to image service selection and composition [3,13]. An image service composition approach has been proposed to form a tapestry in the spatial aspect and a storyboard in the temporal aspect [2]. The focus of most existing work on image services has hitherto been to reconstruct a scene. A fundamental assumption in this regard has so far been that the participating image services are intrinsically *trustworthy*. However, the *trust* issue becomes paramount when image services are assumed to be crowdsourced [20]. For instance, a crime scene analysis relying on crowdsourced image services may contain untrustworthy images which may lead to wrong conclusions. Untrustworthy image services can be avoided by analyzing different versions of a social media image to find the most trustworthy version for the scene reconstruction.

Detecting untrustworthy image services has traditionally been addressed using image processing and information retrieval techniques [11]. These approaches are usually costly and computationally expensive. A preliminary service-based trust framework is proposed in [1,4] which is based on users' comments and stances in an image service to assess its credibility. However, the credibility of image services may not be completely assessed based only on the user's stance. *Fake* posts on social media can get supportive comments from other users [8]. The stance of credible users may also be biased [25]. Moreover, these approaches focus on changes in an individual image service. Whereas, multiple social media images are being forged in conjunction to manipulate information about an incident. To address these limitations, *we propose to assess trust among image services using a more objective and holistic framework consisting of changes and updates in different versions of the image services.* In this regard, we leverage non-functional attributes of different versions of an image to detect changes in image services. *we operate under the assumption that the non-functional attributes, encompassing critical technical details, can be seamlessly accessed through the image service.*

We propose a novel approach to detect changes in the non-functional attributes of an image service, as a first step towards ascertaining whether an image service is fake. Editing an image service may make it inconsistent with its non-functional attributes. An attempt to hide the facts in metadata may create some discrepancies among non-functional attributes. These discrepancies are not straightforward to identify as they are usually embedded in the non-functional attributes. We utilize these inconsistencies to detect changes in an image service. In this respect, we form different groups of image non-functional attributes such that analyzing each group collectively provides useful insights on inconsistencies.

For instance, *shutter speed*, *exposure time* and *aperture size* are the attributes that inform about the intake of light while capturing an image. Analyzing them collectively may indirectly reflect the *time of day* while the image service was captured. Changes in different versions of an image service are also investigated to get more insights about the transformation of different versions from the original image. In this regard, we assume that the provided image service is not the only version of an image upload on social media. We use an image-based search i.e., Reverse Image Search (RIS) to collect all versions of an image service available on social media. A temporal sorting is then performed to arrange them in a sequence they were uploaded on social media. We propose a novel representation of changes in an image service in terms of a *version tree*. The version tree is constructed in a way such that the information about changes in a specific version is implicit in its position/placement in the tree. Therefore, one of the main contribution of this paper is to propose a framework to build the version tree. Afterwards, a state-of-the-art semantic similarity measure is used to find semantic differences between an image and its versions. The proposed framework is a kind of image provenance analysis based only on the non-functional attributes. The proposed approach is validated on 5849 images collected from an image metadata dataset. Below, we summarize our main contributions:

- A framework is proposed to detect changes in different versions of an image service using only the non-functional attributes.
- We introduce a unique way of reporting changes in different versions of an image service in terms of a version tree. Knowledge about changes in all versions is implicit in the tree.
- The proposed framework also provides a serendipitous image provenance analysis using the version tree.

The proposed method effectively handles a typical set of modifications that are reflected in the non-functional attributes. Although, the non-functional attributes may not completely capture certain changes within the image itself, such as alterations in shades, intensity of colors, or distortion, it remains well-suited for a wide range of image modifications. It is worth noting that the proposed framework's performance may be influenced by the availability of non-functional attributes. In cases where a limited number of such attributes are available, an alternative approach involves obtaining meta-information from the social media post. While this alternative approach may be less precise due to potential questions about the accuracy of meta-information, it still offers valuable insights.

2   Motivating Scenario

We consider a scene of a plane crash in New York that happened in 2009 as our motivating scenario. Figure 1 shows evacuation of US Airways Flight 1549 as it floats on the Hudson River. This image was falsely claimed as the lost Malaysian aircraft MH370 in many social media posts in 2014. In those misleading posts, the images are original but they contain a false claim. Many state-of-the-art solutions rely on image processing to identify untrustworthy social media images [19]. These solutions focus on the content within the images and hence, they may fail to identify changes which are not in images. Moreover, these solutions consider changes in a single image and provide no knowledge about the image provenance. To address these limitations, we propose a unique way of identifying untrustworthy images by doing image provenance analysis using only the non-functional attributes of an image and its different versions. Exploring the non-functional attributes of different versions of an image may reveal a lot of inconsistencies among them. These inconsistencies reflect the *trust* of an image. For instance, in Fig. 1, metadata of different versions of an image is inconsistent and is reflective of the modifications in different versions.

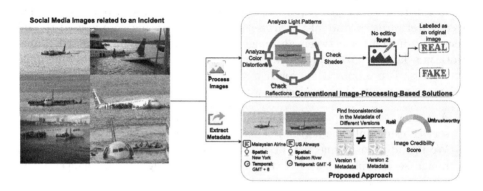

Fig. 1. Motivating Scenario

3   Related Work

Existing work on image services is related to image service selection and composition strategies. A context and direction aware spatio-temporal clustering is proposed in [3]. The proposed approach helps to compose the relevant images to form a tapestry in the spatial aspect and a story in the temporal aspect. A fundamental assumption in this work has hitherto been that images participating in scene reconstruction are trustworthy. However, image services in a crowd-sourced environment can be untrustworthy. Traditional approaches to identify untrustworthy images are based on image processing and machine learning [15]. Moreover, some text classification techniques are also available in the literature that can be employed to classify fake text with an image [23]. The aforementioned image processing based technique has high accuracies in determining the fakes in an image but require high computational power.

Some recent studies claim that a subset of *trust* can be derived using light weight service-oriented approaches [1,4]. A new image services *trust* model is proposed in [4]. The trustworthiness of an image service is measured based on the users' stance. Textual features of the image services, i.e., comments are utilized to determine the trust of the service. Another users' stance and credibility-based image service's trust model is proposed in [1]. The proposed model considers various indicators such as the stance embedded in the services' comments, their meta-data, e.g., time, along with the users' credibility. These approaches are unable to capture modifications in an image service because the misleading content on social media may receive positive comments from other users [8]. Moreover, comments from credible users can be biased.

We propose a relatively more objective and holistic approach that considers modifications and updates introduced in an image service to determine the trust of an image service. This paper focuses on detecting the changes, as a first step towards determining the trust. In this regard, different versions of an image are investigated to get more insights on image provenance details. Versions of an image are being utilized in many state-of-the-art solutions to identify changes in an image. For instance, an image provenance analysis is proposed in [6] using the metadata. Different versions of an image are investigated in [18] to explore different contexts in which the image was shared. Different versions of video clips are analyzed in [9] to detect misinformation in videos. A framework is proposed in [16] that relies on different versions of images to determine if they are shared out of context. The difference between these approaches and our proposed framework is that these approaches majorly rely on computer vision to determine fake images, whereas, our proposed approach is completely based on analyzing metadata of different versions to determine changes in an image. It is worth clarifying that the proposed framework is different from object versioning. The focus of object versioning systems is the creation and management of versions. Whereas, the focus of the proposed framework is to find image versions based on the changes in the non-functional attributes of an image service.

4   Image Service Model

We represent an image service in terms of its functional and non-functional attributes:

$$ImgServ = \{f\} \cup \{nf\} \tag{1}$$

where f and nf represent the set of functional and non-functional attributes respectively. Functional attributes represent the actions involved in capturing an image. Functional attributes can be formalized as:

$$f = \{\alpha, \mu, \gamma\} \tag{2}$$

where α represents the action of capturing an image, i.e., pressing the shutter, μ is the action to switch from one capturing mode to another i.e., switching from picture to video and vice versa, and γ represents the time delay in taking a picture. Non-functional part of an image service consists of spatio-temporal, contextual and intrinsic attributes as listed in Table 1.

$$nf = \{\zeta, \tau, c, \iota\} \tag{3}$$

where ζ represents the set of spatial attributes, τ is the set of temporal attributes, c contains contextual attributes, and ι represents intrinsic attributes. Intrinsic attributes reflect changes inside the images i.e., changes in the visual content.

Non-functional Attributes of an Image Service: We identify different non-functional attributes of an image service that may indicate changes within an image (refer to Table 1). We group the non-functional attributes into the following categories:

Table 1. Description of Non-functional Attributes

Categories	Description	Example Attributes
Spatial Features	Spatial metadata tags describe the location at which the image was taken.	GPS Coordinates
		City, Sate, Country
Temporal Features	Temporal metadata tags describe the date and time when the image was taken.	GPS Timezone Offset
		GPS Timestamp
Contextual Features	Contextual features define the context of an image. Contextual attributes may also contain the details of the ambiance.	Title
		Caption
		Headline

- *Spatial Features*: Spatial attributes represent the location where the image was captured. Modified spatial tags may be an indication of fake background.
- *Temporal Features*: Temporal attributes represent the date and time when the image was captured. Forged temporal metadata tags develop a fake story.
- *Contextual Features*: Contextual features are related to the context of an image. Fake context may support fake spatio-temporal tags of an image.

Potential Modifications in Non-functional Attributes: We propose a categorization of potential modifications that may exist in an image service. The following are the possible changes in image's non-functional attributes:

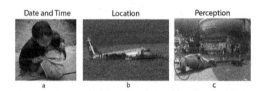

Fig. 2. Potential Changes in Images' Non-functional Attributes

- *Modified Date and Time*: Figure 2a claims two children in 2015 Nepal earthquake. It is actually a picture of two Vietnamese taken in 2007.
- *Modified Location*: Figure 2b was a viral photo in 2014 claiming the picture of the lost Malaysian MH370 plane. It turned out to be a photo of a plane crash in New York in 2009.
- *Modified Context*: Figure 2c claims a camel with limbs cut off used for begging. The camel is actually resting with legs bent under itself.

5   Proposed Framework

This Section provides details of our novel framework (shown in Fig. 3).

5.1   Feature Extraction

The proposed framework takes non-functional attributes of an image service as an input and determines whether the image is modified. The first step is to extract the meta-information available with the image which resides in the metadata of the uploaded image and the information posted with the image. We propose to perform image provenance analysis using the metadata of different versions. In this regard, we assume that the provided image is not the only version available on social media. Therefore, we utilize *Reverse Image Search* to collect all versions of the provided image along with their metadata.

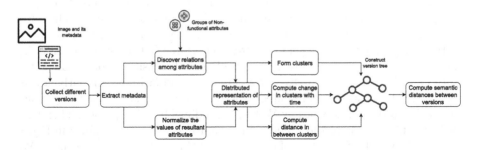

Fig. 3. The Proposed Framework

5.2   Grouping the Non-functional Attributes

We propose to determine changes in an image service using only the non-functional attributes, i.e., without using the image itself. The non-functional attributes should ideally be completely reflective of the content in the picture to correctly reflect on the changes in an image. However, state-of-the-art representation of non-functional attributes is not well-reflective of the semantics of an image. Therefore, we propose a novel representation of these non-functional attributes in form of different groups in Table 2. The attributes are placed in a same group if observing them collectively can provide some useful insights about the changes. Analyzing each group reveals useful insights about the picture. These insights are mostly related to spatio-temporal and contextual parameters of an image service. For instance, *shutter speed* and *exposure time* are placed in a same group because analyzing these attributes collectively indicates the intake of light while capturing an image. It is indirectly reflective of the *time of day* when the picture was captured.

5.3 Normalizing the Non-functional Attributes

Attributes in a group may have different units and scales. The attributes in each group are first normalized on a common scale. In this regard, we transform information provided by each group shown in Table 2 in to their normalized values. For instance, if we have three attributes i.e., ζ, τ and c, then these attributes can be normalized using the following equation:

$$\hat{\zeta} = \frac{\zeta_i - min(\zeta, \tau, c)}{max(\zeta, \tau, c) - min(\zeta, \tau, c)} \tag{4}$$

where $\hat{\zeta}$ represents the normalized value of ζ. τ and c can be normalized similarly.

5.4 Creating a Distributed Representation of Attributes

We create a distributed representation of the normalized non-functional attributes. Each attribute is represented on a high dimensional space. The number of dimensions depends on the types of attributes in a group. In most cases, spatio-temporal and contextual attributes constitute the Cartesian space. These dimensions are further composed of multiple sub-dimensions. For instance, the spatial axis is represented by two axes: longitude and latitude. Similarly, a contextual attribute can be represented as a multi-dimensional vector using either Latent Semantic Analysis or any Word-Embeddings-based approach. Therefore, the contextual axis is further divided in to multiple sub-axes as shown in Fig. 4. Afterwards, we plot the values of each group in this high dimensional space. We then cluster the attribute values of each group for a specific version. The same process is repeated for each group. As a result, we get different clusters plotted in this distributed space as shown in Fig. 4. Each cluster corresponds to a single version of an image. It is worth mentioning that there is an additional time axis (t_{upload}) in the distributed space that informs the time of upload of a specific version. Due to this axis, clusters cannot be overlapped completely. For two clusters to overlap, their versions should be uploaded at exactly the same time. The clusters projected in this space provides a holistic view of non-functional attributes of all versions. The differences in placements and shapes of clusters reflect discrepancies among the versions. Moreover, on time axis, it also reflects the evolution of different versions from an image. However, this sequence of uploads may not accurately inform about the sequence of changes introduced in

Table 2. Grouping of Non-functional Attributes

Attributes	Description
DateTimeOriginal, DateTimeDigitized, DateTime	An image metadata contains various timestamps. By comparing these timestamps, we can see whether the image has been modified.
Make, Model, Other attributes (focal length, aperture, etc.)	A camera's make and model can be compared with different attributes i.e., focal length, aperture size, and resolution etc. to check whether the camera supports these attribute values.
Aperture, Shutter speed, Exposure value	Exposure value is calculated from aperture and shutter speed. We can re-compute exposure value and compare it with the attributes.
Shutter speed, Aperture, ISO	The three pillars of exposure are shutter speed, aperture, and ISO. These three attributes are interconnected and changing one affects the others. For example, increasing the shutter speed may require a wider aperture or higher ISO to compensate for the reduced amount of light reaching the sensor. Similarly, using a narrow aperture for a deeper depth of field may require a slower shutter speed or higher ISO to compensate for the reduced amount of light.
Aperture, Exposure Time, Shutter speed, Datetime	Exposure time and shutter speed reflects the light intake in a picture. It can be transformed to the time of day based on the following: Noon: high f/stop, fast shutter speed; Night: low f/stop, slow shutter speed to let more light in. However, it depends on the environment (indoor/outdoor) and purpose of shooting.
GPS info, TimeZoneOffset, DateTime, Location	We analyze these attributes to see whether the GPS is consistent with the timezone. Moreover, we check whether the datetime is consistent with the timezone.
Datetime, GPS info, ISO, white balance and other camera settings	By using the datetime and GPS info, we can find weather conditions of the shooting location. The white balance and ISO depends on the weather.
Temperature, Humidity, Pressure, Weather	Using GPS and timestamp, we can retrieve weather information of location of shooting using online APIs.
WaterDepth, GPS info	Using GPS info, we can get the water depth information of the shooting location that can be compared with the given WaterDepth to see if it is consistent.

an image. For instance, version corresponding to cluster C3 in Fig. 4 is uploaded after C2, however, in reality, C3 may be the predecessor of C2. To address it, we transform the sequence of uploads to the sequence of changes.

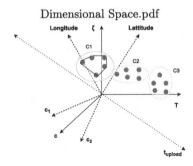

Fig. 4. Distributed Representation of Attributes

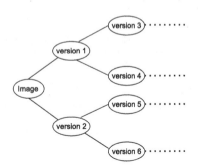

Fig. 5. Version Tree

5.5 Version Tree

Most viral fake social media images are usually related to a specific incident i.e., a road accident, a natural disaster, a man-made disaster etc. Manipulating facts about these incidents may involve sharing relevant fake posts. We consider *relevant images* and *versions of an image* to be two different entities. Relevant images contain relevant stuff but they are not originated from a same image. Whereas, an image b is a version of another image a if b is originated from a. It is crucial to analyze different versions of an image to detect changes in an image service because it provides a holistic view of manipulations about a specific incident. We propose an image provenance analysis based only on the image metadata. The provenance analysis results in a tree because of the fact that an image version can only be originated from one single image. Therefore, we propose to construct a version tree which is reflective of the modifications introduced in each version of an image. It also informs about the transformation of different attributes in that image. Figure 5 shows a generic version tree.

Definition 1: An *image b* is assumed to be version of another *image a* if

- *Image b* originated from *image a*.
- Attributes in *image a* can be transformed to attributes in *image b*. We leverage the concept of transformation matrix to analyze the nature of transform. Equation 5 shows the linear transformations of one cluster to another.

$$\Delta_t \times I_a = I_b \ where \ \Delta_t = \begin{bmatrix} w & x & . \\ y & z & . \\ . & . & . \end{bmatrix} \ and \ I_a = \begin{bmatrix} attr_1 \\ attr_2 \\ . \end{bmatrix} \quad (5)$$

where *attr* stands for attribute, I_a is an attribute matrix for image a, I_b is an attribute matrix for image b, and Δ_t is a linear transformation matrix. According to this statement, even if two images $image_b$ and $image_c$ are originated from $image_a$, if $\Delta_t \times I_b = I_c$ is satisfied, then $image_c$ will be considered as a version of $image_b$.

– Linear transformation can cover the following transformations: translation, scaling, rotation, reflection, shearing, projection, orthogonal projection and affine transformation. If the relationship between the two clusters is inherently nonlinear, a quadratic transformation (shown in Eq. 6) may better capture the underlying transformation. Therefore, we consider the matrix form of quadratic transformations if the linear transformation of an attribute matrix can not be found or is too complex. The criteria to select linear or quadratic transformation depends on the complexity of the transformation. We choose the transform with a simpler transformation matrix.

$$I_a^t \times \Delta_t \times I_a = Quadratic\ form\ of\ I_b \qquad (6)$$

We consider the complexity of Δ_t to check if $\Delta_t \times I_a = I_b$ is satisfied. The lower the complexity, higher will be the likelihood for $image_b$ to be version of $image_a$. The complexity is determined by the similarity of the transformation matrix with the identity matrix (the matrix that, if used as a transformation matrix, returns the same input matrix). However, to determine the complexity of quadratic transformation, we compute the difference of the transformation matrix with the matrix that, if used as a transformation matrix, returns quadratic form of the input matrix. It is worth mentioning that the tree proposed in Fig. 5 is implicitly directional. In the process of constructing the version tree, it automatically determines the origin of the image. However, in case of a linear tree i.e., if there is a single path from root to a leaf node, then the direction of the tree can be deduced from the order of uploads of images.

The version tree provides a holistic view of the changes introduced in different versions of an image. More importantly, it informs about the transformation of an image in to different versions that serves as a tool for image provenance analysis. The depth of each node in the tree is reflective of the extent of changes in the corresponding version. These insights can not be reflected by reporting changes in each version individually.

5.6 Heuristics to Construct a Version Tree

We propose novel heuristics to construct version tree for an image. We utilize the clustering and the transformation matrix proposed in the previous Sections to construct the version tree. The clusters projected on the Cartesian space are the groups of attributes of different versions. Each cluster corresponds to a specific group of a specific version. The distance between these clusters reflect the changes among versions. The variations in the clusters actually represent the transformation of a version in to another. As stated earlier, we consider the sequence of uploads of image versions as a baseline solution. Therefore, we propose reordering of the clusters on the time axes to make it accurate. It will result in a sequence of edits/updates in an image. The criteria to start the swapping is to check whether attributes in a version are being transformed from another version. To ensure it, we rely on the transformation matrix proposed in Eq. 6. According to Eq. 6, there will be multiple transformation matrices for each version because we have a transformation matrix for each group of non-functional attributes. Therefore, for each version, we have Δ_1 to Δ_n matrices where n represents the total number of groups. In the next step, we find the nearest neighbors for each Δ using the Frobenius Distance:

$$F_{a,b} = \sqrt{trace((a - b) \times (a - b)')} \tag{7}$$

Next, we need to decide the sequence of versions, V_1 is placed before V_2 if Δ_1 to Δ_n of V_2 can be derived using either linear or quadratic transformation. The reordering is only possible if Eq. 5 or 6 is satisfied for two consecutive versions on a time axis. Another factor, on which we rely to decide about swapping is the similarity between two versions. If the clusters shapes are similar for two distant versions, we do reordering to make them closer. The following equation is used to check this criterion:

$$if \quad C_{n+1} \cap C_n \geq C_n \cap C_{n-1} \tag{8}$$

We need a control statement to decide how many iterations are required to reach an optimal sequence of versions. In this regard, we introduce a threshold in Eq. 9 to control the reordering:

$$if \quad (C_{n+1} \cap C_n) - (C_n \cap C_{n-1}) \geq Threshold \tag{9}$$

The value of threshold is assigned in a way that the criterion for reordering becomes relatively strict after every swap. As evident from Fig. 6, the threshold follows an exponential trend. The exponential trend is reflective of the fact that the reordering becomes relatively less likely after each iteration. However, the difference/increase in threshold is not linear. Therefore, the change in threshold must be computed after each interval. We calculate this gap based on the similarity of changes between two consecutive clusters/versions on the time axis. The less similar the changes are in two versions, the more likely should be the swap, so we can assign a higher increase in threshold. The idea about the design of the threshold is presented in [22, 24].

$$\Delta Threshold \propto (\Delta C_n - \Delta C_{n-1}) \tag{10}$$

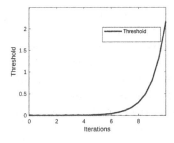

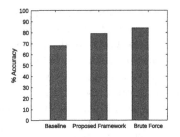

Fig. 6. Trend of Threshold   **Fig. 7.** Accuracy

This procedure constructs one branch of the version tree. To construct other branches, the same procedure is repeated for the remaining nodes/versions. Once a version tree is constructed, the consecutive version nodes can be compared using any semantic similarity measure to find its semantic difference with the previous version. Comparing different nodes in the version tree results in $\delta\zeta$, $\delta\tau$ and δc, where δ represents a change. The proposed framework is self-configurable. Whenever, it encounters a distinct type of version, it becomes part of its learning. The concept of self-configurable algorithms is presented in [21].

6   Experimentation and Results

We use a real image metadata dataset to conduct experiments [14]. The dataset contains images and videos along with their metadata. The dataset includes a wide range of images covering various subjects, scenes, and visual characteristics. We use the metadata-extractor library, which is a Java-based library for reading metadata from image files. The extracted metadata encompasses information such as camera make and model, image dimensions, capture date and time, GPS coordinates, and other technical details. Although, the dataset provides images, however, we only exploit their metadata. We use ChatGPT to generate different versions of images contained in this metadata dataset. ChatGPT can be effectively utilized to generate versions of image metadata due to its language generation capabilities and understanding of contextual information. We also leverage ChatGPT to introduce systematic changes in the sample metadata of different image versions. Instructions are provided to the ChatGPT to create different types of variations in between metadata of different versions of an image. For instance, in some images, shutter speed and exposure time have been made inconsistent. By leveraging its language generation capabilities, ChatGPT can produce altered metadata such as updated timestamps, modified camera settings, or edited descriptions, providing an indication that the image has undergone changes. Figure 8 shows a sample metadata of two versions generated by ChatGPT. It also shows inconsistencies introduced by ChatGPT. The inconsistencies are shown in highlighted text in Fig. 8.

The experiments are completely scalable as we use an API provided by OpenAI to execute text commands on ChatGPT. The API allows us to make requests to the ChatGPT model hosted on OpenAI's servers and receive responses in real-time, enabling interactive and dynamic conversations with the language model. By utilizing the API, we leverage OpenAI's infrastructure to handle the computational resources required for generating versions of an image metadata, ensuring scalability and availability. Moreover, the API provides quick responses, allowing for real-time interactions and dynamic conversations with ChatGPT. We use the HTTP POST method to send a request to the API endpoint. We structure the request payload in JSON format. The payload may contain a list of message objects with a role (either "system", "user", or "assistant") and content (the text of the message). We cluster the attributes of each version for each group. We use the clustering approach proposed in [17]. The distance between the clusters and the dissimilarities among them are leveraged to determine the transformation matrix to build the version tree.

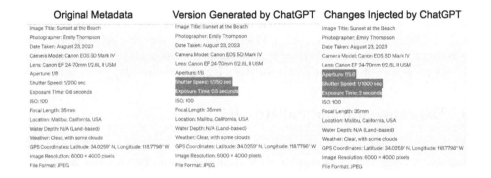

Fig. 8. A Sample Metadata and Changes Introduced by ChatGPT

Effectiveness. We report the performance of the proposed approach in terms of accuracy (in Fig. 7) and run-time. The ground truth of metadata is known from the metadata dataset. Accuracy is calculated as the percentage of correctly classified image versions. We compare our approach with a baseline and a brute force approach. Sequence of uploads of an image (the order in which the image versions were originally uploaded) on social media is regarded as the baseline solution, whereas, the brute force approach doesn't consider the criteria defined in Eq. 9 and 10. The proposed framework achieves an accuracy of 76%. Whereas, the baseline approach is correct 64% of the times. Brute force performs better than the proposed framework but at the cost of additional computations. We also report the run-time complexity and the time consumed (in nano seconds) for brute force and our proposed approach as shown in Table 3. Time complexity is computed by counting units of time. Moreover, the increase in run-time with the increase in the number of inconsistencies is reported in Fig. 9.

Table 3. Run Time Efficiency

	Baseline	Brute-force	Heuristics
Run-time Complexity	1	$O(N^2)$	$O(N^{1/2})$
Time Consumed (ns)	309	26500	15300

Comparison. We compare the accuracy of our proposed framework with a state-of-the-art that uses image metadata along with image content to perform image provenance analysis [6]. The framework proposed in [6] has three variants: a complete image-based solution; Kruskal's maximum spanning tree algorithm based only on image metadata; and Cluster-SURF which utilizes both images and their metadata. The accuracy of the approach is computed in terms of the overlap between the original version tree and the constructed version tree. Our proposed approach outperforms all variants as reflected in Fig. 10.

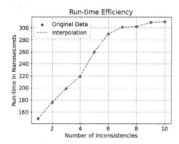

Fig. 9. Run-time Efficiency

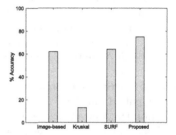

Fig. 10. Comparison with State-of-the-art

7 Conclusion

We propose a novel framework to detect changes in an image service using only the non-functional attributes. The proposed model returns a version tree for an image service. Theory of matrix transformation is leveraged in this paper to model the transformation of one image version to another. The results validate the proposed approach. This work can be further extended to investigate the detected changes to check whether the changes are constituting a fake. One aspect to consider is that run-time may increase with a larger scale of images.

Acknowledgment. This research was partly made possible by LE220100078 and DP220101823 grants from the Australian Research Council. The statements made herein are solely the responsibility of the authors.

References

1. Aamir, T., Dong, H., Bouguettaya, A.: Stance and credibility based trust in social-sensor cloud services. In: Hacid, H., Cellary, W., Wang, H., Paik, H.-Y., Zhou, R. (eds.) WISE 2018. LNCS, vol. 11234, pp. 178–189. Springer, Cham (2018). https://doi.org/10.1007/978-3-030-02925-8_13

2. Aamir, T., Dong, H., Bouguettaya, A.: Heuristics based mosaic of social-sensor services for scene reconstruction. In: Huang, Z., Beek, W., Wang, H., Zhou, R., Zhang, Y. (eds.) WISE 2020. LNCS, vol. 12342, pp. 503–515. Springer, Cham (2020). https://doi.org/10.1007/978-3-030-62005-9_36

3. Aamir, T., Dong, H., Bouguettaya, A.: Social-sensor composition for tapestry scenes. IEEE Trans. Serv. Comput. **15**(2), 1059–1073 (2020)

4. Aamir, T., et al.: Trust in social-sensor cloud service. In: 2018 IEEE International Conference on Web Services (ICWS), pp. 359–362. IEEE (2018)

5. Ali, K., Dong, H., Bouguettaya, A., Erradi, A., Hadjidj, R.: Sentiment analysis as a service: a social media based sentiment analysis framework. In: 2017 IEEE International Conference on Web Services (ICWS), pp. 660–667. IEEE (2017)

6. Bharati, A., et al.: Beyond pixels: image provenance analysis leveraging metadata. In: 2019 IEEE Winter Conference on Applications of Computer Vision (WACV), pp. 1692–1702. IEEE (2019)

7. Chae, J., et al.: Spatiotemporal social media analytics for abnormal event detection and examination using seasonal-trend decomposition. In: 2012 IEEE Conference on Visual Analytics Science and Technology (VAST), pp. 143–152. IEEE (2012)

8. Colliander, J.: "this is fake news": investigating the role of conformity to other users' views when commenting on and spreading disinformation in social media. Comput. Hum. Behav. **97**, 202–215 (2019)

9. Ganti, D.: A novel method for detecting misinformation in videos, utilizing reverse image search, semantic analysis, and sentiment comparison of metadata. Utilizing Reverse Image Search, Semantic Analysis, and Sentiment Comparison of Metadata (2022)

10. Griffis, H.M., et al.: Use of social media across us hospitals: descriptive analysis of adoption and utilization. J. Med. Internet Res. **16**(11), e3758 (2014)

11. Gupta, A., Lamba, H., Kumaraguru, P., Joshi, A.: Faking sandy: characterizing and identifying fake images on twitter during hurricane sandy. In: Proceedings of the 22nd International Conference on World Wide Web, pp. 729–736 (2013)

12. Liu, X., Troncy, R., Huet, B.: Using social media to identify events. In: Proceedings of the 3rd ACM SIGMM International Workshop on Social Media, pp. 3–8 (2011)

13. Mistry, S., Bouguettaya, A., Dong, H., Qin, A.K.: Metaheuristic optimization for long-term IAAS service composition. IEEE Trans. Serv. Comput. **11**(1), 131–143 (2016)

14. Noakes, D.: Database of images from various digital cameras (2019). https://github.com/drewnoakes/metadata-extractor-images

15. Patel, M., Padiya, J., Singh, M.: Fake news detection using machine learning and natural language processing. In: Lahby, M., Pathan, A.-S.K., Maleh, Y., Yafooz, W.M.S. (eds.) Combating Fake News with Computational Intelligence Techniques. SCI, vol. 1001, pp. 127–148. Springer, Cham (2022). https://doi.org/10.1007/978-3-030-90087-8_6

16. Qian, S., Shen, C., Zhang, J.: Fighting cheapfakes: using a digital media literacy intervention to motivate reverse search of out-of-context visual misinformation. J. Comput.-Mediated Commun. **28**(1), zmac024 (2023)

17. Rizvi, S.A., Umair, M., Cheema, M.A.: Clustering of countries for covid-19 cases based on disease prevalence, health systems and environmental indicators. Chaos Solitons Fractals **151**, 111240 (2021)
18. Saez-Trumper, D.: Fake tweet buster: a webtool to identify users promoting fake news on twitter. In: Proceedings of the 25th ACM Conference on Hypertext and Social Media, pp. 316–317 (2014)
19. Shahzad, H.F., Rustam, F., Flores, E.S., Luís Vidal Mazón, J., de la Torre Diez, I., Ashraf, I.: A review of image processing techniques for deepfakes. Sensors **22**(12), 4556 (2022)
20. Shen, C., Kasra, M., Pan, W., Bassett, G.A., Malloch, Y., O'Brien, J.F.: Fake images: the effects of source, intermediary, and digital media literacy on contextual assessment of image credibility online. New Media Soc. **21**(2), 438–463 (2019)
21. Umair, M., Afzal, B., Khan, A., Rehman, A.U., Sekercioglu, Y.A., Shah, G.A.: Self-configurable hybrid energy management system for smart buildings. In: 2018 15th International Conference on Control, Automation, Robotics and Vision (ICARCV), pp. 1241–1246. IEEE (2018)
22. Umair, M., Cheema, M.A., Afzal, B., Shah, G.: Energy management of smart homes over fog-based IoT architecture. Sustain. Comput. Inf. Syst. **39**, 100898 (2023)
23. Umair, M., Saeed, Z., Ahmad, M., Amir, H., Akmal, B., Ahmad, N.: Multi-class classification of bi-lingual SMS using Naive Bayes algorithm. In: 2020 IEEE 23rd International Multitopic Conference (INMIC), pp. 1–5. IEEE (2020)
24. Umair, M., Shah, G.A.: Energy management of smart homes. In: 2020 IEEE International Conference on Smart Computing (SMARTCOMP), pp. 247–249. IEEE (2020)
25. Zimmer, F., Scheibe, K., Stock, M., Stock, W.G.: Fake news in social media: bad algorithms or biased users? J. Inf. Sci. Theory Pract. **7**(2), 40–53 (2019)

Fast Configuring and Training for Providing Context-Aware Personalized Intelligent Driver Assistance Services

Jun Na$^{(\boxtimes)}$, Handuo Zhang, Ouwen Zhu, Weiye Xie, Bin Zhang,
and Changsheng Zhang

Software College, Northeastern University, Shenyang, China
{najun,zhangbin}@mail.neu.edu.cn

Abstract. Intelligent Driver Assistance Services (IDAS) strongly emphasize leveraging artificial intelligence (AI) technology to enhance driver assistance systems' capabilities, enabling drivers to operate their vehicles more safely and comfortably. Despite significant advancements in Advanced Driving Assistance Systems (ADAS) over the past decade, efficiently providing personalized decision-making for all kinds of drivers is still a far-reaching challenge. This paper proposes a novel framework for rapidly configuring and training context-aware personalized intelligent driver assistance services. Based on the cloud-edge collaboration, we investigate the efficient generation and updating of personalized decision models on the edge and the effective integration of personalized experiences in the cloud, forming a complete closed loop of driving experience accumulation. In addition, a method for configuring the driving environment perception model is proposed, considering the variations in different edge environments and edge equipment. This ensures the contextual relevance of the personalized decision-making model and enhances its effectiveness. The proposed approach is evaluated in CARLA, an open urban driving simulator. The results demonstrate that our approach surpasses other methods regarding training time, communication cost, and convergence.

Keywords: Edge AI · Machine learning · Context-adaptation · Personalization

This work is supported in part by National Nature Science Foundation of China under Grant No. U1908212 and Liaoning Scientific And Technological Project No. 1653137155953.

1   Introduction

Advanced driver assistance system (ADAS) aims to improve vehicle safety by repeatedly warning the driver or operating the vehicle's control system based on automatic speed adoption, lane departure assistance, collision alters, blind-spot monitoring, etc. [12]. It incorporates several technologies, such as auto-motive electronics, vehicle-to-vehicle (V2V) communication, RADAR, LIDAR, computer vision, and machine learning. Although the ADAS concept has evolved significantly over the last decade, and techniques like AI, Deep Neural Networks (DNN), and the Internet of Things (IoT) [3,17] have been rapidly developing, it is still a far-reaching challenge to efficiently generate comfortable and intu-itive driving decisions for drivers with different preferences and styles in various driving environments [1].

To provide context-aware personalized intelligent driver assistance services, an agent is required to learn diverse and dynamic configurations of the driving environment and predict optimal on the given driver's preferences. This decision making task is typically formalized as a sequential decision process and addressed by Reinforcement Learning (RL) [7,12]. Since an optimal driving decision not only requires suitability for the given environmental state but also needs to accommodate various driver preferences, RL algorithms designed to assist drivers often operate within a high-dimensional state space, which usually necessitates a sufficiently large model.

Considering the common consensus that achieving greater AI power usually requires more samples and computing resources, assigning affordable training tasks to a single vehicle becomes crucial. Unlike existing solutions that run a Deep Reinforcement Learning (DRL) [8] model independently on an edge device, we propose a novel framework to enable fast configuring and training of a context-aware personalized decision-making model, whose main features are as follows.

- We facilitate a rapid construction mechanism of context-adaptive perception systems by selecting and constructing existing data processing units (algo-rithms or DNNs) according to different model inputs. This opens up numerous possibilities for constructing complex, intelligent sensing systems in scenarios with no unified hardware setting, such as driving assistance systems, smart homes, intelligent healthcare systems, etc.
- Our approach enables edge devices to fast and personally update local decision-making models based on their specific preferences with low inference delays. Unlike traditional federated learning (FL) [10], our approach classi-fies and considers different user preferences during parameter integration to enhance the inference accuracy and convergence speed for local model updat-ing and inferencing, which is crucial for providing personalized AI services.
- We propose a novel framework to construct a closed loop from initial-izing an edge model, sharing emerging edge experiences to enhancing the global model for generating a better initial model in the future.

We provide all the key details in building and applying the proposed framework and test the actual effects in an open urban driving simulator, CARLA (https://carla.readthedocs.io/en/latest/).

2 Related Work

Reinforcement learning employs sequential actions based on the Markov Decision Process (MDP), which is widely utilized in autonomous driving applications. For instance, Min et al. [11] proposed the utilization of quantile regression DQN to control lane keeping, lane changing, and acceleration in driver assistant systems. Wu et al. [15] adopted an Actor-Critic continuous control scheme to regulate limits for enhancing flow rate and reducing emission rate. Ye et al. [18] investigated car following and lane changing behaviors of autonomous vehicles using DDDP. Huang et al. [6] developed a DDPG-based agent and experimented its ability in a human-in-the-loop dynamical simulator. However, few studies pay attention to the dynamic adaptability and transferability of a well-trained model.

Besides, achieving greater AI power usually requires more samples and computing resources, which is often unfeasible for a single-end device. To get a smaller model, some researchers propose compressing a pre-trained "large" DNN into a smaller one [2] that may compromise the accuracy of machine learning inference. Conversely, other researchers suggest partitioning a DNN into several small pieces and deploying them distributedly [13,16]. However, it may incur additional communication costs.

To share edge samples and experiences, Federated Learning (FL) [10] has been widely adopted. FL enables a group of distributed participators to collaboratively train a powerful global model on their private dataset, regardless of whether they possess identical features or samples [10]. However, it is challenging for conventional FL algorithms to obtain an effective global model if their participants' data are unbalanced and not Independent and Identically Distributed (Non-IID) [5,14,19].

A feasible personalized driving assistance service must generate comfortable and intuitive driving decisions based on perceived driving context according to the installed sensors and specific driver preferences. As far as we know, this issue still needs to be solved.

3 Our Basic Idea

To facilitate context-aware personalized DNN configuration and updating, we propose a framework based on federated reinforcement learning (FRL) [20]. As depicted in Fig. 1, it comprises two primary components: a parameter server and an edge device.

As illustrated in Fig. 1, the parameter server comprises three mutually independent components: a single input processing unit library, a decision parameters library, and a model skeleton.

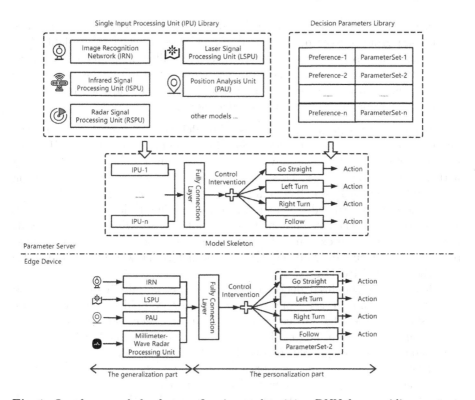

Fig. 1. Our framework for fast configuring and training DNN for providing context-aware personalized intelligent driving assistance services.

- The model skeleton defines the fundamental structure of an edge model. The inputs from various driving environment sensors are incorporated into the model skeleton for personalized driving assistance. Each input will be processed by its corresponding input processing unit (IPU), and the outputs of all these IPUs will then be merged by the fully connected layer in the model skeleton. The control intervention component receives the user's real-time driving behavior, such as going straight, turning left or right, and following. The model generates control actions based on different driving behaviors, including velocity, acceleration, steering angle, etc.
- The single IPU library contains various types of IPUs that an edge device can leverage, including image recognition networks (IRN), infrared signal processing units (ISPU), radar signal processing units (RSPU), laser signal processing units (LSPU), and position analysis units (PAU), etc. Every IPU within the library can be an existing DNN or an algorithm. It can be initialized during parameter server construction, or an edge device can contribute later. Then, these common IPUs can be selected and composed into a given edge model during initialization.

– The decision parameters library maintains multiple sets of model parameters that are grouped according to users' preferences. It clusters available user behaviors into several groups, each capturing a different preference for generating personalized driving actions. Therefore, when initializing a new edge model, one of these parameter sets will be selected and applied to initialize the decision-making network of the edge model.

Therefore, when initiating a new edge model, we can start assembling the input processing part of the edge model by matching corresponding IPUs to sensors installed on the edge device. For instance, if a smart car is equipped with an onboard camera, a radar sensor, and a position sensor, the corresponding IRN, LSPU, and PAU (as depicted in Fig. 1) will be selected from the IPU library and integrated into the edge model. Suppose the edge device is equipped with additional sensors, such as a millimeter-wave radar sensor whose processing unit is not included in the existing IPU library. In that case, the edge device must provide the corresponding processing unit and determine whether to contribute it to the existing IPU library.

Then, the personalized decision-making part is initialized by selecting an appropriate parameter set from the existing library of decision parameters. More specially, the edge device matches the most closely corresponding decision parameter set according to the edge user preference initially collected. The parameter set is subsequently imported into the edge model to accomplish the initialization of decision network parameters in the edge model. Additionally, during the operation of the edge device, the model is adjusted through user interaction to better align with specific preferences. And these adjustments will be shared to update the global decision parameters library further.

In the following sections, we will provide a comprehensive description of the design and implementation of our framework.

4   The DRL-Based Personalized Driving Assisted Model

We adopt DDPG [9] as the fundamental network. It is a model-free Actor-Critic based reinforcement learning approach that can be effectively applied to continuous action space. According to the Markov Decision Process (MDP) definition, a tuple $< S, A, P, R, \gamma >$ can be used to model a decision-making model. Here, S is the state set of a given environment, A is the action set that contains all possible actions the agent can select and perform, P is the probability of transition from one state to another, R is the reward function, and γ is the discount factor.

To ensure compatibility and generalization, we choose the Global Navigation Satellite System (GNSS) sensor and the Inertial Measurement Unit (IMU) sensor as inputs. Therefore, the state of a personalized driving-assisted model is designed as follows.

$$State :< Speed, Accx, Accy, MDistance, LDistance, RDistance, Compass > \tag{1}$$

To adhere to the design principles of action space, which includes integrity, simplicity, and legality, we categorize the actions in a personalized driving assistance model into two distinct parts: steering amplitude (Steer) and acceleration (Acceleration), shown in Eq. 2.

$$Action = \begin{cases} Steer, & 0 < Steer < 1 \\ Acceleration, & -1 < Acceleration < 1 \end{cases}. \tag{2}$$

Theoretically, as the accelerator and brake cannot be pressed simultaneously, we combine the amplitude of the accelerator pedal and the amplitude of the brake pedal into the acceleration term. $[0,1]$ is the amplitude of the accelerator, and $[-1,0)$ is the amplitude of the brake pedal.

Feedback reward plays a crucial role in the design of reinforcement learning algorithms. In complex tasks, it is impractical for agents to freely explore and obtain the main reward due to the vast state set and infinite action space, often leading to non-convergence. Therefore, sub-rewards should be introduced to guide agents toward continuously achieving task objectives. It is necessary to deconstruct the task objective and allocate appropriate rewards or penalties at each step to enhance the likelihood of the agent obtaining the primary reward. Based on repeated experiments, the reward values in the personalized driving-assisted model are defined as follows:

$$R_{steer}(c) = \begin{cases} abs(steer) \times 10, & \text{Steering wheel angle is in optimal range} \\ -abs(steer) \times 10, & otherwise \end{cases} \tag{3}$$

$$R_{location}(c) = \begin{cases} 10, & \text{car is at the best position} \\ -abs(location - bestlocation), & otherwise \end{cases} \tag{4}$$

$$R_{collision}(c) : \begin{cases} -2000, & \text{car crashed} \\ 0, & otherwise \end{cases} \tag{5}$$

$$R_{cross}(c) = \begin{cases} -100, & \text{car crossed the line} \\ 1, & otherwise \end{cases} \tag{6}$$

$$R_{speed}(c) = \begin{cases} s < s_o - 5, & \begin{cases} -10, throttle = 0 \text{ or in } r_o \\ vs + 5, throttle < r_o \\ vs + 10, throttle \text{ is in } r_o \end{cases} \\ s <= s_o, & \begin{cases} -5, & braking > 0 \\ vs., & braking = 0 \end{cases} \\ s > s_o, & \begin{cases} -10, & throttle > 0 \\ vs + 5, & braking \text{ is not in } r_o \\ vs + 10, & braking \text{ is in } r_o \end{cases} \end{cases} \tag{7}$$

The variable c is the branch network selected by the control intervention. R_{steer} is steering angle reward value, $R_{location}$ is car location reward value, $R_{collision}$ is obstacle collision reward value, R_{cross} is crossing line reward value, and R_{speed} is speed reward value. The variable s is speed, s_o is the optimal speed, and r_o is the optimal range. The steering angle, speed, and reward value obtained by obstacle collision can all directly reflect the agent's decision in the current state.

In experiments, we found that more than these are needed to make the car drive usually because as long as it avoids obstacles, it will not get negative rewards. The car often takes an S-shaped route during driving, which does not meet the set task objectives. Additional reward values are needed to limit the driving route of the car, so this paper adds the position reward value and the crossing line reward value on the basis, and the final reward value $R_{total}(c)$ is the sum of the five reward values. The total reward value is shown below.

$$R_{total}(c) = R_{steer}(c) + R_{speed}(c) + R_{location}(c) + \\ R_{collision}(c) + R_{cross}(c) \tag{8}$$

5   FRL-Based Edge Experiences Fusion

According to the characteristics of federated learning, models with similar environments are more likely to learn from each other effectively. Therefore, we adopt model clustering on edge personal driving styles by analyzing driving behaviors collected at each edge. Then, federated learning is conducted among clients in the same cluster to improve the learning effect.

On an edge device, we proposed the following model updating strategy (Eq. 9) to control the cost of updating the local model.

$$CParm = a \times SParm + \\ (1 - a) \times CParm \begin{cases} a = \alpha_1, RDiff < threshold_1 \\ a = \alpha_2, RDiff < threshold_2 \\ a = 0, \text{otherwise} \end{cases} \tag{9}$$

Here, $CParm$ is the personal experience parameter of an edge device. $SParm$ is the original model parameter from the parameter server. a is the fusion ratio of model parameters. $RDiff$ is the difference between the reward value of the current round of reinforcement learning and the last round. $threshold_1$ and $threshold_2$ are the proportional control threshold.

An edge device determines the retention of its differential experience. Suppose the increased amplitude $RDiff$ of the local model in interaction with the environment is somewhat higher than that obtained in the last round. Then, selective retention of part of the differential experience occurs according to the self-defined increase amplitude in the current model. The fusion ratio of model parameters a controls the proportion of edge personal parameters and global decision-making parameters in the new model.

Considering the different improvement amplitudes of decision-making models across edge devices, we propose a model update filtering approach based on reward value fluctuation amplitude, where only selected local models will be considered to update corresponding global decision-making models. The fluctuation range of reward value is determined as shown in Formula 10, where $Rlist$ is the set of model reward values.

$$FluctuationDetection = \sqrt{\frac{\sum_{i=1}^{n}(r_i - \bar{r})^2}{n}}$$
$$Rlist = [r_1, r_2, \cdots, r_n]$$
(10)

Then, the global decision-making model is updated through weighted fusion based on the selected model reward values, as shown in Eq. 11.

$$ServerParm = \sum_{i=1}^{n} \frac{r_i}{R} ClientParam_i \quad R = \sum_{i=1}^{n} r_i \qquad (11)$$

6 Evaluation

To validate the applicability and performance of our approach, we implement, train, and test the personalized driving assistance model in the open urban driving simulator, CARLA [4].

6.1 Experiment Setup

Running an FRL algorithm requires a parameter server and multiple edge devices. We use a desktop computer with an I5-7200u processor, 8GB memory, and an RTX 2080Ti GPU as the parameter server, primarily handling model training, parameter fusion, model delivery, and other related operations. Meanwhile, we deploy virtual machines as edge devices to execute the CARLA simulator (version 0.9.11), dynamically construct personalized driver assistance models, and run online learning and parameter uploading. All the programs are written in Python 3.7 on TensorFlow.

CARLA is an open-source autonomous driving simulator that facilitates the construction of environments, model training, and testing for autonomous driving systems. The supported sensor types encompass camera, LIDAR, GNSS, GPS, and IMU. The GNSS and IMU sensors are predominantly employed in this paper.

Various evaluation criteria exist for reinforcement learning algorithms, such as survival time in car poles, number of hits in shooting games, and confrontation duration with opponents in table tennis games. Nevertheless, the most prevalent criterion is an episode-reward graph that exhibits the amplitude and fluctuation degree of reward values across episodes. In addition, we also evaluate communication times and transmission costs during model downloading and updating, the convergence speed of an edge model, as well as training duration for an edge model. The proposed algorithm's robustness is tested on three driving scenarios: straight driving, left turns, and right turns.

6.2 Performance of Edge Model Initialization and Online Training

Experiment Settings. To assess the performance of initializing and online training for an edge personalized decision-making model, we experiment by comparing downloading a suitable pre-trained model with training a model from scratch. We have slightly modified the driving preferences of the edge device in three driving scenarios - going straight, turning left, and turning right - from those of the pre-trained model. Such slight differences can enhance the applicability of deploying a pre-trained model on an edge device. As illustrated in Table 1, the modifications mainly involve five aspects: optimal speed (OS), steering angle (SA), gas pedal amplitude (GPA), brake pedal amplitude (BPA), and distance to the road center (DTRC).

Table 1. Preferences setting in the pre-trained model and the edge model

Driving scenario	Model	OS	SA	GPA	BPA	DTRC
Straight driving	pre-trained model	25	0.3	0.6	0.6	0.5
	edge model	27	0.2	0.7	0.6	0.6
Left turn	pre-trained model	20	0.5	0.5	0.6	0.5
	edge model	18	0.4	0.4	0.6	0.6
Right turn	pre-trained model	25	0.3	0.6	0.6	0.5
	edge model	27	0.2	0.7	0.6	0.6

In each driving scenario, we conducted five experiments with 40 episodes per experiment and plotted the corresponding episode-reward curve graph. Additionally, we compared the average convergence rounds, reward values, and training duration under different scenarios.

Experimental Results and Analysis. The episode-reward curves for the three scenarios of going straight, turning left, and turning right are presented in Fig. 2, Fig. 3, and Fig. 4, respectively.

The comparison of episode rewards for straight driving, as shown in Fig. 2(a), indicates that our approach can achieve a higher reward value within the same number of episodes than basic RL. Additionally, our approach reaches its first highest reward value approximately 5–10 episodes earlier than basic RL. Our approach also attains higher rewards in the other two driving scenarios, namely left and right turns. However, as the effects are not as pronounced as those observed during straight driving, we have omitted the curves that do not exhibit significant differences. By the way, the abnormal reward values at episodes 15 and 30 in Fig. 2(a) are caused by the exploration in RL, which is an inherent problem of RL.

Specifically, Table 2 compares average convergence rounds, reward values, and training duration (TD) across various driving scenarios.

The comparison presented in Table 2 demonstrates that our approach can achieve convergence 2 to 16 rounds faster than basic RL and its training duration for 40 episodes is reduced by 20 to 40 s. This improvement is attributed to

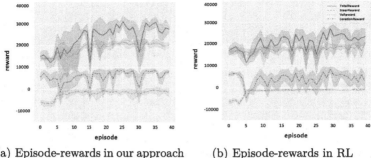

(a) Episode-rewards in our approach   (b) Episode-rewards in RL

Fig. 2. Episode-reward comparison between our approach and traditional RL under straight driving

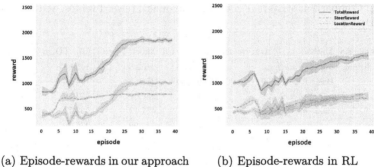

(a) Episode-rewards in our approach   (b) Episode-rewards in RL

Fig. 3. Episode-reward comparison between our approach and traditional RL under left turn

freezing three layers' parameters during online training, which involves approximately 600 parameters. Although this number may seem small, it significantly saves computing resources and training time. Furthermore, this operation results in a reduction of 217 KB in communication costs. In summary, the more network parameters shared by an edge device, the greater the improvement effect of our algorithm.

6.3 Performance of Edge Personal Experiences Fusion

Experiment Settings. To evaluate the performance of personal experiences fusion of our approach, we established a collaborative environment consisting of one pre-trained model and three distinct edges with varying driving preferences, as outlined in Table 3. Similarly, we continue to utilize optimum speed (OS), steering angle (SA), gas pedal amplitude (GPA), brake pedal amplitude (BPA), and distance to the road center (DTRC) to characterize specific driving preferences. Based on this, we compare the performance of our approach, the basic FRL, and the basic RL.

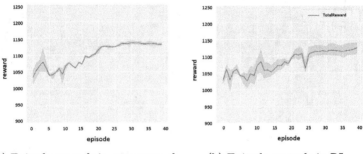

(a) Episode-rewards in our approach   (b) Episode-rewards in RL

Fig. 4. Episode-reward comparison between our approach and traditional RL under right turn

Table 2. Comparison of average convergence rounds, reward values, and training duration (TD)

Driving scenario	Method	Avg. rounds	Avg. reward	Max TD(sec.)	Min TD(sec.)	Avg. TD(sec.)
Straight driving	our approach	14	27006.30	2162.80	1619.87	1930.47
	Basic RL	30	27167.60	2136.33	1642.49	1971.24
Left turn	our approach	22	1507.44	558.61	553.42	557.13
	Basic RL	38	1521.19	582.17	563.71	573.91
Right turn	our approach	20	1104.00	236.99	236.20	236.60
	Basic RL	22	1106.03	258.14	238.56	244.27

In this experiment, we also conducted 40 experiments for each driving scenario: straight driving, left turn, and right turn. As our approach and the basic FRL involve federated learning, every edge was trained for 50 episodes in each experiment. We selected five data groups from these results as training data to perform experience fusion. In the basic RL experiment, each edge was trained 50 episodes under its corresponding optimization objective after downloading the pre-trained model. Based on the experimental results, episode-reward curves were drawn respectively, and the model's training time, communication frequency, and average reward value were calculated and compared.

Experimental Results and Analysis. The episode reward curves for each of the three edges in the straight driving scenario are depicted in Fig. 5, Fig. 6, and Fig. 7, respectively. Each chart within the figures, from left to right, represents the episode reward curves of our approach, basic FRL, and basic RL.

As depicted in Fig. 5, Fig. 6, and Fig. 7, the initial reward value of each edge is determined by its preference, resulting in distinct values. For instance, the total initial reward value for Edge-1 is approximately 20,000, while that of Edge-2 is around 10,000, and that of Edge-3 is roughly 22,000. In addition, based on these episode-reward curves, our approach exhibits significantly improved convergence speed and total reward value compared to basic FRL and RL algorithms. Specif-

Table 3. Preferences setting of the collaborative environment of one pre-trained model and three distinct edges

Driving Scenario	Model	OS	SA	GPA	BPA	DTRC
Straight-driving	Pre-trained model	25	0.3	0.6	0.6	0.5
	Edge-1	27	0.2	0.7	0.6	0.6
	Edge-2	33	0.2	0.6	0.7	0.4
	Edge-3	30	0.3	0.6	0.6	0.5
Left-turn	Pre-trained model	20	0.5	0.5	0.6	0.5
	Edge-1	18	0.4	0.4	0.6	0.6
	Edge-2	25	0.7	0.7	0.8	0.4
	Edge-3	22	0.5	0.5	0.6	0.5
Right-turn	Pre-trained model	25	0.3	0.6	0.6	0.5
	Edge-1	27	0.2	0.7	0.6	0.6
	Edge-2	33	0.2	0.6	0.7	0.4
	Edge-3	30	0.3	0.6	0.6	0.5

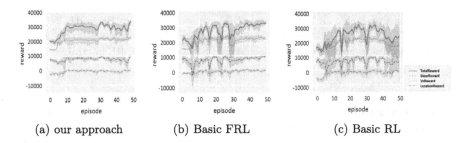

(a) our approach   (b) Basic FRL   (c) Basic RL

Fig. 5. Episode-rewards of our approach, basic FRL, and basic RL in straight-driving on edge-1.

ically, we set the convergence condition in this experiment as when the average reward value obtained over five consecutive episodes meets or exceeds the pre-trained model's reward value. The specific comparison parameters for straight-driving scenarios are presented below.

The column "Avg. Rounds" in Table 4 denotes the algorithm's convergence rate under consideration. Compared with the average convergence rounds on three edges, it is observed that our approach exhibits the fastest convergence speed, which is approximately twice as fast as basic RL and slightly faster than basic FRL. From the perspective of local model updates and cloud-edge communication triggered by these updates, our approach outperforms basic FRL significantly, resulting in a reduction of approximately one-third in total training time for edge models.

We get similar conclusions in the other two scenarios, and the specific comparison parameters for the left turn and right turn are presented in Table 5.

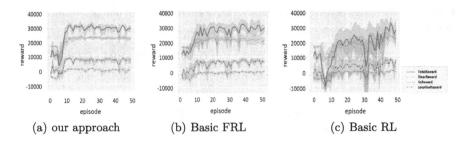

(a) our approach   (b) Basic FRL   (c) Basic RL

Fig. 6. Episode-rewards of our approach, basic FRL, and basic RL in straight-driving on edge-2.

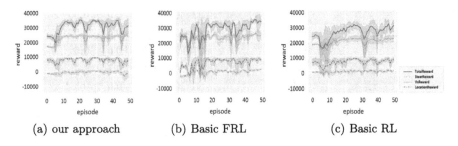

(a) our approach   (b) Basic FRL   (c) Basic RL

Fig. 7. Episode-rewards of our approach, basic FRL, and basic RL in straight-driving on edge-3.

As observed from the specific values in Table 5, it can be noted that while our approach maintains a faster convergence rate and lower communication cost in left-turn and right-turn scenarios, the impact is not as evident as in straight-driving scenarios. This is closely related to the complexity of decision-making and data volume across these three scenarios. For example, when driving straight, the agent interacts with the environment an average of 894 times per episode. In the case of a left turn, the agent interacts with the environment an average of 445 times per episode which is only 170 in a right turn. This results in varying amounts of data obtained per episode across the three driving scenarios, which can impact the algorithm's learning effect. Hence, we filter out dimensions with minimal reward changes and only present those with significant variations in the above figures.

Table 4. Performance comparison on convergence speed and communication cost of our approach, basic FRL, and basic RL for straight driving

Device	Algorithm	Avg.Rounds	Avg.Updates	Avg.Edge-Cloud Comm
Edge-1	our approach	11	2.6	25
	Basic FRL	12	4.6	36
	Basic RL	24	-	-
Edge-2	our approach	12	2.6	16
	Basic FRL	12	5.2	27
	Basic RL	44	-	-
Edge-3	our approach	9	2.4	23
	Basic FRL	11	5.4	32
	Basic RL	20	-	-

Table 5. Performance comparison on convergence speed and communication cost of our approach, basic FRL and basic RL for left turn and right turn

Device	Algorithm	Left-Turn			Right-Turn		
		Avg.Rounds	Avg.Updates	Avg.EC Comm	Avg. Rounds	Avg.Updates	Avg.EC Comm
Edge-1	our approach	23	1.2	8	12	1	7
	basic FRL	23	2.2	11	20	1.8	9
	basic RL	30	-	-	22	-	-
Edge-2	our approach	21	1	6	13	1	8
	basic FRL	24	1.8	13	19	2.2	11
	basic RL	25	-	-	22	-	-
Edge-3	our approach	18	1.2	9	14	1.2	8
	basic FRL	24	2.0	14	19	1.4	8
	basic RL	27	-	-	24	-	-

7   Conclusion

This paper proposes a novel framework for fast configuring context-aware personalized intelligent driver assistance services. It constructs an edge network model skeleton based on reinforcement learning. It divides the network into generalization and personalized parts to emphasize the reuse of existing input processing units while addressing personalized decision requirements. We compare the decision-making effects of our approach, basic FRL, and basic RL in three scenarios: straight, left, and right turns in the CARLA simulator. The experimental results demonstrate that our approach has a significantly faster convergence speed than basic RL. Additionally, compared to basic FRL, there are fewer local model updates and cloud-edge collaboration communication times, reducing communication costs. In the future, we plan to consider other types of inputs, such as images and videos, to investigate the scalability and efficiency of our approach.

References

1. Cao, D., et al.: Future directions of intelligent vehicles: potentials, possibilities, and perspectives. IEEE Trans. Intell. Veh. **7**(1), 7–10 (2022). https://doi.org/10.1109/TIV.2022.3157049
2. Choudhary, T., Mishra, V., Goswami, A., Sarangapani, J.: A comprehensive survey on model compression and acceleration. Artif. Intell. Rev. **53**(7), 5113–5155 (2020)
3. Deng, Q., Söffker, D.: A review of hmm-based approaches of driving behaviors recognition and prediction. IEEE Trans. Intell. Veh. **7**(1), 21–31 (2021)
4. Dosovitskiy, A., Ros, G., Codevilla, F., Lopez, A., Koltun, V.: Carla: an open urban driving simulator. In: Conference on Robot Learning, pp. 1–16. PMLR (2017)
5. Hahn, S.J., Jeong, M., Lee, J.: Connecting low-loss subspace for personalized federated learning. In: Proceedings of the 28th ACM SIGKDD Conference on Knowledge Discovery and Data Mining, pp. 505–515 (2022)
6. Huang, W., Braghin, F., Arrigoni, S.: Autonomous vehicle driving via deep deterministic policy gradient. In: International Design Engineering Technical Conferences and Computers and Information in Engineering Conference, vol. 59216, p. V003T01A017. American Society of Mechanical Engineers (2019)
7. Kiran, B.R., et al.: Deep reinforcement learning for autonomous driving: a survey. IEEE Trans. Intell. Transp. Syst. **23**(6), 4909–4926 (2021)
8. Li, Y.: Deep reinforcement learning: an overview. arXiv preprint arXiv:1701.07274 (2017)
9. Lillicrap, T.P., et al.: Continuous control with deep reinforcement learning. arXiv preprint arXiv:1509.02971 (2015)
10. Liu, J., et al.: From distributed machine learning to federated learning: a survey. Knowl. Inf. Syst. **64**(4), 885–917 (2022)
11. Min, K., Kim, H., Huh, K.: Deep distributional reinforcement learning based high-level driving policy determination. IEEE Trans. Intell. Veh. **4**(3), 416–424 (2019)
12. Nidamanuri, J., Nibhanupudi, C., Assfalg, R., Venkataraman, H.: A progressive review: emerging technologies for ADAS driven solutions. IEEE Trans. Intell. Veh. **7**(2), 326–341 (2021)
13. Ren, W.Q., et al.: A survey on collaborative DNN inference for edge intelligence. Mach. Intell. Res. 1–25 (2023)
14. Tan, A.Z., Yu, H., Cui, L., Yang, Q.: Towards personalized federated learning. IEEE Trans. Neural Netw. Learn. Syst. (2022)
15. Wu, Y., Tan, H., Ran, B.: Differential variable speed limits control for freeway recurrent bottlenecks via deep reinforcement learning. arXiv preprint arXiv:1810.10952 (2018)
16. Xu, D., He, X., Su, T., Wang, Z.: A survey on deep neural network partition over cloud, edge and end devices. arXiv preprint arXiv:2304.10020 (2023)
17. Xu, X., Li, H., Xu, W., Liu, Z., Yao, L., Dai, F.: Artificial intelligence for edge service optimization in internet of vehicles: a survey. Tsinghua Sci. Technol. **27**(2), 270–287 (2021)
18. Ye, Y., Zhang, X., Sun, J.: Automated vehicle's behavior decision making using deep reinforcement learning and high-fidelity simulation environment. Transp. Res. Part C Emerg. Technol. **107**, 155–170 (2019)
19. Zhang, J., et al.: Fedala: adaptive local aggregation for personalized federated learning. arXiv preprint arXiv:2212.01197 (2022)
20. Zhuo, H.H., Feng, W., Lin, Y., Xu, Q., Yang, Q.: Federated deep reinforcement learning. arXiv preprint arXiv:1901.08277 (2019)

Fused User Preference Learning for Task Assignment in Mobile Crowdsourcing

Yue Ma, Li Ma, Xiaofeng Gao$^{(\boxtimes)}$, and Guihai Chen

MoE Key Lab of Artificial Intelligence, Department of Computer Science and
Engineering, Shanghai Jiao Tong University, Shanghai 200240, China
{ma_yue,mali-cs}@sjtu.edu.cn, {gao-xf,gchen}@cs.sjtu.edu.cn

Abstract. With the development of GPS-enabled smart devices and
wireless networks, mobile crowdsourcing (MCS) has received wide attention in assigning location-sensitive tasks to mobile users. The task assignment problem, in which tasks are released on the platforms and then
assigned to available users, is a fundamental problem in MCS. However, existing works generally consider users' category preference and
mobile preference separately. Ignorance of the correlation between them
could lead to poor assignment results. To this end, We propose a framework, *Task Assignment with User Preference Learning*, which consists
of two components: 1) *Fused User Preference Learning* (FUP); and 2)
Preference-Based Task Assignment. The first component called FUP is a
fusion of task-category preference learning and spatial-temporal preference learning. For task-category preference learning, we propose a graph
session-based learning model with attention components to exploit users'
sparse historical records. To our knowledge, we are the first to use a
graph session-based learning model to explore task-category preference
in MCS. Meanwhile, we propose an efficient function metric to characterize the spatial-temporal preference of users. The second component aims
to achieve effective task assignment, in which we give higher priorities to
users with higher preference scores for the tasks. Extensive evaluations of
real data show the effectiveness and efficiency of the proposed solutions.

Keywords: Task assignment · Mobile crowdsourcing · Preference
learning · Session-based learning

1 Introduction

Mobile crowdsourcing (MCS) is an emergent working mode that decomposes
sophisticated tasks into multiple small and easy tasks and then assigns these
tasks to numerous mobile users (i.e., crowd workers). In recent years, MCS has
become a critical building block for the emerging Internet-of-Things in large-scale
sensing applications, such as road condition monitoring [3], crowdsourcing-aided
positioning systems [8], and smart city planning [1].

The major challenge of MCS is how to assign large-scale tasks to users, i.e.,
task assignment. Task assignment is the process of allocating tasks with unique

© The Author(s), under exclusive license to Springer Nature Switzerland AG 2023
F. Monti et al. (Eds.): ICSOC 2023, LNCS 14420, pp. 227–241, 2023.
https://doi.org/10.1007/978-3-031-48424-7_17

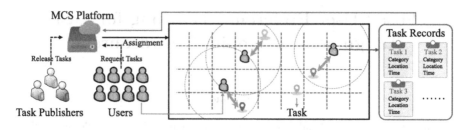

Fig. 1. Illustration of Task Assignment in MCS

characteristics, such as category and location, to users in service who also possess specific characteristics, such as serviceable distance and personal preference. The mentioned task-user matching process is implemented on the MCS platform, as shown in Fig. 1. The MCS platform acts as a broker between the task publishers and users. The task publishers release tasks to be completed with various requirements to the platform, and users participate through the MCS platform. After that, the platform matches suitable tasks with users according to their completed task records, including category, location, and completed time.

There are many existing works on task assignment that attempt to maximize the number of completed tasks [21], maximize the profit of platform [17], or maximize the utility of platform [18]. These works all share the underlying presumption that users are willing to complete the tasks given to them. In practice, this assumption could oversimplify the complicated behaviors of users [5]. Actually, a user may not complete the assigned task honestly and promptly when he/she is not interested, which cannot guarantee the quality of task result. Besides, users' historical records are usually sparse. To preserve their privacy, most users may not be ready to submit all of their mobile data, so the preferred category and spatial-temporal information are recorded only when the user performs a task. Therefore, it is challenging to precisely profile user preferences based on limited records. To tackle these issues, we construct category session graphs and propose a graph session-based model to capture users' dynamic interest patterns.

Meanwhile, most works on task assignment generally consider users' category preference and mobile preference separately [20,22]. Note that conventional assignment models infer user preferences based on past task-performance patterns or explicit feedback [9]. Whereas, in MCS, besides the metric of the users' task-category preferences, we also need to take the spatial-temporal information of historical task records into consideration, because tasks need to be accomplished in a specific location during a valid time. Meanwhile, users have their own mobile preference and prefer to perform tasks in the vicinity of their frequent locations. Thus, it is necessary to jointly consider task-category preference and spatial-temporal preference in task assignment.

To address these challenges, we propose a task assignment framework that considers task-category and spatial-temporal preference to maximize the ratio of completed tasks. This framework, called *Task Assignment with User Preference Learning*, consists of two components: **F**used **U**ser **P**reference Learning

(FUP) and *Preference-Based Task Assignment.* FUP is a fusion of task-category preference learning and spatial-temporal learning. Initially, we transform users' historical records into session graphs and propose a graph session-based learning model to investigate task-category preference. To our best knowledge, this is the first work in MCS that learns users' preferences based on the graph session-based model. Furthermore, we propose an efficient function metric to obtain more auxiliary information for spatial-temporal preference. In the task assignment component, we propose a preference-based greedy algorithm and a preference-based optimized Kuhn-Munkras (KM) algorithm to achieve effective assignment.

To summarize, the main contributions of this work are listed as follows:

- We design a preference learning model, called FUP, which is a fusion of task-category and spatial-temporal preference learning. We create graph sessions to assist in discovering the dynamic category preferences of users.
- We propose two task assignment methods, i.e., preference-based greedy and preference-based optimized KM algorithms, to achieve optimal and efficient task assignment.
- We conduct extensive experiments on real-world datasets, offering evidence of the effectiveness and efficiency of the proposed framework.

2   Related Work

There are many previous studies about task assignment in MCS [12]. Kazemi and Shahabi [6] categorized the MCS based on the publishing mode: *server assigned tasks* (SAT) mode [9,22] and *worker selected tasks* (WST) mode [4], in which tasks are assigned by the MCS server or chosen by users, respectively. Most previous research employed SAT mode, in which the MCS server was responsible for task assignment, but they did not consider whether the task category matched the users' preference during the valid time of tasks. Our model follows SAT mode while considering users' preferences at the same time.

Recently, some studies have explored the variable preferences of users. Mavridis et al. [9] and Cheng et al. [2] stated every user's preference explicitly, so there was no uncertainty regarding the user's preference. ETA2 [20] and HCTD [22] inferred user preferences from historical task-performing patterns. ETA2 [20] relied on a novel semantic analysis method to infer user expertise, estimate truth, and allocate tasks based on the inferred expertise. HCTD [22] incorporated temporal dynamics in preference inference, which constructed two 3-D tensors about recent and historical task-performing data, and two context matrices that provided auxiliary information, but assumed that location had no effect on preference. Moreover, Zhu et al. [23] employed a translation-based recommendation model to learn spatio-temporal effects from the users' historical task-performing activities and then calculate the mobile preference scores of users.

The above works focus on task assignments that generally consider users' category preference and mobile preference separately. Nevertheless, users' category preference and mobile preference are distinct, and ignorance of their combined

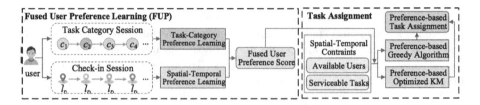

Fig. 2. Framework Overview

effects could reduce the matching number between users and tasks. In this paper, we propose a task assignment framework that takes into account users' category preference and mobile preference simultaneously.

3   Problem Formulation

In this section, we introduce some basic concepts and present the formal definition of our problem. More specifically, the tasks and users are defined as follows:

Definition 1 (Task). *The task set is denoted by $R = \{r_1, \cdots, r_M\}$. Each task r_j is characterized by $r_j = \langle c_j, l_{r_j}, p_j, e_j \rangle$, where c_j is the task category, l_{r_j} is the task location, p_j is publication time, and e_j is expiration time. For each category $c \in C$, $R_c(R_c \subseteq R)$ is the task set belonged to category c.*

Definition 2 (User). *The user set is denoted by $U = \{u_1, \cdots, u_N\}$. A user $u_i = \langle l_{u_i}, sd_i, sp_i, s_i, L_i \rangle$, has a location l_{u_i} at the current time instance, a serviceable distance sd_i, a travel speed sp_i, and a completed task-category session $s_i = [c_1, c_2, \cdots]$ ordered by timestamps, a mobile record $L_i = \left\{ (l_1^i, t_1^i), (l_2^i, t_2^i), \cdots \right\}$ including check-in location and time.*

Definition 3 (Preference-Based Spatial Task Assignment). *Given a set of online users U with recorded data (i.e., historical task records), and a set of tasks R, our problem is to find a task assignment A that maximizes the ratio of completed tasks by considering users' preferences, i.e.,*

$$\max \frac{|A^R|}{|R|} \tag{1}$$

where $|A^R|$ denotes the number of completed tasks in assignment A.

4   Methodology

Our framework, called *Task Assignment with User Preference Learning*, consists of two components: 1) *Fused User Preference Learning* (FUP) including task-category preference learning and spatial-temporal preference learning; and 2) *Preference-Based Task Assignment*, in which we propose preference-based greedy and preference-based optimized KM algorithms to achieve effective task assignment (as shown in Fig. 2).

4.1 Fused User Preference Learning

We aim to learn users' preferences on task category and spatial-temporal information based on the historical data of users, thus we will calculate two preference scores to judge users' interests in different tasks and help us to assign tasks to appropriate users.

Task-Category Preference Learning. Each user corresponds to a list of completed task-category records. To capture user preferences for different task categories, we first construct a session graph for each user and utilize the graph neural network to learn the session embeddings of users. The intricate transitional patterns underlying users' sessions, which are difficult to be exposed by conventional sequential methods, could be found using the graph session-based learning model. Following that, we calculate the user's preference score $p_{i,j}$ for different task categories. Figure 3 shows the workflow of task-category learning.

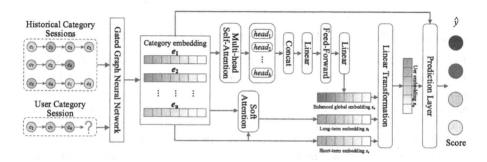

Fig. 3. The Workflow of Task-Category Preference Learning

Constructing Session Graph. Since there are a large number of tasks on the MCS platform, we want to model the user preference for the task category not a specific task. Therefore, we construct a session graph based on each user's historical completed task category. Specifically, a session $s = [c_1, c_2, \cdots, c_n]$ ordered by timestamps is used to construct a directed session graph $\mathcal{G}_s = (\mathcal{C}_s, \mathcal{E}_s)$, where each node $c_i \in \mathcal{C}_s$ indicates a task category, and each edge $(c_{i-1}, c_i) \in \mathcal{E}_s$ indicates that a user completes a task of category c_i after last task of category c_{i-1}. Since some task categories may appear in the session repeatedly, we assign each edge with a normalized weight w, which is calculated as the occurrence of the edge divided by the outdegree of that edge's start node.

Learning Node Embedding. Graph neural network (GNN) [16] is a class of widely used deep learning models to capture complex node connections. Following that, we transform each task category node c_i into a unified embedding space. Specifically, we employ gated graph neural networks (GGNNs) [7] to learn the embeddings $e_1, \cdots, e_n$, where $e_i \in \mathbb{R}^d$, d is the embedding size.

Generating Session Embedding. We further investigate users' short- and long-term preferences exhibited in the current session s and generate an enhanced global embedding by aggregating all node representations in a session.

Short-Term Embedding. As the user's final action is usually determined by her last action, we simply represent the user's short-term preference as a *short-term embedding* s_s as the embedding of last-completed task category c_n, i.e., $s_s = e_n$.

Long-Term Embedding. Users' long-term preference reflect their average interest. After obtaining each task category embedding, now we present the key component for modeling the long-term sequential dependencies. Specifically, we take the entire task category sequence as input and encode the preference long-term embedding representation $s_l \in \mathbb{R}^d$. The encoding process is carried out by a soft-attention mechanism and we draw dependencies between the last-visited task and each task involved in the session, the calculation is defined as follows:

$$\alpha_i = q^\top \sigma \left(W_1 e_n + W_2 e_i + c \right), \; s_l = \sum_{i=1}^{s_n} \alpha_i e_i \tag{2}$$

where $q, c \in \mathbb{R}^d$ and $W_1, W_2 \in \mathbb{R}^{d \times d}$ are weight parameters.

Enhanced Global Embedding. Here we fully consider the relevance of task categories and the dynamic evolution of user preference, then introduce a multi-head self-attention block to calculate an enhanced global embedding. Inspired by the architecture design of Transformer [13], we map the node embedding into key and query vector, and calculate dot product as attention. Then we aggregate the representation constructed by multi-head attention from different subspaces. The multi-head self-attention block could better learn the dependencies among task categories and extract transition patterns, the calculation is defined as follows:

$$head_i(Q, K, V) = softmax(\frac{QK^\top}{\sqrt{d/h}})V, Q = EW^Q, K = EW^K, V = EW^V \tag{3}$$

$$S = Concat(head_1, head_2, \cdots, head_h)W^O \tag{4}$$

where W^Q, W^K, W^V, W^O represent the projection matrices, and h represents the head number. In this way, each task category node learns about its interaction with other task categories and we obtain new representation S for nodes.

Considering the information in these embedding may have different levels of priority, we further adopt the soft-attention mechanism to better represent the global session preference and calculate the enhanced global embedding s_e by the average of category representations, which is defined as follows:

$$F = ReLU(SW_1 + b_1)W_2 + b_2, \; s_e = \frac{1}{n} \sum_{i=1}^{n} f_i \tag{5}$$

where W_1, W_2 are parameter matrices, b_1 and b_2 are bias vectors. To alleviate overfitting problems, we apply dropout techniques during training.

User Session Embedding. Finally, we generate the user session embedding s_u of session s by taking linear transformation over the concatenation of the enhanced global embedding, long-term and short-term embedding:

$$s_u = W_3 [s_e; s_s; s_l] \tag{6}$$

where $W_3 \in \mathbb{R}^{d \times 3d}$ projects the concatenated vectors into $s_u \in \mathbb{R}^d$.

Then, we calculate the preference score $p(i, c)$ of user u_i on task category c by taking the inner-product of category embedding e_c and user session representation s_u, as follows:

$$p(i, c) = s_u^\top e_c \tag{7}$$

whereafter, the task-category preference score of user u_i for task r_j is obtained as $p_{i,j} = p(i, c)$, if $r_j \in R_c$.

Spatial-Temporal Preference Learning. The task's location is an essential factor that might affect the preference of a user for the task. The tasks in the MCS system are location-dependent, and a user needs to move to a specific location to contribute his answer data. People usually have their own mobility laws, and the mobility patterns of users may vary from user to user. Usually, users prefer the tasks in their neighborhood to save on the cost of the transfer. In addition, the platform prefers users who are near the newly published task since they can return results as quickly as possible. Therefore, the matching of spatial-temporal preference between tasks and users can not only bring benefits to users but also improve the utility of the platform.

In the MCS system, when a user accomplishes a task, the location and completed time would be recorded by the platform. The above information would affect users' choices for future tasks, and we use those records as check-in information to learn the spatial-temporal preference of users. To better learn users' historical performances, the overall area is divided into H subareas, denoted as $SA = \{sa_1, \cdots, sa_H\}$. The user u_i's mobile record containing m check-in sessions is denoted as $L_i = \{(l_1^i, t_1^i), (l_2^i, t_2^i), \cdots, (l_m^i, t_m^i)\}$, where the check-in time $t_1^i < t_2^i < \cdots < t_m^i$. The check-in locations are $l_1^i, l_2^i, \cdots, l_m^i$, and any check-in location must belong to one subarea.

The users' check-in locations in frequently visited subareas are indicative of their own interests, and the preference of the subarea may be measured by the session interval between the previous check-in and the next check-in. The smaller session interval between the former check-in and the next check-in indicates the user could more possibly pass by the former check-in subarea in terms of personal interests. Since users who check in at different points may be good candidates to perform tasks in the vicinity of those points, and their current locations are those of the most recent check-in points. Therefore, we give higher preference priority to the subarea with smaller check-in interval and higher check-in frequency.

To quantify the weights of subareas, we create a weighting function $q(\cdot)$ inspired by the logistic function. It decays over the check-in session interval between the previous check-in and the next check-in. In particular, the user u_i's spatial-temporal preference of subarea sa_h could be defined as

$$q(i, h) = \sum_{k=1}^{m} I_{sa_h}(l_k^i) \frac{1}{1 + e^{-\frac{m}{\alpha(m-k+\epsilon)}}}, \tag{8}$$

where α controls the weight of different check-in session intervals of user u_i, ϵ is a tiny number to prevent potential overflow due to division by zero, which is set to 10^{-6} by default. Hence, user u_i's spatial-temporal preference score for each target task r_j can be obtained as $q_{i,j} = q(i, h)$, if $l_{r_j} \in sa_h$.

Fused User Preference Score. So far, we have obtained the two part scores of the user's preference. The fused user preference score $Score(u_i, r_j)$ is a fusion of task-category preference score $p_{i,j}$ and spatial-temporal preference score $q_{i,j}$ of user u_i to task r_j. Here, we employ a linear combination of the two part scores

$$score(u_i, r_j) = \gamma p_{i.j} + (1 - \gamma)q_{i,j} \tag{9}$$

where γ is a hyperparameter.

4.2   Task Assignment

In this section, we first detail how to generate the available user set for each task and the serviceable task set for each user, that would be used throughout the task assignment process, and then propose two algorithms for task assignment, including a Preference-Based Greedy algorithm and a Preference-Based Optimized KM algorithm.

Available User Set and Serviceable Task Set. Because of the constraints of users' serviceable distance as well as tasks' expiration time, we should consider spatial-temporal constraints to filter users and tasks. Given a user set U and a task set R, the available user set for task $r_j \in R$ and the serviceable task set for user $u_i \in U$ are denoted as $AU(r_j)$ and $ST(u_i)$, respectively. Both $AU(r_j)$ ($\forall u_i \in AU(r_j), r_j \in R$) and $ST(u_i)$ ($\forall r_j \in ST(u_i), u_i \in U$) should satisfy the following two conditions:

(1) $d(l_{u_i}, l_{r_j}) < sd_i$, and
(2) $t_{now} + d(l_{u_i}, l_{r_j})/sp_i < e_j$, where $d(l_{u_i}, l_{r_j})$ represents the distance between l_{u_i} and l_{r_j} (e.g., Euclidean distance).

Preference-Based Greedy Task Assignment. The input of the algorithm is a user set U and a task set R. During each iteration, the algorithm begins to randomly select a task r from the remaining ones and assigns the user of $AU(r)$ with the largest preference score to the selected task, and then adds the matching to the task assignment A. Finally, we can obtain the final task assignment A.

Preference-Based Optimized KM Algorithm. Taking users' preference scores as the priority, we transform the Preference-Based Task Assignment problem into a Bipartite Maximum Weight Matching problem and apply the Kuhn-Munkras (KM) algorithm [10] to solve it.

For an undirected bipartite graph, it is represented by $G = (V, E)$, where V is the vertex set and E is the edge set. Given a set of users U and a set of unassigned tasks R, the number of V is equal to the sum of $|U|$ and $|R|$. For the vertex construction, the entire vertex set V is divided into two sets V^U and V^R. Each user u_i maps to a vertex v_i^U, and each task r_j maps to a vertex v_j^R. Due to the spatial-temporal constraints, we add an edge from v_i^U mapped from u_i to the vertex v_j^R mapped from r_j, if r_j can be assigned to u_i, i.e., $r_j \in ST(u_i)$. For each edge (v_i^U, v_j^R), its weight (denoted by $weight(v_i^U, v_j^R)$) can be measured as u_i's preference score (Eq. (9)) of task r_j, i.e., $weight(v_i^U, v_j^R) = score(u_i, r_j)$.

Algorithm 1: Find Matching (FM) Algorithm

Input: The user u_i, the recursion deepth dth
Output: $Bool$

1   $vis_{user}[u_i] \leftarrow True$;
2   **if** $dth > \lambda$ **then**   // dth cannot exceed the upper recursion limit λ
3 | **return** $False$;
4   **else**
5 | **for** $task\ r_j$ is adjacent to u_i in G **do**
6 | | **if** $vis_{task}[r_j]$ **then** continue;
7 | | $gap \leftarrow val_{user}[u_i] + val_{task}[r_j] - weight(v_i^U, v_j^R)$;
8 | | **if** $gap = 0$ **then**
9 | | | **if** $A[r_i] = -1$ or $FM(A[r_i], dth + 1)$ **then**
10 | | | | $A[r_j] = u_i$;   // r_j is assigned to u_i
11 | | | | **return** $True$;
12 | | **else** $slack[r_j] = \min(slack[r_j], gap)$;
13 | **return** $False$;   // u_i fails to match a task

The Preference-Based Task Assignment problem is now converted into a Bipartite Maximum Matching problem in the undirected graph G, which is to achieve the maximum weight matching of G. In our work, we use KM algorithm with a limit of recursion to find the maximal weight matching. For better understanding, we will first introduce the Find Matching algorithm as shown in Algorithm 1. Find Matching (FM) algorithm is a depth-first search algorithm to find a task for a user. In the algorithm, we calculate the difference between the weight of the edge associated with the two vertices and the sum of the expectations of the user and the task. If the difference is equal to 0, the task can be assigned to the user (line 8). If the task has been assigned to another user, we try to assign another task to that user (line 9–11). But the depth of recursion cannot exceed the upper recursion limit λ (line 2–3).

The Preference-Based Optimized KM algorithm is shown in Algorithm 2. Given the bipartite graph G, which is composed of two vertex sets V^R and V^U. First, for each vertex in V^U, its value of expectation is equal to the largest weight

---

Algorithm 2: Preference-Based Optimized KM Algorithm

Input: The weighted bipartite graph G
Output: The task assignment A

1 $A \leftarrow [-1, -1, \ldots];\ val_{task} \leftarrow [0, 0, \ldots];\ slack \leftarrow [INF, INF, \ldots];$
2 **for** *user* $u_i \in U$ **do**
3 $\quad\lfloor\ val_{user}[u_i] \leftarrow \max(weight(v_i^U, v_j^R));$ // Initialize expectation value
4 **for** *user* $u_i \in U$ **do**
5 $\quad\mid$ **while** $val_{user}[u_i] > 0$ **do**   // If value is less than 0, stop matching
6 $\quad\mid\quad\mid\ vis_{task} \leftarrow [False, False, \ldots];\ vis_{user} \leftarrow [False, False, \ldots];$
7 $\quad\mid\quad\mid$ **if** $FindMatching(u_i, 0)$ **then**   // Find whether a task matches u_i
8 $\quad\mid\quad\mid\quad\lfloor$ break;
9 $\quad\mid\quad\mid$ **else**   // u_i fails to match a task
10 $\quad\mid\quad\mid\quad\mid\ d = INF;$
11 $\quad\mid\quad\mid\quad\mid$ **for** *task* $r_j \in R$ **do**
12 $\quad\mid\quad\mid\quad\mid\quad\lfloor$ **if** $!vis_{task}[r_j]$ **then** $d = \min(d, slack[r_j]);$
13 $\quad\mid\quad\mid\quad\mid$ **if** $vis_{user}[u_i]$ **then** $val_{user}[u_i] - = d;$
14 $\quad\mid\quad\mid\quad\mid$ **if** $vis_{task}[r_j]$ **then** $val_{task}[r_j] + = d;$
15 $\quad\mid\quad\mid\quad\lfloor$ **else** $val_{task}[r_j] - = d;$

16 **return** $A;$ // The final task assignment result

---

among the edges associated with it in graph G (lines 2–3). Second, Algorithm 2 recursively finds matching tasks for user u_i through the Find Matching function (line 7). Third, if u_i fails to match a task, we adjust the expectations of users and tasks involved in the last matching to change the competitive relationship among users so that more users can be assigned (lines 9–15).

The original KM algorithm is used to find the perfect matching of a weighted bipartite graph, and it will not stop trying to match tasks for a user until a successful match, which may cause an endless loop in our problem. However, considering that perfect matching may not exist in a user-task bipartite graph, we propose some optimization strategies to improve the KM algorithm. Therefore, if the expectation value is less than 0 in Algorithm 2, we stop matching (line 5).

5 Experiments

In this section, we implement and evaluate the performance of our proposed methods. We first conduct the experiments on user task-category preference learning, and then further examine the performance of task assignment.

5.1 Datasets and Experiment Setting

We conduct evaluations on the real-world datasets crawled from Foursquare [19], which are widely used in the MSC task assignment [22,23]. Here we choose six-month data (from 1 May 2012 to 30 November 2012) of the Foursquare datasets in New York City (NYC) and Tokyo (TKY), which contain check-ins with timestamps, GPS coordinates, and venue categories. We use the venue categories to represent the task categories, and check-in information represents the users' historical task records. To ensure fair comparison, we exclude users with session lengths less than 10 and venue categories that appear less than 10 times. The remaining $133,518$ check-ins and 317 venue categories are in Foursquare-NYC, and $340,260$ check-ins and 293 venue categories are in Foursquare-TKY.

We set the dimensionality of embedding latent vectors $d = 100$ and set $h = 4$. All parameters are initialized using a Gaussian distribution with a mean of 0 and a standard deviation of 0.1. The mini-batch Adam optimizer is exerted to optimize these parameters, where the initial learning rate is set to 0.01 and decays by 0.1 after every 3 epochs. At the same time, the l_2 regularization parameter is set to 10^{-5} to alleviate overfitting.

5.2   Experiment Results

The Correlation Between Two Part Preferences. Here, we investigate the correlation between task-category preference and spatial-temporal preference on Foursquare-NYC dataset, and the experimental results are presented by histogram, as shown in Fig. 4. We use the Pearson correlation coefficient (PCC) [11] to measure the linear correlation of the two part preference scores. From Fig. 4, we can see that the correlation values concentrate between -0.2 and 0.2 with a probability higher than 90%, and there is no obvious linear correlation between the two preferences. Therefore, it is reasonable that we model the two part preferences separately.

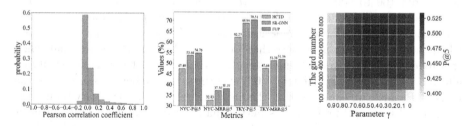

Fig. 4. Histogram of PCC   **Fig. 5.** Experiments on Task-Category Preference   **Fig. 6.** Experiments on Parameter Setting

Experiments on Task-Category Preference Learning. We first evaluate the performance of our proposed task-category preference learning mechanism.

Evaluation Methods. The methods are as followed:

1) HCTD: The latest HCTD [22] models users' temporal preferences by History-based Context-aware Tensor Decomposition.
2) SR-GNN: SR-GNN [15] is a classical session-based learning model.
3) FUP: The task-category preference learning part of FUP (i.e., $\gamma = 1$) is detailed in Sect. 4.1.

Metrics. To evaluate the accuracy of user task-category preference learning, we use P@K and MRR@K as the evaluation metrics. P@K (Precision) metric takes into account the accuracy of predicted tasks. MRR@K (Mean Reciprocal Rank) takes the predicted task ranks into account.

Results. The performance comparison of three methods is shown in Fig. 5. We generate the Top-5 task categories with the highest preference scores on Foursquare-NYC and Foursquare-TKY datasets, and we can observe that four metrics of our model FUP are superior to two benchmarks HCTD and SR-GNN on category preference learning. As we can see, our method achieves the best performance on task-category preference learning in terms of P@5 and MRR@5. Moreover, the accuracy of Foursquare-TKY is higher than Foursquare-NYC among all of the models, we conjecture that Tokyo users' task-category preferences have stronger regularities than New York users.

Experiments on Parameter Setting. To learn the influence of the parameter setting on model performance, we provide each user with a list of 5 tasks with the highest preference scores and check whether the user chooses those tasks in the next action. We adopt the commonly-used metric P@5 (Precision) for evaluation. The choices for the hyperparameters are made by grid search.

As shown in Fig. 6, the parameter γ is set from 0 to 0.9 (the results of $\gamma = 1$ are not shown, because the target tasks in the same category are so numerous that P@5 is low only by category preference). The partition number of the area is set from 100 to 800, which means the whole area is divided into 100×100 to 800×800 girds. The value of P@5 grows with the grid number when it is less than 700. Furthermore, the performance of FUP does not improve anymore, when the gird number is greater than 700. The above results show that when the divided subareas are extremely small, the accuracy of the model would be affected. When the parameter $\gamma = 0.5$ and the grid number is 700, P@5 is the highest. Besides, we could see that the fused strategy of task-category preference and spatial-temporal preference is better than the task-category preference- or spatial-temporal preference-only strategy. Motivated by the results in Fig. 6, we set $\gamma = 0.5$ and the grid number is 700 in the following experiments.

Performance of Task Assignment. We proceed to study the performance of the task assignment on Foursquare-NYC dataset. Table 1 shows our experimental settings, where the default values of all parameters are in bold. Besides, the speed of users is set to 40 km/h and the serviceable distance of users is 1 km.

Table 1. Experiment Parameters for Task Assignment

Parameter	Values
Number of Tasks M	1000, 2000, **3000**, 4000, 5000
Number of Users N	1000, **2000**, 3000, 4000, 5000
Valid Time of Tasks $e - p$ (h)	0.01, 0.02, 0.1, **0.3**, 0.5

Evaluation Methods. We study the following task assignment algorithms.

1) PAR-Greedy [14]: The task assignment algorithm iteratively selects worker-task pairs with the maximum utility increase.
2) PTA [22]: The task assignment algorithm with users' temporal preferences calculated by the HCTD method.
3) FUP+GD: The Greedy algorithm with users' preference calculated by FUP.
4) FUP+KM: The Optimized KM algorithm with users' preferences by FUP.
5) FUP_TC+KM: The Optimized KM algorithm with users' preferences calculated by the task-category preference component of FUP.
6) FUP_ST+KM: The Optimized KM algorithm with users' preferences calculated by the spatial-temporal preference component of FUP.

Metrics. The two main metrics are compared among the above algorithms, i.e., the number of allocated tasks, and the assignment success rate which is the ratio of successful assignments to the total tasks in a certain time instance. In our experiments, if a user performs tasks with the same category in the following three tasks, the assignment of this task can be considered successful.

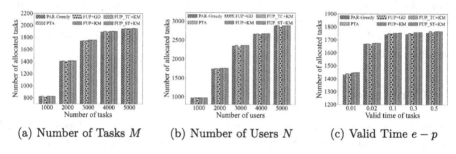

(a) Number of Tasks M (b) Number of Users N (c) Valid Time $e - p$

Fig. 7. Comparison on Allocated Task Number with Various M, N, and $e - p$

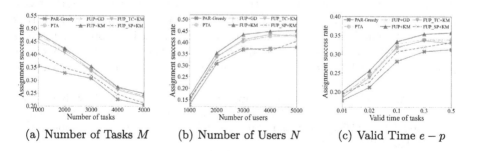

(a) Number of Tasks M (b) Number of Users N (c) Valid Time $e - p$

Fig. 8. Comparison on Assignment Success Rate with Various M, N, and $e - p$

Effect of M. First, we study the effect of the number of tasks M. In Fig. 7(a), the number of allocated tasks assigned by KM is slightly more than those of greedy-based algorithms, which sacrifice the task assignment number in order to improve the total preferences of users. In addition, with the increase of M, the assignment success rate shows a declining trend in Fig. 8(a), due to the limited number of users. As the task number increases, there are a large number of tasks without users to match, which would decrease the assignment success rate. Meanwhile, FUP+KM performs better than FUP_TC+KM and FUP_ST+KM in terms of assignment success rate, indicating that ignorance of the combined effects of two preferences would negatively impact assignment efficiency.

Effect of N. Next, we evaluate the effect of user number N. In Fig. 7(b), the number of allocated tasks increases with the increase of N. In Fig. 8(b), the assignment success rate exhibits an upward trend as the number of users increases, and all preference-based algorithms maintain a high assignment success rate. In summary, FUP+KM obtains the highest assignment success rate.

Effect of $e - p$. We then evaluate the effect of tasks' valid time $e - p$. As shown in Fig. 7(c), with $e - p$ increasing, the number of task assignments increases since users are more likely to be assigned their interested tasks with more tasks available. In Fig. 8(c), FUP+KM achieves the highest assignment success rate, which shows the importance of considering preferences. Besides, as the valid time of tasks extends, the performance gap between FUP+KM and other baselines becomes larger.

6   Conclusion

In this paper, we present solutions to a problem referred to as Preference-Based Saptial Task Assignment in MCS, which aims to maximize the ratio of completed tasks through user preference learning. We propose a framework, Task Assignment with User Preference Learning, that consists of two components: FUP and Preference-Based Task Assignment. FUP is the fusion of task-category preference learning and spatial-temporal preference learning based on historical session records. To our knowledge, we are the first to employ the graph session-based learning model to characterize user preferences. In the Preference-Based Task Assignment component, tasks are assigned to users with higher preference scores first, so that the task assignment can achieve a higher success rate. Extensive experiments on real data demonstrate the effectiveness of our proposed solutions.

Acknowledgment. This work was supported by the National Key R&D Program of China [2020YFB1707900], the National Natural Science Foundation of China [2020YFB1707900], Shanghai Municipal Science and Technology Major Project [2021SHZDZX0102].

References

1. Chen, X., Zhang, L., Pang, Y., Lin, B., Fang, Y.: Timeliness-aware incentive mechanism for vehicular crowdsourcing in smart cities. TMC **21**(9), 3373–3387 (2022)
2. Cheng, P., Lian, X., Chen, L., Han, J., Zhao, J.: Task assignment on multi-skill oriented spatial crowdsourcing. TKDE **28**(8), 2201–2215 (2016)
3. Dai, Z., et al.: Aoi-minimal UAV crowdsensing by model-based graph convolutional reinforcement learning. In: INFOCOM, pp. 1029–1038 (2022)
4. Ji, Y., Mu, C., Qiu, X., Chen, Y.: A task recommendation model in mobile crowdsourcing. WCMC 1–12 (2022)
5. Karaliopoulos, M., Koutsopoulos, I., Titsias, M.: First learn then earn: optimizing mobile crowdsensing campaigns through data-driven user profiling. In: MobiHoc, pp. 271–280 (2016)
6. Kazemi, L., Shahabi, C.: Geocrowd: enabling query answering with spatial crowdsourcing. In: SIGSPATIAL, pp. 189–198 (2012)
7. Li, Y., Zemel, R., Brockschmidt, M., Tarlow, D.: Gated graph sequence neural networks. In: ICLR (2016)
8. Lu, H., Gao, X., Chen, G.: Efficient crowdsourcing-aided positioning and ground-truth-aided truth discovery for mobile wireless sensor networks in urban fields. TWC **21**(3), 1652–1664 (2022)
9. Mavridis, P., Gross-Amblard, D., Miklós, Z.: Using hierarchical skills for optimized task assignment in knowledge-intensive crowdsourcing. In: WWW, pp. 843–853 (2016)
10. Munkres, J.: Algorithms for the assignment and transportation problems. J. Soc. Indust. Appl. Math. **5**(1), 32–38 (1957)
11. Pearson, K.: Vii. mathematical contributions to the theory of evolution.-iii. regression, heredity, and panmixia. Philos. Trans. Royal Soc. A **187**, 253–318 (1896)
12. Tong, Y., Zhou, Z., Zeng, Y., Chen, L., Shahabi, C.: Spatial crowdsourcing: a survey. VLDBJ **29**(1), 217–250 (2020)
13. Vaswani, A., et al.: Attention is all you need. In: NIPS, pp. 6000–6010 (2017)
14. Wang, J., et al.: Hytasker: Hybrid task allocation in mobile crowd sensing. TMC **19**(3), 598–611 (2019)
15. Wu, S., Tang, Y., Zhu, Y., Wang, L., Xie, X., Tan, T.: Session-based recommendation with graph neural networks. In: AAAI, vol. 33, pp. 346–353 (2019)
16. Wu, Z., Pan, S., Chen, F., Long, G., Zhang, C., Yu, P.S.: A comprehensive survey on graph neural networks. TNNLS **32**(1), 4–24 (2021)
17. Xia, J., Zhao, Y., Liu, G., Xu, J., Zhang, M., Zheng, K.: Profit-driven task assignment in spatial crowdsourcing. In: IJCAI, pp. 1914–1920 (2019)
18. Xu, X., Liu, A., Liu, G., Xu, J., Zhao, L.: Acceptance-aware multi-platform cooperative matching in spatial crowdsourcing. In: ICSOC, pp. 300–315 (2022)
19. Yang, D., Zhang, D., Zheng, V.W., Yu, Z.: Modeling user activity preference by leveraging user spatial temporal characteristics in LBSNs. IEEE Trans. Syst. Man Cybern. Syst. **45**(1), 129–142 (2015)
20. Zhang, X., Wu, Y., Huang, L., Ji, H., Cao, G.: Expertise-aware truth analysis and task allocation in mobile crowdsourcing. TMC **20**(3), 1001–1016 (2019)
21. Zhao, Y., Zheng, K., Cui, Y., Su, H., Zhu, F., Zhou, X.: Predictive task assignment in spatial crowdsourcing: a data-driven approach. In: ICDE, pp. 13–24 (2020)
22. Zhao, Y., Zheng, K., Yin, H., Liu, G., Fang, J., Zhou, X.: Preference-aware task assignment in spatial crowdsourcing: from individuals to groups. TKDE **34**(7), 3461–3477 (2022)
23. Zhu, C., Cui, Y., Zhao, Y., Zheng, K.: Task assignment with spatio-temporal recommendation in spatial crowdsourcing. In: APWeb-WAIM, pp. 264–279 (2022)

Octopus: SLO-Aware Progressive Inference Serving via Deep Reinforcement Learning in Multi-tenant Edge Cluster

Ziyang Zhang[1]([✉]) [iD], Yang Zhao[2], and Jie Liu[1,2]

[1] School of Science and Technology, Harbin Institute of Technology, Harbin 150001, China
zhangzy@stu.hit.edu.cn
[2] International Research Institute for Artificial Intelligence, Harbin Institute of Technology, Shenzhen 518055, China
{yang.zhao,jieliu}@hit.edu.cn

Abstract. Deep neural network (DNN) inference service at the edge is promising, but it is still non-trivial to achieve high-throughput for multi-DNN model deployment on resource-constrained edge devices. Furthermore, an edge inference service system must respond to requests with bounded latency to maintain a consistent service-level objective (SLO). To address these challenges, we propose Octopus, a flexible and adaptive SLO-aware progressive inference scheduling framework to support both computer vision (CV) and natural language processing (NLP) DNN models on a multi-tenant heterogeneous edge cluster. Our deep reinforcement learning-based scheduler can automatically determine the optimal joint configuration of 1) DNN batch size, 2) DNN model exit point, and 3) edge node dispatching for each inference request to maximize the overall throughput of edge clusters. We evaluate Octopus using representative CV and NLP DNN models on an edge cluster with various heterogeneous devices. Our extensive experiments reveal that Octopus is adaptive to various requests and dynamic networks, achieving up to a $3.3\times$ improvement in overall throughput compared to state-of-the-art schemes while satisfying soft SLO and maintaining high inference accuracy.

Keywords: Edge computing · Progressive inference · Deep reinforcement learning · Multi-tenant

1 Introduction

Recent advancements in deep learning and Internet of Things (IoT) have facilitated the development of various edge intelligence applications [25], such as autonomous driving [20] and augmented reality [14]. These applications utilize deep neural network (DNN) models to perform various complex tasks. However, it is non-trivial to deploy compute-intensive DNN models to IoT devices due to limited resources. In this case, edge computing [18] has emerged as a promising paradigm for providing low-latency inference services by deploying models to edge devices, which are in closer proximity to users than cloud servers [1].

© The Author(s), under exclusive license to Springer Nature Switzerland AG 2023
F. Monti et al. (Eds.): ICSOC 2023, LNCS 14420, pp. 242–258, 2023.
https://doi.org/10.1007/978-3-031-48424-7_18

As shown in Fig. 1, an edge inference service usually involves a multi-tenant environment [6] comprised of various IoT devices. These IoT devices send their inference requests to a nearby edge device, or in our case an edge cluster, on which computing resources are allocated among multiple tenants and DNN models. Existing edge inference serving systems adopt a wide range of approaches to process as many requests as possible, i.e., achieve high throughput on resource-constrained edge devices. For instance, DeepRT [23] adopts batching to provide soft real-time inference services. Edgent [11] leverages multi-exit DNN models for collaborative inference. MAEL [17] uses cross-processor scheduling to satisfy service level objectives (SLO) of various requests. Indeed, a high-throughput edge inference serving system needs to trade-off among inference accuracy, latency and throughput. However, none of the works mentioned above targets inference serving on an edge cluster, which poses new challenges in optimizing in multi-dimensional search spaces.

An edge cluster equipped with GPUs located close to user devices can be used to improve throughput of DNN inference serving. Furthermore, edge inference services must be flexible to accommodate SLO budget, heterogeneous hardware accelerator, and inference accuracy requirement. Thus, for an SLO-aware inference serving system on an edge cluster, the scheduler should be capable of dispatching inference requests from IoT devices to appropriate edge nodes, where multiple DNN models are deployed, to satisfy different SLOs while maintaining high inference accuracy.

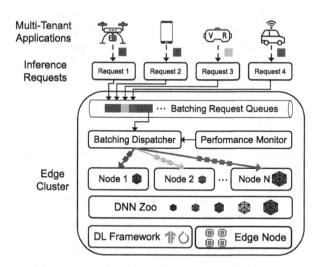

Fig. 1. Deep learning (DL) inference serving on a multi-tenant edge cluster.

To address these challenges, we propose Octopus, the first progressive inference serving system designed for a multi-tenant edge cluster, which aims at maximizing the overall throughput of the edge cluster while satisfying soft SLO budget and inference accuracy. Octopus adopts the multi-exit DNN inference approach [19], i.e., progressive inference, a mechanism that enables early exit at different points during DNN inference [10], given the request budget. The scheduler in Octopus utilizes deep reinforcement learning to efficiently schedule resources for inference requests. More precisely, Octopus automatically learns the optimal joint configuration of exit point, batch size, and node dispatching, in order to provide high-throughput progressive inference serving while taking into account SLO and accuracy budget. Additionally, the latency predictor in Octopus leverages an attention-based long short-term memory (LSTM) to achieve SLO awareness, and ensure bounded response latency for inference requests.

Overall, this paper makes the following contributions:

- We propose a novel multi-exit DNN-based progressive edge inference serving system, aiming to maximize the overall throughput of a heterogeneous edge cluster while satisfying SLO budget and maintaining high accuracy.
- We design a deep reinforcement learning-based scheduler that automatically co-optimizes a three-dimensional search space with batch size, exit point, and node dispatching to provide high-throughput inference services for multi-tenant edge intelligence applications.
- We implement a system prototype of Octopus on a heterogeneous edge cluster, deploying three representative CV and NLP DNN models. Extensive evaluations show that Octopus achieves up to 3.3× in overall throughput compared to state-of-the-art schemes, while maintaining high inference accuracy and low SLO violation rate below 5%.

The rest of this paper is organized as follows: Sect. 2 introduces related work. Section 3 illustrates the system architecture and formulates the optimization problem. Section 4 proposes an SLO-aware latency predictor. Section 5 details the design of the learning-based scheduler. Section 6 provides the system prototype and performance comparison. Section 7 summarizes our work.

2   Related Work

Edge inference services have recently attracted great attention among researchers. Prior work utilizes multi-exit DNN to efficiently share limited resources on edge devices. For instance, Delen [12] adopts multi-exit DNN to adaptively control inference requests with SLO, accuracy, and energy budget. Edgent [11] leverages an early exit mechanism to achieves collaborative inference between end devices and edge servers, balancing latency and accuracy. MAMO [3] proposes a bidirectional dynamic programming approach to determine the optimal exit point, and utilizes deep reinforcement learning to co-optimize resource allocation and model partitioning. However, none of these works provides SLO budget. In practice, edge devices must respond to inference requests within bounded latency, so as to provide QoS consistent with SLO budget.

Prior work also proposes various scheduling algorithms for single-device edge inference services. For instance, DeepRT [23] proposes a scheduler based on earliest-deadline-first (EDF) [4], which aims to provide soft real-time inference services. Jellyfish [16] leverages dynamic programming that adapt input data and

DNNs, so as to provide soft SLOs while maintaining high accuracy. HiTDL [22] proposes a latency-based performance model that considers resource availability, DNN exit points, and cross-DNN interference, in order to improve throughput while satisfying SLO. However, these works only provide limited inference services due to the lack of an efficient resource sharing.

Additionally, some research focus on scheduling heterogeneous multiprocessor to provide on-device edge inference. For instance, BlastNet [13] introduces a priority-driven algorithm for block-level scheduling across CPU-GPU processors. Similarly, Band [9] schedules the subgraphs of DNN model on heterogeneous multiprocessor to coordinate multi-DNN inference. MAEL [17] proposes a heterogeneous multiprocessor-aware scheduling strategy for edge devices equipped with CPU, GPU, and DSP, using a minimum-average-expected-latency algorithm to satisfy SLO while reducing energy consumption. Note that these works are orthogonal to Octopus, which can be used to further improve throughput.

3 System Architecture and Problem Formulation

In this section, we illustrate the workflow procedure of our proposed progressive inference serving framework for multi-tenant edge cluster, and formulate the scheduling problem as an optimization problem.

3.1 System Overview

Figure 2 shows an overview of the proposed Octopus system, which comprises multiple clients and an edge cluster with heterogeneous devices. When multiple clients ❶ send batch inference requests to the edge cluster via a network, the monitor ❷ in Octopus generates configuration files that specify the SLO budget and accuracy threshold for each request. Meanwhile, the latency predictor ❸ utilizes historical data to estimate the end-to-end latency of subsequent requests, thereby achieving SLO awareness (Sect. 4). The learning-based scheduler ❹ then learns the optimal batch size, exit point, and node dispatching for each request based on the collected request information and predicted latency (Sect. 5). Next, each edge node ❺ deploys multi-exit DNN models using the joint optimal configuration from the scheduler. Finally, the inference results ❻ are sent back to clients, thus completing an end-to-end inference request.

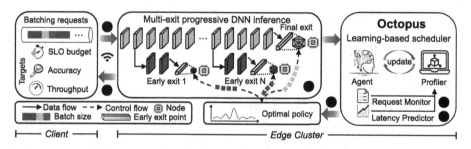

Fig. 2. Overview of Octopus system architecture.

3.2   Problem Formulation

Let $\mathbb{K} = \{1, 2, \ldots, K\}$ represent the set of inference requests. Each request $k \in \mathbb{K}$ has its input data size D_k, network bandwidth $\mathcal{B}_k$, expected accuracy ξ_k, request rate τ_k and SLO budget s_k. The edge cluster comprises multiple heterogeneous edge nodes, denoted as $\mathbb{N} = \{1, 2, \ldots, N\}$, The computility (i.e., floating point operations per second) and hardware clock frequency of each edge node $n \in \mathbb{N}$ are represented by C_n and f_n, respectively. The higher the hardware clock frequency, the bigger the computility. An ensemble of domain-specific DNN models (such as CV and NLP) forms a DNN Zoo, denoted as $\mathbb{M} = \{1, 2, \ldots, M\}$. The inference latency of each DNN model $m \in \mathbb{M}$ is related to the batch size b and exit point q. The set of batch sizes is denoted as $\mathbb{B} = \{1, 2, \ldots, B\}$. The larger the batch size, the higher the throughput. The set of exit points for a DNN model is denoted as $\mathbb{Q} = \{1, 2, \ldots, Q\}$. Each exit point $q(q \in \mathbb{Q})$ is sorted in ascending order according to inference latency. Note that the later the exit point, the higher the latency and the accuracy.

The end-to-end latency of the i-th request k comprises network latency and inference latency. More precisely, network latency is modeled as a function of input data size D_k and network bandwidth $\mathcal{B}_k$. Inference latency is related to the input data size D_k, the computility C_n and the clock frequency f_n of each edge node, and the batch size b_k, which can be formulated as:

$$t_k(b, n, m, q) = \frac{D_k}{\mathcal{B}_k} + \frac{D_k \cdot C_n}{f_k \cdot b_k}, \tag{1}$$

Inspired by [16], we introduce a binary decision variable $\psi_{b,n,m,q} \in \{0, 1\}$ to indicate whether a request k is dispatched to DNN m with exit point q and batch size b deployed on edge node n. We first model the throughput on a single edge node. Each edge node deploys multiple DNN models with varying exit points and batch sizes. The throughput of each node processing K inference requests can be formulated as:

$$rps_k(b, n, m, q) = \frac{K}{\sum_K t_k(b, n, m, q)} \cdot \psi_{b,n,m,q}, \tag{2}$$

The goal of Octopus is to maximize the overall throughput of the edge cluster while satisfying the SLO budget and maintaining high accuracy for each inference request. Based on the throughput of an individual edge node as defined in Eq. (2), the scheduling problem can be formulated as:

$$\min_{\psi} \sum_{n=1}^{N} rps_k(b, n, m, q) \cdot \tau_k \cdot \psi_{b,n,m,q} \tag{3}$$

$$s.t. \sum_{b=1}^{B} \sum_{n=1}^{N} \sum_{m=1}^{M} \sum_{q=1}^{Q} \psi_{b,n,m,q} = 1, \forall k \in K \tag{4}$$

$$ITA_k(b, n, m, q) \geq \xi_k, \forall k \in K \tag{5}$$

$$t_k(b, n, m, q) \leq s_k, \forall k \in K \tag{6}$$

$$\tau_k \cdot \psi_{b,n,m,q} \leq rps_k(b, n, m, q), \forall k \in K \tag{7}$$

$$\psi_{b,n,m,q} \in \{0, 1\}, \forall b \in B, \forall n \in N, \forall m \in M, \forall q \in Q \tag{8}$$

$$ModelSize(m_q) + PeakSize(m_q) + BufSize(m_q) \leq Memory_{avl}^{n} \tag{9}$$

where Eq. (3) defines the maximizing overall throughput as the optimization objective. Equation (4) ensures that each inference request can only be dispatched to a single edge node. $ITA_k(b, n, m, q)$ is the inference-to-accuracy of request k on DNN m_q deployed on node n with exit point q. Equation (5) specifies that $ITA_k(b, n, m, q)$ is higher than the accuracy budget ξ_k. Equation (6) enforces latency budget, that is, the end-to-end latency should not exceed the SLO budget. Equation (7) ensures that each edge node has enough resources to support batch inference. Equation (8) illustrates that the dispatch of request is a binary variable, meaning that a DNN model cannot be partitioned for distributed inference. Equation (9) considers the limited memory resources of edge nodes. Since multi-exit DNN models require intensive memory for inference [8], it is necessary to load the weight matrix $ModelSize(m_q)$, the intermediate feature matrix $PeakSize(m_q)$, and the buffer size $BufSize(m_q)$ into memory to speed up inference. The total memory requirement should not exceed the available memory of the edge device $Memory_{avl}^n$.

4   SLO-Aware Latency Predictor

Octopus predicts the latency of the current batch requests based on the previous batches. Prior work [5] has revealed that DNN inference is highly predictable. Importantly, there is a highly correlated temporal relationship between consecutive requests, such as video streams for object monitoring. Attention mechanism [21] and long short-term memory (LSTM) [7] have shown impressive effectiveness in predicting long- and short-term time series data, respectively. Inspired by [24], we adopt an attention-based LSTM as latency predictor, to achieve SLO-awareness for batch requests. The latency predictor aims to minimize the error between the predicted and actual latency for batch requests:

$$\min_{\sigma} \mathcal{L}(\hat{L}_b^t, L_b^t) = \min \sum_b [(\hat{l}_b^t - l_b^t)^2] \tag{10}$$

$$s.t. \ \hat{L}_b^t = f(\{l_b^{t-N}, l_b^{t-N+1}, , l_b^{t-1}, \dots\}, \sigma) \tag{11}$$

where L_b^t is the actual latency of batch requests with batch size b at time slot t, and $\hat{L}_b^t$ is the corresponding predicted latency. l_b^t and $\hat{l}_b^t$ represent the actual and predicted latency of the b-th inference request in the batch requests, respectively. σ is the LSTM parameter, and N represents the number of previous batch requests used in the prediction network $f(\cdot)$.

As shown in Fig. 3, the attention-based LSTM-based latency predictor is composed of an encoder, an attention module and a decoder.

Encoder. The encoder is implemented using a two-layer LSTM. To accurately predict the latency of the b-th request in the current batch requests, the encoder takes as input the latency corresponding to the b-th request in the past N batches of requests, and encodes it into a feature map $\{Y_t\}$:

$$Y_t = f(Y_{t_1}, L_b^N) \tag{12}$$

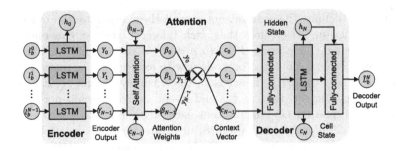

Fig. 3. Overview of the attention-based LSTM for latency predictor.

where $f(\cdot, \cdot)$ denotes the LSTM network.

Attention Module. We use an attention module with a fully-connected layer to evaluate the importance of encoded feature maps. The weight of the feature map generated by the attention module can be formulated as:

$$\mu_t = W_1 \tanh(W_2[Y; c_{N-1}; h_{N-1}]) \tag{13}$$

$$\beta(Attn)_t = \frac{\exp(\mu_t)}{\sum_t \exp(\mu_t)} \tag{14}$$

where $[Y; c_(N-1); h_(N-1)]$ represents the encoder output Y, the state vector $c_(N-1)$ of decoder unit, and the hidden state vector of decoder $h_(N-1)$. W_1 and W_2 are the weights that need to be optimized. $\beta(Attn)_t$ is the normalized weight of different feature maps. The context vector $c_(N-1)$ is used to evaluate the contribution of each feature map.

Decoder. The decoder is implemented using two fully-connected layers and an LSTM, which processes the context vectors.

5   Learning-Based Scheduler

Complexity Analysis: Octopus aims to find the optimal batch size, exit point and node assignment for each inference request to maximize the overall throughput of the edge cluster. The challenge with the three-dimensional scheduling space for Octopus is that scheduling decisions are affected by several interdependent variables. More precisely, the batch size and exit point depend on the computing resources of the allocated nodes to ensure SLO and accuracy. To represent the search space, suppose Q is the number of exit points in a DNN model, M is the number of DNN models to serve, and B is the number of batch sizes on each multi-exit DNN model. Therefore, there are a total of $B^M Q^M$ possible options to configure M DNN models. Since there are N edge nodes in an edge cluster, the complexity of the search space is as follows:

$$Total\ Search\ Space = O(NQ^M B^M) \tag{15}$$

Solving such a huge search space is non-trivial. Exhaustively search and heuristic-based approaches are unable to handle the problem in polynomial time. In contrast, deep reinforcement learning (DRL) considers the impact of current decisions on future outcomes by using Markov decision process (MDP), and learns the optimal policy to maximize cumulative returns, enabling it to be suitable for complex decision problems in multi-dimensional search spaces. Consequently, we propose leveraging DRL to automatically learn the optimal joint configuration of batch size, exit point, and node dispatching.

Markov Decision Process. In DRL, the agent continuously interacts with the environment and makes decisions via a policy, which is achieved using Markov decision process (MDP). Consequently, we first transform the scheduling problem in Eq. (3) into an MDP. An MDP can be represented as a three-tuple: state space $\mathcal{S}$, action space $\mathcal{A}$ and reward function r, which are described as follows:

- **State:** At each scheduling time slot t, the agent in DRL constructs a state $s_t(s_t \in \mathcal{S})$ to periodically collect the information of inference requests. We define the state s_t using four components: (I) Input data size D_t. (II) Bandwidth $\mathcal{B}_k$. (III) Request rate τ_k. (IV) Predicted latency $\hat{L}_b^{N+1}$.
- **Action:** The action represents a decision made by the agent based on the current state. We define the action as the choosing of the appropriate batch size b, exit point q, and edge node n for each multi-exit DNN model, which can be denoted as $a_t = (b, q, n)$.
- **Reward:** The agent aims to maximize the cumulative expected reward $\mathbb{E}\left[\sum_{t=0}^{T} \gamma^t r_t\right]$, where $\gamma \in [0, 1]$ is a discount factor. r_t denotes the immediate reward obtained when the agent executes inference after choosing the appropriate batch size, exit point, and edge node. We define the reward function r_t using the accuracy τ_k and SLO violation rate s_k, based on Eq. (3):

$$r_t(\xi; \eta) = \frac{1}{1 + e^{-\xi/\eta}} \sum_{n=1}^{N} rps_k(b, n, m, q) \cdot \tau_k \cdot \psi_{b,n,m,q} \qquad (16)$$

Maximum Entropy Reinforcement Learning-Based Scheduling Algorithm. Our proposed scheduling algorithm is based on the discrete soft Actor-Critic (SAC) [2] framework. SAC is maximum entropy DRL algorithm, which aims to maximize both the reward and the entropy of the visited states, enabling the agent in DRL to learn more near-optimal actions and accelerating the learning process. Meanwhile, it also allows the agent to explore a larger search space and enhances the robustness of the system.

The policy π is the function that determines the next action chosen by the agent based on current state. The optimal strategy π^* can be formulated as:

$$\pi^* = \arg\max_{\pi} \sum_{t=0}^{T} E_{(s_t, a_t) \sim \rho_\pi} [r(s_t, a_t) + \alpha \mathcal{H}(\pi(\cdot \mid s_t))] \qquad (17)$$

where ρ_π is the trace distribution generated by the policy π. α is the temperature parameter that balances the relative importance of entropy and reward. $\mathcal{H}(\pi(\cdot \mid s_t)) = -\log \pi(\cdot \mid s_t)$ denotes the entropy of policy π with state s_t.

We utilize soft policy iteration [2] to achieve the optimal policy, which consists of soft policy evaluation and soft policy improvement. These two steps are alternated during the training process.

Soft policy evaluation involves the calculation of the policy value, that is, soft state value function (V-function) and soft action-state value function (Q-function). The discrete V-function with entropy is defined as:

$$V(s_t) := \pi(s_t)^T [Q(s_t) - \alpha \log(\pi(s_t))] \tag{18}$$

We then obtain the soft Q-function using the soft Bellman equation:

$$\mathcal{T}^\pi Q(s_t, a_t) \triangleq r(s_t, a_t) + \gamma \mathbb{E}_{s_{t+1} \sim p}[V(s_{t+1})] \tag{19}$$

where $\mathcal{T}_\pi$ is the modified Bellman backup operator. Based on the soft Bellman equation in Eq. (19), soft policy evaluation can converge to the soft Q-function of the optimal policy π^* under limited state and action spaces.

We update the policy using the following soft policy improvement:

$$\pi_{new} = \arg \min_{\pi' \in \Pi} D_{KL}\left(\pi'(\cdot \mid s_t) \left\| \frac{\exp\left(\frac{1}{\alpha} Q^{\pi_{old}}(s_t, \cdot)\right)}{Z^{\pi_{old}}(s_t)}\right.\right) \tag{20}$$

where D_{KL} denotes the KL divergence, and $Z^{\pi_{old}}(s_t)$ is the partition function.

In our approach, we utilize two Q-networks, and for each training step, we select the network with the lower Q-value, in order to alleviate the overestimation of Q-values. The loss function of any Q-network $\mathcal{L}_Q(\theta)$ is calculated by minimizing the soft Bellman residual in Eq. (19):

$$\begin{aligned}
\mathcal{L}_Q(\theta) = E_{(s_t,a_t) \sim \mathcal{D}, a_{t+1} \sim \pi_\theta(\cdot \mid s_{t+1})}[\frac{1}{2}(Q_\theta(s_t, a_t) - (r(s_t, a_t) \\
+ \gamma(\min_{j=1,2} Q_{\theta_j}(s_{t+1}, a_{t+1}) - \alpha \log_\pi(a_{t+1} \mid s_{t+1}))))^2]
\end{aligned} \tag{21}$$

where $\mathcal{D}$ is the replay buffer that used to store the collected historical traces. To facilitate more stable training, we utilize two target Q-networks $\bar{Q}_{\bar{\theta}_j} (j = 1, 2)$ that correspond to the two Q-networks used to calculate Q-values.

The loss function of policy $\mathcal{L}_\pi(\varphi)$ is calculated by minimizing the KL divergence in Eq. (20):

$$\mathcal{L}_\pi(\varphi) = E_{s_t \sim D}\left[\pi_t(s_t)^T [\alpha \log(\pi_\varphi(s_t)) - Q_\theta(s_t)]\right] \tag{22}$$

Note that it is critical to choose the appropriate temperature parameter α. For instance, in states where the optimal action is highly uncertain, the importance of entropy should be increased. As a reference [2], the loss function of the temperature parameter $\mathcal{L}_\alpha$ is formulated as:

$$\mathcal{L}_\alpha = \pi_t(s_t)^T[-\alpha(\log(\pi_t(s_t)) + \bar{H})] \tag{23}$$

where $\bar{H}$ is a constant vector. More precisely, when the entropy of the policy is lower than $\bar{H}$, the loss function $\mathcal{L}_{(\alpha)}$ will increase the value of α, thereby enhancing the importance of entropy during training.

Algorithm 1 provides an overview of our proposed learning-based scheduling search algorithm. We take as input the request information collected by the profiler and the latency predicted by the latency predictor. Before training, we first initialize all network weights and the replay buffer (*line 1~3*). For each training episode, we take the current request as the initial state of the environment (*line 5*). At each environment step, we select an action a_t (*line 7*) based on the current policy $\pi_\varphi(a_t \mid s_t)$, and execute the action while receiving a reward (*line 8*). Next, the scheduler feeds back the decisions made by the DRL to the corresponding edge nodes for progressive inference (*line 9*). When inference is complete, DRL updates the environment state (*line 10*) while storing the current trajectory in the replay buffer (*line 11*). For each gradient step, we calculate the soft state value and Q value by random sampling (*line 14~15*), and update all network weights and the temperature parameter (*line 16~19*). As this process repeats, the learning-based algorithm eventually converges on the optimal policy that maximizes the overall throughput of the edge cluster.

Algorithm 1: Learning-based scheduling search algorithm.

Input : set of requests $\mathbb{K} = \{1, 2, \ldots, K\}$, information per request k with input data size D_k, bandwidth $\mathcal{B}_k$, predicted latency $\hat{L}_b^N$ and request rate τ_k, target budget with accuracy ξ_k and SLO s_k

Output: the optimal schedule $\{b_k, n_k, q_k\}$ for each request k

1 Initialize actor network $\pi(s \mid \varphi)$ with φ and critic network $Q_{\theta_1}, Q_{\theta_2}$ with θ_1 and θ_2, respectively

2 Initialize target network $\bar{Q}_{\bar{\theta}_1}, \bar{Q}_{\bar{\theta}_2}$: $\bar{\theta}_1 \leftarrow \theta_1, \bar{\theta}_2 \leftarrow \theta_2$

3 Initialize an empty replay buffer $\mathcal{D} \leftarrow \emptyset$

4 **for** *each epoch* $e = 1 \to E$ **do**

5   Generate current request $k(D_k, \mathcal{B}_k, tau_k, \hat{L}_b^N)$ with target budget $\{\tau_k, s_k\}$ as the initial state of the environment s_1

6   **for** *each environment step* $t = 1 \to T$ **do**

7   Sample action $a_t = s_t(b_k, n_k, q_k) \sim \pi_\varphi(a_t \mid s_t)$

8   Execute action a_t and obtain instant reward $r_t(a_t \mid s_t)$ using Eq. (16)

9   Execute progressive inference with action $a_t(b_k, n_k, q_k)$

10   Update state $s_t \leftarrow s_{t+1}$

11   Store the transition $(s_t, a_t, r(s_t, a_t), s_{t+1})$ in the replay buffer $\mathcal{D}$

12   **end**

13   **for** *each gradient step* $g = 1 \to G$ **do**

14   Sample transition from the environment $s_{t+1} \sim p(s_{t+1} \mid s_t, a_t)$

15   Calculate the soft state value $V(s_t)$ with policy π using Eq. (18) and the soft Q-function $Q(s_t, a_t)$ using Eq. (19), respectively

16   Update critic network weights θ_i for $i \in \{1, 2\}$ using Eq. (21)

17   Update actor network weight φ using Eq. (22)

18   Update temperature parameter α using Eq. (23)

19   Update target network weights $\bar{Q}_{\bar{\theta}_1} \leftarrow \lambda Q_{\theta_i} + (1 - \lambda)\bar{Q}_{\bar{\theta}_1}$ for $i \in \{1, 2\}$

20   **end**

21 **end**

---

6 Prototype and Performance Evaluation

6.1 Implementation

Octopus Prototype. Octopus is implemented using PyTorch. We use an NVIDIA Xavier NX as the master node to receive inference requests from multiple clients. Additionally, we employ three heterogeneous edge devices as nodes to execute inference for specific multi-exit DNN models. The detailed configurations of each edge device are detailed in Table 1. For offline training of Algorithm 1, we use an edge server equipped with four NVIDIA GeForce GTX 3080 GPUs, using a mini-batch size of 128 for 2000 epochs. All networks are trained using the Adam optimizer with a learning rate of 10^{-3}. Each network comprises a two-layer ReLU neural network with 64 and 32 hidden units, respectively. The size of the replay buffer is fixed at 10^6. The trained learning-based scheduler is ultimately deployed online on the master node.

Table 1. The detailed configurations of edge devices.

Edge Device	CPU	GPU	Memory	Computility
NVIDIA Jetson Nano	ARM Cortex-A57	128-core Maxwell	4 GB	0.47TFLOPS
NVIDIA Jetson TX2	ARM Cortex-A57	256-core Pascal	8 GB	1.33TFLOPS
NVIDIA Xavier NX	Carmel ARMv8.2	384-core Volta	8 GB	21TOPS

DNN Zoo and Datasets. Three domain-specific DNN models are used to process image and speech data, as summarized in Table 2. We adopt the BranchyNet framework [19], which supports multi-exit DNN training with five early exit points per DNN model. The DNN Zoo, comprising these multi-exit DNN models, is deployed on each edge node.

Table 2. The specific information for inference requests.

Request Type	DNN Model	Dataset	SLO(ms)	Accuracy(%)
Object Detection	YOLOv4-Tiny	VOC-2012	50	64.31
Semantic Segmentation	EfficientViT-B1	Cityscapes	75	81.65
Natural Language Processing	BERT-Base	SQuAD v1.1	25	79.52

Baselines. We compare Octopus with three baselines: DeepRT [23] develops a soft real-time scheduler for single edge device that leverages earliest-deadline-first (EDF) [4] to schedule batch requests. DINA [15] utilizes matching theory to achieve distributed inference with adaptive DNN partitioning and offloading. Edgent [11] proposes a regression-based predictive model for multi-exit DNN inference through device-edge synergy. Since our proposed Octopus is the first framework for multi-tenant progressive inference serving on heterogeneous edge clusters, we scale three baselines to the edge cluster in Table 1 and compare the sum of their throughput on each edge node, for a fair comparison.

Workloads and Network. We synthesize workloads using the three datasets detailed in Table 2, and use three Jetson Nano edge devices as multi-clients to generate inference requests based on these synthetic workloads. Note that inference requests arrive randomly to simulate the real-world applications, and each client always submits inference requests for a specific DNN model. The default request rate is fixed at $30rps$, unless otherwise specified. Besides, we use $WiFi$ to connect clients and edge devices, with available bandwidth ranging from 2 Mbps to 24 Mbps to simulate fluctuations in dynamic network conditions.

6.2   End-to-End Performance

Overall Throughput Improvement. As shown in Fig. 4(a), the overall throughput of Octopus, as detailed in Table 2, consistently outperforms the baselines. More precisely, Octopus achieves 1.3×–3.3× improvement in overall throughput. Although DeepRT utilizes batching to improve throughput, it suffers from resource-constrained edge devices and high memory overhead associated with executing entire DNN models. As a result, its throughput is lower than those of the two multi-exit DNN-based methods, Edgent and DINA, which do not utilize batching. Octopus takes advantage of both batching and multi-exit inference to improve the overall throughput of the edge cluster while significantly reducing resource occupancy.

SLO Violation Rate. We also analyzed the SLO violation rate of Octopus at a request rate of $30rps$. As shown in Fig. 4(b), Octopus exhibits the lowest SLO violation rate, below 5%, thanks to its SLO-aware latency predictor. The admission control module in DeepRT aims to reduce the SLO violation rate by analyzing the schedulability of inference requests, but it ignores the temporal relationship between inference requests, resulting in a higher SLO violation rate than Octopus. Edgent and DINA do not focus on SLO awareness for inference requests, and thus have significantly higher SLO violation rates.

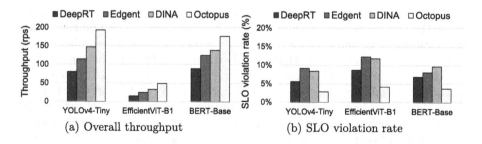

(a) Overall throughput   (b) SLO violation rate

Fig. 4. The end-to-end performance of Octopus.

6.3 Visualization of Scheduler in Three-Dimensional Search Space

As shown in Fig. 5(a), within the complex three-dimensional search space, the scheduler chooses the Jetson Nano with the lowest computility, a moderate batch size, and a moderate exit point for YOLOv4-Tiny, which has the lowest computing density. For EfficientViT-B1 in Fig. 5(b), which has the highest computing density, the optimal configuration, is a larger batch size, the Xavier NX with the highest computility, and a later exit point. For BERT-Base, which has a computing density between that of YOLOv4-Tiny and EfficientViT-B1, as shown in Fig. 5(c), the scheduler chooses the Jetson TX2 with moderate computility, a larger batch size and a later exit point. Overall, Octopus can seamlessly adapt to heterogeneous edge nodes and different multi-exit DNN models for various inference requests, choosing the optimal batch size and exit point to maximize throughput while satisfying SLO budget and accuracy requirement.

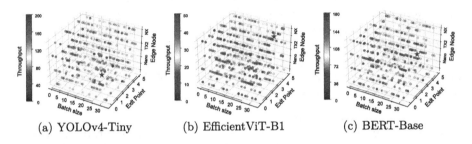

(a) YOLOv4-Tiny   (b) EfficientViT-B1   (c) BERT-Base

Fig. 5. The learning process of sheduler. ⋆ represents the optimal joint configuration.

6.4 Impact of Latency Predictor

To evaluate the effect of proposed SLO-aware latency predictor, we collected end-to-end latency and SLO for a total of 500 inference requests. We randomly selected 400 information of requests as training data and 100 data for validation. Figure 6(a) presents the training loss curve over 120 epochs. The results demonstrate that Octopus enables more accurate SLO-awareness based on contextual historical requests compared to the widely adopted linear regression-based predictive model used in prior work [1]. Furthermore, benefit from the combination of lightweight LSTM and attention, Octopus significantly reduces training loss and achieves similar convergence to linear regression. We also report the SLO violation rate in Fig. 6(b), which shows that the attention-based LSTM reduces the average SLO violation rate from 7.9% to 3.5%, compared with linear regression. It reveals that linear regression is inefficient for accurately predicting the SLO of unknown inference requests. In contrast, the attention-based LSTM focuses on the temporal relationship between inference requests, which utilizes neural networks to model the nonlinear relationship between inference latency and complex influencing factors, thereby effectively avoiding SLO violations.

6.5   Impact of Network Bandwidth

In this section, we evaluate the impact of dynamic network conditions on the optimal configuration chosen by the scheduler in Octopus. The trend in Fig. 7(a) indicates that the batch size increases as network bandwidth improves, allowing more requests to be processed and resulting in higher throughput. Figure 7(b) shows that the scheduler chooses the earliest exit point for all requests when the available bandwidth is only 2 Mbps. Similarly, as the network bandwidth improves, the position of exit point is gradually moved back to improve accuracy while satisfying SLO. The results in Fig. 7(c) demonstrate that Octopus tends to schedule requests to edge nodes with high computility, such as Xavier NX, under poor network bandwidth conditions. In contrast, when bandwidth is not the bottleneck, Octopus schedules requests to edge nodes with low computility, such as Jetson Nano or TX2, to achieve load balancing of edge cluster.

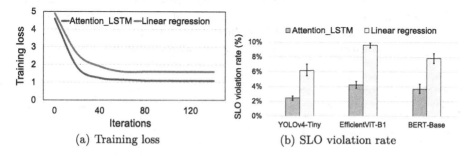

(a) Training loss   (b) SLO violation rate

Fig. 6. The performance of the proposed latency predictor.

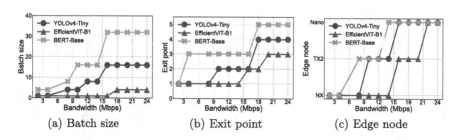

(a) Batch size   (b) Exit point   (c) Edge node

Fig. 7. The impact of dynamic network on the optimal configuration.

6.6   Evaluation of Scalability

Different Request Rates. Since the performance of scheduler, especially the position of the exit point, is affected by the request rate, we evaluate inference accuracy by gradually increasing the request rate. Note that DeepRT, which does not employ multi-exit DNNs, exhibits the highest accuracy. Figure 8 shows that Octopus outperforms Edgent and DINA in terms of accuracy, with the performance improvement increases as the request rate increases. For instance, at 50*rps* request rate, the average accuracy improvement of Octopus is up to 10.6% and 7.6% compared to Edgent and DINA, respectively. Additionally, the accuracy loss of Octopus remains within 5%. The results indicate that the SLO-aware latency predictor and learning-based scheduler enable Octopus to handle high request rates while maintaining high accuracy.

Number of Edge Nodes. We evaluate the scalability of Octopus by scaling the number of edge nodes. As shown in Fig. 9(a), the average overall throughput improvement of Octopus with eight nodes is 3.1×, 2.1× and 1.2× that of two, four and six nodes, respectively. This indicates that the number of edge nodes is highly linear with the overall throughput of edge cluster. We also report the effect of the number of edge nodes on SLO violation rate and inference accuracy in Fig. 9(b). Intuitively, inference accuracy gradually improves as the number of edge nodes increases. For instance, the average accuracy of Octopus with eight nodes is 2.6%, 1.8% and 1% higher than that of two, four and six nodes, respectively. Additionally, the SLO violation rate at the default request rate (30*rps*) remains within 5%, demonstrating the flexible scalability of Octopus.

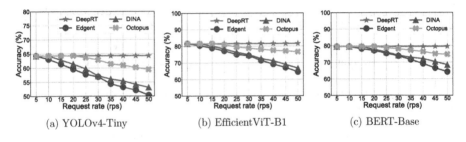

Fig. 8. The impact of different request rates on inference accuracy.

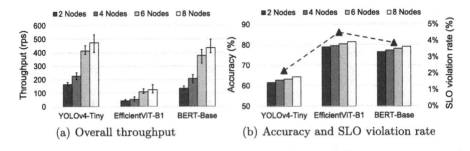

Fig. 9. The impact of number of edge nodes on throughput and inference accuracy.

7 Conclusion

In this paper, we propose Octopus, a multi-exit DNN-based progressive inference serving system for heterogeneous edge clusters. The learning-based scheduler in Octopus aims to maximize the overall throughput of edge clusters by automatically co-optimizing the joint configuration of batch size, exit point, and node dispatching for each inference request. Additionally, Octopus leverages an attention-based LSTM as a latency predictor to achieve SLO-aware. Our prototype implementation illustrates that Octopus has flexible scalability, and it can improve the overall inference serving throughput by up to 3.3× compared to the state-of-the-art schemes, while satisfying SLO and maintaining high inference accuracy. We emphasize that Octopus is primarily targets edge clusters, but is also applicable to individual edge devices. For the future work, Octopus can be combined with various inference optimization technologies (such as cloud-edge collaborative inference, compilation optimization, model compression, etc.) to further improve inference performance.

Acknowledgment. We thank our anonymous reviewers for their helpful comments and feedback. This work is partly supported by the National Key R&D Program of China under Grant No. 2021ZD0110905, and An Open Competition Project of Heilongjiang Province, China, on Research and Application of Key Technologies for Intelligent Farming Decision Platform, under Grant No. 2021ZXJ05A03.

References

1. Choi, S., Lee, S., Kim, Y., Park, J., Kwon, Y., Huh, J.: Serving heterogeneous machine learning models on {Multi-GPU} servers with {Spatio-Temporal} sharing. In: 2022 USENIX Annual Technical Conference (USENIX ATC 2022), pp. 199–216 (2022)
2. Christodoulou, P.: Soft actor-critic for discrete action settings. arXiv preprint arXiv:1910.07207 (2019)
3. Dong, F., et al.: Multi-exit DNN inference acceleration based on multi-dimensional optimization for edge intelligence. IEEE Trans. Mob. Comput. (2022)
4. Faggioli, D., Trimarchi, M., Checconi, F., Bertogna, M., Mancina, A.: An implementation of the earliest deadline first algorithm in linux. In: Proceedings of the 2009 ACM Symposium on Applied Computing, pp. 1984–1989 (2009)
5. Gujarati, A., et al.: Serving {DNNs} like clockwork: performance predictability from the bottom up. In: 14th USENIX Symposium on Operating Systems Design and Implementation (OSDI 2020), pp. 443–462 (2020)
6. Hao, J., Subedi, P., Ramaswamy, L., Kim, I.K.: Reaching for the sky: maximizing deep learning inference throughput on edge devices with AI multi-tenancy. ACM Trans. Internet Technol. **23**(1), 1–33 (2023)
7. Hochreiter, S., Schmidhuber, J.: Long short-term memory. Neural Comput. **9**(8), 1735–1780 (1997)
8. Jeon, S., Choi, Y., Cho, Y., Cha, H.: Harvnet: resource-optimized operation of multi-exit deep neural networks on energy harvesting devices. In: Proceedings of the 21st Annual International Conference on Mobile Systems, Applications and Services, pp. 42–55 (2023)

9. Jeong, J.S., et al.: Band: coordinated multi-DNN inference on heterogeneous mobile processors. In: Proceedings of the 20th Annual International Conference on Mobile Systems, Applications and Services, pp. 235–247 (2022)

10. Laskaridis, S., Venieris, S.I., Almeida, M., Leontiadis, I., Lane, N.D.: Spinn: synergistic progressive inference of neural networks over device and cloud. In: Proceedings of the 26th Annual International Conference on Mobile Computing and Networking, pp. 1–15 (2020)

11. Li, E., Zeng, L., Zhou, Z., Chen, X.: Edge AI: on-demand accelerating deep neural network inference via edge computing. IEEE Trans. Wireless Commun. **19**(1), 447–457 (2019)

12. Liang, Q., Hanafy, W.A., Bashir, N., Ali-Eldin, A., Irwin, D., Shenoy, P.: Dĕlen: enabling flexible and adaptive model-serving for multi-tenant edge AI. In: Proceedings of the 8th ACM/IEEE Conference on Internet of Things Design and Implementation, pp. 209–221 (2023)

13. Ling, N., Huang, X., Zhao, Z., Guan, N., Yan, Z., Xing, G.: Blastnet: exploiting duo-blocks for cross-processor real-time DNN inference. In: Proceedings of the 20th ACM Conference on Embedded Networked Sensor Systems, pp. 91–105 (2022)

14. Liu, Z., Lan, G., Stojkovic, J., Zhang, Y., Joe-Wong, C., Gorlatova, M.: Collabar: edge-assisted collaborative image recognition for mobile augmented reality. In: 2020 19th ACM/IEEE International Conference on Information Processing in Sensor Networks (IPSN), pp. 301–312. IEEE (2020)

15. Mohammed, T., Joe-Wong, C., Babbar, R., Di Francesco, M.: Distributed inference acceleration with adaptive DNN partitioning and offloading. In: IEEE INFOCOM 2020-IEEE Conference on Computer Communications, pp. 854–863. IEEE (2020)

16. Nigade, V., Bauszat, P., Bal, H., Wang, L.: Jellyfish: timely inference serving for dynamic edge networks. In: 2022 IEEE Real-Time Systems Symposium (RTSS), pp. 277–290. IEEE (2022)

17. Seo, W., Cha, S., Kim, Y., Huh, J., Park, J.: SLO-aware inference scheduler for heterogeneous processors in edge platforms. ACM Trans. Archit. Code Optim. **18**(4), 1–26 (2021)

18. Shi, W., Cao, J., Zhang, Q., Li, Y., Xu, L.: Edge computing: vision and challenges. IEEE Internet Things J. **3**(5), 637–646 (2016)

19. Teerapittayanon, S., McDanel, B., Kung, H.T.: Branchynet: fast inference via early exiting from deep neural networks. In: 2016 23rd International Conference on Pattern Recognition (ICPR), pp. 2464–2469. IEEE (2016)

20. Teng, S., et al.: Motion planning for autonomous driving: the state of the art and future perspectives. IEEE Trans. Intell. Veh. (2023)

21. Vaswani, A., et al.: Attention is all you need. In: Advances in Neural Information Processing Systems, vol. 30 (2017)

22. Wu, J., Wang, L., Pei, Q., Cui, X., Liu, F., Yang, T.: HiTDL: high-throughput deep learning inference at the hybrid mobile edge. IEEE Trans. Parallel Distrib. Syst. **33**(12), 4499–4514 (2022)

23. Yang, Z., Nahrstedt, K., Guo, H., Zhou, Q.: Deeprt: a soft real time scheduler for computer vision applications on the edge. In: 2021 IEEE/ACM Symposium on Edge Computing (SEC), pp. 271–284. IEEE (2021)

24. Zhang, W., et al.: ELF: accelerate high-resolution mobile deep vision with content-aware parallel offloading. In: Proceedings of the 27th Annual International Conference on Mobile Computing and Networking, pp. 201–214 (2021)

25. Zhou, Z., Chen, X., Li, E., Zeng, L., Luo, K., Zhang, J.: Edge intelligence: paving the last mile of artificial intelligence with edge computing. Proc. IEEE **107**(8), 1738–1762 (2019)

Industrial Papers

Anonymization-as-a-Service: The Service Center Transcripts Industrial Case

Nemania Borovits[1]([✉]), Gianluigi Bardelloni[2], Damian Andrew Tamburri[1], and Willem-Jan Van Den Heuvel[3]

[1] Eindhoven University of Technology, Eindhoven, Netherlands
n.borovits@tue.nl, d.a.tamburri@tue.nl
[2] KPN, Amsterdam, Netherlands
gianluigi.bardelloni@kpn.com
[3] Tilburg University, Tilburg, Netherlands
W.J.A.M.vdnHeuvel@tilburguniversity.edu

Abstract. Modern Big Data Analytics services require compliance with non-functional requirements such as privacy, in order to align with the introduced legislation such as the General Data Protection Regulation (GDPR). Specifically, the Telco industry has been using Big Data Analytics solutions for service continuity, whose basic steps revolve around automatically transcribing call center text data to extract valuable insights and enhance customer service. Such data obviously contains Personal Identifiable Information (PII) which hampers privacy-sensitive service operations if not handled properly. To meet these requirements we created Deperson—an efficient rule-based data anonymization service—which enables companies to anonymize customer data effectively while preserving its utility for further analysis. As a proof-of-concept, Deperson has been integrated into an existing Big Data Analytics solution in the Customer Contact Analytics department of a major Dutch Telco provider to ensure compliance with GDPR regulations. Based on dictionary look-ups and pattern-matching rules Deperson effectively removes PII achieving an accuracy of 0.82 while maintaining the essential information necessary for analysis. Our concept shows that Deperson plays a significant role in enabling the extraction and further processing of valuable insights from customer data without risking non-compliance with GDPR.

Keywords: Data Anonymization · Anonymization as a Service · Natural Language Processing

1 Introduction

The "Big Data" age is characterized by the amount, diversity, velocity, and veracity of data generated between individuals and numerous end-point devices and censors [11]. Beyond the technological constraints, data overflow and insight extraction create a number of challenges that might make it difficult to comply

F. Monti et al. (Eds.): ICSOC 2023, LNCS 14420, pp. 261–275, 2023.
https://doi.org/10.1007/978-3-031-48424-7_19

with regulations. Privacy preservation is one such challenge [33]. Data privacy has been characterized as the most important challenge for this decade [24]. As privacy legislation is implemented globally organizations are required to take action to comply with legal privacy regulations and individuals' privacy preferences [16]. In Computer Science and Information Systems, privacy is realized within the context of personal data. Personal data, which contains Personal Identifiable Information (PII), is any information about an identified or identifiable natural person, called data subject, according to the General Data Protection Regulation (GDPR) [1]. Companies are frequently required to remove or mask the PII contained within their data in order to perform lawfully the corresponding data processing operations. Data anonymization is a common practice used by companies across various industries to comply with privacy laws that involve removing or obscuring PII from the collected data in order to process the obtained data lawfully [15].

In the telco industry, it is common practice to analyze customer and agent conversations that take place in call centers. Telco companies perform data anonymization to ensure they comply with the relevant data privacy laws [20]. In this work, we utilize a real-life industrial setting from a Dutch Telco provider. The provider has developed a Big Data Analytics solution based on transcribed call center text with the goals of improving the process of customer service and extracting insights from customers about the offered products and services. In most cases when the calls between customers and agents occur, customers have to disclose certain PII as part of the customer service process. Nevertheless, in instances where the collected data lacks synchronization with the subsequent data processing operations, it becomes imperative to exclude such data from the textual corpus. To accomplish this, data anonymization techniques are employed to remove sensitive information within the call center transcripts.

The recent advancements in Natural Language Processing (NLP), exemplified by the Transformer architecture and the development of the BERT model [35], have revolutionized the field of Large Language Models (LLMs), particularly in the context of data anonymization in text documents. However, recent studies have demonstrated that pre-trained models are susceptible to privacy attacks [31] due to their inclination to memorize training data without overfitting, commonly referred to as the "memorization issue" [8]. This concern gives rise to three primary types of privacy attacks: membership inference [17], model inversion [14], and training data extraction [9].

Furthermore, there has been a notable increase in data protection fines, reaching a record high of approximately 1.6 billion in 2023 [2]. As a result of these circumstances, the industrial sector has experienced a surge in concerns regarding the implementation of LLMs and is actively seeking alternatives to mitigate potential financial consequences and reputation damage [7,34]. Consequently, we propose the introduction of a rule-based data anonymization system as a solution to address these pressing concerns and attain a lightweight and scalable approach to the problem.

Our solution was integrated into the Telco provider's Big Data Analytics solution. We show our emerging results regarding data anonymization from the Dutch telco industry. Motivated by the existing academic literature on rule-based data anonymization [21,27,28,32,36] we developed Deperson, a service that removes PII from corpora so that data analysis carried out at a later stage complies with the law, in this case, the GDPR. In Fig. 1 we illustrate Deperson's integration into the Telco provider's Big Data Analytics solution. The Telco provider's Data Analytics Hub consists of various NLP services that support decisions aiming for customer service process improvement and knowledge extraction for the provider's offered products and services improvement. The Deperson service assures that anonymized text data is provided for the aforementioned data processing goals.

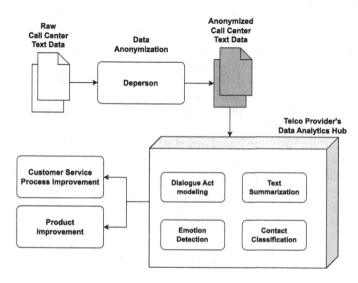

Fig. 1. Deperson's Integration into the Telco Provider's Big Data Analytics Solution.

The rest of the paper is organized as follows. Section 2 discusses the background and some significant related work. Section 3 elaborates on the research methodology used to build Deperson. Section 4 presents the data anonymization methodology. Section 5 elaborates on the data anonymization as a service integration to a Big Data Analytics solution. Section 6 presents Deperson's results regarding data anonymization. Section 7 discusses the results, the advantages and shortcomings of Deperson. Section 8 concludes the paper with future research directions.

2 Backround and Related Work

Data anonymization is essential for protecting the privacy of individuals whose data is collected and used for various purposes [32]. In this context, the most common solutions for data anonymization in text documents are either Language Models (LLMs) or rule-based approaches.

Prior works studied the privacy leakage issues of LLMs and claimed that memorizing training data leads to private data leakage [9,18,23,25,30]. Moreover, increasing apprehensions have emerged from multiple viewpoints that encompass the entire lifecycle of LLMs development. For instance, the acquisition and handling of data for LLM training necessitate meticulous adherence to privacy-preserving protocols [5]. Protecting user privacy throughout the lifecycle is essential, involving secure data transmission, encryption, and access controls [29]. Algorithmic transparency is vital to address biases or discriminatory behavior in LLMs while data minimization required for training should be considered to reduce privacy risks [13].

Rule-based approaches rely on a set of predefined rules to identify and replace personally identifiable information (PII) in text documents with more general and less identifiable terms. These rules can be customized for different types of data and use cases, making them flexible and adaptable. One example of a rule-based approach for data anonymization in text documents is the system developed by [27]. In this word, they used a set of pre-defined rules to detect and replace PII in text documents with more general terms. The system allows users to specify their own custom rules and thresholds for anonymization, as well as to manually review and edit anonymized text. Another example is the one developed by [21], which uses rule-based and statistical methods to identify and mask sensitive information in text documents. The system is designed to be scalable and can handle large volumes of data, making it suitable for enterprise-level data anonymization. Other related works in this area include the rule-based Chinese clinical text de-identification system proposed by [19], and the privacy-preserving classification of customer data without loss of accuracy system proposed by [36].

3   Research Context and Methods

3.1   Industrial Context

For the adoption of our data anonymization service, we engaged the Data Science Lab (DSL) of the Customer Contact Analytics (CCA) department within a prominent Dutch Telco provider, which we refer to as the DSL Team. The company has established itself as one of the pioneers of the Privacy by Design framework, exhibiting a firm commitment to ensuring that all processing operations are conducted lawfully and in compliance with the GDPR. Our collaboration with the DSL Team stemmed from our shared objectives of safeguarding privacy and upholding legal obligations within the context of Big Data analytics.

With hundreds of branches, a vast workforce comprising hundreds of thousands of employees, and an extensive customer base spanning both the Business-to-Business (B2B) and Business-to-Consumer (B2C) domains, the Telco provider holds a prominent position in the telecommunications industry. As part of their strategic decision-making processes, they have harnessed a sophisticated streaming platform designed to analyze data derived from call centers. By transcribing this data into text and subjecting it to comprehensive analysis, the company gains invaluable insights into customer opinions regarding their products and services, enabling them to make informed improvements. Furthermore, this platform enables the identification of potential bottlenecks in customer service processes, facilitating the enhancement of speed and efficiency.

Throughout the development process, we collaborated closely with the DSL Team, the IT department, Subject Matter Experts (SMEs), and the Legal Department to create a lightweight data anonymization service. Table 1 presents the comprehensive roster of experts with whom we engaged in collaborative endeavors. Our primary aim was to ensure that this solution seamlessly integrates with the existing streaming platform, thereby preserving its performance capabilities. Crucially, this anonymization service was meticulously designed to adhere to the GDPR regulations, thereby upholding the Telco provider's commitment to privacy protection and legal compliance.

Table 1. Overview of the experts we collaborated with to develop Deperson.

Job Title	Work Experience	Department
Project Manager	10 years	Data Science Lab
Data Scientist	7 years	Data Science Lab
Data Engineer	8 years	IT Product Engineering
Security engineer	12 years	IT Product Engineering
IT Administrator	23 Years	IT Product Engineering
Quality Assurance Specialist	8 years	Data Science Lab
Data Privacy Officer	10 years	Compliance & Legal Department
Legal Counsel	27 years	Legal Department
Subject Matter Experts	20–29 years	Product Development

3.2   Research Method

This paper addresses the problem of anonymizing sensitive PII from call center text data and integrating it into a Big Data Analytics solution. With this goal, we developed Deperson adopting Action Research (AR) [4] to refine and further prototype the working solution. AR was well-suited for developing our solution due to its participatory and iterative nature. By involving the key stakeholders mentioned in Sect. 3.1 throughout the research process, AR ensured that the solution aligned with real-world needs and challenges. The iterative nature of AR allowed for continuous feedback and adaptation, enabling the refinement of the approach to meet the industry requirements and compliance standards. AR encompasses distinct steps including problem identification, planning, action, reflection, and iteration [12]. Figure 2 provides a succinct overview of the undertaken actions corresponding to each phase throughout the iterative cycles of the AR methodology.

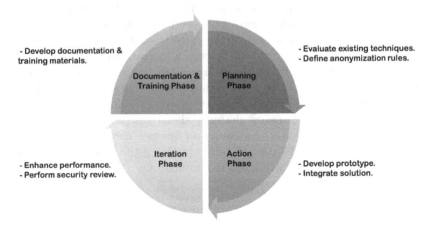

Fig. 2. The adoption of Action Research cycle for developing Deperson.

During the planning phase, we rigorously evaluated anonymization techniques, conducting a comprehensive assessment of diverse approaches. We meticulously examined the suitability of each technique to address specific privacy concerns in the industrial context and paid detailed attention to the definition and documentation of anonymization rules. This established a robust framework for data transformation and protection. This phase laid a solid foundation and set a well-informed, purposeful direction for subsequent actions in the project.

In the action phase, we prioritized practical implementation. We developed a finely crafted prototype of the anonymization tool, which incorporated the identified techniques and strictly adhered to the established rules. Moreover, we seamlessly integrated the tool into the existing Big Data Analytics Solution within the Telco provider's infrastructure during this phase.

The subsequent iteration phase emphasized refining the anonymization tool, focusing on incorporating efficiency-enhancing features like parallel processing to optimize performance and expedite the process. We also conducted a thorough security review to fortify the tool against potential vulnerabilities. This phase allowed for continuous improvements, effectively addressing emerging challenges and incorporating stakeholder insights.

The final phase centered on developing concise documentation and training materials, crucial for facilitating the tool's seamless adoption and effective utilization within the industrial environment. These materials provided comprehensive instructions and best practices, enabling users to leverage the tool's full potential with confidence. The thorough development of these materials underscored the commitment to academic rigor, ensuring knowledge dissemination to support successful implementation and sustainability.

4 Solution Design for Rule-Based Data Anonymization: The Deperson Approach

As illustrated in Fig. 1, the Big Data Analytics solution of the Telco Provider incorporates services designed to identify customer opinions on offered services or products and uncover potential bottlenecks in customer service processes. This solution subjects transcribed dialogues between customers and call center agents to NLP analysis. For optimal assistance, customers disclose specific PII, necessitating its removal to comply with legal justifications for data processing objectives. Additionally, language models, with a tendency to memorize phrases from training sets, can inadvertently reveal sensitive contexts, enabling potential reconstruction of original transcriptions by adversaries [8]. Hence, the removal of PII from our corpora is imperative for legislative compliance and to avert unintended PII disclosures.

To address these challenges, we developed *Deperson*. Deperson[1] is a data anonymization service that removes personal data from the unstructured text for the Dutch language. Examples of such data in our corpora are:

- Names of persons and places.
- Street names and house numbers.
- Postal codes.
- Phone numbers.
- Bank account numbers.
- Dates (e.g. of birth).

We removed the aforementioned PII in collaboration with the company's legal department and SMEs who manually assessed and reviewed the transcribed conversations. As a result, the subsequent NLP tasks became compliant with the law by the specified data processing goals after the PII has been removed.

Deperson's functionality is based on dictionary look-ups and pattern-matching rules via regular expressions. In practical terms, we whitelisted all parts of the text that are considered non-sensitive. This way, anything not explicitly approved is assumed to be sensitive information; e.g. a name shall be blocked no matter its specific spelling. Employing rule-based approaches, such as whitelisting, is not something new in academic literature [28]. Whitelisting requires a comprehensive dictionary of valid words to whitelist. The whitelist utilized in Deperson is generated by combining the Dutch dictionary sourced from an open-source spellchecker and publicly available datasets offered by the Dutch government. We used pattern-matching rules and regular expressions to identify indirect PII words that are language-specific and also not to falsely flag words as PII.

---

[1] available online at: https://github.com/kpnDataScienceLab/deperson.

Let $C = (c_1, c_2, \ldots, c_m)$ be a sequence of m conversations, where $c_i = (w_{i,1}, w_{i,2}, \ldots, w_{i,n_i})$ represents the i-th conversation with n_i words, where n_i is the number of words in the i-th conversation. Let $D_{\text{spellchecker}}$ be the dictionary obtained from the spellchecker data. Let D_{public} be the dictionary obtained from the publicly available dataset. The reference dictionary $D_{\text{reference}}$ is defined as the union of $D_{\text{spellchecker}}$ and D_{public}:

$$D_{\text{reference}} = D_{\text{spellchecker}} \cup D_{\text{public}}$$

In addition, let $P = \{q_1, q_2, \ldots, q_k\}$ be a set of pattern matching rules, where q_i represents the i-th rule in the set. An example of such a pattern-matching rule is the Dutch surname recognition. Dutch surnames typically include words like 'van der' or 'van den'.

For each word w_i in C, we can determine if the word is PII by checking if it satisfies either of these 2 conditions:

1. w_i is in the reference dictionary $D_{\text{reference}}$.
2. There exists a combination of words before or after w_i that matches any of the pattern rules in P, then w_i is also marked as PII.

We outline Deperson's data anonymization process in Algorithm 1. The algorithm takes as input a stream of customer conversations C. For each word w_j of each conversation c_i, it checks whether w_j is within the dictionary $D_{\text{reference}}$ or matches any of the pattern-matching rules in P. If w_j matches either of these conditions, it is replaced with the symbol $****$ otherwise, it is left unchanged. The resulting modified stream of conversations is then returned. The algorithm operates in $O(n)$ time complexity, where n is the number of words in the input stream.

Algorithm 1. Rule-based Data Anonymization Algorithm

1: **procedure** DEPERSON($c_1, c_2, \ldots, c_n$)
2:     **for all** conversation c_i **do**
3:         **for all** word w_j in c_i **do**
4:             **if** w_j is in dictionary $D_{\text{reference}}$ **OR** matches any pattern-matching rule in P **then**
5:                 replace w_j with ****
6:             **end if**
7:         **end for**
8:     **end for**
9:     **return** modified conversations $c_1', c_2', \ldots, c_n'$
10: **end procedure**

---

5   Anonymization-as-a-Service in Action

Motivated by the previous work [10], we integrated the Deperson text anonymization as a service into our Big Data Analytics solution to ensure data privacy as illustrated in Fig. 3.

The main orchestrating API called by the Big Data Analytics solution is responsible for importing the unstructured text and delivering the anonymized output. When the API receives the raw text, it calls the library that we have developed, which contains the Anonymize function. This function is modularized to ensure that each step is executed sequentially.

The first step in the Anonymize function is to tokenize the text. The next step is to flag each token as PII based on the outcome of two subsequent functions. The first function is a Dutch dictionary lookup function that identifies PII based on the presence of certain words in the dictionary. The second function is a pattern-matching rule function that uses regular expressions to identify PII based on a set of predefined rules. If the flag given to each token is TRUE, then the token is considered PII and is removed by the subsequent corresponding function.

After the PII tokens are removed, the anonymized text is returned as the output by the main orchestrating API. This output can be used as input for the following data preparation and preprocessing steps in the Big Data Analytics solution. The Deperson text anonymization as a service can be easily integrated into any existing data pipelines using a REST API.

By integrating the Deperson service into our Big Data Analytics solution, we were able to provide a seamless and effective way for anonymizing unstructured call center text data. With Deperson's modular design, this service can be easily customized to meet the specific needs of any Big Data Analytics solution.

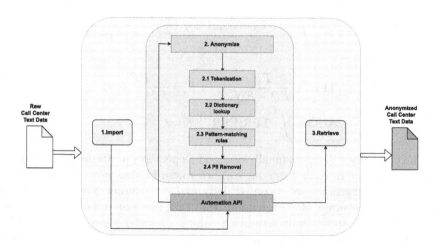

Fig. 3. Deperson's Anonymization-as-a-Service process.

6   Results

For the implementation of Deperson we used Python as the programming language. To construct the Dutch look-up dictionaries we used the open-source spellchecker Hunspell[2] and publicly available datasets from the Dutch government[3]. Motivated by the previous work [26], we formulate the PII removal task as a binary classification task where each word in our corpora that is considered PII is removed otherwise is not. There are four possible outcomes when obfuscating a word in sentences:

- True Positive (TP): when the actual word is recognized as PII and removed in the sentence.
- False Negative (FN): when the actual word is PII but not removed in the sentence.
- True Negative (TN): when the actual word is not PII and not removed in the sentence.
- False Positive (FP): when the actual word is not PII but removed in the sentence.

To assess the performance of Deperson, we employed widely adopted metrics commonly utilized in binary classification problems [6], namely *accuracy, precision, recall, F1-score* and *Area Under the ROC Curve (AUC)* score. We define them as follows:

$$\text{Accuracy} = \frac{TP + TN}{TP + TN + FP + FN}, \quad \text{Precision} = \frac{TP}{TP + FP},$$

$$\text{Recall} = \frac{TP}{TP + FN}, \quad \text{F1-score} = 2 \times \frac{\text{precision} \times \text{recall}}{\text{precision} + \text{recall}}$$

$$\text{TPR} = \frac{TP}{TP + FN}, \quad \text{FPR} = \frac{FP}{FP + TN},$$

$$\text{AUC} = \int_0^1 \text{TPR}(\text{FPR}^{-1}(t)) \, dt$$

The company's SMEs manually assessed Deperson's performance by looking at every sentence in chats from our corpora where PII has been removed. Since customer conversations are recorded daily and considering SME's availability we sampled an average of conversations that take place on a daily basis and we evaluated only a statistically significant sample of sentences considering a 95% confidence level and a 5% margin of error. The total number of sentences was 493, and 13% of the words were PII, in the amount of 9000 PII words.

The results of Deperson's performance are illustrated in Table 2 and Fig. 4. Deperson removed PII from our corpora with an accuracy of 0.82 and the Area under the ROC Curve (AUC) score was 0.63.

---

[2] https://github.com/OpenTaal/opentaal-hunspell.
[3] https://data.overheid.nl/.

Table 2. Deperson's anonymization performance.

Accuracy	Precision	Recall	F1-score	AUC
0.82	0.29	0.40	0.33	0.63

Deperson Area Under the ROC Curve

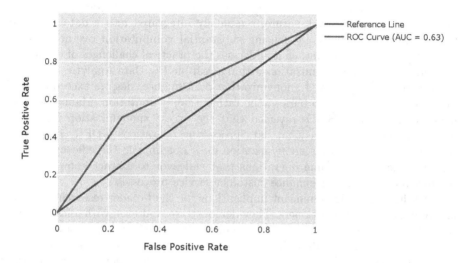

Fig. 4. The Receiver Operating Characteristic (ROC) Curve for Deperson

7 Discussion

7.1 Insights: Evaluating Rule-Based Data Anonymization in an Industrial Context

We showcased the implementation of a rule-based data anonymization service within an actualized Big Data Analytics solution operating under the context of an industrial setting. We engaged in collaboration with multiple teams within the industrial partner, including the DSL Team, the IT Department, SMEs, and the Legal department.

Interpreting the findings derived from Sect. 6, we expected relatively low values for precision, recall and F1-score since these metrics do not take into account the TNs. The number of terms identified as TN was anticipated to be very large because 88% of the words were not PII. The greater AUC metric value, as illustrated also in Fig. 4, reflects the fact that this is the case. Deperson's performance is decreasing primarily due to a higher number of FPs. The most prominent example of FP occurs with numbers. When a customer spells the bank account or the address this is successfully obscured but when he needs to state a number e.g. the times he tried to log in this gets falsely obscured.

FN account for 10% of total falsely predicted values. A typical example of FN is surnames. Some Dutch surnames can be common nouns or adjectives such as "groot" which means large. This type of error is explained by the rule-based nature that Deperson operates which completely ignores semantics in the corpora which is a known shortcoming in the academic literature [26].

The significance of our research lies in the evaluation of a rule-based anonymization service and its implications in an industrial context. While its accuracy of 0.82 may fall short of state-of-the-art LLMs, the noteworthy advantage lies in its lightweight nature, seamlessly integrated into a data-intensive streaming platform without causing substantial computation overhead. This characteristic is paramount, as it addresses the practical challenges of efficiently implementing data anonymization within a real-life Big Data Analytics solution.

Moreover, the observed anonymization performance, despite exceeding certain thresholds, proves to be a virtue rather than a limitation. Manual assessments conducted by SMEs revealed that the excess anonymization is instrumental in rendering subsequent data processing operations GDPR compliant. Importantly, this rigorous anonymization does not impede the efficacy of subsequent language modeling operations that endeavor to extract knowledge for product improvement or enhance customer service processes.

Such findings hold significant implications for the broader research community and industrial practitioners. They demonstrate that even with a less sophisticated rule-based approach, data anonymization can effectively achieve GDPR compliance and support data-driven operations, without necessitating the adoption of more complex and resource-intensive LLMs. This knowledge is particularly valuable for industries seeking privacy-preserving solutions while retaining operational efficiency and streamlining data-handling practices. Researchers and data privacy practitioners can draw insights from this study to tailor anonymization strategies based on contextual requirements, balancing compliance and utility within their specific domains. This aligns with the broader aim of enhancing data protection measures while optimizing data utilization for innovative endeavors and customer-oriented services.

7.2   Critical Insights: Design Principles for Data Anonymization

Motivated by the existing academic literature and based on a comprehensive performance evaluation and astute observations within an industrial context, we propose two distinctive design principles to guide the development of robust data anonymization tools. These principles aim to strike a harmonious balance between regulatory compliance, pragmatic usability, and strategic privacy measures, catering to the specific demands of real-world applications.

The first design principle, "Strive for Practicality and Compliance", accentuates the paramount importance of optimizing anonymization solutions for seamless integration within existing infrastructures while scrupulously adhering to pertinent data protection regulations like GDPR [22]. This approach places emphasis on practical usability, ensuring that anonymization tools can be readily deployed within industrial environments without compromising operational efficiency or data handling practices.

Design Principle 1: Strive for Practicality and Compliance. Optimize anonymization solutions by emphasizing lightweight integration into existing infrastructures, ensuring GDPR compliance, and balancing accuracy with practical utility for real-life industrial applications.

The second design principle, "Prudent Anonymization with Strategic Overreach", advocates for a judicious calibration of anonymization strategies that transcend mere minimal compliance [3]. Deliberately exceeding standard requirements, this approach seeks to enhance data privacy while strategically considering the downstream impact on data processing tasks. By taking a meticulous approach to anonymization, the aim is to maintain the utmost data utility for vital insights and continuous improvements in language modeling operations and customer-centric services.

Design Principle 2: Prudent Anonymization with Strategic Overreach. Incorporate a carefully calibrated anonymization strategy that goes beyond minimal compliance to enhance data privacy, while strategically considering the impact on downstream data processing tasks, ensuring they remain unobstructed and useful for valuable insights and improvements.

---

8   Conclusions and Future Work

In this work, we have presented the outcomes of successfully integrating a rule-based data anonymization service into a Big Analytics solution, establishing a foundational baseline for future developments in this domain. Our findings will serve as a benchmark to guide the formulation of more robust and sophisticated solutions. One promising avenue for improvement lies in the incorporation of advanced modeling techniques, exemplified by Named Entity Recognition (NER), which has demonstrated compelling performance in relevant academic investigations. Additionally, we acknowledge the paramount significance of addressing privacy preservation not solely at the input data level but also throughout all subsequent stages, encompassing model training, deployment, and inference. Looking ahead, we envisage conducting further research to investigate additional design principles and innovative methodologies, aiming to fortify data anonymization practices and optimize privacy preservation across the entire data lifecycle. These endeavors are pivotal in advancing the field of data anonymization within industrial settings and beyond.

References

1. Regulation (EU) 2016/679 of the European Parliament and of the Council of 27 April 2016 on the protection of natural persons with regard to the processing of personal data and on the free movement of such data, and repealing Directive 95/46/EC (General Data Protection Regulation). Official Journal of the European Union L 119 4 May 2016; pp. 1–88 (2016)
2. Armstrong, M.: Infographic: Data Protection Fines Reach Record High in 2023. Statista Daily Data (2023). https://www.statista.com/chart/30053/gdpr-data-protection-fines-timeline
3. Ataei, M., Degbelo, A., Kray, C., Santos, V.: Complying with privacy legislation: from legal text to implementation of privacy-aware location-based services. ISPRS Int. J. Geo Inf. **7**(11), 442 (2018)
4. Avison, D.E., Lau, F., Myers, M.D., Nielsen, P.A.: Action research. Commun. ACM **42**(1), 94–97 (1999)
5. Barreno, M., Nelson, B., Joseph, A.D., Tygar, J.D.: The security of machine learning. Mach. Learn. **81**, 121–148 (2010)
6. Borovits, N., et al.: FindICI: using machine learning to detect linguistic inconsistencies between code and natural language descriptions in infrastructure-as-code. Empir. Softw. Eng. **27**(7), 1–30 (2022)
7. Burgess, M.: CHATGPT has a big privacy problem. Wired (2023). https://www.wired.com/story/italy-ban-chatgpt-privacy-gdpr/
8. Carlini, N., Liu, C., Erlingsson, Ú., Kos, J., Song, D.: The secret sharer: Evaluating and testing unintended memorization in neural networks. In: 28th USENIX Security Symposium (USENIX Security 2019), pp. 267–284 (2019)
9. Carlini, N., et al.: Extracting training data from large language models. In: 30th USENIX Security Symposium (USENIX Security 2021), pp. 2633–2650 (2021)
10. Chen, W.Y., Yu, M., Sun, C.: Architecture and building the medical image anonymization service: cloud, big data and automation. In: 2021 International Conference on Electronic Communications, Internet of Things and Big Data (ICEIB), pp. 149–153. IEEE (2021)
11. Chen, C.P., Zhang, C.Y.: Data-intensive applications, challenges, techniques and technologies: a survey on big data. Inf. Sci. **275**, 314–347 (2014)
12. Coughlan, P., Coghlan, D.: Action research for operations management. Int. J. Oper. Prod. Manag. **22**(2), 220–240 (2002)
13. Dwork, C., Roth, A.: The algorithmic foundations of differential privacy. Found. Trends® Theor. Comput. Sci. **9**(3–4), 211–407 (2014)
14. Fredrikson, M., Jha, S., Ristenpart, T.: Model inversion attacks that exploit confidence information and basic countermeasures. In: Proceedings of the 22nd ACM SIGSAC Conference on Computer and Communications Security, pp. 1322–1333 (2015)
15. Ghinita, G., Karras, P., Kalnis, P., Mamoulis, N.: Fast data anonymization with low information loss. In: Proceedings of the 33rd International Conference on Very Large Data Bases, pp. 758–769 (2007)
16. Guerriero, M., Tamburri, D.A., Di Nitto, E.: Defining, enforcing and checking privacy policies in data-intensive applications. In: Proceedings of the 13th International Conference on Software Engineering for Adaptive and Self-Managing Systems, pp. 172–182 (2018)
17. Hisamoto, S., Post, M., Duh, K.: Membership inference attacks on sequence-to-sequence models: is my data in your machine translation system? Trans. Assoc. Comput. Linguist. **8**, 49–63 (2020)

18. Huang, J., Shao, H., Chang, K.C.C.: Are Large Pre-Trained Language Models Leaking Your Personal Information? arXiv preprint arXiv:2205.12628 (2022)

19. Jian, Z., et al.: A cascaded approach for Chinese clinical text de-identification with less annotation effort. J. Biomed. Inform. **73**, 76–83 (2017)

20. Kaplan, M.: May I Ask Who's Calling? Named Entity Recognition on Call Center Transcripts for Privacy Law Compliance. arXiv preprint arXiv:2010.15598 (2020)

21. Li, N., Li, T., Venkatasubramanian, S.: t-closeness: privacy beyond k-anonymity and l-diversity. In: 2007 IEEE 23rd International Conference on Data Engineering, pp. 106–115. IEEE (2006)

22. Li, Z.S., Werner, C., Ernst, N., Damian, D.: Towards privacy compliance: a design science study in a small organization. Inf. Softw. Technol. **146**, 106868 (2022)

23. Lukas, N., Salem, A., Sim, R., Tople, S., Wutschitz, L., Zanella-Béguelin, S.: Analyzing leakage of personally identifiable information in language models. arXiv preprint arXiv:2302.00539 (2023)

24. Meehan, M.: Data Privacy shall Be The Most Important Issue In The Next Decade. Forbes (2019). https://www.forbes.com/sites/marymeehan/2019/11/26/data-privacy-shall-be-the-most-important-issue-in-the-next-decade/

25. Mireshghallah, F., Uniyal, A., Wang, T., Evans, D.K., Berg-Kirkpatrick, T.: An empirical analysis of memorization in fine-tuned autoregressive language models. In: Proceedings of the 2022 Conference on Empirical Methods in Natural Language Processing, pp. 1816–1826 (2022)

26. Murugadoss, K., et al.: Building a best-in-class automated de-identification tool for electronic health records through ensemble learning. Patterns **2**(6), 100255 (2021)

27. Narayanan, A., Shmatikov, V.: De-anonymizing social networks. In: 2009 30th IEEE Symposium on Security and Privacy, pp. 173–187. IEEE (2009)

28. Neamatullah, I., et al.: Automated de-identification of free-text medical records. BMC Med. Inform. Decis. Mak. **8**(1), 1–17 (2008)

29. Paleyes, A., Urma, R.G., Lawrence, N.D.: Challenges in deploying machine learning: a survey of case studies. ACM Comput. Surv. **55**(6), 1–29 (2022)

30. Pan, X., Zhang, M., Ji, S., Yang, M.: Privacy risks of general-purpose language models. In: 2020 IEEE Symposium on Security and Privacy (SP), pp. 1314–1331. IEEE (2020)

31. Papernot, N., McDaniel, P., Sinha, A., Wellman, M.P.: SoK: security and privacy in machine learning. In: 2018 IEEE European Symposium on Security and Privacy (EuroS&P), pp. 399–414. IEEE (2018)

32. Solove, D.J.: Why privacy matters even if you have 'nothing to hide'. Chronicle High. Educ. **15** (2011)

33. Soria-Comas, J., Domingo-Ferrer, J.: Big data privacy: challenges to privacy principles and models. Data Sci. Eng. **1**(1), 21–28 (2016)

34. Turrecha, L.M.: AI has a privacy problem, and the solution is privacy tech, not more Red Tape. AI Has A Privacy Problem, And The Solution is Privacy Tech, Not More Red Tape (2023). https://lourdesmturrecha.substack.com/p/title-ai-has-a-privacy-problem-and

35. Vaswani, A., et al.: Attention is all you need. In: Advances in Neural Information Processing Systems, vol. 30 (2017)

36. Zhong, Z.Y.S., Wright, R.N.: Privacy-preserving classification of customer data without loss of accuracy. In: SIAM International Conference on Data Mining, pp. 1–11 (2005)

Attribute Authorization - A Novel Enhancement to API Gateways

Archana Sulebele[(⊠)] [iD] and Sai Krishna Munnangi[iD]

1 Apple Park Way, Cupertino, CA 95014, USA
{asulebele,saikrishna}@apple.com

Abstract. With the growth of microservice-based architectures, API Gateways have proven to be a viable intermediary service for enforcing security policies including authentication, authorization, and access control. Checking if a caller is entitled to invoke an API (API Level Authorization) is available in many API Gateway solutions, however, inspecting if the caller is entitled to specific attributes of the response (Attribute Authorization) is not supported and is an unexplored problem in the literature. This paper formally introduces the Attribute Authorization problem and presents two real-time scalable low latency solutions, that effectively process large responses. The first algorithm leverages a traditional Trie-based approach to enforce attribute authorization and the second utilizes a Tree representation coupled with traditional Depth First Search (DFS) to speed up response transformation.

Keywords: Attribute Authorization · Response Transformation · API Gateway · Service Oriented Architecture

1 Introduction

In micro-service based architectures [9,10], an application is divided into several loosely coupled collaborating services that communicate with each other using application programming interfaces (APIs) [11]. While this approach simplifies the development, deployment, and maintenance of individual application components at scale, it also introduces additional complexities including security considerations [28,30] such as authentication and authorization. API Gateways [22,26,27] play a vital role in addressing these challenges by streamlining enforcement of security policies [8]. An API Gateway is a single point of entry for API requests into an application. As illustrated in Fig. 1, it sits in between clients and service providers [26,31], receiving API requests and providing capabilities like authentication, authorization, routing, composition, and response transformation.

Authorization in the context of API security typically refers to API Level Authorization [1,3] - providing access to specific services to a client. However, service providers cater to multiple clients and hence need to manage differential client responses for each API as well. Managing API access restrictions and

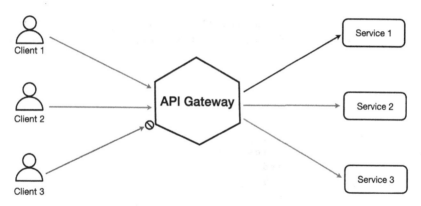

Fig. 1. API Gateway

providing tailored responses per client, per API, at the service level can be challenging to both developer and operation teams [21]. Being an intermediary between the client and service providers, an API Gateway can offer an efficient solution to address these tasks. In the absence of this feature, service providers are limited in enforcing security policies at the attribute level in the response within each service. Our research indicates that this problem of attribute level authorization is largely unexplored in the current literature. Within the API Gateway context, we formally introduce the Attribute Authorization problem that refers to providing filtered responses to the clients, with only specific data elements that are approved for the client.

In this paper, we propose two scalable low latency solutions for the Attribute Authorization problem, which can be easily incorporated into an API Gateway. The first approach uses a Trie [12] based strategy to determine authorized attributes and the second uses a Tree [16] based strategy with customized Depth First Search [5] for this task. We also present our API Gateway architecture tailored to solve the Attribute Authorization problem. The adaptability of the attribute selection and filtering process to various use cases has made it highly impactful and well received.

2 Preliminary

JavaScript Object Notation (JSON) [2,25] and Extensible Markup Language (XML) [23,29] have become de-facto formats for information exchange between micro services. Attribute Authorization involves parsing the incoming JSON or XML response from the provider and applying filter criteria to only allow authorized attributes. However, parsing JSON or XML data is expensive [6, 7,18,19] since the hierarchical complexity of the response document could be unlimited. Likewise, as the size of the response increases, Attribute Authorization becomes expensive and slow [24].

Throughout this paper, we depict JSON as the default response format from an API and use the following running JSON example representing an online music store:

```
{
  "library": {
    "albums": [
      {
        "genre": "jazz",
        "singer": "Miles Davis",
        "title": "Kind of Blue",
        "price": 18.95,
        "releaseDates": {
          "US": 1959,
          "UK": 1959
        }
      },
      {
        "genre": "country",
        "singer": "Shania Twain",
        "title": "Come On Over",
        "price": 10.99,
        "releaseDates": {
          "US": 1997
        }
      }
    ],
    "sales": 248000,
    "revenue": 300000
  }
}
```

JSONPath [13,14] expressions provide a flexible way to address different parts of the JSON and navigate to an element in the JSON structure. The root member in a JSONPath expression is referred to as $ and subsequent child elements are represented with the dot-notation (.). The JSONPath operators are elaborated in Table 1. Analogous to JSONPath, XPath [4] expressions are utilized in XML to address elements in the structure.

For example, the JSONPath expression to access the singer of the first album is given by - $.library.albums[0].singer. Wildcard characters are also supported. For example, $.library.albums[*].singer defines the singers of all albums.

3   Architecture

3.1   Overview

The architecture of our proposed API Gateway system with support for Attribute Authorization (refer to Fig. 2), consists of four major components,

Table 1. JSONPath Expressions

Expression	Description
$	Root Element
@	Current Element
*	Wildcard
.	Child Operator
.parent	Selects specified property in parent
..	Recursive descendant
[ ]	Subscript Operator
[start: end]	Selects array elements from start to end
[?(expression)]	Filter expression

namely the Loader, Index Builder, and a custom Gateway Filter with Mapper and Transformer. The data flow is as follows: (1) The service provider loads the attribute authorization records structured as JSONPath expressions into a data source. Upon system startup, two steps are performed: (2) first, the Loader reads authorization records from the data source and provides it to the Index Builder. (3) Next, the Index Builder builds an index [5, 20] for each of the authorization records that maps the client to the list of authorized APIs and attributes for each of those APIs. (4) Upon receiving an API invocation from the client, the gateway intercepts the request and routes it to the service provider. (5) The service provider processes the request and sends the response to the API gateway. (6) Within the API gateway, we define a custom filter for each API route which intercepts the response and invokes the Mapper to map the incoming API response to pre-configured attribute authorizations in the index. (7) Finally, the Transformer deletes attributes that are not entitled and returns the modified response back to the client.

3.2 Data Setup

The service provider determines the services as well as the attributes of the service endpoint a client is entitled to. For example, the provider may choose to provide access to only a few of the attributes in an API response. This information is stored in the data source as a JSON document where each record defines the JSONPath expressions of the authorized attributes for the specified client. For example, consider a GET call to service /api/v1/lookup/{album_name}.

The authorization record is setup in the database as below:

```
{
    "clientId": "123",
    "method": "GET",
    "path": "/api/v1/lookup/{album_name}",
    "authorizedAttributes": [
        "$.library.albums[*].genre",
        "$.library.albums[*].singer",
        "$.library.albums[*].title"
    ]
}
```

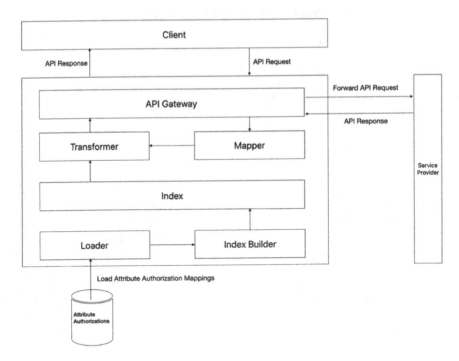

Fig. 2. API Gateway Architecture

In this example, the client with `clientId` as 123 is entitled to the `genre`, `singer`, and `title` attributes in the response JSON of the API endpoint `GET /api/v1/lookup/{album_name}`.

3.3   Components

Loader. The Loader module retrieves the authorizations provided by the service provider from the data source. The output of the Loader module is a list of JSON documents representing authorized attributes for a client, for specific API endpoints.

Index Builder. The Index Builder takes the output of the Loader module and adds each record to an in memory index. The index maps the client to the list of authorized request URIs as well as authorized attributes associated with each of those URIs. The index is an extension of a simple map or dictionary. The contents of the index can be logically represented in Table 2. The Loader and Index Builder are preprocessing steps that occur upon startup of the system. Index is refreshed periodically at configured intervals, which helps with dynamic client authorization changes.

Table 2. Index Setup

Key	Value	
	Key	Value
{$clientId='123'$, $method='GET'$}	/$api/v1/lookup/\{album\_name\}$	[$.$library.albums$[*].genre$, $.$library.albums$[*].singer$, $.$library.albums$[*].title$]
	/$api/v1/lookup/price/\{album\_name\}$	[$.$library.albums$[*].title$, $.$library.albums$[*].price$]
	/$api/v1/lookup/sales$	[$.$library.sales$]

Mapper. The Mapper takes the original response and generates a list of JSON-Path expressions for all attributes in the JSON response. To achieve this, we flatten the JSON into JSONPath expressions. During the flattening process, we replace any array indices with the wildcard '*'. The process is outlined in Algorithm 1. For instance, the field `sales` in the attribute `library` within the example JSON is converted into `$.library.sales`, with corresponding value 248000.

Algorithm 1. Map of JSONPaths

Input: *originalResponse*: Original JSON response from service provider
Output: *paths*: List of JSONPaths of attributes of response
1: **function** GETJSONPATHS(*originalResponse*)
2:     *dom* ←parse(*originalResponse*)
3:     *paths* ←flatten(*dom*)   ▷ Replace array indices in keys of map with *
4:     **return** *paths*
5: **end function**

Transformer. The Transformer is responsible for filtering the original response. The transformation pipeline consists of two modules, namely Retriever and Response Builder.

Retriever. The Retriever builds the index lookup key as a JSON document consisting of the *clientId* and the method type, from the incoming request. For example, for the incoming request `GET /api/v1/lookup/Come+On+Over` from client App Id `123`, the lookup key built by the retriever module can be represented as: `clientId='123', method='GET'`.

Next, the module performs a lookup in the index using the lookup key to retrieve the corresponding value for the client. Since the value is a map itself, the Retriever then iterates through all the keys of the map to find the matching incoming request URI. We use template matching [15,17] to identify the key corresponding to the incoming request URI. The value corresponding to the key is the list of authorized attributes. In the above example, the Retriever returns authorized attributes as [$.library.albums[*].genre, $.library.albums[*].singer, $.library.albums[*].title] specifying that client 123 is authorized for the genre, singer, and title fields in the response of the request URI GET /api/v1/lookup/Come+On+Over.

Response Builder. The Response Builder module takes the list of authorized attributes and the original response from the service, performs Attribute Authorization, and then returns the transformed response. We implemented three different approaches to solve the Attribute Authorization problem, which we present in the subsequent section.

4   Solution Approaches

4.1   Trie-Based Approach

The solution approach is defined in Algorithm 2. We build a Trie [12] with patterns of authorized attributes. Next, we invoke the Mapper to get the JSONPaths associated with each attribute in the response and search each against entries stored in the Trie. Finally, those attributes not found in the Trie are added to the list of forbidden attributes for deletion.

Algorithm 2. Build Response

   Input: $originalResponse$: Original JSON response from service provider
   Input: $authorizationConfiguration$: JSONPaths of authorized attributes
   Output: $finalResponse$: Modified JSON with only authorized attributes

1: **function** BUILDRESPONSE($originalResponse, authorizationConfiguration$)
2:     $head \leftarrow$ BuildPatternTrie($authorizationConfiguration$)
3:     $allAttributes \leftarrow$ getJSONPaths($originalResponse$)   ▷ Retrieve from Mapper
4:     **for** $j = 1$ to $len(allAttributes)$ **do**
5:         **if not** SearchPatternTrie($head, allAttributes[j]$) **then**
6:             $forbiddenAttributes$.append($allAttributes[j]$)
7:         **end if**
8:         $j \leftarrow j + 1$
9:     **end for**
10:     $dom \leftarrow$ jsonToDom($originalResponse$)
11:     **for** $j = 1$ to $len(forbiddenAttributes)$ **do**
12:         dom.delete($forbiddenAttributes[j]$)
13:         $j \leftarrow j + 1$
14:     **end for**
15:     $finalResponse \leftarrow$ domToJson(dom)
16:     **return** $finalResponse$
17: **end function**

Algorithm 3. Build Pattern Trie

Input: *jsonpaths*: List of authorized attributes in JSONPath format
Output: Trie of authorized attributes

```
1: function BUILDPATTERNTRIE(jsonpaths)
2:     head ← new Node()
3:     for i = 1 to len(jsonpaths) do:
4:         currentNode ← head
5:         tokens ← split(jsonpaths[i], ".")          ▷ Tokenize on '.'
6:         for j = 1 to len(tokens) do:
7:             if currentNode.child = tokens(j) then
8:                 currentNode ← currentNode.child        ▷ Traverse to child
9:                 j ← j + 1
10:            else
11:                node ← new Node(tokens(j))            ▷ Create a new node
12:                currentNode.child ← node              ▷ Add node as child
13:                currentNode ← node                    ▷ Recurse
14:                j ← j + 1
15:            end if
16:        end for
17:        i ← i + 1
18:    end for
19:    return head
20: end function
```

Algorithm 4. Search Pattern Trie

Input: *head*: Root node of Trie
Input: *jsonpath*: JSONPath representation of attribute path in response
Output: True if JSONPath expression is found in Trie

```
1: function SEARCHPATTERNTRIE(head, jsonpath)
2:     currentNode ← head
3:     tokens ← split(jsonpath, ".")               ▷ Tokenize on '.'
4:     for j = 1 to len(tokens) do:
5:         if currentNode.child = tokens(j) then
6:             currentNode ← currentNode.child        ▷ Traverse to child
7:         else
8:             return false
9:         end if
10:        j ← j + 1
11:    end for
12:    return true
13: end function
```

Algorithm 3 defines building the Trie with patterns of authorized attributes. We first create the root node with the token ('$') since all expressions begin with '$'. Then for each JSONPath expression, we tokenize and split it on '.'. For each of these tokens, we recursively traverse the Trie checking if the token exists in the Trie. When we reach a leaf node, we create a new node with the token adding it as a child of the node. Therefore, the subsequent tokens become the children of the node with the current token.

Algorithm 4 outlines how we can search the Trie for a JSONPath expression. The input to the algorithm is a JSONPath expression representing a path in the JSON response body. The JSONPath expression is tokenized and split on '.'. For each of these tokens, we start from the root node and recursively traverse the Trie checking if the token exists in the Trie i.e., we check if there is any node with the current token as its value. If the node exists, we proceed to its children. If not, we return *false* signifying that the current JSONPath expression is not found in the Trie and add it to the forbidden attributes list for deletion. When we have exhausted all the tokens, this means that we have found the current JSONPath expression in the Trie and hence we return *true*. This signifies that the current JSONPath expression is an allowed attribute and hence must be included in the filtered response.

4.2   Tree-Based Solution - Approach 1

While the Trie algorithm is highly performant for smaller inputs, in practice, the initial step of flattening the JSON is time intensive even for medium sized inputs. Additionally the subsequent search process over the constructed Trie is equally slow, resulting in execution times exceeding 1 s for inputs with over 100K attributes. In order to efficiently filter the response JSON with low latency on Gateway's end, we need a customized mechanism that can quickly parse input and identify authorized attributes.

To realize the goal of efficient parsing, we implement a JSON parser that constructs a Tree representation of the input JSON. Each node of the JSONTree uniquely corresponds to an attribute within the JSON and holds references to nodes corresponding to the attribute's children within the JSON. In addition, each node holds a boolean variable *flag* representing if the node is an authorized attribute. Nodes with *flag* value 1 are authorized attributes and considered to be marked, while the *flag* value 0 represents a forbidden attribute. The JSONTree representation for the sample JSON is illustrated in Fig. 3.

Once the JSONTree is constructed, for each authorized attribute, we then retrieve the corresponding tree nodes and set their *flag* value to 1. Once all the authorized nodes have been marked, we traverse the entire tree using a depth-first search (DFS) based approach and delete those nodes that are neither themselves marked nor have any marked children. After this step, the remaining tree solely consists of the authorized attributes, representing the filtered JSON. Refer to Algorithms 5 and 6 for the pseudo-code outlining this process.

4.3   Complexity Analysis

Time Complexity

The first step in the algorithm is construction of the JSONTree based on the input JSON. The time complexity (T_1) of this step is proportional to the number

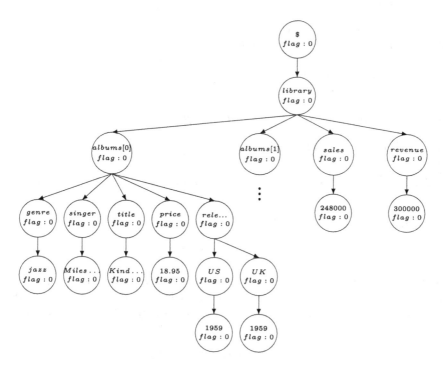

Fig. 3. Tree representation of the sample JSON

Algorithm 5. JSONTree Filtering Approach 1

Input: $originalResponse$ - JSON
Input: $authorizedAttributes$ - list of JSONPaths
Output: $filteredResponse$ - JSON string

1: **function** BUILDRESPONSEAPPROACH1($originalResponse, authorizedAttributes$)
2:    Build $JSONTree$ on the input $originalResponse$
3:    $root \leftarrow JSONTree.getRoot()$;
4:    **for all** attribute $a_i \in authorizedAttributes$ **do**
5:       $matchingNodes \leftarrow root.getMatchingNodes(a_i)$;
6:       **for all** $node \in matchingNodes$ **do**
7:          $node.flag \leftarrow 1$;
8:       **end for**
9:    **end for**
10:   $deleteUnmarkedNodes(root)$;
11:   **return** $Serialize(root)$;
12: **end function**

Algorithm 6. Delete Forbidden Attributes

    Input: *node* - JSONTree node
    Output: *delete* - boolean flag
 1: **function** DELETEUNMARKEDNODES($node$)
 2:    **if** $node.flag == true$ **then**
 3:        **return false**
 4:    **else**
 5:        $deleteThisNode \leftarrow$ **true**
 6:        **for each** child $c_j \in node.children$ **do**
 7:            $deleteThisChild \leftarrow deleteUnmarkedNodes(c_j)$
 8:            **if** $deleteThisChild$ **then**
 9:                delete c_j
10:            **end if**
11:            $deleteThisNode \mathrel{\&=} deleteThisChild$
12:        **end for**
13:        **return** $deleteThisNode$
14:    **end if**
15: **end function**

---

of attributes (N) in the input i.e.

$$T_1 \propto N \approx kN = \mathcal{O}(N)$$

In the subsequent step, while marking a node is an instantaneous operation, retrieving the nodes matching with the provided JSONPath is a linear time operation. Hence the total time complexity (T_2) for marking all the nodes matching with given M authorized attributes is

$$T_2 \propto M \times N \approx M \times hN = \mathcal{O}(MN)$$

In the final step of DFS traversal, we visit each node at most once. Hence

$$T_3 = \mathcal{O}(N)$$

Therefore the overall complexity of this whole approach is

$$T = T_1 + T_2 + T_3 = \mathcal{O}(MN)$$

Space Complexity
The space requirement of this algorithm is proportional to the memory required for the input JSON, as we construct and store only the JSONTree.

4.4 Tree-Based Solution - Approach 2

A drawback of the previous algorithm is its inability to handle missing fields. Consider the sample JSON as an API response and the authorized attributes as [$.library.albums[*].title, $.library.albums[*].releaseDates.UK].

The first authorized attribute gets matched with `$.library.albums[0].title` - *Kind of Blue* and `$.library.albums[1].title` - *Come On Over*. However the second authorized attribute only gets matched with `$.library.albums[0].releaseDates.UK` because the object `$.library.albums[1].releaseDates` does not have the nested field UK. Hence the filtered response returned by this algorithm is:

```
{
    "library": {
    "albums": [
        {
            "title": "Kind of Blue",
            "releaseDates": {
                "UK": 1959
            }
        },
        {
            "title": "Come On Over"
        }
    ]
    }
}
```

Note that the filtered response does not contain the *releaseDates* field in the second element of the *albums* array. This disruption in structural symmetry might be undesired and can have unintended consequences on the client's side. To address this problem of missing fields, we provide a solution by marking all the ancestors of the authorized attributes nodes. Then, we identify forbidden nodes as those that are not marked and proceed to delete them. This exercise reduces the JSONTree to only contain authorized and empty nodes where the fields are missing from the input JSON.

Given the hierarchical structure of JSONPaths, the ancestor JSON-Paths can be easily derived from a given JSONPath. For instance, if `$.library.albums[*].title` is the given JSONPath, the ancestor paths {`$`, `$.library`, `$.library.albums[*]`} can be computed by simply removing the suffix after the last '.'. For all the authorized attributes, we generate a set (to avoid duplicates) of ancestor attributes and mark all the nodes matching the JSONPaths within this set. The complete algorithm is outlined in Algorithms 7 and 8.

4.5   Complexity Analysis

Time Complexity. In this variant, the only change is the inclusion of ancestor attributes as authorized attributes. As a result, the time complexity of the algorithm increases proportionally to the number of new paths added. However, it remains bounded by $\mathcal{O}(MN)$, where M represents the number of attributes and N denotes the number of fields in the input JSON.

Algorithm 7. MarkableJsonNode Filtering Approach - Missing Fields Included

---

Input: $originalResponse$ - JSON string
Input: $authorizedAttributes$ - list of JSONPaths
Output: $filteredResponse$ - JSON string

1: **function** BUILDRESPONSEAPPROACH2($originalResponse, authorizedAttributes$)
2:     Build the $JSONTree$ on the input $originalResponse$
3:     $root \leftarrow JSONTree.getRoot()$;
4:     $authorizedAttributes \leftarrow generateAncestorPaths(authorizedAttributes)$;
5:     **for all** attribute $a_i \in authorizedAttributes$ **do**
6:         $matchingNodes \leftarrow root.getMatchingNodes(a_i)$;
7:         **for all** $node \in matchingNodes$ **do**
8:             $node.flag \leftarrow 1$;
9:         **end for**
10:    **end for**
11:    $deleteUnmarkedNodes(root)$;
12:    **return** $Serialize(root)$;
13: **end function**

Algorithm 8. Delete Forbidden Attributes - Missing Fields Included

---

Input: $node$ - JSONTree node

1: **function** DELETEUNMARKEDNODES($node$)
2:     **if not** $node.isMarked$ **then**
3:         delete node
4:     **else**
5:         **for each** child $c_j \in node.children$ **do**
6:             $deleteUnmarkedNodes(c_j)$
7:         **end for**
8:     **end if**
9: **end function**

Space Complexity. The space requirement of this variant remains unchanged from Approach 1.

4.6   Performance Comparison

We evaluate performance of the three Response Builders on four different JSON responses from three service providers, across total execution time, the most critical metric for Gateways. We curated the input to contain JSON responses with increasing size and total number of attributes. All the tests have been performed under similar conditions. The results are summarized in Table 3.

From these benchmark results, we find that the eligibility Tree based algorithms outperform the Trie algorithm and are at least 4 times faster on average. We also establish that the Tree based algorithms are capable of processing over 2 Million attributes in under 1 s. Note that the runtime of the variant (Approach 2) of Tree based algorithm is slightly higher due to the additional computation of generating parent attributes and further marking them.

Table 3. Evaluation Test Results

Input		Filtered Response		Runtime		
Size	Total Attributes	Size	Total Attributes	Trie	Tree Approach 1	Tree Approach 2
40 KB	678	2 KB	54	168 ms	128 ms	129 ms
3.7 MB	161,708	369 KB	9,547	754 ms	208 ms	223 ms
25.5 MB	574,706	2.8 MB	80,558	1900 ms	474 ms	521 ms
102 MB	2,298,824	11.2 MB	322,232	5717 ms	1065 ms	1129 ms

5   Conclusion and Future Work

In this paper, we address the challenge of Attribute Authorization in API Gateways, where each attribute in the response is selectively filtered based on specific client entitlements. To provide a comprehensive solution for precise access control and enhanced security, we propose two solution approaches: a Trie-based strategy and a novel Tree-based strategy. We also create a variant of the Tree-based algorithm that preserves structural integrity of the input in the filtered response. Our research shows that while both the Trie and Tree-based approaches are highly scalable, the Tree-based method is at least four times faster than the former.

As part of future work, we plan to develop a distributed algorithm for inputs that do not fit into the memory.

References

1. Barabanov, A., Makrushin, D.: Authentication and authorization in microservice-based systems: survey of architecture patterns. arXiv preprint arXiv:2009.02114 (2020)
2. Bray, T.: The javascript object notation (JSON) data interchange format. Technical report (2014)
3. Christie, M.A., et al.: Managing authentication and authorization in distributed science gateway middleware. Futur. Gener. Comput. Syst. **111**, 780–785 (2020)
4. Clark, J., DeRose, S., et al.: XML path language (XPath) (1999)
5. Cormen, T.H., Leiserson, C.E., Rivest, R.L., Stein, C.: Introduction to Algorithms. MIT Press, Cambridge (2022)
6. Davis, D., Parashar, M.P.: Latency performance of soap implementations. In: 2nd IEEE/ACM International Symposium on Cluster Computing and the Grid (CCGRID 2002), p. 407. IEEE (2002)
7. Dhalla, H.K.: A performance analysis of native JSON parsers in Java, Python, MS.NET Core, Javascript, and PHP. In: 2020 16th International Conference on Network and Service Management (CNSM), pp. 1–5. IEEE (2020)
8. Dias, W.K.A.N., Siriwardena, P.: Microservices Security in Action. Simon and Schuster, New York (2020)
9. Dragoni, N., et al.: Microservices: yesterday, today, and tomorrow. Present and Ulterior Software Engineering, pp. 195–216 (2017)
10. Erl, T.: Service-oriented architecture. Citeseer (1900)
11. Fielding, R.: Representational state transfer. Architectural Styles and the Design of Network-Based Software Architecture, pp. 76–85 (2000)

12. Fredkin, E.: Trie memory. Commun. ACM **3**(9), 490–499 (1960)
13. Friesen, J., Friesen, J.: Extracting JSON values with JSONpath. Java XML and JSON: Document Processing for Java SE, pp. 299–322 (2019)
14. Gössner, S.: JSONPath-XPath for JSON, p. 48 (2007). http://goessner.net/articles/JsonPath
15. Gregorio, J., Fielding, R., Hadley, M., Nottingham, M., Orchard, D.: URI template. Technical report (2012)
16. Knuth, D.E.: The Art of Computer Programming, vol. 3. Pearson Education, London (1997)
17. Leung, H.: Regular languages and finite automata. AMC **10**, 12 (2010)
18. Li, Y., Katsipoulakis, N.R., Chandramouli, B., Goldstein, J., Kossmann, D.: Mison: a fast JSON parser for data analytics. Proc. VLDB Endow. **10**(10), 1118–1129 (2017)
19. Maeda, K.: Performance evaluation of object serialization libraries in XML, JSON and binary formats. In: 2012 Second International Conference on Digital Information and Communication Technology and it's Applications (DICTAP), pp. 177–182. IEEE (2012)
20. Mehlhorn, K., Sanders, P., Sanders, P.: Algorithms and Data Structures: The Basic Toolbox, vol. 55. Springer, Heidelberg (2008). https://doi.org/10.1007/978-3-540-77978-0
21. Meng, N., Nagy, S., Yao, D., Zhuang, W., Argoty, G.A.: Secure coding practices in java: challenges and vulnerabilities. In: Proceedings of the 40th International Conference on Software Engineering, pp. 372–383 (2018)
22. Microsoft: Use API gateways in microservices (2022). https://learn.microsoft.com/en-us/azure/architecture/microservices/design/gateway
23. Murata, M., Laurent, S.S., Kohn, D.: XML media types. Technical report (2001)
24. Palkar, S., Abuzaid, F., Bailis, P., Zaharia, M.: Filter before you parse: faster analytics on raw data with sparser. Proc. VLDB Endow. **11**(11), 1576–1589 (2018)
25. Peng, D., Cao, L., Xu, W.: Using JSON for data exchanging in web service applications. J. Comput. Inf. Syst. **7**(16), 5883–5890 (2011)
26. Reese, W.: Nginx: the high-performance web server and reverse proxy. Linux J. **2008**(173), 2 (2008)
27. Richardson, C.: Pattern: API gateway/backends for frontends (2018). https://microservices.io/patterns/apigateway.html
28. Sun, Y., Nanda, S., Jaeger, T.: Security-as-a-service for microservices-based cloud applications. In: 2015 IEEE 7th International Conference on Cloud Computing Technology and Science (CloudCom), pp. 50–57. IEEE (2015)
29. Thompson, H., Lilley, C.: RFC 7303: XML media types (2014)
30. Yu, D., Jin, Y., Zhang, Y., Zheng, X.: A survey on security issues in services communication of microservices-enabled fog applications. Concurr. Comput. Pract. Exp. **31**(22), e4436 (2019)
31. Zhao, J., Jing, S., Jiang, L.: Management of API gateway based on micro-service architecture. In: Journal of Physics: Conference Series, vol. 1087, p. 032032. IOP Publishing (2018)

Unveiling Bottlenecks in Logistics: A Case Study on Process Mining for Root Cause Identification and Diagnostics in an Air Cargo Terminal

Chiao-Yun Li[1,2]([✉])(ID), Tejaswini Shinde[1](ID), Wanyi He[3], Sean Shing Fung Lau[3], Morgan Xian Biao Hiew[3], Nicholas T. L. Tam[3], Aparna Joshi[1], and Wil M. P. van der Aalst[1,2](ID)

[1] RWTH Aachen University, Aachen, Germany
{tejaswini.shinde,aparna.joshi}@rwth-aachen.de,
wvdaalst@pads.rwth-aachen.de
[2] Fraunhofer FIT, Birlinghoven Castle, Sankt Augustin, Germany
chiaoyun.li@pads.rwth-aachen.de
[3] Hong Kong Industrial Artificial Intelligence and Robotics Centre Limited, Shatin, NT, Hong Kong
{dorahe,seanlau,morganhiew,nicholastam}@hkflair.org

Abstract. To improve processes in logistics, it is crucial to understand the factors influencing performance. To achieve this, process mining utilizes *event data* to extract insights into operational processes. In this paper, we present a case study conducted in an air cargo terminal, where process mining is applied to event data collected during package distribution. The primary objective is to identify the root causes of bottlenecks in the system. However, practical limitations, including noisy sensor data, scalability challenges, and abstraction limitations, require a different approach than conventional process mining projects. Building upon existing process mining techniques, we develop a two-fold approach to identify root causes at the data level and provide diagnostics at the business level. Through a comprehensive analysis of the provided datasets, we substantiate the effectiveness and practical applicability of our approach in analyzing root causes.

Keywords: Process mining · Logistic · Root cause identification · Root cause diagnostics · Performance Spectrum · Case study

1 Introduction

Efficient processes are crucial for success in the logistics industry. Businesses must understand their process performance to attain this objective. Material

This work was supported by the InnoHK funding launched by Innovation and Technology Commission, Hong Kong SAR. Additionally, we thank Sebastiaan van Zelst for his support.

Handling Systems (MHS) are vital to efficient logistics management, facilitating the timely movement of materials. Evaluating MHS performance enables organizations to optimize their operational processes by minimizing delays, reducing manual labor, and overcoming obstacles encountered during the distribution [11].

Process mining aims to enhance the understanding of operational processes by utilizing *event data*, consisting of records of process execution stored in information systems. A process mining project typically involves discovering a process model, which abstracts the process behavior, from event data using *discovery techniques* [2,14]. The model is then compared with the expectations to identify deviations or to *repair* the model [3,18]. Process efficiency is evaluated by analyzing the model annotated with performance information derived from the event data [10]. In the case of a large system, activities (i.e., well-defined process steps) can be abstracted, alongside performance information aggregated, to reduce the process complexity for human analysis [4]. Leveraging the context provided by the model and domain knowledge, one can diagnose bottlenecks and optimize processes. Throughout the process described, it is evident that a reliable model depicting the behavior in real life is central to a process mining project.

In this study, we aim to discern the underlying causes of bottlenecks affecting the distribution of packages within the MHS of an air cargo terminal, as depicted in Fig. 1. The figure delineates our specific focus and case study scope. Using a logistic log, which captures package distribution data, and a fault log, encompassing information on equipment malfunctions and maintenance, we identify and diagnose the root causes of detected bottlenecks. Subsequently, these identified root causes are mapped onto the transport layout for business owners to gain a visual understanding, aiding them in monitoring and further controlling the system effectively. However, we encounter challenges that compel us to deviate from the conventional process mining approach [7].

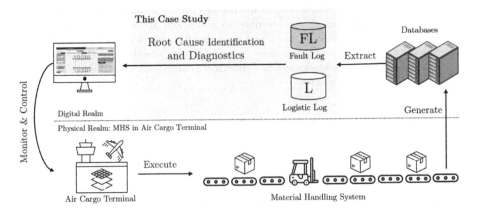

Fig. 1. In this case study, we aim to uncover package distribution inefficiencies at an air cargo terminal by analyzing logistic and fault logs. The resulting insights will inform an integrated solution for optimizing the distribution process.

– Noisy event data: The system consists of thousands of equipment pieces with sensors generating event data. Sensor data are prone to noise [12], which can distort the actual relationships between different pieces of equipment.
– Scalability limitations: Given the large number of pieces of equipment and the substantial volume of event data, existing open-source tools [17] cannot adequately support the performance requirements to discover a model and to interactively explore the process performance using the model.
– Abstraction limitations: Typically, abstraction resolves complexity and scalability challenges caused by the excessive number of concepts in a process, like the conveyor equipment in this case study. Yet, due to the queuing behavior and equipment faults within the process, abstraction may lead to misleading conclusions since it does not fully capture the queuing phenomenon.

To address these challenges, we devised a solution that delivers transparent and reliable results, empowering business owners to make well-informed decisions regarding their service efficiency. We uncover unbiased behavior and identify incidents that contribute to bottlenecks, including identifying package distributions that cause bottlenecks on specific pieces of equipment at particular points in time. Despite the constraints, we devise a two-fold approach that uncovers inefficiencies and provides explanations without relying on a process model. First, we programmatically detect the root causes of bottlenecks at the *data level* to narrow down the analysis scope. Building upon the findings, we derive diagnostics at the *business level*, leveraging the *Performance Spectrum Miner* (PSM) [5]. Our approach is quantitatively evaluated and integrated into the system, aiming to enhance the overall service performance within the air cargo terminal.

In Sect. 2, we introduce the techniques and notations applied. Section 3 describes the available datasets in the case study. Package distribution behavior is depicted in Sect. 4, while root cause identification is in Sect. 5. Sect. 6 demonstrates the results. We discuss the related work in Sect. 7. Lastly, Sect. 8 summarizes the case study and discusses future work.

2   Background

In this section, we introduce the techniques applied for root cause analysis and mathematical notations.

2.1   Performance Spectrum

PSM is a visual analytic tool that formats the performance of activities in a process within the context of a *case* (i.e., a process instance) [5]. By visualizing how cases progress through activities over time, the tool enables the observation of efficiency dynamics and facilitates the analysis of interactions between cases. Numerous extensions have been developed to quantify [5], predict [6], and visualize the performance within the context of a process model [1]. In our case study, we employed the implementation which enables the interactive exploration of performance based on a process model supported by PSM [1].

However, scalability emerges as a practical challenge in this case study. First, the existing discovery techniques within the tool exhibit limited scalability when faced with a significant number of activities, as exemplified in the case study with thousands of equipment pieces. As the complexity of the model increases, it progressively poses greater challenges for human analysts to effectively identify all root causes effectively. Given the case study's scale, it is challenging to pinpoint the areas requiring analysis without adequate guidance for navigating the process model. To address these issues, we have devised a programmatic approach that detects root causes at the data level. By narrowing down the analysis scope, we leverage PSM to facilitate the subsequent diagnosis at the business level.

2.2 Notations

Let X be an arbitrary set. A sequence is a function $\sigma \colon \{1, 2, ..., n\} \to X$, where $\sigma = \langle x_1, x_2, x_2, .., x_n \rangle$ is a sequence over X, and $\sigma(i) = x_i$ denotes the ith element in σ. We denote $|\sigma|$ as the length of σ and X^* as the set of all possible sequences over X. We write $x \in \sigma \iff \exists k \in \mathbb{N}$ s.t. $1 \leq k \leq |\sigma|$ and $\sigma(k) = x$. The index of $x \in \sigma$ is denoted as $\sigma^{-1}(x) \in \mathbb{N}$ and $\sigma^{-1}(x) = min\{1 \leq i \leq |\sigma| \mid \sigma(i) = x\}$. A path from m to n in σ, where $1 \leq m < n \leq |\sigma|$, refers to a segment of σ, written as $path_\sigma(m, n) = \langle x_m, x_{m+1}, ..., x_n \rangle$. Note that $path_\sigma(1, |\sigma|) = \sigma$.

3 Datasets

The case study incorporates two logs: a logistic log and a fault log.[1] The logistic log captures the package distribution within the system and the fault log documents fault instances related to the conveyor equipment.

3.1 Representation of Logistic Log

We represent the logistic log as an *event log*, i.e., a typical input for most process mining techniques. $\mathcal{U}_{pkg}$ is the universe of package identifiers, $\mathcal{U}_{eqt}$ is the universe of equipment identifiers, and $\mathcal{U}_{time}$ is the universe of timestamps.

Definition 1 (Event Log). $\mathcal{E}$ *is the universe of events.* $e \in \mathcal{E}$ *represents a data sample collected by sensors for the package distribution, which is characterized with the corresponding package identifier* $\pi_{pkg}(e) \in \mathcal{U}_{pkg}$, *equipment identifier* $\pi_{eqt}(e) \in \mathcal{U}_{eqt}$, *and the arrival timestamp* $\pi_{arr}(e) \in \mathcal{U}_{time}$ *of* $\pi_{pkg}(e)$ *on* $\pi_{eqt}(e)$. *An event log L is a set of events $L \subseteq \mathcal{E}$.*

A case is a collection of events describing a complete package distribution, i.e., given pid $\in \mathcal{U}_{pkg}$, *the case of* pid *is* $c = \{e \in L \mid \pi_{pkg}(e) = $ pid$\}$. *The trace of a case c, denoted as $\pi_{trace}(c)$, is a chronologically ordered sequence of events in a case, where $\pi_{trace}(c) = \langle e_1, e_2, ..., e_{|c|} \rangle$ such that $\forall 1 \leq i < j \leq |c|, \pi_{arr}(e_i) \leq \pi_{arr}(e_j)$. Additionally, the time that a package distribution exits the system is provided and we write as $\pi_{exit}(c) \in \mathcal{U}_{time}$, where $\pi_{exit}(c) \geq max\{\pi_{arr}(e) \mid e \in c\}$.*

---

[1] For confidentiality, we pseudo-anonymized the datasets, preserving the relative relation between incidents. In this case study, we only present pertinent attributes.

Table 1. An excerpt of an event log L. Each row represents an event describing the arrival of a package (represented by PKG) on a specific piece of equipment (represented by EQT) at a particular time (represented by ARR). For ease of reference, the event identifier (represented by Event ID) is provided using the row index, e.g., the first event is labeled as e_1. The completion time of the distribution is also included, denoted as EXIT, providing additional details about the distribution.

Event ID	PKG ($\pi_{pkg}(e)$)	EQT ($\pi_{eqt}(e)$)	ARR ($\pi_{arr}(e)$)	EXIT ($\pi_{exit}(c)$)
1	2365884457	HXUF1928	2023-05-05 12:12:34	2023-05-05 14:00:31
2	2365884457	TFGT3578	2023-05-05 12:12:53	2023-05-05 14:00:31
3	2365884457	UENF3008	2023-05-05 13:59:51	2023-05-05 14:00:31
4	2459856232	GJWK4805	2023-05-05 13:33:56	2023-05-05 17:44:28
5	2459856232	UENF3008	2023-05-05 17:38:00	2023-05-05 17:44:28
6	2459856232	ITSC0915	2023-05-05 17:38:41	2023-05-05 17:44:28
7	2459856232	LKHS8902	2023-05-05 17:38:54	2023-05-05 17:44:28
8	2459856232	CJIF5952	2023-05-05 17:39:06	2023-05-05 17:44:28

Table 1 displays an excerpt from the event log, illustrating the package distribution. For example, the case $c = \{e_1, e_2, e_3\}$ describes the distribution of package 2365884457, which undergoes three pieces of equipment in the system. It first arrives on $\pi_{eqt}(e_1) =$ HXUF1928 at $\pi_{arr}(e_1) =$ 12:12:34, then moves to $\pi_{eqt}(e_2) =$ TFGT3578 at $\pi_{arr}(e_2) =$ 12:12:53, and finally reaches $\pi_{eqt}(e_3) =$ UENF3008 at $\pi_{arr}(e_3) =$ 12:59:51 before leaving the system at $\pi_{exit}(c) =$ 14:00:31.

3.2 Fault Log

A fault refers to an incident that occurs on a piece of equipment and is unrelated to the package distribution process. A fault log is a compilation of such incidents, which we formalize as follows.

Definition 2 (Fault Log). $\mathcal{F}$ *is the universe of faults.* $f \in \mathcal{F}$ *is a fault, which is characterized by the corresponding equipment identifier* $\pi_{eqt}(f) \in \mathcal{U}_{eqt}$, *downtime of* $\pi_{dt}(f) \in \mathcal{U}_{time}$, *and the corresponding uptime* $\pi_{ut}(f) \in \mathcal{U}_{time}$ *where* $\pi_{dt}(f) < \pi_{ut}(f)$. *A fault log* FL *is a set of faults* $FL \subseteq \mathcal{F}$. *Since at most one fault can occur on a piece of equipment at any point in time, the faults on the equipment form a sequence of faults in time, i.e.,* $\forall f_1 \in FL \forall f_2 \in FL, f_1 \neq f_2 \implies (\pi_{dt}(f_1) \geq \pi_{ut}(f_2)) \vee (\pi_{dt}(f_2) \geq \pi_{ut}(f_1))$.

Table 2 showcases a sample from the fault log, with each row depicting an instance of a fault occurrence. For instance, equipment UENF3008 experiences a fault from 12:15:23 to 12:16:49. Notably, the excerpt demonstrates a sequential occurrence of five faults on UENF3008.

4 Behavioral Analysis

This section introduces identified constraints and outlines the assumptions of the system behavior, which serve as the basis for defining the bottlenecks.

Table 2. Every row in the dataset represents a fault occurrence in the system. A fault is uniquely identified by three key pieces of information: the piece of equipment where the fault happens (represented by EQT), the start time of the fault (represented by DOWN), and the end time of the fault (represented by UP). Likewise, we provide the fault identifier (represented by Fault ID) using the row index for ease of reference.

Fault ID	EQT ($\pi_{eqt}(f)$)	DOWN ($\pi_{dt}(f)$)	UP ($\pi_{ut}(f)$)
1	UENF3008	2023-05-05 12:15:23	2023-05-05 12:16:49
2	UENF3008	2023-05-05 12:28:07	2023-05-05 12:30:26
3	UENF3008	2023-05-05 12:31:16	2023-05-05 12:38:00
4	UENF3008	2023-05-05 12:47:23	2023-05-05 12:49:49
5	UENF3008	2023-05-05 13:11:40	2023-05-05 13:30:00
6	UAZB1814	2023-05-05 14:58:35	2023-05-05 15:16:05

4.1   Package Distribution – Constraints and Assumptions

The analysis reveals the following constraints of the package distribution. In collaboration with domain experts, we validate the constraints and impose specific assumptions to facilitate the identification of bottlenecks.

Departure Time. We assume that a package departs from one piece of equipment at the same time as it arrives on the next piece of equipment along its trajectory. Let $L \subseteq \mathcal{E}$. Given a case $c \subseteq L$, let $\sigma = \pi_{trace}(c)$. For an event $e \in \sigma$, we define the function $dep_c(e) = \pi_{arr}(\sigma(\sigma^{-1}(e) + 1)) \iff \sigma^{-1}(e) < |\sigma|$ and $dep_c(e) = \pi_{exit}(c) \iff \sigma(|\sigma|) = e$. We name the duration as the *dwell time* of a package on a piece of equipment. As an illustration, considering Table 1, we assume that package 2365884457 departs TFGT3578 at 13:59:51, and the dwell time of 2365884457 on TFGT3578 is 1 h, 46 min, and 58 s.

Equipment Capacity. At any given time, one equipment piece can accommodate a maximum of one package. Let $L \subseteq \mathcal{E}$ denote an event log. Given eqt $\in \mathcal{U}_{eqt}$, $\forall e_1 \in L(\pi_{eqt}(e_1) = \text{eqt}) \; \forall e_2 \in L(\pi_{eqt}(e_2) = \text{eqt}), e_1 \neq e_2 \implies (\pi_{arr}(e_1) > dep_c(e_2))$ $\vee (\pi_{arr}(e_2) > dep_c(e_1))$. This constraint leads to a queuing behavior in the system, wherein packages are distributed in a sequential manner, allowing a package to move to the next piece of equipment only when the preceding package in its trajectory departs from that piece of equipment.

Fault Impact on Package Distribution. The faults in the fault log can be classified into three categories: warning, maintenance, and *real* fault. Warning and maintenance faults do not have any impact on package distribution. However, a real fault disrupts the distribution process and may also affect the overall system performance. Considering a real fault $f \in \mathcal{F}$ and an event log $L \subseteq \mathcal{E}$, during the fault, $\pi_{eqt}(f)$ is unable to send or receive any packages. In other words, there does not exist an event $e \in L$ such that $\pi_{dt}(f) < \pi_{arr}(e) < \pi_{ut}(f)$ or $\pi_{dt}(f) < dep_c(e) < \pi_{ut}(f)$. Since there are no specific attributes available to directly determine the category of a fault in the fault log $f \in FL$, we define a real fault using the function $real(f, L) \nrightarrow \mathcal{F}$ if there are no packages arriving or departing from $\pi_{eqt}(f)$ during the time period of $\pi_{dt}(f)$ and $\pi_{ut}(f)$.

4.2 Bottleneck Definition

A *bottleneck event* refers to an event indicating that a package remains on a piece of equipment for a longer duration than anticipated. Let $\mathcal{U}_{dur}$ be the universe of time durations, e.g., 5 min, 3 s, etc. A bottleneck event in the system is defined as follows.

Definition 3 (Bottleneck Event). *Let* eqt $\in \mathcal{U}_{eqt}$ *be a piece of equipment identifier, and* $thr(\mathsf{eqt}) \in \mathcal{U}_{dur}$ *denotes the theoretical service time of* eqt*. Let* L *be an event log. Given an event* $e \in L$ *and a case* c*, where* $e \in \pi_{trace}(c)$*,* e *is a bottleneck event iff* $dep_c(e) - \pi_{arr}(e) > thr(\pi_{eqt}(e))$*.*

A baseline for comparison is crucial when evaluating process performance. In this case study, since the efficiency is significantly influenced by the dynamic nature of cases within the system, a rigid benchmark is impractical. Therefore, we employ statistical metrics as a benchmark to evaluate the performance of the equipment. Specifically, we establish benchmarks for each equipment type by examining the first quartile of dwell time per equipment type, recognizing that the dwell time of a piece of equipment varies depending on its type. For instance, the dwell time of a package on a lift shaft differs from that on a conveyor belt. Bottleneck events are identified when the corresponding dwell times exceed the benchmark. Throughout the paper, we refer to these events as bottlenecks.

5 Root Cause Identification and Diagnostics

Considering the inherent complexity of the system, we devise a two-stage approach for root cause analysis, as illustrated in Fig. 2. In the first stage, given a bottleneck, we narrow down the scope by identifying the root cause at the data level—extracting specific location and timing information that triggers the bottlenecks. Next, we gather the relevant incidents and collaborate with domain experts to visualize the entire process leading to the bottleneck using PSM. This collaborative process facilitates a comprehensive examination and diagnosis of the identified root causes from a business perspective. We integrate root cause identification into our partner's system, visually displaying the bottleneck and its cause on their logistic map, enhancing stakeholder understanding.

5.1 Root Cause Identification

The scale and complexity of the system, comprising approximately 800,000 events from around 5,700 equipment pieces, present significant challenges in

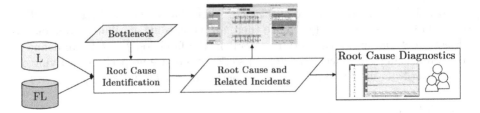

Fig. 2. Two-Stage Root Cause Analysis. The first stage involves narrowing down the scope through root cause identification. The resulting root cause is visualized on the logistic map, while the process leading to the bottleneck is visualized with PSM, allowing for collaborative discussions with stakeholders.

systematically uncovering the underlying causes of bottlenecks. To address this, root cause identification narrows down and extracts a subset of events and/or faults that contribute to bottleneck occurrences. By focusing on this subset, we efficiently pinpoint the incidents that are most relevant to our analysis, ensuring a more targeted approach. In this context, a root cause is defined as an incident on a piece of equipment that triggers a specific bottleneck. The formal definition of a root cause is outlined below.

Definition 4 (Root Cause). *Let* $L \subseteq \mathcal{E}$ *and* $FL \in \mathcal{F}$. *Given a bottleneck* $bn \in L$, *a root cause* rc *is an incident occurring on a piece of equipment in the system* $rc \in L \cup FL$ *that causes* bn.

Prior to the algorithm, we establish two conditions for identifying root causes. First, we determine if a bottleneck occurs due to a fault occurring on the piece of equipment associated with it. Since real faults do not allow for package reception nor sending, a package gets *stuck due to fault* if it arrives on the piece of equipment before a fault happens and remains there until the fault is repaired. During this period, the fault prevents the piece of equipment from processing any packages, resulting in packages becoming *stuck* until the fault is resolved.

Definition 5 (Stuck due to Fault). *Let* $L \subseteq \mathcal{E}$ *and* $FL \subseteq \mathcal{F}$. *Given a bottleneck* $bn \in L$, $stuck(bn, FL) = \sigma \in \mathcal{F}^*$ *extracts a sequence of root causes where* $1 \leq i \leq |\sigma|(\pi_{eqt}(\sigma(i)) = \pi_{eqt}(bn) \wedge \pi_{arr}(bn) < \pi_{dt}(\sigma(i)) \wedge dep_c(bn) > \pi_{ut}(\sigma(i)))$.

If a bottleneck is not due to a fault in the associated equipment piece, we investigate the condition of the subsequent equipment along its trajectory. Equipment condition is determined by the incidents at a specific time. In this case study, two types of incidents are considered: an event indicating the availability of the equipment piece (i.e., a package is present on the equipment piece) and a fault indicating the unavailability of the equipment piece.

Definition 6 (Equipment Condition). *Let* $L \subseteq \mathcal{E}$, $eqt \in \mathcal{U}_{eqt}$, *and* $t \in \mathcal{U}_{time}$. $CON_{occ} \colon \mathcal{U}_{eqt} \times \mathcal{U}_{time} \times \mathcal{E} \nrightarrow \mathcal{E}$, *where* $CON_{occ}(eqt, t, L) = e \in L \iff \pi_{eqt}(e) = eqt \wedge \pi_{arr}(e) < t < dep_c(e)$. *Given* $FL \subseteq \mathcal{F}$, $CON_{flt} \colon \mathcal{U}_{eqt} \times \mathcal{U}_{time} \times \mathcal{F} \nrightarrow \mathcal{F}$, *where* $CON_{flt}(eqt, t, FL) = f \in FL \iff \pi_{eqt}(f) = eqt \wedge \pi_{dt}(f) < t < \pi_{ut}(f)$.

Algorithm 1 outlines the identification of the root cause given a bottleneck. The algorithm checks if the bottleneck is caused by being stuck on the associated equipment piece. If no faults are detected, the algorithm proceeds to examine the condition of the equipment on the trajectory of the bottleneck and extracts the last incident until one of the following final conditions is met:

– The associated equipment piece is the last equipment piece on its trajectory;
– The associated equipment piece is empty and without a real fault;
– The associated equipment piece is at real fault.

A piece of equipment can be both at fault and occupied simultaneously. However, considering that the business owner's primary interest lies in identifying and addressing faults, the developed method places a stronger emphasis on identifying root causes related to faults. This focus allows for a more targeted approach in determining the actions to be taken to address the identified faults.

Algorithm 1. Root Cause Identification

Require: event log L, fault log FL, bottleneck $bn \in L$
Ensure: a root cause $rc \in \mathcal{E} \cup \mathcal{F}$
1: **if** $|stuck(bn, FL)| > 0$ **then return** $stuck(bn, FL)(1)$
2: $c \leftarrow$ the corresponding case of bn
3: $\sigma \leftarrow \pi_{trace}(c)$
4: $\sigma' \leftarrow path_\sigma(\sigma^{-1}(bn), |\sigma|)$
5: $current \leftarrow bn$
6: **for** $1 \leq i < |\sigma'|$ **do**
7:     **if** $\pi_{eqt}(current) = \pi_{eqt}(\sigma'(|\sigma'|))$ **then return** current
8:     $time \leftarrow \pi_{arr}(current) + thr(\pi_{eqt}(current))$
9:     $next \leftarrow \pi_{eqt}(\sigma'(i + 1))$
10:    $f \leftarrow CON_{flt}(next, time, FL)$
11:    **if** $real(f, L)$ **then return** f
12:    $e \leftarrow CON_{occ}(next, time, L)$
13:    **if** $e = \bot$ **then return** $current$
14:    $current \leftarrow e$

5.2   Root Cause Diagnostics

In this section, we delve into a comprehensive analysis of the process leading to bottlenecks, going beyond the identification of the root cause. We collect and analyze incidents contributing to the bottleneck since the identified root cause. This enables us to uncover the cause-effect relationships that influence bottleneck occurrences, facilitating a more profound understanding of the underlying process. To strengthen our analysis, we utilize PSM to visually represent the behavior of the incidents. Furthermore, engaging in effective discussions with domain experts provides valuable insights and perspectives. The following diagnostics illustrate their implications from a business standpoint.

Diagnosis 1 (Stuck on Faulty Equipment). Figure 3 depicts the diagnosis of an internal root cause where a piece of faulty equipment causes a package to be *stuck* on it, as described in Definition 5. The performance spectrum displayed on the right side depicts the efficiency of the selected places in the discovered Petri net shown on the left side. Selected places representing a single path are colored in green, while aggregated paths are colored in blue. The example shows that faulty equipment SRFH2430 *blocks* the package distribution, which is impossible to reroute without human intervention.

We project the faults onto the timeline, displaying the downtime and uptime for the respective piece of equipment. We utilize blue and red arrows to highlight bottlenecks and the corresponding root causes. This visualization is consistently applied across figures throughout the subsequent diagnostics.

Diagnosis 2 (Waiting for Repair). Figure 4 depicts a scenario with two bottlenecks stemming from the same root cause, specifically a fault on equipment UAZB1814. Once the fault is fixed, the distribution process resumes. Furthermore, Fig. 5 illustrates two bottlenecks resulting from a sequence of faults on equipment UENF3008. For the bottleneck on equipment LFYV0354 in case 2654852459, the first fault is the root cause, while for the bottleneck in case 2365884457, the second fault is identified as its root cause. The figure also highlights distribution prioritization, with package 2365884457 being given higher priority despite arriving later on equipment TFGT3578 due to its importance.

Diagnosis 3 (Waiting to Exit). Figure 6 showcases the cascading package waiting, highlighting the impact of capacity constraints on the distribution. The packages queue to exit, resulting in a sequence of bottlenecks. The root cause of the bottlenecks is identified as the package 2968579218 on equipment KXLJ5003, which is also a bottleneck itself and is observed waiting at the last piece of equipment along the distribution trajectory of the bottlenecks. The visualization emphasizes how the waiting of a single package on a piece of equipment affects subsequent distributions, leading to inefficiencies propagating throughout the system. Further investigation reveals that the root cause originates from the package 2968579218 waiting to be loaded onto an aircraft.

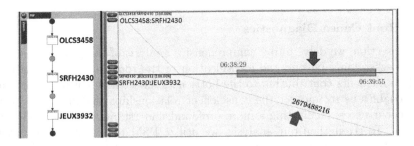

Fig. 3. Package distribution of package 2679488216 gets *stuck* at faulty equipment SRFH2430 during the distribution process. (Color figure online)

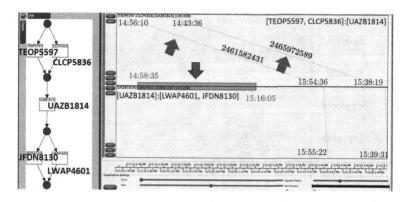

Fig. 4. Two bottlenecks waiting for faulty equipment UAZB1814 to be repaired.

Diagnosis 4 (Unjustified Waiting). If no incidents are identified for a bottleneck, the root cause is defined as unjustified waiting, indicating the next piece of equipment on the package's trajectory is available for transfer without any detected incidents. Nevertheless, the distribution inexplicably ceases. While one reason could be the equipment piece serving as a storage place within the system, there are root causes that remain unexplainable from a business perspective.

By gathering and analyzing the incidents that contribute to a bottleneck, we facilitate the diagnostic at the business level through the utilization of a visual analytic method inspired by PSM. This enables the process owner to identify the appropriate measures to address the identified bottlenecks effectively.

5.3   Impact of Bottlenecks

Some bottlenecks may be circumvented by navigating around the identified obstacles. To identify potential *detours* and their relationship with bottlenecks,

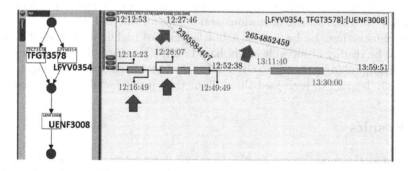

Fig. 5. Two bottlenecks due to waiting for sequential faults to be repaired. The intersection highlights the distribution priority of packages. Specific timestamps are annotated to demonstrate the relationship between the arrival time of the packages and the downtime and uptime of the faults.

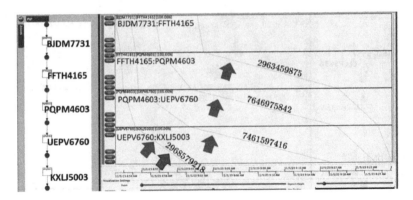

Fig. 6. Packages waiting to be loaded onto an aircraft, where the inefficiency cascades through the equipment.

we make an assumption that cases with the same source and destination pieces of equipment follow the same *planned* route if no obstacles are encountered during distribution. Building upon this assumption, first, we extract cases that share the same source and destination as the trajectory of a bottleneck. Next, we identify the *change points* of these cases, i.e., the equipment piece where a case deviates from the originally planned route. To relate the detour with the bottleneck, we select the cases with the change points preceding the bottleneck on the route, and the events at these change points temporally take place *after* the bottleneck.

Figure 7 exemplifies the impact of a bottleneck, which results in a detour within the system. In this example, case 2159753596 *detours* on LHWU9366, i.e., the change point for its distribution, due to the bottleneck caused by the distribution of package 2736942968 on equipment PGUL9655. Additionally, package 2159753596 experiences a temporary waiting period on LHWU9366 until the decision to detour is made. As a result, the distribution of 2159753596 is compelled to deviate from its initial planned route, leading to a longer path to reach its destination. This scenario highlights how bottlenecks impact the overall distribution process, causing deviations and delays for affected cases.

By illustrating the impact of a bottleneck, we highlight that inefficiencies may not be readily observable solely based on the presence of a bottleneck. The distribution, taking a detour to circumvent the bottleneck, follows a longer route, ultimately leading to increased throughput time in its distribution process.

6   Results

We present the quantitative results from our diagnostics, as depicted in Fig. 8. The figure provides insights into the distribution of bottlenecks based on their root causes. Notably, as the number of bottlenecks increased, we observed a trend where multiple bottlenecks shared the same root causes, highlighting their interconnectedness and shared contributing factors within the system.

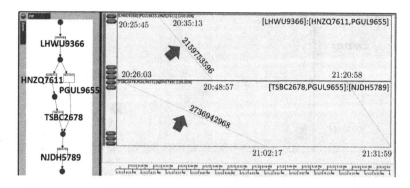

Fig. 7. An example highlighting the impact of a bottleneck: package 2736942968 on equipment PGUL9655 triggers a cascading effect, causing 2159753596 to experience additional waiting and detour, resulting in extended throughput time.

Interestingly, although only a small portion of bottlenecks appeared to be attributed to equipment faults, our analysis of the root causes of unjustified waiting reveals another possibility. Approximately 3% of the root causes of the unjustified waiting could be attributed to storage-related reasons, which are regarded as more of a business decision rather than operational inefficiencies. For other root causes, we identified an example that illustrates the impact of design decisions on threshold settings, as shown in Fig. 9. This instance resulted in unde-tected root causes, where equipment ZGNT4301 was evaluated at 17:27:20 with a 14-s threshold, while the fault occurred 17 s later, causing package 2736942868 to become stuck on equipment ZGNT4301. These findings highlight the impor-tance of thoroughly considering design choices to accurately detect and address root causes.

The identification of root causes demonstrates efficiency, with an average time of approximately 0.2 s and a maximum of 2 s per bottleneck. These metrics highlight a rapid identification process, influential in preserving optimal system performance. Leveraging this efficiency, the root cause identification developed is

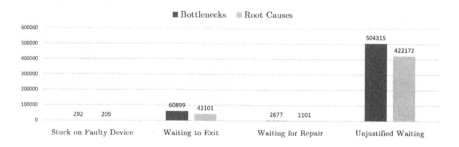

Fig. 8. The number of bottlenecks and the corresponding root causes based on diag-nostics.

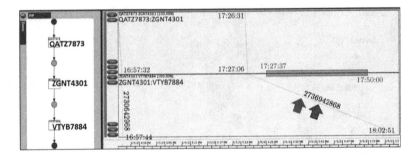

Fig. 9. An example of unjustified waiting, highlighting the impact of design decisions where the equipment fault occurred after evaluating the equipment condition.

integrated into the system, as exemplified in Fig. 10. Utilizing a logistic map that visually represents the equipment layout and relationships within the system, the root causes are swiftly detected based on the bottlenecks highlighted on the map. The right panel provides an interactive interface for exploring the detected root causes, enabling a comprehensive analysis of the distribution process. This integration emphasizes its practical applicability and highlights its potential to enhance operational efficiency.

7   Related Work

Diagnosing the root cause is crucial for optimizing service performance. Comprehensive process models are typically seen as essential for root cause diagnostics [8,13,16]. For instance, in one study [13], a descriptive process model with statistical metrics is used to identify root causes by observing resource status during the bottleneck time periods. Another work in [8] employs conformance checking

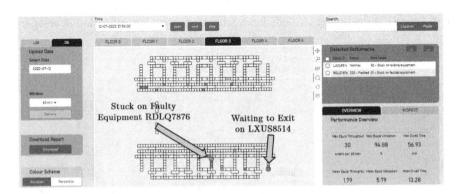

Fig. 10. Visualizing root causes of bottlenecks in the distribution process on the logistic map. note that the diagnostics are renamed for user clarity.

to diagnose bottlenecks through deviations and cause-effect correlations, demonstrated through an offshore oil and gas industry case study. However, discovering a suitable process model is often challenging due to scalability issues with discovery algorithms. Additionally, these models require a substantial amount of data for each resource, making them less applicable in scenarios where resource utilization is sparse, as presented in our case study.

Certain approaches rely heavily on knowledge-intensive domain understanding, demanding significant effort and expertise to represent complex causal relationships. While innovative methodologies show promise in representing knowledge [9,15,16], their effective implementation requires a high level of expertise. For example, in an approach [15], fusion-based clustering and a hyperbolic neural network are utilized to represent domain knowledge. Inspired by causality theory, the authors [9] strive to avoid imposing assumptions on the data, enhancing reliability in practical applications. In the work by Unger et al. [16], an event log derived from business lawsuits is defined and subsequently analyzed using process mining techniques. Although the analysis yields valuable insights, identifying the root causes necessitates human analysis and a profound understanding of the domain to interpret the performance metrics accurately and diagnose the underlying reasons for bottlenecks. These methods demand specialized knowledge, limiting their practical adoption and applicability.

In practical applications, scalability, accessibility to domain knowledge, and the necessity of a process model pose significant challenges. In contrast, the proposed solution automatically identifies root causes at the data level, demonstrating scalability and potential for real-time application. We emphasize transparency based on unbiased raw data and facilitate business-level interpretation through visualization using PSM.

8   Conclusion

In this paper, we presented a case study focusing on the identification and diagnostics of root causes in the package distribution process of an air cargo terminal. The process efficiency is closely tied to the dynamic nature of the system. We formalized the provided datasets and analyzed the observed behavior within the system. By identifying bottlenecks, we proposed a data-level method for extracting root causes and conducting targeted diagnostics. Moreover, we demonstrated the effectiveness of the visualization inspired by PSM in aiding the diagnostic process. Additionally, we showcased the impact of bottlenecks, which led to inefficiencies in the system that cannot be directly observed in individual package distributions. The results of the case study further establish the practicality and relevance of our method in real-world scenarios. For future work, we aim to extend the visualization to include the status of the equipment, which can be seen as the concept of resources in process mining, as it significantly impacts the system. Developing a visual analytic tool considering equipment or resource status would benefit scenarios similar to this case study.

References

1. van der Aalst, W.M.P., Tacke Genannt Unterberg, D., Denisov, V., Fahland, D.: Visualizing token flows using interactive performance spectra. In: Janicki, R., Sidorova, N., Chatain, T. (eds.) PETRI NETS 2020. LNCS, vol. 12152, pp. 369–380. Springer, Cham (2020). https://doi.org/10.1007/978-3-030-51831-8_18

2. Burke, A., Leemans, S.J.J., Wynn, M.T.: Stochastic process discovery by weight estimation. In: Leemans, S., Leopold, H. (eds.) ICPM 2020. LNBIP, vol. 406, pp. 260–272. Springer, Cham (2021). https://doi.org/10.1007/978-3-030-72693-5_20

3. Carmona, J., van Dongen, B.F., Solti, A., Weidlich, M.: Conformance Checking - Relating Processes and Models. Springer, Cham (2018). https://doi.org/10.1007/978-3-319-99414-7

4. Chapela-Campa, D., Mucientes, M., Lama, M.: Simplification of complex process models by abstracting infrequent behaviour. In: Yangui, S., Bouassida Rodriguez, I., Drira, K., Tari, Z. (eds.) ICSOC 2019. LNCS, vol. 11895, pp. 415–430. Springer, Cham (2019). https://doi.org/10.1007/978-3-030-33702-5_32

5. Denisov, V., Belkina, E., Fahland, D., van der Aalst, W.M.P.: The performance spectrum miner: visual analytics for fine-grained performance analysis of processes. In: International Conference on Business Process Management (Dissertation/Demos/Industry), vol. 2196 (2018)

6. Denisov, V., Fahland, D., van der Aalst, W.M.P.: Predictive performance monitoring of material handling systems using the performance spectrum. In: International Conference on Process Mining (2019)

7. van Eck, M.L., Lu, X., Leemans, S.J.J., van der Aalst, W.M.P.: PM^2: a process mining project methodology. In: Zdravkovic, J., Kirikova, M., Johannesson, P. (eds.) CAiSE 2015. LNCS, vol. 9097, pp. 297–313. Springer, Cham (2015). https://doi.org/10.1007/978-3-319-19069-3_19

8. Ge, J., Sigsgaard, K.W., Mortensen, N.H., Hansen, K.B., Agergaard, J.K.: Structured process mining in maintenance performance analysis: a case study in the offshore oil and gas industry. In: International Symposium on System Security, Safety, and Reliability (2023)

9. Van Houdt, G., Depaire, B., Martin, N.: Root cause analysis in process mining with probabilistic temporal logic. In: Munoz-Gama, J., Lu, X. (eds.) ICPM 2021. LNBIP, vol. 433, pp. 73–84. Springer, Cham (2022). https://doi.org/10.1007/978-3-030-98581-3_6

10. de Leoni, M., Maggi, F.M., van der Aalst, W.M.P.: Aligning event logs and declarative process models for conformance checking. In: Barros, A., Gal, A., Kindler, E. (eds.) BPM 2012. LNCS, vol. 7481, pp. 82–97. Springer, Heidelberg (2012). https://doi.org/10.1007/978-3-642-32885-5_6

11. Leung, C.S.K., Lau, H.Y.K.: Simulation-based optimization for material handling systems in manufacturing and distribution industries. Wirel. Netw. **26**(7), 4839–4860 (2020)

12. Mansouri, T., Moghadam, M.R.S., Monshizadeh, F., Zareravasan, A.: IOT data quality issues and potential solutions: a literature review. Comput. J. **66**(3), 615–625 (2023)

13. Rudnitckaia, J., Venkatachalam, H.S., Essmann, R., Hruska, T., Colombo, A.W.: Screening process mining and value stream techniques on industrial manufacturing processes: process modelling and bottleneck analysis. IEEE Access **10**, 24203–24214 (2022)

14. Sommers, D., Menkovski, V., Fahland, D.: Process discovery using graph neural networks. In: International Conference on Process Mining (2021)
15. Tang, J., Liu, Y., Lin, K., Li, L.: Process bottlenecks identification and its root cause analysis using fusion-based clustering and knowledge graph. Adv. Eng. Inform. **55**, 101862 (2023)
16. Unger, A.J., dos Santos Neto, J.F., Fantinato, M., Peres, S.M., Trecenti, J., Hirota, R.: Process mining-enabled jurimetrics: analysis of a Brazilian court's judicial performance in the business law processing. In: International Conference for Artificial Intelligence and Law (2021)
17. Verbeek, E., Buijs, J.C.A.M., van Dongen, B.F., van der Aalst, W.M.P.: Prom 6: the process mining toolkit. In: International Conference on Business Process Management, vol. 615 (2010)
18. Yasmin, F.A., Bukhsh, F.A., de Alencar Silva, P.: Process enhancement in process mining: a literature review. In: CEUR Workshop Proceedings, vol. 2270 (2018)

Author Index

Printed in the United States
by Baker & Taylor Publisher Services